SPEAK·TRUTH·TO·POWER·

COMMANDER
STEVEN HAINES
ROYAL NAVY

LITERATURE AND THE LAW OF NATIONS,
1580–1680

Literature and
the Law of Nations,
1580–1680

CHRISTOPHER N. WARREN

OXFORD
UNIVERSITY PRESS

OXFORD
UNIVERSITY PRESS

Great Clarendon Street, Oxford, OX2 6DP,
United Kingdom

Oxford University Press is a department of the University of Oxford.
It furthers the University's objective of excellence in research, scholarship,
and education by publishing worldwide. Oxford is a registered trade mark of
Oxford University Press in the UK and in certain other countries

Published in the United States of America by Oxford University Press
198 Madison Avenue, New York, NY 10016, United States of America

British Library Cataloguing in Publication Data
Data available

Library of Congress Control Number: 2014951321

ISBN 978–0–19–871934–2

Printed and bound by
CPI Group (UK) Ltd, Croydon, CR0 4YY

Links to third party websites are provided by Oxford in good faith and
for information only. Oxford disclaims any responsibility for the materials
contained in any third party website referenced in this work.

Acknowledgments

It is a pleasure to thank the many friends, family, and colleagues in Pittsburgh, Chicago, Oxford, and many other places who have lent time and energy to the writing of this book. I thank my colleagues at Carnegie Mellon University, in the University of Chicago Society of Fellows, and at Oxford University, above all my wise and learned D.Phil. supervisor Sharon Achinstein. The list of those who have provided friendship, advice, thoughtful criticism, and acts of generosity while this book was in progress is a long one. Meriting special mention are Marian Aguiar, Matthew Stembridge Anderson, Cliff Ando, Lauren Benton, David Bevington, Eyona Bivins, Bradin Cormack, Andrew Dilts, Michael Fakhri, Stephen Fallon, Ed Gordon, Kinch Hoekstra, Paul Hopper, Elizabeth Hutcheon, Matt Jenkinson, Richard Joyce, Victoria Kahn, Margaret Kinsky, Jon Klancher, Peggy Knapp, Dino Kritsiotis, Christine Lee, John Lehoczky, Fritz Levy, Noel Malcolm, Matt McHale, Vickie McKay, Tim Michael, Jeff Miller, Sophie Murray, Sanjay Narayan, Mark Neustadt, Chris Neuwirth, Marisa O'Connor, John Oddo, Anne Orford, Umut Oszu, Jessica Otis, Alex Porcaro, Joanna Picciotto, Ethan Pullman, Rich Purcell, Andreea Ritivoi, Jason Rosenblatt, Shalini Satkunanandan, Jonathan Scott, Barbara Sebak, Daniel Shore, Tracey Sowerby, David Shumway, Jonathan Stainsby, Paul Stevens, Benjamin Straumann, Richard Strier, Antti Tahvanaihen, Premala Thiagarajan, Rachel Trubowitz, Katie Wade, and Jeff Williams. David Norbrook and Lorna Hutson examined the Oxford D.Phil. thesis where I first explored many of the ideas in this book, and I am grateful to both for excellent suggestions at a formative moment. Rare Books Librarians at the Folger Shakespeare Library, the Bodleian Library, the Dutch Royal Library, the Newberry Library, CMU's Hunt Library, the University of Chicago's Regenstein Library, the British Library, and Chatsworth House assisted with research. I owe special thanks to Andrew Marshall in Interlibrary Loans at CMU. Since excellent academic bookstores are fading fast, I also register here my deep gratitude to two great ones, Blackwell's (Oxford) and the Seminary Co-Op (Hyde Park, Chicago). I thank my tremendous editors and staff at Oxford University Press, especially Jaqueline Baker and Rachel Platt, and Deborah Hey, who was responsible for copyediting. I thank Oxford University Press and Taylor & Francis for permission to publish in revised form material appearing initially in *The Seventeenth Century*, *The European Journal of International Law*, and *The Roman Foundations of the Law of Nations: Alberico Gentili and the Justice of Empire*, edited by Benjamin Struamann and Benedict Kingsbury.

For opportunities to air work in progress, I'm grateful to Paul Stevens and the Toronto Milton Seminar, to Jason Rosenblatt and the Northeast Milton Seminar, to Benjamin Struamann, Benedict Kingsbury, and NYU Law School, to the University of Chicago Renaissance Workshop, to Anne Orford, Dino Kritsiotis, and J. H. H. Weiler and the Junior Faculty Forum for International Law, and to Jo Craigwood and Tracey Sowerby and the Textual Ambassadors Network, kindly supported by the AHRC. I gratefully acknowledge an Erwin R. Steinberg Summer Fellowship from the Carnegie Mellon Department of English, an appointment as Visiting Scholar at the University of Chicago in 2011–2012, and an appointment as Senior Research Visitor at Keble College, Oxford in 2013. My graduate students have helped me think through many of the issues in this book—sometimes, much more than they know—and I thank in particular Julie Bowman, Marisa Colabuono, Kate Hamilton, Stephen Rosnick, D. J. Schuldt, Natalie Suzelis, and Pavithra Tantrigoda. For some late encouragement and suggestions, I am grateful to Peggy Knapp, Kristina Straub, Leah Whittington, Jason Rosenblatt, and Sharon Achinstein. For support that only family can provide, I thank my mom and dad, Katherine Norton Warren and Paul Warren, Timothy and Sunni Warren, Marie and Gerald O'Hara, Lucy Warren, and Steve and Nancy Kachniasz. Above all, I am grateful to Julie Kachniasz and Gabriel Matthew Warren for abiding love and laughter. Annabel Marie Warren was born in this book's final stages. It delights me to think that she and it will share a world together.

Contents

List of Figures

1

The Stakes of International Law and Literature

The terms *international* and *globalization* are everywhere today, yet they have distinct histories, imaginaries, and politics. Globalization, some say, began in 1571, the year in which silver from the New World was first traded in China.[1] But the term wasn't widely used until the 1980s and now usually invokes a homogenized dreamscape populated by ever more McDonalds', Coca-Colas, and global English. And while *international* can today be used in contexts ranging from "international relations" to the North American restaurant chain the "International House of Pancakes," it is in fact a considerably older term. It was coined in 1780, by Jeremy Bentham, and its linguistic and conceptual roots extend further into the Renaissance terrain at the heart of this book.

The original context for Bentham's coinage is illuminating. "The word international...is a new one," he wrote, "though, it is hoped, sufficiently analogous and intelligible. It is calculated to express, in a more significant way, the branch of law which goes commonly under the name of the law of nations."[2] If *globalization* commonly privileges faceless, de-politicized economic forces, *international* in 1780 invoked a different family of concepts, ones that literary scholars neglect at our peril. Law and the plurality of nations fade to the background in discussions of globalization. By contrast, they were hardwired into the concept of the *international* at its beginning. *International* and *law* now often float free of one another, of course. But Bentham's reference to the law of nations marks an important earlier tradition of thinking about law, politics, and the world. This book investigates literary history in light of that tradition. Its fundamental argument is that early modern literary genres helped generate and systematize some of the most important categories and suppositions of modern international law.

---

[1] Dennis O. Flynn and Arturo Giraldez, "Globalization Began in 1571," in *Globalization and Global History*, ed. Barry K. Gills and William R. Thompson (New York: Routledge, 2006), 232–47; David Armitage, "Is There a Pre-History of Globalization?," in *Comparison and History*, ed. Maura O'Connor and Deborah Cohen (London: Routledge, 2004), 165–76. For a useful taxonomy of globalization historiographies, see Duncan S. A. Bell, "History and Globalization: Reflections on Temporality," *International Affairs* 79, no. 4 (July 2003): 801–14.

[2] Jeremy Bentham, *An Introduction to the Principles of Morals and Legislation*, ed. J. H. Baker, H. L. A. Hart, and F. Rosen (Oxford: Clarendon Press, 1996), 296. For discussion, see especially M. W. Janis, "Jeremy Bentham and the Fashioning of 'International Law,'" *The American Journal of International Law* 78, no. 2 (April 1, 1984): 405–18; Hidemi Suganami, "A Note on the Origin of the Word 'International,'" *British Journal of International Studies* 4, no. 3 (October 1, 1978): 226–32; David Armitage, *Foundations of Modern International Thought* (Cambridge: Cambridge University Press, 2012), 42–3, 151.

Since it's not exactly obvious that 400-year-old literature should tell us anything about international law, this chapter develops a broad rationale for a more literary history of international law and sets the conceptual groundwork for the chapters that follow. It uses a range of examples from law and literature to sketch the book's premises, argument, key terms, and methodology. It explains how the book's fundamental argument might join up with prior work in law and literature and connect, especially, to work by eighteenth-century scholars on the novel's contributions to the history of human rights. It gives an overview of chapters to come, and it concludes with some preliminary examples of early modern genres that enrich our genealogies of contemporary international law.

Reflexively, many people would say that international law began in 1945, or maybe 1919. Some argue human rights began in earnest in the 1970s.[3] Literature and law, meanwhile, enjoy at best a "misunderstood relationship," and Richard Posner has even argued literature and law have little in common at all.[4] I proceed on the basis of three interrelated propositions. First, early modernists and other literary scholars have long studied the relations between law and literature; but they have not fully recognized the challenges and possibilities posed by the history of *international* law. Second, though modern international law emerged in the early modern period, our abilities to see literature and law beyond national borders have been constrained by nationalist tendencies. Finally, I propose that once we give the history of international law the prominence it deserves in our analysis, scholars can better understand the early modern nexus of law and literature, most importantly by recognizing the fundamentally international legal questions at the heart of many major literary texts and, more broadly, by appreciating the international legal entailments of several significant early modern poetic genres.

The pages that follow discuss well-known and less-well-known texts by Sidney, Shakespeare, Milton, Hobbes, and Grotius, among others, but this book is concerned as much with the history and theory of genre as it is with reinterpreting individual texts or with the history and theory of international law. Indeed, demonstrating how the genres of epic, comedy, tragicomedy, history, and biblical tragedy organized persons, actions, events, and evidence into recognizably modern legal categories like the laws of war, private international law, and human rights can be seen as the main burden of subsequent chapters.

Those who might already think that early modern literature and the history of international law seem like strange bedfellows will probably see little connection between international jurisprudence and early modern genre theory. But such distinctions fade considerably under scrutiny. In fact, early modern theories of genres, or kinds, regularly doubled as international legal theory. Generic types like epic or tragedy pointed not only to constitutive literary conventions—say, beginning *in medias res* or ending in *catharsis*—but to a broader world of communication from

³ Samuel Moyn, *The Last Utopia: Human Rights in History* (Cambridge, MA: Harvard University Press, 2010).
⁴ Richard A. Posner, *Law and Literature*, 1st edn. (Cambridge, MA: Harvard University Press, 1988).

which such conventions necessarily departed. *Ius gentium*, the Latin term for which "law of nations" has long been the standard translation, retains important evidence of the link with genre in the concept of the *gens*, which translates as *nation* but also as *kind, house, family*, or *people*. Such associative terms remind us that early modern genres, etymologically, were mechanisms for organizing kinship. Though they kept domestic order, they had international relations too. Like their etymological cousins, nations and peoples (*gentes*), genres/kinds existed only in relation to other such types. Conventions of tragedy, for example, existed in complex relations of similarity and difference to those of contiguous literary kinds like comedy. "The most profoundly social aspect of literature," as Franco Moretti puts it, genre prevails on interpreters to attend to the "boundaries" that separate one work of literature from another.[5]

If generic boundaries operate like tribal or national distinctions, creating identities by positing difference from adjacent "supplements" or "constitutive outsides," the early modern law of nations itself operated as a jurisprudence of kinds.[6] Not only did it consider kin groups, peoples, or nations (*gentes*) in their relations with one another, it also concerned itself with human kinds writ large: *le genre humain, humani generis*, mankind. Early modern lawyers and moral philosophers theorized kinds in a legal register. But poets, playwrights, and genre theorists performed related intellectual work under the broad term of poetics, where they theorized kinds of literature in both their internal and external respects. The conventions regarding persons, actions, relations, and evidence that would come to dominate international law developed in literary theory and practice. Tracts of early modern poetics, therefore, form an unexpectedly rich archive of international legal thought. Indeed, the early modern Italian theorist of tragicomedy Giambattista Guarini wrote explicitly of the "jurisdiction" of genres, and similar views can be found in other major works of early modern poetics, from Sidney's *Apology for Poetry*, to Daniel Heinsius' *De Tragoediae Constitutione*, to Tasso's *Discourses on the Heroic Poem*.

Of course, such texts have received considerable prior attention. The book's argument about literary genres and legal taxonomies thus incorporates two foundational lines of scholarship: work in the history of genre; and work in law and literature. Scholars including Mikhail Bakhtin, Kenneth Burke, Hayden White, Barbara Lewalski, Raymond Williams, Alastair Fowler, Rosalie Colie, Richard Strier, and Heather Dubrow have long been interested in what Williams called the early modern period's "community of forms."[7] Such scholars have taught us how

---

[5] Franco Moretti, *Graphs, Maps, Trees: Abstract Models for Literary History* (London: Verso, 2007); Mikhail Bakhtin, "The Problem of Speech Genres," in *Speech Genres and Other Late Essays*, ed. Caryl Emerson and Michael Holquist, trans. Vern W. McGee (Austin, TX: University of Texas Press, 1986), 60–102.

[6] Jacques Derrida, "The Law of Genre," in *Modern Genre Theory* (Harlow: Longman, 2000), 219–31; Judith Butler, *Bodies That Matter: On the Discursive Limits of "Sex"* (New York: Routledge, 1993), 140–8.

[7] Raymond Williams, *The Sociology of Culture*, 2nd edn. (Chicago, IL: University of Chicago Press, 1995), 156. In his landmark *Keywords* (1976), Williams neglected to include an entry for "law," but scholars like Naomi Mezey and Peter Goodrich have usefully approached law through the lens of cultural studies. See Naomi Mezey, "Law as Culture," *Yale Journal of Law & the Humanities* 13 (2001): 35; Peter Goodrich, "Law," in *Critical Terms for Media Studies*, ed. W. J. T. Mitchell and Mark B. N. Hansen (Chicago, IL: University of Chicago Press, 2010).

genres "often carry along strong hypotheses about their fictional worlds"; that "substantive concerns are built into the formal signatures of... genre"; and that we can learn to analyze "the content of the form."[8]

Building on the work of such scholars along with recent scholarship in early modern law and literature, I aim to illuminate here some specific *legal* entailments of particular literary forms. Amidst what might be called a recent "legal turn" in English Renaissance literary studies, scholars including Victoria Kahn, Lorna Hutson, and Bradin Cormack have admirably illustrated how certain generic practices could critique state-based legal processes, enact quasi-judicial judgments, theorize contracts, and adapt formally and mimetically alongside legal doctrine and practice. For Kahn, the English romance is a key site for producing the contracting subjects of liberal political theory.[9] For Hutson, it is primarily the English Renaissance comedy that stoked growing "evidential awareness" fundamental to common law legal epistemology.[10] Bradin Cormack has proposed that "kinds of literary production grappled with kinds of legal discourse and legal problems," and this is a suggestion I take up at length.[11]

But the history of international law offers a valuable opportunity to test, critique, and potentially alter law and literature's rarely acknowledged attachments to the nation-state. Even major studies of law and literature have found little to say about international law. A touchstone of early modern scholarship is tellingly called *Forms of Nationhood*.[12] We have no parallel cultural history of international law.[13] Scholarship in law and literature tacitly affirms that law and literature is one thing, literature and international relations another. Purposefully or not, literary scholars seem to have accepted the assumptions of the Victorian arch-positivist

---

[8] Thomas G. Pavel, *Fictional Worlds* (Cambridge, MA: Harvard University Press, 1986), 129; Stanley Fish, "Why Milton Matters; Or, Against Historicism," *Milton Studies* 44 (2005): 6; Hayden White, *The Content of the Form: Narrative Discourse and Historical Representation* (Baltimore, MD: Johns Hopkins University Press, 1987); Hayden White, *Metahistory: The Historical Imagination in Nineteenth-Century Europe* (Baltimore, MD: Johns Hopkins University Press, 1973).

[9] Victoria Kahn, *Wayward Contracts: The Crisis of Political Obligation in England, 1640–1674* (Princeton, NJ: Princeton University Press, 2004).

[10] Lorna Hutson, *The Invention of Suspicion* (Oxford: Oxford University Press, 2007).

[11] Bradin Cormack, *A Power to Do Justice: Jurisdiction, English Literature, and the Rise of Common Law* (Chicago, IL: University of Chicago Press, 2008), 22.

[12] Richard Helgerson, *Forms of Nationhood: The Elizabethan Writing of England* (Chicago, IL: University of Chicago Press, 1992).

[13] Valuable contributions in that direction, however, include Theodor Meron, *Henry's Wars and Shakespeare's Laws: Perspectives on the Law of War in the Later Middle Ages* (Oxford: Oxford University Press, 1993); Theodor Meron, *Bloody Constraint: War and Chivalry in Shakespeare* (New York: Oxford University Press, 1998); Julie Stone Peters, "A 'Bridge over Chaos': De Jure Belli, Paradise Lost, Terror, Sovereignty, Globalism, and the Modern Law of Nations," *Comparative Literature* 57, no. 4 (January 2005): 273–93; Brian Lockey, *Law and Empire in English Renaissance Literature* (Cambridge: Cambridge University Press, 2006); Edward Morgan, *The Aesthetics of International Law* (Toronto: University of Toronto Press, 2007); Chenxi Tang, "Re-Imagining World Order: From International Law to Romantic Poetics," *Deutsche Vierteljahrsschrift Fur Literaturwissenschaft Und Geistesgeschichte* 84, no. 4 (2010): 526–79; Chenxi Tang, "The Transformation of the Law of Nations and the Reinvention of the Novella: Legal History and Literary Innovation from Boccaccio's Decameron to Goethe's Unterhaltungen Deutscher Ausgewanderten," *Goethe Yearbook: Publications of the Goethe Society of North America* 19 (2012): 67–92.

John Austin, who notoriously claimed in 1832 that international law is not "law."[14] John Bolton's more recent question—"Is There Really 'Law' in International Affairs?," in which typography recapitulates ontology for this George W. Bush United Nations appointee—is met with awkward silence.[15] As Kahn reminds us, Robert Filmer, author of *Patriarcha*, had written in 1652, "where there is no supreme power that extends over all or many nations . . . there can be no laws made to bind nations."[16] Insofar as the view shared by Austin, Bolton, and Filmer remains the default view today, we early modernists might pause over the company we keep.

A helpful way to see the need for further work on the law of nations is to consider the phrase "national law." In so doing, we should reorient ourselves, however, because "national law" in the early modern period could mean the very opposite of what most would now expect. Even so, thinkers like Austin, Bolton, and Filmer have influenced us so thoroughly that the Oxford English Dictionary (OED) gives no indication of the antithetical usage. The OED A1a definition of "national" (adj.) gives roughly what one might imagine: "Of or relating to a nation or country, esp. as a whole; affecting or shared by a whole nation." But as used by writers as diverse as Richard Hooker, Francis Bacon, John Cowell, and John Milton, the adjective "national" meant something not captured by OED A1a, nor indeed any of the OED's thirteen other definitions. For many Latinate Renaissance writers, "national law" did not mean the law of *a* nation—civil or municipal law. Rather, it referred to the law of nations (*ius gentium*), a legal order far closer to "law between nations" or "international law." "National" in "national law," in other words, functioned like the adjective "ancestral" in "ancestral home": the home is the home of the ancestors; the law is the law of the nations.

Examples from early modern usage abound, absent though they are from the OED. In *Areopagitica*, Milton translated John Selden's *De Jure Naturali et Gentium* (1640), as Selden's "volume of naturall & national laws."[17] John Cowell spoke of the "National Law or the Law of Nations," Richard Hooker referred to "the national laws of mutual commerce between societies," while a letter from Louis XIII supposedly described "the firme League made between [Louis and Charles I] (which by the Nationall Law of Kingdomes we are bound to observe)."[18] A late

---

[14] John Austin, *The Province of Jurisprudence Determined*, ed. Wilfrid E. Rumble (Cambridge: Cambridge University Press, 1995), 20.

[15] John R. Bolton, "Is There Really 'Law' in International Affairs?," *Transnational Law & Contemporary Problems* 10 (2000): 1.

[16] Robert Filmer, *Patriarcha and Other Writings*, ed. J. P. Sommerville (Cambridge: Cambridge University Press, 1991), 216. For discussion, see Victoria Kahn, "Disappointed Nationalism: Milton in the Context of Seventeenth-Century Debates about the Nation-State," in *Early Modern Nationalism and Milton's England*, ed. David Loewenstein and Paul Stevens (Toronto: University of Toronto Press, 2008), 249–72.

[17] John Milton, *Complete Prose Works*, ed. Don M. Wolfe (New Haven, CT: Yale University Press, 1953), 2.513.

[18] Richard Hooker, *Of the Laws of Ecclesiastical Polity: Preface, Book I, Book VIII*, ed. Arthur Stephen McGrade (Cambridge: Cambridge University Press, 1989), 97–8; John Cowell, *The Interpreter* (Amsterdam: Theatrum Orbis Terrarum, 1970; orig. 1607), 3; Louis XIII, *Admirable and Notable Things of Note* (London: Francis Coules and Thomas Banks, 1642), a2r.

seventeenth-century writer's "Fountain from whence all our Civil, and National Laws do flow" was a translation of *Fons ex quo manat totum jus civile, & jus Gentium*.[19] National law was important, powerful, and pervasive, but it was not what we would expect.

Linguists would identify the phenomenon of "national law" as a case of "neutralization," one in which the movement from Latin's genitive noun to the English adjective neutralized *gentium*'s collective force in the original Latin. But since early modern English writers heard and deployed its collective force, we're left with some important questions. Has the nation-state in the interim so captured our imaginations that we're incapable of hearing anything else? What would it mean to recover this earlier sense of "national law"? How closely must the law and literature enterprise hew to the intellectual preferences of the nation-state? Could we dispense with the presumption of geographically stable, territorially bound citizens and start instead from the reality that early modern merchants, servants, lovers, mariners, diplomats, warriors, scholars, students, and sovereigns regularly crossed national borders, and that they were developing international legal structures and adjudicatory mechanisms for their support?

Even though the history of international law has received relatively little attention from literary scholars, prior work in law and literature does indeed offer considerable resources for addressing such questions. Cormack has provided a compelling view of literature as "radical jurisprudence" that "looks within law for what the law does not see"—"an intensified account of the practical dynamic through which the law itself emerges."[20] Hutson explores the legal and cultural consequences of Renaissance rhetorical education in which mid-sixteenth-century schoolrooms, saturated with what she calls a "judicial pedagogy of narrative," compelled formal innovations on the English stage.[21] Such approaches are models of how literary criticism can powerfully engage with early modern legal history.

For Cormack, it is the idea of jurisdiction that facilities analysis of literature's critical engagements with the "mundane process of administrative distribution and management."[22] Explicitly turning away from abstract questions of sovereignty, Cormack analyzes literature at various "threshold[s] *between* sovereign spaces" including, powerfully, "the sea's disruptive energies."[23] "Jurisdiction," as he helpfully puts it, "is the starting point for political discourse."[24] At stake in the turn to jurisdiction for Cormack is the English common law's story of its own hegemony. Literary texts are critical in this endeavor, for they give us common law not in its own blustery terms and self-protective genres (reports, opinions, pleadings, etc.) but instead in a field of alternative symbolic orders—Celtic custom, French historicism, canon law, Roman civil law, *lex mercatoria*, Revelation, and imaginative literature itself. A common law that from certain angles appears an indomitable

---

[19] Henry Glover, *Ekdikesis or A Discourse of Vengeance* (London: Henry Brome, 1664), 8.
[20] Bradin Cormack, "Practicing Law and Literature in Early Modern Studies," *Modern Philology* 101, no. 1 (August 1, 2003): 79–91; Cormack, *A Power to Do Justice*, 23.
[21] Hutson, *The Invention of Suspicion*, 7, 122, 146.
[22] Cormack, *A Power to Do Justice*, 9.   [23] Cormack, *A Power to Do Justice*, 42.
[24] Cormack, *A Power to Do Justice*, 233.

fortress of strength looks from the perspective of early modern literature unusually playful, contingent, contradictory, and fragile—even tender. Cormack shows how literature, in key words that straddle multiple legal and literary fields, remains uniquely capable of telling "law's buried history."[25]

In Lorna Hutson's work, the growing "evidential awareness" that she brilliantly highlights in early modern drama arises most powerfully at the intersection of the comic plot and English criminal law.[26] As Hutson argues, English dramatists fostered a unique epistemology crucially related to the English system of the popular jury trial. Presented with plots of astonishing legal artistry, playgoers learned to evaluate evidentiary questions—questions regarding circumstance, probability, hearsay, character, and proof—at striking levels of granularity.

Such summaries cannot capture the full depth and breadth of the recent legal turn in early modern studies, but they can illustrate that scholars are now in an excellent position to explore the possibilities and challenges posed by an enriched legal historiography that includes the history of international law. As we shall see in further detail later on, early modern readers of Vergil or Sidney, developing understandings of the law of war, themselves paid careful attention to plot elements like treaties made and broken or customs upheld or violated. Readers of Hebrew scripture, too, explained events like the plagues in Exodus with legal arguments about Pharaoh's purported breach of contract with the sojourning Israelites. Exemplary heroes such as Aeneas and Moses were often cast as those most capable of attending to evidentiary detail in international contexts. Plot events including promises, oaths, slanders, and lies that were perhaps forgotten or overlooked by lesser characters informed and justified heroes' later responses to exigencies.

Expert reading, meanwhile, exercised a similar historical plot-memory that illuminated legal bases for heroic action. This meant that many readers—and not all of them English—took forensic approaches at least superficially resembling those emerging from the English jury trial system. What I find particularly compelling about Hutson's work is that it alerts us to plot's role as a legal archive for many readers. And while comedy and English criminal law drive Hutson's inquiry, her work can be extended to observe how the deep temporal archive of narrative informed determinations of crime and virtue in international contexts as well.

The reasons why international law has received little attention from literary scholars are complex, but I would argue that a significant factor is that international law has seemed uncomfortably anomalous. Julie Stone Peters points out that one reason literary critics have often turned to the law is for a perceived engagement with the "real world."[27] If domestic law—rightly or wrongly—has enjoyed strong association with the "real," critics like Bolton who suggest international law is a fiction have successfully made international law's association with the "real" seem less straightforward. "No other area of law is compelled to justify its very ontology and existence," Bederman observes, "and yet international law seems

---

[25] Cormack, *A Power to Do Justice*, 324.   [26] Hutson, *The Invention of Suspicion*, 4, 45.
[27] Julie Stone Peters, "Law, Literature, and the Vanishing Real: On the Future of an Interdisciplinary Illusion," *PMLA* 120, no. 2 (March 2005): 442–53.

condemned perpetually to do so."[28] Literary critics who have generally preferred to ignore or sidestep international law, then, may not have been doing so because international law seemed too far from imaginative literature. International law may instead have seemed too close.

Thinkers on the Right have of course long accounted international law as a fiction—the Nazi jurist Carl Schmitt famously endorsed the proposition that "whoever invokes humanity wants to cheat"—but that phrase originated on the Left, with Proudhon.[29] Many on the Left, too, consider law the wrong path entirely. The Marxist social critic and novelist China Miéville finds international law too tied to the history of capitalism for much contemporary use.[30] Foucault argued that law and absolute monarchic power were so closely aligned that one should speak of a "juridico-monarchic sphere."[31] "The theoretical privilege of law" is an "image we must break free of," Foucault wrote in the first volume of his *History of Sexuality* (1976).[32] In his reasoning, "juridico-political discourse" "went hand in hand" with monarchy's "covering up of the facts and procedures of power"; he therefore argued that "we must construct an analytics of power that no longer takes law as a model and a code."[33] Foucault concluded that "law was not simply a weapon skillfully wielded by monarchs; it was the monarchic system's mode of manifestation and the form of its acceptability."[34] Other critical theorists have treated law with a similarly broad brush. For Althusser, law was an "ideological state apparatus" *tout court*.[35] According to Bourdieu, "law consecrates the established

[28] David J. Bederman, *The Spirit of International Law* (Athens, GA: University of Georgia Press, 2002), 1. For a particularly effective example of international law advocacy, see the pamphlet distributed by the American Society of International Law, *International Law: 100 Ways It Shapes Our Lives* (Washington, DC: American Society of International Law, 2006).

[29] Carl Schmitt, *The Concept of the Political*, trans. George Schwab (Chicago, IL: University of Chicago Press, 1996), 54. Schmitt's contributions to Nazi legal propaganda led to his inclusion on early lists for prosecution at Nuremberg. See Kevin Jon Heller, *The Nuremberg Military Tribunals and the Origins of International Criminal Law* (Oxford: Oxford University Press, 2011), 64. See further Jürgen Habermas, "The Horrors of Autonomy: Carl Schmitt in English," in *The New Conservatism: Cultural Criticism and the Historians' Debate*, trans. Shierry Weber Nicholsen (Cambridge, MA: MIT Press, 1989), 128–39; Perry Anderson, "The Intransigent Right: Michael Oakeshott, Leo Strauss, Carl Schmitt, Friedrich Von Hayek," in *Spectrum: From Left to Right in the World of Ideas* (London: Verso, 2005); Bardo Fassbender, "Stories of War and Peace: On Writing the History of International Law in the 'Third Reich' and After," *European Journal of International Law* 13, no. 2 (April 1, 2002): 479–512.

[30] China Miéville, *Between Equal Rights: A Marxist Theory Of International Law* (Chicago, IL: Haymarket Books, 2006). For an equally subtle reconsideration, see Robert Knox, "Marxism, International Law, and Political Strategy," *Leiden Journal of International Law* 22, no. 03 (2009): 413–36.

[31] Michel Foucault, *The History of Sexuality, Volume 1: The Will to Knowledge*, trans. Robert Hurley (London: Penguin Books, 1990), 88.

[32] Foucault, *The Will to Knowledge*, 90.   [33] Foucault, *The Will to Knowledge*, 88, 80.

[34] Foucault, *The Will to Knowledge*, 87.

[35] Louis Althusser, "Ideology and Ideological State Apparatuses: Notes Toward an Investigation," in *Lenin and Philosophy, and Other Essays*, trans. Ben Brewster (London: New Left Books, 1971), 85–126. The Marxist historian E. P. Thompson issued a stirring rejoinder to Althusser in the postscript to his *Whigs and Hunters* (1975). Even as he acknowledged that law's forms and languages were subject to manipulation, law for Thompson was not "another mask for the rule of a class" but, very much to the contrary, "an unqualified human good." "[P]eople are not as stupid as some structuralist philosophers suppose them to be," he wrote. "[T]hey will not be mystified by the first man who puts on a wig." See E. P. Thompson, *Whigs and Hunters: The Origin of the Black Act* (New York: Pantheon Books, 1975), 261–6.

order by consecrating the vision of that order which is held by the State."[36] Law *in general* was caught up in critical theory's critique of the state. Scholars influenced by critical theory, then, can find themselves in one of two odd positions. Either they join thinkers like Bolton, Filmer, and Schmitt as opponents of international law, or they treat international law with a conceptual solidity they typically withhold from law in domestic contexts.

Jürgen Habermas, a major theorist of international law as well as the public sphere, has observed that "the constellation formed by the Cold War and the impotence of international law [in that period] could not fail to favor a theory that... international institutions are chronically ineffectual."[37] When New Historicism reigned in early modern literary studies during the Cold War, it may then have seemed preferable to sidestep the anomaly of international law. But the years since the George W. Bush administration have made the silences and paradoxes acute. As critics on the Left have variously described waterboarding and drone warfare as "violations of human rights," the Iraq war as an "illegal war," and Bush administration lawyers as "war criminals," it has been difficult not to feel that the Right's own contradictions regarding law have salient counterparts on the Left. Right-wing regimes most prone to imposing the "rule of law" are quickest to question the force and validity of international law. But left-leaning critics of the War on Terror and drone warfare have endowed "international law" with a numinous legitimacy standing in marked tension with critical theories long devoted to unmasking the power, capital, and sovereign decisions behind the mostly undifferentiated category of "law." Given the need to consider law in more nuanced ways, international law challenges early modernists to pay closer attention to what we talk about when we talk about law.

As we look more explicitly to literature and international law, the connection Cormack draws between jurisdiction and political discourse helps us see the plural jurisdictions of genres, which is to say their competing, overlapping norms and procedural requirements. If jurisdiction is the starting point for political discourse, genres themselves emerge by extension as distinctive sites of international political thought in which authors situate certain characters as either subjects or objects in international law, charge particular actions with distinctive juridical salience, and render events as comprehensible or incomprehensible at law.

"To draw a line between public and private rights [*publica privatis secernere*]," Horace suggested, was a basic function of poetry.[38] Genres, we should understand,

---

[36] Pierre Bourdieu, "The Force of Law: Toward a Sociology of the Juridical Field," trans. Richard Terdiman, *Hastings Law Journal* 38 (1987): 838. Foucault argued influentially in *Discipline and Punish* (London: Allen Lane, 1977) that what's ultimately at stake in the punishment of criminals is the state's legal claim to power. In his late lectures at the College de France, he emphasized the way "governmentality" emerged with the state "as far as possible employing laws as tactics." See Michel Foucault, *Security, Territory, Population: Lectures at the Collège De France, 1977–1978* (Basingstoke: Palgrave Macmillan, 2007), 99.

[37] Habermas further observes that the annual budget for the United Nations is roughly 4% of that of New York City. Jürgen Habermas, *The Divided West* (Cambridge: Polity, 2006), 167, 207 n. 97.

[38] Horace, "De Arte Poetica," in *Satires, Epistles and Ars Poetica, with an English Translation*, trans. H. Rushton Fairclough, Loeb Classical Library (Cambridge, MA: Harvard University Press, 1926), 482–3 (397).

are resources whose law-saying (*juris dictio*) distributed publicity and privacy, opening and closing possible orders of international duties and rights. They are alternative configurations of what international lawyers call the subjects and objects of international law. Bederman explains, "The subjects of international law are the actors, or players, on the international scene. In contrast, the objects of international law are the who, what, and where that are being acted on. The objects of international law are the legitimate topics of international regulation."[39] Differences between, say, *King Lear* and *The Merchant of Venice*, speak to larger distinctions between the subjects and objects in differing conceptions of the law of nations. As federated but distinct archives of international legal thought, genres provide alternative traditions of who and what matters on the world stage.

IF THE PAST IS A DIFFERENT COUNTRY, ALL LAW IS INTERNATIONAL LAW

International law can of course mean many different things. If the past is a different country, *all* law is international law. We regularly obey people who lived long ago, typically in other lands. Language clarifies what national traditions obscure: The Anglophone world's common law tradition has come down to us in law French; legal maxims are typically Latin, the language of ancient Romans; the *admiral* of admiralty law—maritime law—derives from Arabic. Like air, water, and language itself, law drifts, soars, tunnels, and glides beyond national and temporal boundaries. Richard Helgerson's *Forms of Nationhood* (1992) focused on a generation of Elizabethans eager to prove that "England's law is homegrown, continuous, insular, and unique."[40] Helgerson's subjects were nervous because the evidence suggested precisely the opposite—that law in core respects was imported, discontinuous, international, and derivative.[41]

The case known as Aldred's Case (1610) helps illustrate the international sources, afterlives, and consequences of a law that might on its surface look exclusively local. Fracturing myths of legal nationalism, it further illuminates the stakes of international law and literature. In 1609 or thereabouts, a man in a small town in Norfolk, England, Thomas Benton, converted an orchard into a pig sty. To his neighbor, William Aldred, this was an unwelcome development. Pigs stink. No longer enjoying what Edward Coke in his *Reports* called *salubritas aeris*, wholesomeness of air, Aldred filed suit.[42] While his opponent Benton argued "one ought not to be of so delicate nosed, that he cannot endure the scent of hoggs," Aldred persuaded the King's Bench that Benton had no right to pollute an environment that included Aldred's own habitat.[43] Benton was hardly less responsible for the nuisance than the tanner who polluted upstream water or the dyer whose runoff

---

[39] Bederman, *The Spirit of International Law*, 79.   [40] Helgerson, *Forms of Nationhood*, 67.
[41] Cormack, *A Power to Do Justice*, 177–226.
[42] Edward Coke, *The Selected Writings of Sir Edward Coke*, ed. Steve Sheppard (Indianapolis, IN: Liberty Fund, 2003), 1.310.
[43] Coke, *The Selected Writings of Sir Edward Coke*, 1.310.

contaminated a fishing hole. All of these, the King's Bench insisted, were actionable at law.

Cases like Aldred's Case limn thought-worlds and precedents whose effects can hardly be predicted. Sometimes centuries later, often in radically different places and circumstances, people—even peoples—put highly interested pressure on cases' language, images, and logic. Law travels too. As a result of the British Empire, Aldred's Case is today studied in law schools around the world, and many see in it an embedded theory of interconnected life, one whose logic compels us to re-consider rights and responsibilities in the context of pollution and climate change.

In 1928, the great literary critic and poet William Empson drew other lessons from early modern property law. His much-anthologized poem "Legal Fiction" satirized Aldred's logic using a conceit derived from the great jurist Edward Coke. "He who owns the land, owns it to the skies" (*cujus est solum ejus est usque ad coelum*), Coke wrote in his *Institutes*, adapting a maxim from the thirteenth-century Roman law glossator Accursius that was itself, we might say, in the air.[44] "Land, in the legall signification comprehendeth..., a great extent, upwards as well as downwards, not only of water...but of ayre even up to heaven," Coke wrote.[45] "So that the word 'land' includes not only the face of the earth, but also every thing under or over it," Blackstone explained.[46] Though not mentioned explicitly in Aldred's Case, such principles had underpinned Aldred's rights in clean air and Benton's duties toward Aldred's environment.

In Empson's wry four quatrain lyric—Donnian in form, Miltonic in diction, and tinged with the author's "left-wing" suspicion of *mine* and *thine*—the legal fiction of ownership meant that landowners' "rights reach down where all owners meet, in Hell's / Pointed exclusive conclave, at earth's center /... And up, through galaxies, a growing sector."[47] Law's fictions configured space—downwards and outwards—and time—present and past. "Law," Empson had begun, "makes long spokes of short stakes of men." "Short stakes" referred partially, of course, to boundary markers like the fence between Aldred's and Benton's properties, but "long" and "short" marked duration as well.

As Empson understood, law, like literature, carries embodied mortal selves across artificial boundaries. Much as literary "genre is not just a theory of classification but perhaps even more crucially, a theory of interconnection," legal cases, maxims, analogies, and fictions mediate between present and past to stitch the fabric of culture.[48] "Class[es] of objects that," in Wai-Chi Dimock's words, "fail to

[44] On Accursius and other early modern uses of the maxim, see Clement L. Bouvé, "Private Ownership in Airspace," *Air Law Review* 1 (1930): 243–8.

[45] Edward Coke Sir, *The First Part of the Institutes of the Lawes of England. Or, A Commentarie Upon Littleton, Not the Name of a Lawyer Onely, but of the Law It Selfe* (London: [Adam Islip] for the Society of Stationers, 1628), 4.

[46] William Blackstone, *Commentaries on the Laws of England*, 2nd edn., vol. II (Oxford, 1766), 18.

[47] William Empson, *The Complete Poems of William Empson*, ed. John Haffenden (Gainesville, FL: University Press of Florida, 2001), 37; Marcus Waithe, "Empson's Legal Fiction," *Essays in Criticism* 62, no. 3 (July 1, 2012): 279–301.

[48] Wai-chee Dimock, *Through Other Continents: American Literature across Deep Time* (Princeton, NJ: Princeton University Press, 2006), 74.

shut up, fail to restrict their resonance over time," law and literature both help us share air-time with the dead.[49]

Probably in the 1950s or 1960s, "a group of American international lawyers...doing a brochure about space travel" paid William Empson five dollars to reproduce his "Legal Fiction."[50] In doing so, they didn't just print Empson but—intertextually—Donne, Milton, Aldred, and Coke, too. Donne, a lawyer-poet, spoke through the genre of the metaphysical conceit. Abetting Empson's playfulness with physical and temporal scale, Milton's *Paradise Lost* spoke through the poem's Christian metaphysics and the language of the "exclusive conclave," which echoes Milton's "secret conclave" of Books 1 and 2, where Hell's "incorporeal Spirits to smallest forms / Reduced their shapes immense."[51] In the years before "Legal Fiction" attracted the interest of the American international lawyers, early modern court decisions for landholders like Aldred continued to resonate. As if to illustrate the temporal as well as spatial protraction of early modern property doctrine, the legal historian Stuart Banner traces the *cujus est solum* maxim into vigorous twentieth-century debates over air travel. From time out of mind, didn't owners—farmers, sovereigns—own to the sky? Coke's maxim haunted early air travel advocates and enthusiasts. For nation-states and property owners endangered by roaring airplanes overhead, however, Coke was a welcome visitor from the past. Sovereigns and proprietors spoke with him and through him to say that overhead flights were nuisances, trespasses, or invasions. Even Milton's Satan at the end of Book 2 of *Paradise Lost*, they might have said, negotiated flyover rights with Chaos, Milton's umpire of the deep.

Aldred, Donne, Coke, and Milton are hardly the only early modern figures whose stakes prick, sometimes uncomfortably, at modernity. The so-called father of international law, Hugo Grotius, a onetime spokesman for the Dutch East Indies Company and a contemporary of Donne, Aldred, Coke, and Milton, has also had long spokes. Grotius' *Mare Liberum* (1608), composed originally to aid the Dutch trade in the East Indies against Portuguese competitors, had advanced the potentially equally applicable doctrine of the free sea. To his twentieth-century advocates, the sky was more like water than an appendage to land. "Nature has not made the sun private to any, nor the air, nor...water," Grotius quoted Ovid to say.[52] In the twentieth century, the precedent of *Mare Liberum* involved not only a very different judgment about the *kind* of thing air travel was; it also meant a radically alternative outcome. Whereas Aldred's "rights extend[ed] under and above [his] claim / Without bound," as Empson put it, Grotius helped ensure that air space above a certain height would remain *res communis*, something common.

---

[49] Wai-chee Dimock, "A Theory of Resonance," *PMLA* 112, no. 5 (October 1997): 10. Early modernists will inevitably note the echo of Stephen Greenblatt's *Shakespearean Negotiations*, "I began with the desire to speak with the dead." See *Shakespearean Negotiations: The Circulation of Social Energy in Renaissance England* (Berkeley, CA: University of California Press, 1989).

[50] Empson, *The Complete Poems of William Empson*, 230.

[51] John Milton, *Paradise Lost*, ed. Alastair Fowler, 2nd edn. (London: Longman, 1998), 1.795, 1.789–790.

[52] Hugo Grotius, *The Free Sea*, ed. David Armitage, trans. Richard Hakluyt (Indianapolis, IN: Liberty Fund, 2004), 25.

To suggest, then, that all law is international law is to remind ourselves that much of the basic order of our lives comes from other times and places, or at least that we negotiate our laws with the dead. The U.S. Supreme Court may presently chafe even at *citations* of foreign law, but that hardly changes the fact that today's commercial flights from Pittsburgh to Chicago are happening because a seventeenth-century Dutch author, citing ancient Roman law and poetry against Portuguese claims in Southeast Asia, prevailed against an early modern Englishman quoting a thirteenth-century Italian to defend property from the likes of stinky pigs.[53]

That last sentence was of course a playful formulation intended to challenge self-serious fictions of national autonomy. But related points can be made more solemnly. The more international approach to law that I advance follows through on an under-emphasized dimension of landmarks on nationalism like Benedict Anderson's *Imagined Communities* (1983) and Helgerson's *Forms of Nationhood* (1992). Anderson's *Imagined Communities* emphasized nations' artificiality, their roots not in nature but in shared human fictions. Helgerson's *Forms of Nationhood* showed powerfully how early modern English "poetry, law,... antiquarian study," and several other practices "were given a single, apparently co-terminous national base."[54] Such work followed from deep ambivalences about the nation long present in the so-called "national question."[55] Though Helgerson analyzed this "co-terminous national base" of Elizabethan England, his "Afterword" reveals a largely unelaborated international vision. The book's aim, Helgerson allows, is "to unmask the nation's claim to a 'natural' or 'immemorial' origin," to identify the cultural forms "that *replaced* the various overlapping local and international jurisdictions that had previously predominated in one cultural field or another" (emphasis added).[56] Here Helgerson's repressed "utopian impulse" bubbles to the surface.[57] Helgerson has taught us so much about what Rosa Luxemburg called the "misty veil" of nationalism precisely because he finds nationalism, like the state, so troublingly *made*.[58] With a possible nod to Jacob Burkhard's famous chapter "The State as a Work of Art," Helgerson admonishes, "Neither the nation nor the state has always been there."[59] I do not share Helgerson's sense that something is inherently less legitimate because it is made or constructed.[60] But I do consider law far

---

[53] On debates about foreign law in U.S. courts, see Jeremy Waldron, "Foreign Law and the Modern Ius Gentium," *Harvard Law Review* 119, no. 1 (November 1, 2005): 129–47.

[54] Helgerson, *Forms of Nationhood*, 300.

[55] On the national question, see *inter alia* Rosa Luxemburg, *The National Question: Selected Writings*, ed. Horace B. Davis (New York: Monthly Review Press, 1976); Hannah Arendt, "The Decline of the Nation-State and the End of the Rights of Man," in *The Origins of Totalitarianism*, 2nd edn. (New York: Harcourt, Brace and Co., 1951), 267–302; Tom Nairn, "Internationalism: A Critique," in *Faces of Nationalism: Janus Revisited* (London: Verso, 1998), 25–46; Joan Cocks, *Passion and Paradox: Intellectuals Confront the National Question* (Princeton, NJ: Princeton University Press, 2002).

[56] Helgerson, *Forms of Nationhood*, 300.

[57] Fredric Jameson, *Archaeologies of the Future: The Desire Called Utopia and Other Science Fictions* (London: Verso, 2007), 3.

[58] Luxemburg, *The National Question*, 135.   [59] Helgerson, *Forms of Nationhood*, 301.

[60] I am influenced here by Elaine Scarry's reflections on the "made-up" and the "made-real." In a discussion of Scarry, Stone Peters also wonders why "exposure of the fact that things were once created

stranger and more complex than national mythologies allow. And I begin, as Luxemburg, Helgerson, and Anderson all did, from the broad sense that the nation has too often been an artifact of "shrunken," "limited imaginings."[61]

THE EARLY MODERN LAW OF NATIONS AND THE PROBLEMATIC OF THE MADE

Even if all law might justifiably be classified as "international law," this book uses that term more conventionally. What's most distinctive and important about the early modern period is—*pace* Helgerson—the increasing awareness of human agency and artistry in the history of international law—that humanity had made laws for itself. The law of nations, as Richard Hooker put it, was increasingly understood as "built."[62] If international law has since appeared as "a different and spectral law, an object of vigorous theoretical construction," we can trace this sense of constructed-ness directly to the sixteenth and seventeenth centuries through the law of nations.[63] This law of nations as used and imagined in the early modern period was consequential and expansive. It encompassed no less than "Embassies, courteous entertainment of foreigners and strangers, Laws of Arms, freedom of Traffique, right of Contracts, free passage through each others Borders, Reprizalls, the preserving and redemption of Captives, Leagues, [and] Truces..."[64] And like a poem or a play, the law of nations was widely considered an object of collective *poiesis* or making.

Early modern literature, then, provides special access to questions of art, fiction, and invention—in short, what I would call the problematic of the made—in the history of international law. For if international law has suffered from the sense that it is, in some way, a fiction—that "there is no such thing as international law"—we need only recall fiction's Latin roots in fashioning or sculpting (*fict-*) to see a conceptual alliance between literature and the law of nations through the category of the *made*. "Fine word, legitimate!" scoffs *King Lear*'s villain Edmund, deriding the "curiosity of nations" in favor of nature's seemingly preferable "law" (1.2.4, 1.2.1).[65] Shakespeare was already registering the moral difficulties

[should] necessarily mean that their authority should be downgraded? Why should the realization that aesthetic things have something in common with other created things lessen the prestige of the aesthetic generally?" Elaine Scarry, "The Made-Up and the Made-Real," in *Field Work: Sites in Literary and Cultural Studies*, ed. Marjorie Garber, Paul Franklin, and Rebecca Walkowitz (New York: Routledge, 1996), 214–24; Peters, "Law, Literature, and the Vanishing Real," 450.

[61] Benedict Anderson, *Imagined Communities: Reflections on the Origin and Spread of Nationalism*, Rev. edn. (London: Verso, 2006), 7.

[62] Hooker, *Of the Laws of Ecclesiastical Polity*, 98.

[63] Peter Goodrich, "On the Relational Aesthetics of International Law," *Journal of the History of International Law* 10 (2008): 324.

[64] Robert Wiseman, *The Law of Laws, Or, The Excellencie of the Civil Law above All Humane Laws Whatsoever* (London: R. Royston, 1664), 60.

[65] Unless otherwise specified, all references to Shakespeare are to William Shakespeare, *The Norton Shakespeare*, ed. Stephen Greenblatt, Jean E. Howard, and Katharine Eisaman Maus (London: W. W. Norton & Company, 1997). Quoted lines from *King Lear* appear in both Q1 and the Folio.

introduced by the law of nations. Typically contrasted with natural law ("a law not specific to mankind... but common to all animals," according to the Roman *Digest*) and civil law (the unique code of a given society), the law of nations, it was claimed, was "common only to human beings among themselves."[66] Literature and the law of nations, to their credit and occasional shame, were the work of *homo faber*. They challenged humans—no small task—to love what they had made. Theologically, the law of nations was an uneasy treaty between divine perfection and human depravity. Temporally, it was belated. Morally, it was between two straights.

The edifice Hooker acknowledged as "built" was experienced by others— Edmund among them—as a sinful "plague of custom" (1.2.4). Gonzalo's famous speech in Act 2, Scene 1 in *The Tempest*, where Gonzalo entertains the striking possibility of "no sovereignty," offers rich illustration. "Judged by the principles of natural law, the world of early modern politics and economy could only be viewed as a moral abomination," writes Martti Koskenniemi.[67] Although it is often emphasized that Gonzalo's speech borrows language from Montaigne's essay "On Cannibals," we should also know that the speech undoes, line by line, one of the most familiar definitions of the law of nations circulating in early modern England. Like Empson's "Legal Fiction," Gonzalo's speech illustrates how the law of nations vied conceptually with natural liberty or a state of nature. When Gonzalo imagines having "plantation of this isle," he says he

> ...would by contraries
> Execute all things; for no kind of traffic,
> Would I admit; no name of magistrate,
> Letters should not be known, riches, poverty,
> And use of service, none; contract, succession,
> Bourn, bound of land, tilth, vineyard, none;
> No use of metal, corn, or wine, or oil;
> No occupation; all men idle, all,
> And women too, but innocent and pure;
> No sovereignty –
>
> (2.1.144–153)

Shakespeare engages here with a foundational passage compiled in Justinian's *Digest* (I.5), where the Roman jurist Hermogenian points out the gap between a putatively innocent state of nature and the order pertaining to a human world of nations. "As a consequence of this *jus gentium*, wars were introduced, nations differentiated, kingdoms founded, properties individuated, estate boundaries settled, buildings set up, and commerce established, including contracts of buying and selling and letting and hiring."[68] Sovereignty, property, borders, contracts: all of

---

[66] Justinian, *The Digest of Justinian*, trans. Alan Watson (Philadelphia, PA: University of Pennsylvania Press, 1985), I.1.3–4.

[67] Martti Koskenniemi, "The Political Theology of Trade Law: The Scholastic Contribution," in *From Bilateralism to Community Interest*, ed. Ulrich Fastenrath et al. (Oxford: Oxford University Press, 2011), 94.

[68] Justinian, *The Digest of Justinian*, 1.2.

these were human addenda supplementing or modifying nature—not in conflict with the law of nations but authorized by that law. Slavery too—which Gonzalo calls "service"—was caught up in such accounts. "Slavery [*servitus*] is an institution of the law of nations," affirmed *Digest* I.5.4.1. Gonzalo's utopianism was therefore a utopianism developed dialectically with the law of nations, or at least a version of it received in Renaissance England through Roman law. John Cowell's *Interpreter* (1607), one of several possible sources for Shakespeare, had recently observed, "From the Law of Nations...are servitudes, wars, distinct and divided Nations, severall distinguisht Kingdomes and Dominions, Manumissions, setting of bounds to Land, the building together, and neighbouring of houses, by which means we have our Cities, boroughs, and Villiages."[69] Thinkers far more politically radical than Cowell happily endorsed similar claims, deeming it absurd for "subjective authority formally to flow from Nature."[70]

Ancient Roman jurists themselves were poly-vocal on whether law fell into two or three broad categories. The tripartite account of law introduced earlier—*ius naturae, ius gentium*, and *ius civile*—was advanced in the *Corpus Juris Civilis* by the jurists Ulpian and Hermogenian, but contributions by Gaius side by side with theirs treated the law of nations and the law of nature synonymously. Tensions between such accounts made legal taxonomy in early modern England a surprisingly contentious issue. Milton in his divorce tracts of the 1640s was able to add divorce to the conventions brought in by the "secondary" law of nations because divorce in his account shared an essential similarity with other conventions like property, captivity, and laws of war. It was part of the broad set of imperfect remedies that helped mitigate the generalized state of human vulnerability that Milton and many other Christians thought had been occasioned by the Fall.

The Fall's role in the disjunction between natural law and the law of nations meant that the *ius gentium* occupied an uneasy place. Law of nations discourse wasn't exclusively a discourse of making. It was also a discourse of humility, impotence, and lack. Seen as "humane inventions," remedies of the law of nations were inventions to protect against dangers like malice, insufficiency of resources, and "weather on skin."[71] Milton was one of many thinkers who came to distinguish between a "primary law of nature" and a "secondary law of nature," using the latter term synonymously with the law of nations. Maneuvers such as these point toward two kinds of discomfort about the law of nations: first, that institutions like property, commerce, and the laws of war might be mistaken as natural; but second, that they may be seen as altogether anathema to the nature God had made. Walter Raleigh, who observed in his *History of the World* (1617) that "Nationall law [i.e., the law of nations], according to divers acceptions, and divers considerations...may be sometime taken for a *Species* of the Naturall, sometime of the Humane," suggested

---

[69] Cowell, *The Interpreter*, 3.

[70] Peter English, *The Survey of Policy: Or, A Free Vindication of the Commonwealth of England, against Salmasius, and Other Royallists* (Leith, 1654), 167.

[71] Christopher Elderfield, *The Civil Right of Tythes* (London: Tho. Newcomb, for John Holden, 1650), 14; Laurie Shannon, "Poor, Bare, Forked: Animal Sovereignty, Human Negative Exceptionalism, and the Natural History of King Lear," *Shakespeare Quarterly* 60, no. 2 (2009): 178.

like many that the law of nations was ultimately law seen through a dark glass.[72] "The law of Nations properly taken, is that *dictate,* or *sentence,* which is drawne from a very probable, though not from an evident principle, yet so probable, that all Nations doe assent unto the conclusion."[73] The association with the human acknowledged—in fact, was premised on—the possibility of error. An inbuilt humility helped distinguish the historically constituted law of nations from the divine and natural laws that in most accounts were seen to transcend human time and agency.

Saying something was consistent with the law of nations was almost always part of an attempt to justify it (for example, Milton and divorce), yet the law of nations was often, too, a discourse of "pathology," remaining uniquely vulnerable to critiques from two sides: on the one hand, for normalizing felt injustices, on the other hand, for wanting too much.[74] Some critics saw the law of nations as impairing the godly endeavor to walk once again with God in the garden, giving undue quarter to violence and destruction. Others insisted the Fall had been a decisive break in legal epochs. Showing both embers of the former light and evidence of human corruption, then, the law of nations was perceived as attractive and dangerous in equal measures.

In Miltonic terms, the emphasis for some was on *Paradise,* for others it was *Lost.* Writers of the latter disposition viewed the law of nations as *too* connected to an unattainable innocence, its danger flowing from the perilous conjunction of its attractiveness and unattainability. For such writers, there was no path back to the garden of Genesis. When Gonzalo's interlocutor mocks Gonzalo, joking, "The latter end of his commonwealth forgets the beginning," the accusation is that Gonzalo has forgotten the lessons of the Fall—"in the beginning," of course, is the English translation of *Genesis.*

In his famous discussion of sovereignty in *Six Livres de la République* (I.8), Jean Bodin treated the law of nations with circumspection. He quarreled with those claiming that the sovereign prince was somehow bound by the law of nations to keep his predecessor's agreements. Defining "law of nations" as "human laws common to all nations," Bodin argued, "the prince is bound ... by the law of nations [*droit des gens*], but no more than by any of his own enactments. If the law of nations is iniquitous in any respect, he can disallow it within his own kingdom, and forbid his subjects to observe it..."[75] Iniquitous [*inique*] was not a word theorists were tempted to apply to *ius naturae.*[76] Unlike natural law, which was noted

---

[72] Walter Raleigh, *The History of the World* (London: [William Stansby] for Walter Burr, 1617), 289.

[73] Raleigh, *The History of the World,* 289.

[74] Annabel Brett, *Changes of State: Nature and the Limits of the City in Early Modern Natural Law* (Princeton, NJ: Princeton University Press, 2011), 115.

[75] Jean Bodin, *On Sovereignty: Six Books of the Commonwealth,* trans. M. J. Tooley (United States of America: Seven Treasures, 2009), 68, 75.

[76] Bodin interestingly anticipates late work by Derrida, who likewise observes in *Rogues* that "Nation-state sovereignty can even itself, in certain conditions, become an indispensable bulwark against certain international powers." Jacques Derrida, *Rogues: Two Essays on Reason,* trans. Pascale-Anne Brault and Michael Nass (Stanford, CA: Stanford University Press, 2005), 158. The external

for its permanence, the law of nations was associated with contingency, mutability, custom, and history. It wasn't quite that the law of nations wasn't a valid source of authority. For most writers, it was. Rather, it was what Bruce Robbins terms a "dirty universalism."[77] Its authority remained suspect and provisional, its norms and permissions always bracketed by the *ius gentium's* avowedly human origins.

The questions of epistemology, human artistry, and convention raised by the law of nations aren't the only reasons we need a more literary history of international law, however. I aim to show in this book that literature was an important engine for thinking about the law of nations and that poetry offered compelling resources for intervening in international legal controversies. The law may wish to have a formal existence, as Stanley Fish once commented, but the chapters of this book will suggest that law and literature in the early modern period were more like different states of matter than fundamentally different elements.[78] In the heat of international controversy, words of law sublimated to become powerful literature. Under pressure, literature solidified into law.

KINDS OF INTERNATIONAL LAW

The fullest way to understand the literary history of the law of nations is to look carefully at the early modern community of genres. For historians of international law, it is often the Peace of Westphalia of 1648 that inaugurates the modern order. Ending the Thirty Years' War, Westphalia is seen as formalizing the separation of religion and politics under the principle *Cuius regio, eius religio*: whose is the region, his is the religion. But accounts dominated by Westphalia can be too quick to forget that modern international law involves far more than territory and religion. Today, an everyday occurrence such as the transport of hazardous chemicals at sea may be "narrate[d] as part of... different set[s] of human pursuits, values, and priorities," which might include trade law, human rights law, environmental law, law of the sea, transport law, or public international law.[79] Each of these kinds of law organizes persons, events, and evidence in a distinctive way. The *homo economicus* of international trade law is a legal person only insofar as she is a "market-oriented consumer"; to the exclusion of other aspects of his being, the "subject" of human rights is addressed as "a passive, helpless entity [who] requires protection,

threats against which sovereignty might provide a bulwark for Derrida include "certain ideological, religious, or capitalist, indeed linguistic, hegemonies that, under the cover of liberalism or universalism, would still represent, in a world that would be little more than a marketplace, a rationalization in the service of particular interest." While Derrida does not explicitly name "law" in his catalogue, it is easy to imagine how it could meet such criteria. See also J. Butler and G. C. Spivak, *Who Sings the Nation-State?: Language, Politics, Belonging* (London; New York: Seagull Books, 2007), for whom the nation-state remains an institution worthy to be sung.

[77] Bruce Robbins, *Feeling Global: Internationalism in Distress* (New York: New York University Press, 1999), 75.

[78] Stanley Fish, "The Law Wishes to Have a Formal Existence," in *The Fate of Law*, ed. Austin Sarat and Thomas R. Kearns (Ann Arbor, MI: University of Michigan Press, 1991), 159–208. See further Bourdieu, "The Force of Law."

[79] Martti Koskenniemi, *The Politics of International Law* (Oxford: Hart, 2011), 279.

[as] an individual in need [of] a mediator."[80] Contemporary international law is riven by fault lines and complexities.

The Renaissance literary field of proximate and complexly differentiated genres offers a new genealogy for this tense plurality of contemporary international law. I advance here a critical method that illuminates the stakes of genre using the political and intellectual history of international law. My contention is that epic, comic, tragicomic, historical, and tragic *topoi* hardened into recognizable kinds of international law like laws of war, treaty law, private international law, trade law, and human rights. By organizing persons, actions, and evidence in distinctive ways, early modern genres anticipate but also create the multiplicity of contemporary international law, in which subfields like human rights, the laws of war, international commercial law, and so forth, co-exist in uneasy proximate relation.

The book's argument about kinds and the history of international law connects to work by eighteenth-century specialists like Joseph Slaughter, Lynn Hunt, and Julie Stone Peters, who have persuasively linked the eighteenth-century rise of the novel with the concurrent rise of philosophical aesthetics and of human rights.[81] Peters persuasively argues that the rise of human rights helped create a new category of aestheticized literature, one newly dissociated from politics and international legal controversy. Slaughter tracks the novel's inbuilt version of the human into the Universal Declaration of Human Rights (UDHR). In a deft piece of reception history, he reminds us that we owe the UDHR's precise wording to drafters' ideological debates over the meaning of Daniel Defoe's novel *Robinson Crusoe*. Given this important strain in eighteenth-century studies, I focus here on early modern genres historically prior to the novel, with a view towards enriching the already subtle accounts by Peters, Slaughter, and others.

Literature could be established as aesthetic and fundamentally distinct from the law of nations only when the law of nations had developed its own institutional kinds. To better understand such a claim, a brief comparison may be helpful: The early modern contours appear more clearly through the perspective of the eighteenth century. "In early modern England the distinction between history and literature was, at least technically, an anachronism."[82] "In fact," as Donald R. Kelley and David Harris Sacks observe, "'literature' encompassed history, since

---

[80] Rene Urueña, *No Citizens Here: Global Subjects and Participation in International Law* (Leiden; Boston, MA: M. Nijhoff Publishers, 2012), 60, 105.

[81] Joseph R. Slaughter, *Human Rights, Inc.: The World Novel, Narrative Form, and International Law* (New York: Fordham University Press, 2007); Lynn Hunt, *Inventing Human Rights: A History* (New York: W.W. Norton & Co, 2007); Julie Stone Peters, "'Literature,' the 'Rights of Man,' and Narratives of Atrocity: Historical Backgrounds to the Culture of Testimony," *Yale Journal of Law & the Humanities* 17, no. 2 (2005). See also Thomas Laqueur, "Bodies, Details, and the Humanitarian Narrative," in *The New Cultural History: Essays*, ed. Aletta Biersack and Lynn Hunt (Berkeley, CA: University of California Press, 1989); Susan Maslan, "The Anti-Human: Man and Citizen before the Declaration of the Rights of Man and of the Citizen," *South Atlantic Quarterly* 103, no. 2/3 (2004): 357–74.

[82] Donald R. Kelley and David Harris Sacks, "Introduction," in *The Historical Imagination in Early Modern Britain: History, Rhetoric, and Fiction, 1500–1800* (Cambridge: Cambridge University Press, 1997), 2.

the term conventionally signified anything preserved in writing."[83] By the end of the eighteenth century, however, literature was taking on a more restricted meaning. English had developed the "modern sense of literature as having something to do with imaginative writing."[84] In the process, strong associations with forensic and deliberative rhetoric were overshadowed by growing concerns with imagination and sentiment. Broadly stated, rhetorical dimensions that had characterized literature in the sixteenth and seventeenth centuries resolved over the long eighteenth century into a more disinterested philosophical aesthetics founded on the narration of the feeling human *as such*.[85] Such developments coincided almost exactly with the first mention of "international law," in 1780. Along with the emergence of the novel, the eighteenth century saw the professionalization and systemization of the law of nations.

A proleptic vision of the age of Defoe, Richardson, and Fielding reminds us that it was also in a sense the age of Grotius and Pufendorf—more specifically, Grotius' *De Jure Belli ac Pacis* and Pufendorf's *De Jure Naturae et Gentium*, treatises granted an increasingly prominent role in specialized eighteenth-century law curricula. The career of someone like the jurist Jean Barbeyrac (1674–1744), who translated both Pufendorf and Grotius into French, suggests that translating and annotating seventeenth-century treatises on the law of nations garnered much of the prestige once given to translating and annotating classical texts.[86] Pufendorf's work had become part of the law curriculum at Glasgow; Edinburgh established the Regius Chair of Public Law and the Law of Nature and Nations in 1707; and thinkers like Christian Wolff and Emer de Vattel became authorities on world affairs, the latter principally through his *Le Droit des Gens* of 1758.[87] The University of Kraków converted a professorship of canon law to one dedicated to the law of nations in the mid-eighteenth century, and Spain created a chaired professorship in 1770.[88] The collection and publication of treaties, an activity that occupied both Leibniz and the early Shakespeare critic Thomas Rymer in the early Enlightenment, became over the eighteenth century a "growth industry."[89] By the late eighteenth

[83] Kelley and Sacks, "Introduction," 2.

[84] Stephen Greenblatt, "What Is the History of Literature?," *Critical Inquiry* 23, no. 3 (April 1, 1997): 469.

[85] Peters, "'Literature,' the 'Rights of Man,' and Narratives of Atrocity"; Slaughter, *Human Rights, Inc.*; Hunt, *Inventing Human Rights*; Laqueur, "Bodies, Details, and the Humanitarian Narrative."

[86] Meri Päivärinne, "Translating Grotius's De Jure Belli Ac Pacis: Courtin vs Barbeyrac," *Translation Studies* 5, no. 1 (2012): 33–47.

[87] John W. Cairns, "Scottish Law, Scottish Lawyers and the Status of the Union," in *A Union for Empire: Political Thought and the British Union of 1707*, ed. John Robertson (Cambridge: Cambridge University Press, 1995), 258; David Armitage, *The Declaration of Independence: A Global History* (Cambridge, MA: Harvard University Press, 2007), 38–41; Theodore Christov, "Vattel's Rousseau: Ius Gentium and the Natural Liberty of States," in *Freedom and the Construction of Europe*, 2 vols. (Cambridge: Cambridge University Press, 2013), 2167–87.

[88] Ludwik Erlich, "The Development of International Law as a Science," *Recueil Des Cours* 105 (1962): 230; Ignacio de la Rasilla del Moral, "The Study of International Law in the Spanish Short Nineteenth Century (1808–1898)," *Chicago Kent Journal of International and Comparative Law* 13, no. 2 (2013): 125.

[89] Jennifer Pitts, "Empire and Legal Universalisms in the Eighteenth Century," *American Historical Review* 117, no. 1 (2012): 100.

century in Britain, "citations from continental authorities on the law of nature and of nations...bec[a]me an essential part of the oratorical arsenal of the well-prepared parliamentary debater."[90] Edmund Burke wielded powerful anti-imperial arguments from the law of nations. The text of the U.S. Constitution (1787), too, testifies to the rise of the law of nations: Congress in Article 1 Section 8 is given the power to "to define and punish Piracies and Felonies committed on the high Seas, and Offences against the Law of Nations." Bentham could coin "international law" "to express, in a more significant way, the branch of law which goes commonly under the name of the law of nations" precisely because the law of nations had by this period matured into institutional forms.

In broadest outlines, then, the story of literature and the law of nations in the eighteenth century is one of bifurcation. Literary practices that in the early modern period were channeled into dramatic and poetic genres increasingly in the long eighteenth century were directed toward the fresh new genre of the *bildungsroman*, which invested in a particular version of individualized humanity and "project[ed] the social and cultural conditions out of which human rights might be recognized as commonsensical."[91] Over this period, the law of nations gained institutional stature but, in so doing, it shed previously strong affinities with genres with competing ontologies like biblical tragedy and epic. Until the mid-eighteenth century, "a sort of interchange and osmosis...characterised the link between the literary genres of biblical commentary and of juridical-political compositions, even...textbooks on the law of nature and of nations."[92] Even more specifically, biblical tragedy was a key site of exchange. Had they been writing a century earlier, thinkers like Vattel, Wolff, and Cornelis van Bynkershock may well have gained fame composing plays and poems or translating classical histories before writing treatises on the law of nations. Although Vattel, for one, remained interested in comedy and tragedy, the law of nations in general became too professionalized for the rich engagements with literary forms seen in previous centuries. The longstanding practice of quoting classical poets and orators fell out of fashion—Hobbes and Bynkershock both denounced it—and the very term "literature" that in the arts was increasingly linked with sensation and imagination took on an independent meaning within the institutionalized context of the law of nations, where one could now speak of the prior history of a specialized discourse.[93]

By 1800, the year Wordsworth composed his famous *Preface to the Lyrical Ballads*, teaching and publishing on the law of nations had become widespread but also highly controversial. Following the likes of English republicans like Milton and Algernon Sidney, French revolutionaries had accounted tyrants as enemies of

---

[90] Armitage, *Foundations of Modern International Thought*, 149.
[91] Slaughter, *Human Rights, Inc.*, 29.
[92] Gabriella Silvestrini, "With Grotius against Grotius: Jephtha's 'Appeal to Heaven' in John Locke's *Two Treatises of Government*," in *The Roots of International Law: Liber Amicorum for Peter Haggenmacher*, ed. Pierre-Marie Dupuy and Vincent Chetail (Leiden: Martinus Nijhoff, 2014), 94.
[93] Thus the title of D. H. L. Ompteda's German language work, *Litteratur des gesammten sowohl natüirlichen als positiven Völkerrechts* (1785).

all mankind, outlaws of the law of nations.[94] Counter-revolutionary tracts on the law of nations, such as Robert Ward's *Enquiry into the Foundation and History of the Law of Nations in Europe, From the Time of the Greeks and Romans, to the Age of Grotius* (1795), and Sir James Mackintosh's *Discourse on the Study of the Law of Nature and Nations* (1799), were written in response. While the French Assembly seriously debated a *Declaration of the Law of Nations* (1793) to supplement the *Declaration of the Rights of Man and Citizen*, Spain shuttered its crown-sponsored professorship in the law of nations, on the grounds that teachings on law of nations "bring with them the almost unavoidable risk that youth, imbued with principles that are contrary to our constitutions could draw pernicious consequences which can spread and produce an upheaval in the way of thinking of the nation."[95] In some eyes, the law of nations had gained *too much* institutional legitimacy.

Returning to the early modern terrain from the eighteenth century landscape allows us to see that the split between literature and international law enacted in the eighteenth century was not limited to human rights. The emergence of the novel increasingly challenged the cultural esteem of several early modern genres, including epic, tragedy, and comedy. The disparate cultural work each of those genres did in theorizing and disputing international law, therefore, was increasingly done elsewhere. In sum, the eighteenth century saw the rise of the *bildungsroman* and the rise of human rights, but it also saw the law of nations take on institutional legitimacy in textbooks, professorships, and finally, with Bentham, its modern moniker "international law." Fundamentally, there is a shift in the eighteenth century from literature *as* international jurisprudence to literature *and* international jurisprudence. This book is possible, however, because literature and international law still bear unmistakable marks of their once-stronger imbrication.

THE ROAD AHEAD

The role of this introduction so far has been to open conceptual space for the chapters that follow. Having connected the *gens* of genre to the *gens* of *ius gentium*, I examined some contemporary assumptions and biases through the phrase "national law." I then proposed that bringing literary history into closer conversation with the history of international law usefully challenges shibboleths across the political spectrum. My discussions of William Aldred's Case and William Empson's "Legal Fiction" suggested that if the past is a different country, all law is international law.

---

[94] Dan Edelstein, "War and Terror: The Law of Nations from Grotius to the French Revolution," *French Historical Studies* 31, no. 2 (Spring 2008): 229–62; Rachel Hammersley, *French Revolutionaries and English Republicans: The Cordeliers Club, 1790–1794* (Rochester, NY: Boydell Press, 2005).

[95] Abbe Gregoire, "Declaration of the Law of Nations," in *The Progressive Development of International Law; Proposed Declaration on Rights and Duties of States*, trans. Manley O. Hudson (Boston, MA: American Bar Association, Committee for Peace and Law Through United Nations, 1947), 1–2; Quotation of the Spanish decree from del Moral, "The Study of International Law in the Spanish Short Nineteenth Century (1808–1898)," 125–6.

Turning then to the early modern law of nations with help from Helgerson, *The Tempest*, and *King Lear*, I introduced what I called the *ius gentium*'s problematic of the made. We saw how early modern legal theory and poetics teamed up in a jurisprudence of kinds, and we then looked to the eighteenth century to see how philosophical aesthetics and a professionalized field of international law altered the relations of literature and the law of nations. In the remainder of this chapter, I give an overview of the following chapters and then conclude with some preliminary examples of the ways differing genres distribute international subject-hood and object-hood. Even in the short space I dedicate to the topic there, it may be possible to see how tragedy, comedy, and tragicomedy might give us fuller genealogies for our contemporary international institutions.

Methodologically, each of the following chapters engages with what Aristotle's *Nicomachean Ethics* calls "ultimate particulars."[96] No critic can do justice to every particular of a complex literary work, at least as long as the map is distinguishable from the territory. Treating singular literary tokens as representative of generic types necessarily subordinates important details and contexts. If I therefore abstract some of the ultimate particulars of works like Sidney's *New Arcadia* in calling it an epic or Shakespeare's *The Tempest* by calling it a comedy, I do so in a way not dissimilar from international law itself, which relies on ultimately contestable judgments about the *kind* of facts at hand. As Lauren Berlant puts it, law and genre are both "way[s] of rationalizing and debating about how to manage singularity."[97] Since early modern writers articulated principles of the law of nations most forcefully in fundamentally singular moments, often with particular interests under threat, topicality thus represents a second kind of ultimate particular. Taking a cue from Hannah Arendt, who observed that an "interest[ ] constitute[s], in the word's most literal significance, something which *inter-est*, which lies between people and therefore can relate and bind them together," I devote considerable space here to topical interests and circumstances.[98] The rationale—borne out in what follows— is that authors chose genres in response to legal-historical exigencies and political horizons.[99] Attention to writers' topical interests is fundamental to my approach to law and literature for the way it allows us to unravel contingent, specific configurations of facts and norms.

I argue in the next chapter that legally-minded attention to English Renaissance epic furnishes a surprising genealogy for public international law. At the heart of the chapter is a particular international network of humanists whose legal, philosophical, and diplomatic interests cohered in the early 1580s around epic. When the novel supplanted epic as the dominant genre, I contend, legal concerns long organized by the world of epic came dislodged. Ultimately, they found institutional

[96] Aristotle, *Nicomachean Ethics*, trans. Martin Ostwald (Upper Saddle River, NJ: Prentice Hall, 1999), 160 (1142a).
[97] Lauren Berlant, "On the Case," *Critical Inquiry* 33, no. 4 (June 1, 2007): 664.
[98] Hannah Arendt, *The Human Condition* (Chicago, IL: University of Chicago Press, 1958), 182.
[99] This relation between genre and political horizons is a point made elegantly by David Scott in *Conscripts of Modernity: The Tragedy of Colonial Enlightenment* (Durham, NC: Duke University Press, 2004), whose inspirations include Quentin Skinner and Northrop Frye.

refuge in the discipline of "public international law." *Topoi* of public international law, made relevant by the challenging legal and diplomatic contexts of the late sixteenth century, then, illuminate the shared concerns of works like Torquato Tasso's *Gerusalemme Liberata*, Alberico Gentili's *De Jure Belli*, and especially Philip Sidney's *New Arcadia*. While Austin argued that international law could be seen as law only "by analogy," such works prove that the conventions of genre were not merely logically similar to the conventions of international law. The tight overlap of epic conventions and conventions of the law of nations emerges here as homology—no longer a "confrontation of resemblances across space," as Foucault once described analogy, but a co-evolution from the common source of humanist *praxis*.[100] Although only Gentili has remained an important figure in the history of international law, the humanist network at the heart of Chapter 2 helps to explain why epic's conventional plots so surprisingly anticipate and so easily map onto the now canonical concerns of public international law—the formation and recognition of states, acquisition of territory, the drafting and interpretation of treaties, and the laws of war. One of Gentili's most important sources was Vergil's *Aeneid*, and he drew deeply from Homer's *Iliad* and Tasso's *Jerusalemme Liberata*. Sidney, a reader of Vergil and Tasso, corresponded with Gentili and was the dedicatee of Gentili's *De Legationibus Libri Tres* (1585). Tropes of supplication, enmity, and diplomacy constitute the "feigned examples" in the epic law of nations, suggesting that the would-be diplomats of the Sidney circle treasured epic for presenting international law in its most heroic dimensions.

Chapter 2's literary history of public international law is closely connected to the history of reading. Early modern receptions of ancient supplication scenes became central to the *topoi* of modern public international law. Roman comedy in the history of private international law works in parallel. In Chapter 3, "Jacobean Comedy and the *Anagnorisis* of Private International Law," Renaissance lawyers' debates over the Roman comedian Plautus inform the analysis of Plautine Jacobean dramas *Pericles*, *The Tempest*, and *The Captives*. Whereas Shakespeare's late plays have come to be seen as romances following Edward Dowden's Victorian taxonomy, this chapter treats these plays as comedies in order to make the legal-literary Plautus allusions legible. To further detail the productive topical synergy between private international law and English Renaissance comedy, the chapter looks to an important but little-studied English admiralty court case, *Venetian Ambassador v. Brooke* (1608–1611). It was alleged in this case that 30,000 crowns worth of goods on a Venetian ship had been stolen by Mediterranean pirates, sold to Turks in Tunis, and then bought by English merchants who transported the goods to England. On the basis of the case's high stakes and difficult questions about contracts, property, and proof, the chapter argues that the case serves as an important aid for understanding Jacobean comedy, particularly Jacobean comedy's heretofore under-acknowledged preoccupations with the canonical concerns of private international law, especially the emerging conflict of laws doctrines of *lex loci contractus*,

---

[100] Michel Foucault, *The Order of Things: An Archaeology of the Human Sciences* (New York: Vintage Books, 1970), 21.

lex rei sitae (law of the place where an object is situated), and *lex loci delicti commissi* (law of the place in which a tort is committed). While scholars have rightly pointed out the forensic energy in *Pericles, The Tempest*, and *The Captives*, these private international law contexts accompanying adaptations of Plautine Roman comedy have generally been less well understood. The new understanding of Renaissance comedy developed in this chapter points toward private international law's recognition that traders, exiles, expatriates, and migrants were ordinary facts of legal life. Not only was a vast area of the law premised on such fundamental realities, so too was much English Renaissance comedy.

Some of the better-known discussions of the law of nations in the English Renaissance came in the context of the Union debates of the early Jacobean period. Chapter 4 examines the law of nations in its tragicomic aspects during this period. It looks at the tragicomic law of nations through *The Winter's Tale* and argues that the play's remarkable spatiality is informed by the generic dimensions of the law of nations in the context of the Union debates. By using Francis Bacon's emphasis on "new forms," I argue that it becomes possible to see how the generic experiment of *The Winter's Tale* is related to the proposed "new forms" of law based on the law of nations that would bind English and Scots citizens together. The argument for new forms in both cases had to do with the power of old forms. What became clear in the Union debates was that legal conventions, like literary conventions, could generate unthinking or illicit allegiance. New forms, by contrast, challenged customary patterns of identification and, even more, provoked vibrant new bonds. Already existing as a notion and a geographical unit, Britain, according to its advocates, merely needed to make itself. Bacon and Shakespeare were some of the few to understand the symbolic and constitutive role of legal forms in this geopolitical self-fashioning. What *The Winter's Tale* does, above all, is to link the legal conventions with literary conventions and to come down, with Bacon, on the side of the novel—even as the play's title associates that novelty with long-held custom through the bardic tradition of storytelling. The result is to put a new emphasis on middles—as legal forms and literary conventions are re-imagined to turn the barren and contested middle spaces of genre and geography into the rich and festive spaces of community. Thus do the law of nations and geography find representation in *The Winter's Tale*'s generic movement from international tragedy to transnational comedy.

It is the aim in what then follows in Chapter 5 to return humanist philological *praxis*, history, and translation to the important places they once held in the early modern making of international law. Thomas Hobbes is a figure more often credited with destroying the law of nations than with making it, but this chapter reveals Hobbes entering an emerging debate between Gentili and Grotius on history in the law of nations. Hobbes published his famous translation of Thucydides, *Eight Bookes of the Peloponesian Warres*, in 1628. "From Imperial History to Colonial International law: Thucydides, Hobbes, and the Law of Nations" augments existing scholarship, much of which has focused on Hobbes' royalism, by emphasizing how Hobbes' translation of classical history steered between the Scylla of antiquarianism and the Charybdis of baldly instrumental rhetoric. The chapter shows the formidable interventions a translator could make amidst the seventeenth-century *poiesis* of international law. The stakes of Thucydides included the accuracy of the Genesis story, the extent or existence of natural obligations, and the capacity of men, as one of Hobbes' marginal notes put it, to "gr[o]w...civil." Reading Hobbes' translation in the context of seventeenth-century debates over the law of nations offers a chance to see how history and humanism intersected in the making of international law.

For Hobbes, international history would become proof of his state of nature, famously characterized as a war of all against all. According to some writers, that state of nature was exemplified most strongly in the sixteenth and seventeenth centuries by the figures of pirates, described at least since Cicero's *De Officiis* as the "enemies of all mankind." While Chapters 3, 4, and 5 all touch on piracy in one way or another, these chapters also indicate major differences in how different genres conceive of the so-called right to have rights.[101] Chapter 6 follows this thread into a broader exploration of questions about what would come to be called "international legal personality." The explicit focus here is on who has standing in the eyes of international law. "From Biblical Tragedy to Human Rights: International Legal Personality in Grotius' *Sophompaneas* and Milton's *Samson Agonistes*" turns to biblical tragedy and with it, to heretofore underdeveloped scriptural contexts.[102] Revealing the interlocking concerns of biblical tragedy and the law of nations are two works in particular: Hugo Grotius' *Sophompaneas* (1635; English trans., 1652), a learned dramatization of Genesis 39–50 that deserves to be much better known, and Milton's much-debated *Samson Agonistes*. Reading *Samson Agonistes* with Grotius' biblical tragedy helps us not only to see Hebrew scripture's influence on emerging global norms, but also how biblical tragedy develops into two competing orders: a flat, unmediated politics of human rights and the highly allegorized mimetic structure of international legal personality.

As quasi-public figures acting on the international stage, Grotius' Joseph and Milton's Samson both dramatize traditional problems in the law of nations and also challenge pervasive distinctions between public and private. Even as the two dramas illuminate Isidore of Seville's oft-reproduced suggestion in the *Etymologies* that "the law of nations concerns the occupation of territory, building, fortification, wars, captivities, enslavements, the right of return, treaties of peace, truces, the pledge not to molest embassies, the prohibition of marriages between different races," they also show broadening conceptions of international legal personality that help shed light on the eighteenth-century emergence of human rights.

The previously described chapters on the international legal dimensions of epic, comedy, history, and tragedy yield new insights into *Paradise Lost*. We know of Milton's interest in the law of nations from such sources as his meeting with

---

[101] Arendt, "The Decline of the Nation-State and the End of the Rights of Man," 296.

[102] For international law's often repressed religious history, see James St. Leger, *The "Etiamsi Daremus" of Hugo Grotius: A Study in the Origins of International Law* (Rome: Typis Pontificiae Universitatis Gregorianae, 1962); David Kennedy, "Images of Religion in International Law," in *Religion and International Law*, ed. Mark W. Janis and Carolyn Evans (The Hague: Martinus Nijhoff Publishers, 1999), 145–53; Goodrich, "On the Relational Aesthetics of International Law"; J. Muldoon, "Medieval Canon Law and the Formation of International Law," *Zeitschrift Der Savigny-Stiftung Für Rechtsgeschichte. Kanonistische Abteilung* 125 (1995): 64–82.

Grotius in Paris in the 1630s, his readings of John Selden, and most explicitly from his argument in *Tetrachordon* that our "imperfect and degenerate condition" left us capable of horrific, "intolerable wrong." Mitigating this condition, he wrote, required pragmatic, human conventions like divorce, property, captivity, and war—called collectively "by Civilians...the secondary Law of Nature and of Nations." The secondary law of nations, for Milton, was non-utopian and indeed tragicomic. God "suffered" these non-utopian conventions because they diminished those terrifying risks of human freedom that for Milton were signified by the scriptural phrase "hardness of heart." Chapter 7, "'A Problem From Hell': From *Paradise Lost* to the Responsibility to Protect," reads the poem in light of the canonical problems of public international law—the formation and recognition of states, the laws of war, acquisition of territory, and the drafting and interpretation of treaties—but it does so by placing Milton's epic jurisprudence in the context of recent discussions in public international law and international humanitarian law concerning the "responsibility to protect." "Responsibility to protect" has been proposed as a new alternative to the language of "humanitarian intervention" and has been lauded as a new norm in international law. Challenging the view that the responsibility to protect is a modern idea, however, I contend that protection was a key element of Milton's thinking on the law of nations since the early 1630s and that *Paradise Lost* offers a distinctly republican analytic of protection. The chapter further sheds new light on Milton's *Second Defense* by attending to Milton's activities as Latin Secretary and the legal controversies surrounding a 1653 murder committed in London by Don Pantaleon de Sá, the brother of the Portuguese ambassador, João Rodrigues de Sá. Milton's poem, I suggest, rejects Westphalian distinctions between inside and outside and puts human jurisdiction over tyranny at the center of its epic jurisprudence.

I leave until the book's conclusion a final example of an early modern author whose surprising role in twenty-first-century international affairs illustrates the contemporary stakes of literature and international law in a new way.

TOWARDS A LITERARY HISTORY
OF INTERNATIONAL LAW

While the primary aim of this introduction has been to prepare the ground for the chapters that follow, I want to conclude with slightly more detail about how three specific early modern genres—tragedy, comedy, and tragicomedy—might enrich our genealogies of contemporary international law. In early modern tragedy, we see elements that continue to shape contemporary debates over questions of war crimes and sovereign immunity.[103] It's hardly news that early modern tragedy

[103] This formulation adds a literary dimension to an argument made by Bruce Rosenstock, "Against Sovereign Impunity: The Political Theology of the ICC," in *After Secular Law*, ed. Winnifred Fallers Sullivan, Robert A. Yelle, and Mateo Taussig-Rubbo (Stanford, CA: Stanford University Press, 2011), 160–77.

concerns the legal entailments of sovereignty, but tragic sovereignty isn't always appreciated in its necessarily international dimensions.[104] The encroaching French in *King Lear*, Norwegians in *Hamlet*, and Ottoman Turks in *Othello* all situate sovereignty in an international context. Even within such international contexts, however, the jurisdiction over sovereignty is narratively bound with catastrophic woe: tragic catastrophes are often depicted as the punishment of the gods. To recognize as much is to gain a new foothold on controversies such as that surrounding the International Criminal Court (ICC). The ICC, founded in 2002, takes jurisdiction over genocide, crimes against humanity, war crimes, and crimes of aggression. Theoretically, and no less controversially, the Rome Statute underpinning the ICC puts almost all sovereigns and their representatives at risk of prosecution. Critics like John Bolton see the ICC as wrongheadedly subjecting sovereigns to universal jurisdiction.[105] Bolton has argued that the ICC expresses "utopian zeal," in the process setting his own view up as realism; but Bolton's objections can be framed more accurately as tragic jurisprudence. In tragic terms, the ICC's very raison d'être means its activities cannot end in anything other than catastrophe. The ICC's putative utopianism, in this view, is a generic wrong—a crime against the higher law of genre.[106] We are better positioned to understand contemporary debates when we recognize the surprising role of poetics: de-coupling jurisdiction over sovereigns from the narrative *telos* of catastrophe could well be the primary ideological challenge that the ICC faces.

Comedy makes its own claims on contemporary institutions. International law is often thought to begin and end with heroic *personae* and grand questions of war and peace, but early modern comedy teaches us to recognize commerce, travel, and family as meaningful sites of international law.[107] *The Merchant of Venice* is a comedy not simply because Antonio escapes death and because Bassanio, Portia, Jessica, and Lorenzo all get married. It is a comedy because of the international legal matters the play organizes.[108] "Private international law" came to be associated with "wills, people's marriages, and disputes about ships and boats," as Dickens described the remit of Doctors' Commons in *David Copperfield*.[109] The *topoi* of

---

[104] See, for example, Franco Moretti, "The Great Eclipse: Tragic Form as the Deconsecration of Sovereignty," in *Signs Taken for Wonders: Essays in the Sociology of Literary Forms*, Rev. edn. (London: Verso, 1988), 42–82.

[105] John R. Bolton, "The Global Prosecutors: Hunting War Criminals in the Name of Utopia," *Foreign Affairs*, January 1999, www.foreignaffairs.com/print/54634?page=2; Derrida, "The Law of Genre."

[106] Bolton, "The Global Prosecutors: Hunting War Criminals in the Name of Utopia"; Derrida, "The Law of Genre."

[107] That comedy concerns private affairs is an early modern commonplace. I quote here from Giambattista Guarini, "The Compendium of Tragicomic Poetry," in *Literary Criticism: Plato to Dryden*, ed. and trans. Allan H. Gilbert (Detroit, MI: Wayne State University Press, 1962), 509. "I...am content to hand over to tragedy kings, serious actions, the terrible, and the piteous; to comedy I assign private affairs, laughter, and jests; in these things are the specific differences between the two."

[108] Antonio, we should recall, is a stranger to Shylock's "sacred nation" (1.3.43).

[109] Charles Dickens, *David Copperfield*, ed. Jeremy Tambling (New York: Penguin, 2004), 352. I am influenced here by Luke Wilson, "Drama and Marine Insurance in Shakespeare's London," in *The Law in Shakespeare*, ed. Constance Jordan and Karen Cunningham (New York: Palgrave Macmillan, 2007).

early modern comedy help us think about how this came to be. The history of comedy is an enormous archive for private law questions of contracts, adoption, human trafficking, and property, and it can inform and challenge our contemporary thinking about privacy and authority in contemporary international law. Tragedy and comedy, then, register distinct but important traditions of international thought.

Blending comedy and tragedy, the early modern rise of tragicomedy registers commerce's increasing authority in international affairs.[110] As a hybrid form, tragicomedy mixed jurisdictions and orders, creating deeply complex worlds with multiple sources of authority, a range of actors, competing popular and elite power structures, and multiple laws across time and space. It takes seriously a kind of legal complexity that legal scholars now term "global legal pluralism."[111] Tragicomedy developed alongside the rise of a merchant class increasingly organizing itself as a "jurisgenerative community," one capable of articulating values and norms and offering reasons that those values and norms might be seen as laws.[112] Sovereign attempts to exert control over trade and commerce, heroic in a certain light, could be re-categorized as grandiose buffoonery. Those *personae juris gentium* exalted by the heroic suppositions of tragedy could seem, from another perspective, like "rude mechanicals" playing at tragedy in *A Midsummer Night's Dream*—that is, awkwardly imitating authority but hardly instantiating it. The title of Shakespeare's *Pericles, Prince of Tyre*, a play often read as a tragicomedy, in fact derives in part from Isaiah 23:8 where Isaiah calls the Biblical Tyre a place where the "merchants are princes." John Calvin's commentary on the passage confirms the growing authority of European merchants in relation to their customary betters: "[Isaiah] calls the Merchants *Princes*: as at this day the Merchants of Venice thinke themselves to surmount Princes in dignitie."[113] Tragicomedy, then, gives access to how early modern culture theorized the inevitable conflicts that arose with competing or overlapping legal ideologies, presenting new avenues into what Martti Koskenniemi has recently termed the "political theology of trade law," an early modern discourse of faith concerning the "miraculous coincidence of private and public good" attendant upon free trade.[114]

---

[110] A. Claire Cutler, "Private Authority in International Trade Relations: The Case of Maritime Transport," in *Private Authority and International Affairs*, ed. Virginia Haufler, Tony Porter, and A. Claire Cutler (Albany, NY: State University of New York Press, 1999), 283–328; Zachary Lesser, "Tragical-Comical-Pastoral-Colonial: Economic Sovereignty, Globalization, and the Form of Tragicomedy," *ELH* 74 (2007): 881–908; Valerie Forman, *Tragicomic Redemptions: Global Economics and the Early Modern English Stage* (Philadelphia, PA: University of Pennsylvania Press, 2008); Philip J. Stern, *The Company-State: Corporate Sovereignty and the Early Modern Foundations of the British Empire in India* (Oxford: Oxford University Press, 2012).

[111] Benedict Kingsbury, "Confronting Difference: The Puzzling Durability of Gentili's Combination of Pragmatic Pluralism and Normative Judgment," *The American Journal of International Law* 92, no. 4 (October 1, 1998): 713–23; Paul Schiff Berman, *Global Legal Pluralism: A Jurisprudence of Law beyond Borders* (Cambridge: Cambridge University Press, 2012).

[112] Robert M. Cover, "Nomos and Narrative," *Harvard Law Review* 97, no. 1 (November 1983): 4–64.

[113] Jean Calvin, *A Commentary upon the Prophecie of Isaiah*, trans. Clement Cotton (London: Felix Kyngston, 1609), 225.

[114] Koskenniemi, "The Political Theology of Trade Law: The Scholastic Contribution," 112.

The paths from early modern tragicomedy to global legal pluralism and the contemporary theology of trade law are not straightforward, nor is it possible to do any more than gesture to them in the confines of this introduction, or even a single book. My hope is that other scholars will join me in the work I begin in these pages. Even beyond the following chapters, much work would need to be done to connect tragedy and the ICC more fully, or to develop the full and far more complicated story of comedy and private international law. The point, however, as we turn to the chapters that follow, is to see the possible fruits of joining law and literature, genre studies, and the history of international law. A new literary history of international law might turn out to give us significant purchase on our twenty-first-century world.

2

From Epic to Public International Law
Philip Sidney, Alberico Gentili, and "Intercourse Among Enemies"

The 1580s offered no shortage of hard cases for Elizabethan Protestants like Philip Sidney and Alberico Gentili. Real, feared, and proposed assassinations, rebellions, and humanitarian interventions pervaded the Elizabethan geopolitical landscape. Over the decade that would culminate with the attack of the Spanish Armada in 1588, and in the midst of which Sidney would lose his life on the battlefield fighting against Spanish oppression of Dutch Protestants in the Low Countries, Elizabethans encountered deeply felt tensions among Protestantism, Christianity, and humanity as a whole. They confronted competing obligations to nation and to neighbor, to equity and to the self, to godly piety and to global primacy. Interpersonally, lines of kinship and confession crisscrossed, as with the Protestant Elizabeth and her Catholic cousin, Mary Stuart, whom Elizabeth finally agreed to have executed in 1587. Internationally, the world was populated with both friends in need and inconvenient inhabitants of strategic beachheads. Rebellion was at once the baleful political theory of Jesuitical papists in the British Isles, and the pathway to religious liberty in the Low Countries and in France. Beyond Europe, Iberian claims to legitimate dominion in the New World were as risible as they were reproducible: Before long, the English were making similar claims regarding the islands in the Caribbean and trade routes in Southeast Asia. In 1580, Lord Grey de Wilton, acting as Lord Deputy of Ireland with young Edmund Spenser as his Secretary, executed over 500 Spanish and Italian prisoners at Smerwick on the grounds, as Spenser put it in *A View of the Present State of Ireland,* that they were "not lawful enemies" but "adventurers" and therefore not entitled to "either custom of war or law of nations."[1] It was during this period, which Roger Kuin has provocatively called World War Zero, when a handgun was first used to assassinate a world leader—William the Silent, in 1584.[2] Poisoning was regularly feared. The challenges of "do[ing] justice to all aspects of a hard case, seeing and feeling in all its conflicted many sidedness" in this period were acute.[3]

---

[1] Edmund Spenser, *A View of the State of Ireland: From the First Printed Edition (1633)*, ed. Andrew Hadfield and Willy Maley (Oxford: Blackwell, 1997), 105.
[2] Roger Kuin, "Sir Philip Sidney and World War Zero: Implications of the Dutch Revolt," *Sidney Journal* 30, no. 2 (July 2012): 33–55.
[3] Martha Craven Nussbaum, *The Fragility of Goodness: Luck and Ethics in Greek Tragedy and Philosophy* (Cambridge; New York: Cambridge University Press, 1986), 45.

For two Elizabethan writers with more in common than is generally acknowledged, Philip Sidney and Alberico Gentili, I want to suggest now, the hard case in the law of nations was what epic poetry was for. As scholars of the epic genre have so powerfully shown, epic's formal signatures carried strong hypotheses of what the world was like and set the momentum of any individual post-Homeric epic toward some particular substantive concerns.[4] When Philip Sidney in the early 1580s revised his *Arcadia* to look more like Vergil's *Aeneid*, therefore, he did so knowing that the altered form brought different expectations from the comedic structure underpinning his earlier version of the poem.[5] The new structure oriented the poem more firmly toward an international tradition of aristocratic heroes overcoming private barriers and foreign enemies in a collective quest toward empire.[6]

In this new order, whose *topoi* favored trials by battle over the courtroom justice at the end of the *Old Arcadia*, events came charged with a distinctive type of representative meaning. Epic form implicitly asked its readers to understand its heroes ultimately in their public character, as representatives of larger collective destinies. Violence and peacemaking in epic took on a mimetic structure. If the characteristic epic actions of war-making and peacemaking started, as in the case of Homer's Achilles, in private affections, epic moved to reorient those actions toward mimesis, actions taken on behalf of the *genos*, *gens*, or collectivity. To use Thomas Hobbes' somewhat later language of representation, one of the things that made epic heroes *epic* was that they eventually "personated" their "kin" in international affairs. Stylistically, readers encounter what Mikhail Bakhtin called "epic distance." The sense that epic worlds are "closed" and "inaccessible to personal experience," in Bakhtin's influential account, can be attributed to epic's constitutive convention of heroic actions performed at a remove from the collectivities whose destinies are at stake.[7]

Epic's imaginative worlds, then, involved heroes and their enemies performing acts of legitimized mimetic violence alongside what might be called representative acts of kindness. Bakhtin's "epic distance," a term I take to assimilate this full structure of publicity and representation, has implications for what international lawyers would call epic's subjects and objects. Through the eyes of international law, subjects are entities recognized as having rights and duties in themselves, without further need for mimetic representation. Objects, we recall from Chapter 1, are

---

[4] David Quint, *Epic and Empire: Politics and Generic Form from Virgil to Milton* (Princeton, NJ: Princeton University Press, 1993); Thomas G. Pavel, *Fictional Worlds* (Cambridge, MA: Harvard University Press, 1986), 129; Hayden White, *The Content of the Form: Narrative Discourse and Historical Representation* (Baltimore, MD: Johns Hopkins University Press, 1987); Hayden White, *Metahistory: The Historical Imagination in Nineteenth-Century Europe* (Baltimore, MD: Johns Hopkins University Press, 1973).

[5] Lorna Hutson, *The Invention of Suspicion* (Oxford: Oxford University Press, 2007), 123.

[6] Quint, *Epic and Empire: Politics and Generic Form from Virgil to Milton*.

[7] Mikhail Bakhtin, "Epic and Novel," in *The Dialogic Imagination: Four Essays*, trans. Michael Holquist (Austin, TX: University of Texas Press, 1981), 16.

"the who, what and where... being acted on."[8] These objects of international law are the "legitimate topics" in respect to which rights and duties are held.[9] I argue that epic's distribution of subjects and objects, a distribution that differs importantly from the distributions of subjects and objects in other genres, helps produce the legitimate *topoi* of public international law. In the legal sense, epic subjects were collectivities, represented though they were in particular warriors, diplomats, and rulers. Epic's objects, "the who, what and where that were being acted on," the "legitimate topics" in respect to which rights and duties were held, included individuals in their private capacities, land, sea, diplomacy, prizes, war-making, and treaties. These, it is evident, have since become canonical subjects and objects of public international law.

The strong connection between the worlds of epic and public international law helps us see how public international law functions within a more or less epic ontology of heroes and enemies. And yet this is very far from suggesting that nothing changes when epic turns, over the eighteenth century, into public international law. The translation from epic to public international law neutralizes the dynamism of the epic plot, for epic is a teleological genre of becoming—the hero becoming public, the *gens* finding its imperial feet. Epic adversaries are not always enemies, in the privileged legal sense, either. Sometimes they too are becoming.

For liminal figures themselves seeking entry into the mimetic structures of international representation like the two Elizabethans at the heart of this chapter, Alberico Gentili and Philip Sidney, these features of epic—its traditional subjects and objects, alongside the challenging dynamism at the heart of the form—meant that epic's imaginative worlds could become schools in which would-be diplomats, warriors, and rulers could procure useful equipment for their difficult age. Situated at the nexus of law of nations theory, moral philosophy, literary criticism, and poetic practice, epic for these and other writers of their humanist networks offered occasions to develop legal literacy alongside moral muscle-building. This chapter argues that by treating epic as the genre of grand, representative persons in morally fraught international relation, Sidney and Gentili in different though connected ways cemented the *topoi* of what would become public international law.

Philip Sidney and Alberico Gentili are both major figures, albeit in divergent and rarely overlapping fields, and they have only occasionally been linked. This fact testifies to the immense—and, I have already suggested, misleading—gulf presently existing between literary history and the history of international law. If historians of international law have had little time for Sidney's fancies, literary history, similarly, has all but ignored Gentili's *De Legationibus Libri Tres* (1585) and *De Jure Belli* (1588), works justly celebrated by the modern experts in public

[8] David J. Bederman, *The Spirit of International Law* (Athens, GA: University of Georgia Press, 2002), 79.

[9] Bederman, *The Spirit of International Law*, 79.

international law who are also, I argue, largely unwitting inheritors of the epic worldview.[10] Even as Gentili's students have included Hugo Grotius and Carl Schmitt, and one of the twentieth century's most remarkable Sidney scholars— James Osborne—was a Yale professor with ties to the CIA and MI6, the overlapping concerns of the two Renaissance figures have nevertheless tended to be kept separate.[11] But partly because epic helped both of these figures probe and theorize the laws of war; partly because embassy itself was regularly described as a "Sort of Fiction" whereby a sovereign was represented in a foreign court; and partly because of Philip Sidney's specific and lifelong hunger for diplomatic missions, studying their works together yields productive conversations across the literature and law of nations divide.[12] As we shall see, the relation between epic conventions and conventions of the law of nations in the case of Sidney, Gentili, and others of their circle is underserved by the term analogy. In fact, the reason epic's plots map so easily onto today's public international law *topoi* of diplomatic recognition, the laws of war, acquisition of territory, and so forth is that epic and the public side of the law of nations in this period were co-constitutive. What might be seen as an analogy between epic conventions and the conventions of the law of nations can now be seen more clearly through Sidney and Gentili as homology, with the laws of war and diplomacy both originating from common sources in Renaissance humanist practices around epic.

Not least among reasons for studying Sidney and Gentili together is Sidney's personal friendship with Gentili. *De Legationibus* was printed by the Huguenot refugee Thomas Vautroullier and appeared with a fulsome dedication to Sidney,

---

[10] For treatment of Gentili in international law, see especially Thomas Erskine Holland, *Studies in International Law* (Oxford: Clarendon Press, 1898) 1–39, which includes a translation of Gentili's will, a bibliography of Gentili's published and unpublished works, as well as a bibliography of late nineteenth-century scholarship on Gentili; Richard Tuck, *The Rights of War and Peace: Political Thought and the International Order from Grotius to Kant* (Oxford: Oxford University Press, 1999), 16–50; Arthur Nussbaum, *A Concise History of the Law of Nations* (New York: Macmillan, 1954), 74–5, 94–5; Edward Adair, *The Extraterratoriality of Ambassadors in the Sixteenth and Seventeenth Centuries* (New York: Longmans Green, 1929), 17–20; Gesina H. J. Van der Molen, *Alberico Gentili and the Development of International Law: His Life, Work and Times* (Amsterdam: H. J. Paris, 1937); Diego Panizza, *Political Theory and Jurisprudence in Gentili's De Jure Belli: The Great Debate between "Theological" and "Humanist" Perspectives from Vitoria to Grotius* (New York: Institute for International Law and Justice, New York University School of Law, 2005); Benedict Kingsbury, "Confronting Difference: The Puzzling Durability of Gentili's Combination of Pragmatic Pluralism and Normative Judgment," *The American Journal of International Law* 92, no. 4 (October 1, 1998): 713–23; Diego Panizza, "The 'Freedom of the Sea' and the 'Modern Cosmopolis' in Alberico Gentili's De Iure Belli," *Grotiana* 30, no. 1 (2009): 88–106; Lauren Benton, *A Search for Sovereignty: Law and Geography in European Empires, 1400–1900* (Cambridge: Cambridge University Press, 2009), 104–31; Benedict Kingsbury and Benjamin Straumann, eds., *The Roman Foundations of the Law of Nations: Alberico Gentili and the Justice of Empire* (Oxford; New York: Oxford University Press, 2011).

[11] Peter Haggenmacher, "Grotius and Gentili: A Reassessment of Thomas E. Holland's Inaugural Lecture," in *Hugo Grotius and International Relations* (Oxford: Oxford University Press, 1992); Carl Schmitt, *The Nomos of the Earth in the International Law of the Jus Publicum Europeaum*, trans. G. L. Ulmen (New York: Telos Press, 2003), 158–62; On Osborn, see Robin W. Winks, *Cloak & Gown: Scholars in the Secret War, 1939–1961* (New Haven, CT: Yale University Press, 1996), 291–2.

[12] Hugo Grotius, *The Rights of War and Peace*, ed. Richard Tuck and Jean Barbeyrac, trans. [John Morris] (Indianapolis, IN: Liberty Fund, 2005), 912; Timothy Hampton, *Fictions of Embassy: Literature and Diplomacy in Early Modern Europe* (Ithaca, NY: Cornell University Press, 2009).

praising Sidney for the wisdom he had demonstrated in his "frequent personal interviews" with Gentili and concluding with a section suggesting Sidney was "a living image and example of the perfect ambassador."[13] While literary scholars have long known of the work, it has only recently begun to receive detailed investigation. Seeing it primarily as Gentili's relatively uncomplicated play for patronage, scholars have correspondingly been slow to explore suggestive links between *De Legationibus* and Sidney's *New Arcadia*.[14] For example, Gentili merits only a single mention in Blair Worden's important 400-page book, *The Sound of Virtue*—a mention demonstrating Sidney's interest in Machiavelli, which is of significance for Worden more for its domestic political implications than for its international ones.[15] Nevertheless, if Philip Sidney's *New Arcadia* amounts to "a work of political theory" whose central point is "that civilized society is not natural, but fragilely imposed," as John Carey puts it, Sidney's epic should be considered with far more attention to the network of lawyers and humanists around him whose own legal theories were premised on the notion that the human-made law of nations fixed international society together.[16] As another of Sidney's lawyer friends, Jean Hotman, would put it, defending diplomatic inviolability, the law of nations should be upheld lest "we should fall againe into that first Chaos."[17]

Gentili's dedication of *De Legationibus* to Sidney signals the political and intellectual milieu in which the two operated in the 1580s. Almost immediately after his arrival in England from Italy in 1580, Gentili became associated with Sidney's network of forward Protestants, a group with a "keen interest...in legal issues," many of whom gathered around Sidney's uncle Robert Dudley, Earl of Leicester, and who were adamant against English links with Catholic France and eager to

---

[13] Denis B. Woodfield, *Surreptitious Printing in England, 1550–1640* (Charlottesville, VA: University of Virginia Press, 1984), 25; Lisa Ferraro Parmelee, *Good Newes from Fraunce: French Anti-League Propaganda in Late Elizabethan England* (Rochester, NY: University of Rochester Press, 1996), 30–1; Alberico Gentili, *De Legationibus Libri Tres*, trans. Gordon Jennings Laing, vol. II (Oxford: Oxford University Press, 1924), iii, 201.

[14] Joanna Craigwood, "Sidney, Gentili, and the Poetics of Embassy," in *Diplomacy and Early Modern Culture*, ed. Robyn Adams and Rosanna Cox (New York: Palgrave Macmillan, 2011), 82–100; Katherine Duncan-Jones, *Sir Philip Sidney: Courtier Poet* (London: Hamish Hamilton, 1991), 271; Dennis Kay, ed., *Sir Philip Sidney: An Anthology of Modern Criticism* (Oxford: Clarendon Press, 1987), 6; Philip Sidney, *The Countess of Pembroke's Arcadia (the New Arcadia)*, ed. Victor Skretkowicz (Oxford: Clarendon Press, 1987), xv; James Marshall Osborn, *Young Philip Sidney, 1572–1577* (New Haven, CT: Yale University Press, 1972), 495 n. 50.

[15] Blair Worden, *The Sound of Virtue: Philip Sidney's Arcadia and Elizabethan Politics* (New Haven, CT: Yale University Press, 1996), 256; Further discussion of Gentili and Machiavelli can be found in Victoria Kahn, *Machiavellian Rhetoric: From the Counter-Reformation to Milton* (Princeton, NJ: Princeton University Press, 1994), 128–30; and in relation to Sidney, F. J. Levy, "Philip Sidney Reconsidered," *English Literary Renaissance* 2, no. 1 (1972): 5–187, 13.

[16] John Carey, "Structure and Rhetoric in Sidney's Arcadia," in *Sir Philip Sidney: An Anthology of Modern Criticism*, ed. Dennis Kay (Oxford: Clarendon Press, 1987), 258, 259. I should clarify here that I take no issue with Colin Burrow's terminology of "epic romance." I use "epic" primarily for succinctness, noting with Tasso, "accidental differences cannot constitute different genres...romance imitates the same actions [as epic], imitates in the same way, and imitates by the same means; it is therefore of the same genre." See Donna B. Hamilton, *Virgil and The Tempest: The Politics of Imitation* (Columbus, OH: Ohio State University Press, 1990), 69. Colin Burrow, *Epic Romance: Homer to Milton* (Oxford: Clarendon Press, 1993).

[17] Jean Hotman, *The Ambassador* (London: James Shawe, 1603), sig. h2v.

support the Dutch revolt against the Spanish.[18] Gentili was admitted into Oxford University in 1580 based on a recommendation from Leicester, then chancellor of the University, and soon became intimate with Sidney and his Oxford friends, a group that included Henry and Thomas Savile, Gabriel Harvey, Richard Hackluyt, the historian William Camden and Jean Hotman, the eldest son of François Hotman, author of the famous Huguenot resistance tract *Francogallia*.[19] Having been appointed professor of Roman law on 6 March 1581, Gentili dedicated his first work in England, his 1582 *De juris interpretibus dialogi sex*, to Leicester. The dedication to Sidney of *De Legationibus* digresses to defend Leicester against "certain unscrupulous persons...howling against a good man and true," a reference to the notorious 1584 Catholic libel of Leicester, *The Copy of a Letter Written by a Master of Art of Cambridge* known as *Leicester's Commonwealth*, a work to which Sidney also responded.[20] According to one scholar, "similarities between Gentili's argument and the opening section of Sidney's defense of his uncle indicate that the two writers had been in consultation, or that one had followed the other's lead in a combined effort to give coherence and emphasis to the official position."[21] While Sidney in 1586 prepared for his fated expedition with Leicester to the Low Countries, Gentili, through the influence of Sidney's father-in-law Francis Walsingham, was part of a diplomatic mission charged with raising German troops for the purpose of an invasion of France on behalf of the Protestant Henry Navarre.[22] Later, after Robert Devereux, Earl of Essex, had assumed the mantle of Leicester's puritan party, Gentili named his son Robert after the Earl.[23] Was Gentili's dedication to Sidney just an appeal for patronage? If over the 1580s Gentili merely wanted patronage, then he tried to secure it by performing valuable and unwavering service to Sidney's political allies, and any obsequiousness was indistinguishable from political and confessional ideological commitment.

Assumptions about patronage, however, are less important here than the gulf currently dividing literary history from the history of international law—metonymically, the gulf between Sidney and Gentili. Analysis of Sidney and Gentili together shows how familiar aspects of Sidney's revised (New) *Arcadia* helped to teach early modern laws of war and peace.

Whereas Sidney's importance to early modern literary and political history has never been disputed, reading the *New Arcadia* through Gentili's conception of the law of nations allows us to consider Sidney's significance—as a poet—to the emergence and practice of public international law. Humanism as lived and practiced

[18] David Norbrook, *Poetry and Politics in the English Renaissance*, rev. edn. (Oxford: Oxford University Press, 2002), 90.
[19] G. H. M. Posthumus Meyjes, *Jean Hotman's English Connection* (Amsterdam: Koninklijke Nederlandse Akademie van Wetenschappen, 1990).
[20] Gentili, *De Legationibus*, 2: v.
[21] Eleanor Rosenberg, *Leicester, Patron of Letters* (New York: Columbia University Press, 1955), 291.
[22] Lawrence Stone, *An Elizabethan: Sir Horatio Palavicino* (Oxford: Clarendon Press, 1956), 38; Holland, *Studies in International Law*, 11.
[23] Artemis Gause, "Gentili, Alberico (1552–1608)", *Oxford Dictionary of National Biography*, Oxford University Press, 2004; online edn, Jan 2008 <http://www.oxforddnb.com/view/article/10522>.

by Sidney and Gentili indeed confounds the modern separation of literature from the law of nations.

The remainder of this chapter has several parts. The first part further bridges the chasm currently separating Sidney's literary activities from Gentili's legal ones by showing how Gentili's laws of war developed in conversation with his readings in Vergil's *Aeneid*. The second part looks in more detail at the humanist reading and writing practices of their circle in order show how interest in the law of nations was part of their network's distinctive emphasis on the preparation of ambassadors. Through analysis of three episodes—the rebel Amphialus' published justification of his actions, the use of heralds in a civil conflict, and Amphialus' grant of liberty to Philanax—the section argues that Sidney sought to sharpen his readers' literacy of international affairs through an imaginative world rife with problems of international legality. By then looking in greater detail at a remarkable episode in which Sidney's princesses decline the opportunity to escape their captors, the chapter studies how exemplarity functions between narrative and the law of nations in Sidney's poetic and legal theory. Finally, discussing Sidney's own engagement with the troubling conclusion of Vergil's *Aeneid*, the chapter concludes by suggesting that even as Sidney's poem operates, like Gentili's international theory, upon a distinction between legal civility and illegal barbarity, the border between the two was porous, and Sidney considered the *New Arcadia* capable of drawing his elite aristocratic readers into a revised framework of legal obligation—one that extended even into the relationship of enmity.

AENEAS ON TRIAL

Among literary scholars, Sidney may be famous for his formidable argument in the *Defence of Poesy* that poetry teaches and delights, but it was Alberico Gentili, rather than Sidney, who contended that epic poetry taught and transmitted the laws of war. According to Gentili, Hannibal "the Carthaginian committed many things against the justice of war [*contra iustitiam bellicam*] since he despised Homer, the most outstanding teacher of his age."[24] Did the laws of war really depend on poetry for Gentili? In a doctrinal legal sense, perhaps only in a weak way. Passages of poetry could indeed be deployed as ornament as classical rhetoricians like Quintilian had advised. But early modern humanists like Andrea Alciato had argued that Vergil purposefully dramatized ambiguous cases in the law of nations.[25] Similarly,

---

[24] See the edition and English translation of Alberico Gentili, *Commentary on the Third Law of the Title of the Code "On Teachers and Doctors"* (Oxford, 1593), 254; in J. W. Binns, "Alberico Gentili in Defense of Poetry and Acting," *Studies in the Renaissance* 19 (1972): 224–72. All further references are to this text, cited hereafter as Gentili, *Commentary*. In a different context, Gentili would redeploy this example, which his modern translator traces to Lucian's *Dialogues of the Dead* 25. See Alberico Gentili, *The Wars of the Romans: A Critical Edition and Translation of De Armis Romanis*, ed. Benedict Kingsbury and Benjamin Straumann, trans. David Lupher (New York: Oxford University Press, 2011), 2.12, 308–9, cited hereafter as *De Armis Romanis*.

[25] Denis L. Drysdall, "Alciato and the Grammarians: The Law and the Humanities in the Parergon Iuris Libri Duodecim," *Renaissance Quarterly* 56, no. 3 (2003): 713.

Thomas Hobbes, who himself later translated Homer's *Iliad* and *Odyssey*, insisted that the "wise men of remotest antiquity believed" that "the elements of the law of nature and of nations" "should be given to posterity only in the pretty forms of poetry."[26] And as Renaissance theorists sought to identify laws of nature and nations that applied in warfare independent of the accidents of birth (*natio*), ancient epic was a convenient and much-used source. In Gentili's eyes, the laws of war depended on what Sidney called the "feigned example" in the sense of practice—what warriors did in war. In the case of Gentili, moreover, assumptions about humanist rhetorical ornamentation mask far deeper engagements with epic poems like Homer's, for Gentili in his own work used epic both inductively and deductively. At the same time that familiar examples from classical epic could illustrate pre-formulated precepts of the laws of war, so too could turning to epic for handy illustrations prompt unexpected new questions and readings, leading to inductive insights about the laws of war as well.

Homer's usefulness, however, was obviously bound by time and custom. Homer was, after all, only the best teacher "of his age." Homeric exemplarity could be a double-edged sword. If it was possible to learn from Homer about the inviolability of heralds or of warriors' shared humanity, lessons that Hannibal had clearly failed to digest in Gentili's view, it was equally possible to learn that it was sometimes permissible to desecrate a corpse, as Achilles had famously done to Hector. Hannibal may have neglected Homer, but Gentili also laments how the real-life Alexander the Great consciously followed Achilles' "example" in parading a dead enemy around the city.[27]

Here Vergil presented an important, if partial solution. Homer might be flawed, but "Vergil is nature," argued the great and influential humanist Julius Caesar Scaliger.[28] In a passage that Gentili would cite approvingly, Scaliger wrote, "all the arts of peace and war [*artes pacis... et belli*] are comprehended [*cognitas*] in Aeneas alone."[29] But what then of Vergil's own historicity? Even if Vergil's Aeneas did not deny enemies burial or desecrate bodies, who could deny that he too was "of his age"? How ultimately was one to know which epic actions to imitate and which to abjure?

For all their similarities, Sidney and Gentili approached this question from quite different directions. Readers could simply be told outright which epic actions to imitate and which to reject. This is primarily what Gentili did in his most famous work, *De Jure Belli*. When approached with assumptions about an autonomous field of international law, *De Jure Belli* devotes surprising space to sorting virtuous epic actions from base actions. Since judging epic actions first required the basic

[26] Thomas Hobbes, *On the Citizen*, ed. Richard Tuck, trans. Michael Silverthorne (Cambridge: Cambridge University Press, 1998), 7. I explore aspects of Gentili's possible influence on Hobbes in Chapter 5.

[27] Alberico Gentili, *De Jure Belli Libri Tres*, trans. John Carew Rolfe (Oxford: Clarendon Press, 1933), 2.24, 460f. Pagination follows the 1612 edition reprinted in vol. I. See also David Quint, "'Alexander the Pig': Shakespeare on History and Poetry," *Boundary 2* 10, no. 3 (April 1, 1982): 56.

[28] Bernard Weinberg, *A History of Literary Criticism in the Italian Renaissance* (Chicago, IL: University of Chicago Press, 1961), 2.747.

[29] Gentili, *Commentary*, 256.

legal procedure of determining facts, this process gave rise to the host of passages in *De Jure Belli* that might today be called literary criticism. Gentili's lawyerly reading of Vergil's *Aeneid* contributed significantly to his laws of war. His chapter "Of Suppliants" (2.20) in *De Jure Belli*, particularly, delved deeply into the *Aeneid*, as we shall see. The second solution to the problem of imitation involves narrative. As Timothy Hampton has noted, the Aristotelian theory of plot dominant in the Renaissance helped "historical material placed in a coherent narrative structure [seem] universal and philosophical rather than ambiguously particular and historical."[30] Partially for this reason, the humanist imitations of Vergil written by Sidney and others in their networks could also teach the laws of war. Gentili's admiring references to Sidney and the Italian epic poet Torquato Tasso remind us that analysis of Vergil and suppliants was not limited in the late sixteenth century to Gentili's tracts on the laws of war, but, rather, could take place in a range of genres. In turning to the fertile nexus of moral philosophy, law, literary criticism, and humanist imitation of Gentili's circle of poets and scholars to help elucidate the textured nature of sixteenth-century thought on the laws of war, I propose that Renaissance humanist literary activities like reading, imitating, and commenting upon Vergil might also be construed as constitutive of the laws of war. The argument is not quite that poets, as Shelley famously suggested, "are the unacknowledged legislators of the World."[31] Rather, it concerns what Quentin Skinner and Mark Goldie have recently called humanism's "generic expansiveness."[32] A better understanding of how interpretation, imitation, and adaptation of Vergilian epic helped Sidney, Gentili, and other Renaissance humanists to analyze and to teach the laws of war makes it possible to better understand public international law's obscured literary history.

The term "humanism" is central to this chapter, but it requires some explanation. Scholars have advanced strong but differing views on whether "humanism" is a term appropriate for Gentili. "Humanism" has most recently been used in two distinct senses. On the one hand is the sense of legal humanism. In Donald Kelley's highly influential account, legal humanism describes a cluster of commitments and practices associated with a number of Renaissance jurists. These commitments and practices included most notably a fierce skepticism towards the Byzantine editor of the Roman *Digest*, Tribonius, who was suspected of meddling with ancient Roman law, and an almost equal skepticism towards scholastic interpreters of the *Digest* such as the fourteenth-century Italian lawyer Bartolus de Saxoferrato. In Kelley's account, legal humanists, mostly in France, developed a powerful philological approach, sensitive to historical linguistic change, that was designed to catch late

---

[30] Timothy Hampton, *Writing from History: The Rhetoric of Exemplarity in Renaissance Literature* (Ithaca, NY: Cornell University Press, 1990), 122–3.

[31] Percy Bysshe Shelley, "A Defense of Poetry," in *Shelley's Poetry and Prose*, ed. Neil Fraistat and Donald H. Reiman (New York: Norton, 2002), 535.

[32] Quentin Skinner, "Surveying 'The Foundations': A Retrospect and Reassessment," in *Rethinking the Foundations of Modern Political Thought*, ed. Annabel S. Brett, James Tully, and Hamilton-Bleakley (Cambridge: Cambridge University Press, 2006), 244; Mark Goldie, "The Context of 'The Foundations,'" in *Rethinking the Foundations of Modern Political Thought*, ed. Annabel S. Brett, James Tully, and Hamilton-Bleakley (Cambridge: Cambridge University Press, 2006), 10.

interpolations in the *Digest*—an approach that would come to be known as the *mos gallicus*. These legal humanists distinguished themselves from those who remained tethered to the so-called Bartolist *mos italicus*. Noting Gentili's early quarrel with the French lawyers associated with the *mos gallicus* in *De iuris interpretibus dialogi sex* (1582), Kelley has argued that Gentili ought to be seen in terms of his "extreme opposition to legal humanism."[33]

The second sense of "humanism" is that used most influentially by Richard Tuck and Diego Panizza.[34] Less interested in the categories of *mos gallicus* and *mos italicus*, Tuck and Panizza have been more concerned with traditions of civic and rhetorical humanism. Whereas Kelley's "legal humanism" focuses on the specialized scholarly methodology practiced by Guillaume Budé, Andrea Alciato, and others, Tuck and Panizza's "humanism" emerges from more widely shared cultural scenes, like the rhetorically-inclined Renaissance schoolroom, in which boys like Gentili used *imitatio* and the translation of Roman poems from Latin to the vernacular and back again—a practice known as double translation—to learn about the ancient world. In Tuck's view, for example, it is Gentili's favorable posture toward the "literary and rhetorical writings of the ancient world" that makes him a "humanist"; *De Jure Belli*, moreover, can "stand as a kind of *summa* of the whole literature" of Renaissance humanism.[35] The import of humanism for Tuck and Panizza is that it profoundly influenced the content of Gentili's writing on the laws of war, leading Gentili in particular to break with scholastic tradition by justifying pre-emptive attacks and wars in defense of natural law.

Both definitions of humanism have had their adherents, although interest in rhetorical humanism is currently especially strong. As this more recent focus on rhetorical humanism potentially masks important differences in legal methodologies, however, Kelley's reading correspondingly grows in significance. But Kelley's reading of Gentili as a staunch opponent of legal humanism may also require some qualification.[36] Since Gentili appears opposed to legal humanism in *De iuris interpretibus dialogi sex*, ascribing such a view to Gentili's later writings depends on omitting Gentili's praise both for Alciato, a key figure of legal humanism, whom Gentili calls "a great jurist," and his general tolerance for Alciato's method of scraping away the accretions of medieval commentators on Roman law. In Gentili's most influential work, *De Jure Belli*, he cites Alciato no fewer than 170 times. Moreover, Gentili

[33] Donald R. Kelley, "Law," in *The Cambridge History of Political Thought, 1450–1700*, ed. J. H. Burns and Mark Goldie (Cambridge: Cambridge University Press, 1991), 76; Donald R. Kelley, *Foundations of Modern Historical Scholarship: Language, Law, and History in the French Renaissance* (New York: Columbia University Press, 1970); Donald R. Kelley, "History, English Law and the Renaissance: A Rejoinder," *Past and Present*, no. 72 (1976): 145; Donald R. Kelley, "The Rise of Legal History in the Renaissance," *History and Theory* 9, no. 2 (1970): 179, 191.

[34] Diego Panizza, "Political Theory and Jurisprudence in Gentili's De Iure Belli: The Great Debate between 'Theological' and 'Humanist' Perspectives from Vitoria to Grotius" (2005), <http://ssrn.com/abstract=871754>; Tuck, *The Rights of War and Peace*, 16–50.

[35] Tuck, *The Rights of War and Peace*, 16–50.

[36] For a critique of Kelley's account of legal humanism, see Douglas J. Osler, "Budaeus and Roman Law," *Ius Commune* 13 (1985): 195–212.

showed little aversion to granting authority to poets and historians in his works, a practice that, according to Kelley, "was most offensive to jurists of the old school."[37] As Benjamin Straumann astutely observes, Gentili could also denounce legal humanist textual criticism when his aims required it, but this fact may suggest the need to look less for Gentili's consistent posture toward legal humanism than to the rhetorical protocols of writing for an occasion heavily emphasized in Renaissance schoolroom humanism.[38]

It may thus be important to qualify the notion that Gentili staunchly and uniformly opposed legal humanism. Gentili's biography also gives a number of reasons to keep his rhetorical humanism in view, not least if it has consequences for his writings on the laws of war. One need not agree that rhetorical humanism as such is what led Gentili to justify pre-emptive attacks, for example, in order to agree with the importance of the *studia humanitatis* for Gentili.[39] Van der Molen relates the following story about young Alberico, his father Matteo, and his brother Scipio, who would become a noted poet and legal scholar:[40]

> One winter evening the three were sitting round the fire when the father said to the sons: "Let each of you take a piece of charcoal and write a Latin poem on the wall. I shall relate the theme in prose." Scipio succeeded in expressing the theme in a few lines of poetry, but the story relates that Alberico covered the entire wall with his poem. The father then encouraged Scipio to continue to cultivate the Muse, but at the same time extracted a promise from Alberico that he should never again turn his mind to verse.[41]

The anecdote speaks to the literary environment in which Alberico Gentili was raised. If true, however, Gentili broke his promise at least five times, writing commendatory poems in Italian for two separate Latin academic dramas by the Christ Church lawyer and dramatist William Gager, capable sonnets for works by John Budden, his successor as Oxford Regius Professor of Civil Law, and John Florio, the famous translator, and an epigrammatic couplet in a work whose publication

---

[37] Kelley, *Foundations of Modern Historical Scholarship: Language, Law, and History in the French Renaissance*, 69.

[38] Benjamin Straumann, "The Corpus Juris as a Source of Law Between Sovereigns in Alberico Gentili's Thought," in *The Roman Foundations of the Law of Nations: Alberico Gentili and the Justice of Empire*, ed. Benedict Kingsbury and Benjamin Straumann (Oxford: Oxford University Press, 2011), 101–25. For Quentin Skinner's now classic defense of this contextualist approach, see his "Meaning and Understanding in the History of Ideas" in Quentin Skinner, *Visions of Politics*, vol. I (Cambridge: Cambridge University Press, 2002), 57–89.

[39] For a critique of Tuck on this point, see Noel Malcolm, "Alberico Gentili and the Ottomans," in *Alberico Gentili: La Salvaguardia Dei Beni Culturali Nel Diritto Internazionale* (Milano: Giuffrè editore, 2008), 65–89.

[40] J.A. Van Dorsten, *Poets, Patrons, and Professors: Sir Philip Sidney, Daniel Rogers, and the Leiden Humanists* (Leiden: University of Leiden, 1962), 90–1; Scipione Gentili, *Scipii Gentilis Nereus Siue De Natali Elizabethæ Illustriss. Philippi Sydnæi Filiæ* (London: John Wolfe, 1585). On Scipio Gentili, see further Anne Pallant, "The Printed Poems of Scipio Gentili" (MA Thesis, University of Birmingham, 1983); Anne Pallant, "Scipione Gentili: A Sixteenth Century Jurist," *The Kingston Law Review* 14–15 (1985).

[41] Gesina H. J. Van der Molen, *Alberico Gentili and the Development of International Law: His Life, Work and Times*, 2nd rev. edn. (Leiden: A.W. Sifthoff, 1968), 41.

he likely financed himself.[42] The first of the Gager commendatory poems introduced Gager's *Mealager*, an Ovidian play performed first in Oxford in 1582 and then again in front of Philip Sidney in 1585 before it was published in 1592 with a dedication to the Earl of Essex. The second introduced Gager's tragicomedy *Ulysses Redux* (1592), at least one copy of which was dedicated to Mary Sidney, the Countess of Pembroke.[43] So long as humanism is understood as the participation in "the revival of classical learning and in particular the arts of language," Gentili's humanism does not end with polite contributions to friends' volumes either.[44] J. W. Binns has analyzed the "cross-fertilization of disciplines" that allowed Gentili to compose a legal commentary on Vergil's *Eclogues* and to employ Petrarch's *Sonnets* in the course of writing about legal methodology.[45] A careful reader of More's *Utopia*, Gentili was also deeply interested in legal conditionals, and, having eloquently praised "the merits of poets," he considered poetry "not an instrument of contemplative, but of active, philosophy."[46] As it had been for Alciato and other legal humanists, classical literature for Gentili was a complement to the law, aiding legal tasks with philological information about usage and, through its plots, providing cases that were common and accessible to all of literate Renaissance society.[47] Following Quintilian, Gentili defended his use of proofs and examples from classical poetry by saying that "[j]urists are not restricted to the books of Justinian, any more than physicians are limited to those of Galen, or Philosophers to the writing of Aristotle."[48] Thus, I refer to Gentili as a humanist in this chapter, even as I flesh out more precisely what humanism meant for Gentili and his circle.

Gentili's humanism is most fully on display in a work rarely cited in connection with his treatises on international law, the work in which he most forcefully tied epic poetry to the laws of war. Published in 1593, though perhaps delivered as a set of lectures somewhat earlier, *Commentatio ad L[egem] III C[odicis] de prof[essoribus] et med[icis]* or *Commentary on the Third Law of the Code on Teachers and Doctors*

---

[42] John Florio, *Queen Anna's New World of Words, or Dictionarie of the Italian and English Tongues, Collected and Newly Much Augmented by Iohn Florio* (London, 1611); J. W. Binns, *Intellectual Culture in Elizabethan and Jacobean England: The Latin Writings of the Age* (Leeds: Francis Cairns, 1990), 348; John Budden, *Gulielmi Patteni* (Oxford: Joseph Barnes, 1602), sig. [a4]; Ian Maclean, "Alberico Gentili, His Publishers, and the Vagaries of the Book Trade between England and Germany, 1580–1614," in *Learning and the Market Place: Essays in the History of the Early Modern Book* (Leiden: Brill, 2009), 299. *William Gager: The Complete Works*, trans. Dana Ferrin Sutton (New York: Garland, 1994), vol. I, 38–9 (Meleager), vol. II, 16–17 (Ulysses Redux).

[43] Binns, *Intellectual Culture in Elizabethan and Jacobean England: The Latin Writings of the Age*, 131.

[44] David Norbrook, *Poetry and Politics in the English Renaissance*, rev. edn. (Oxford: Oxford University Press, 2002), 286.

[45] Binns, *Intellectual Culture in Elizabethan and Jacobean England: The Latin Writings of the Age*, 355–6, 338–59 generally.

[46] Philip Dust, "Alberico Gentili's Commentaries on Utopian War," *Moreana* 37 (1973): 31–40; Gentili, *Commentary*, 258, 261; Tuck, *The Rights of War and Peace*, 49; Michael Wyatt, *The Italian Encounter with Tudor England: A Cultural Politics of Translation* (Cambridge: Cambridge University Press, 2005), 194; Maclean, "Alberico Gentili, His Publishers, and the Vagaries of the Book Trade between England and Germany, 1580–1614," 302–3.

[47] Drysdall, "Alciato and the Grammarians: The Law and the Humanities in the Parergon Iuris Libri Duodecim," 717.

[48] Gentili, *Commentary*, 254; Gentili, *De Jure Belli Libri Tres*, 1.3, 26.

asks why poets enjoyed no immunity from taxation under a Roman law extending such privileges to painters and grammarians. In arguing that poets deserve such immunity, Gentili implores his readers to "look to the glosses of [legal humanists] Alciato and Cujas" while he lays out a literary theory that includes a lengthy discussion of epic poetry.[49] A few aspects of Gentili's *Commentary on the Third Law* warrant special attention before I turn to *De Jure Belli*. The first is Gentili's argument regarding the subject of epics. Epic, he says, portrays "the deeds of princes" in morally idealized fashion.[50] Vergil's Aeneas, for example, is a "prince" about whom some historical facts are known—that he "waged war" with Italy, for instance—but whose full story is "hidden in the darkness of antiquity."[51] If the darkness of antiquity leaves gaps in the historical record, according to Gentili, it also offers the poet an "opportunity" to act as a "moral philosopher" by ensuring that the fictionalized deeds of princes amount to a depiction not of failure or mediocrity but of "the best and most industrious prince."[52] The "invented deeds and fictitious actions" of epic, therefore, have a clear didactic purpose in his conception.[53] Yet epic has a function beyond what Gentili sees as the more general function of poetry to "make...the morals of the citizens good [*bonos*]."[54] More specifically, epic is a mirror for princes: not only is epic's subject the prince, but so too are princes epic's preferred audience. "[T]he best of princes are taught by epic [*Instruuntur principes optimi*]," Gentili writes.[55] In the case of the *Aeneid*, the example for emulation concerns virtue and piety in conquest. Vergil's Aeneas is a "prince of outstanding virtue" who showed "piety" in "seeking the kingdom of Italy [*quaerendo regno Italiae*]."[56] To a certain extent, these are Renaissance commonplaces, but what makes Gentili's theory of the epic especially noteworthy is that the moral register in which it operates is the same register in which Gentili often writes about the laws of war. The clearest example of this moral register may come when Gentili describes the laws of war as a species of goodness, contending (against Machiavelli) that the Roman generals "were all brave and good [*bonos*] and (to mention what we are mainly looking for) upholders of the laws of war [*servantes bellici juris*]."[57] So long as upholding the laws of war forms part of the good, epic, as a teacher of the good, teaches the laws of war.

Gentili explores related themes in *De Jure Belli*, particularly in Book 2, Chapter 20, entitled "Of Suppliants." Supplication—pleading for mercy or aid—has been called "the epic motif par excellence," and Gentili embarks on this discussion, he says, because supplication "frequently happen[s] amid arms and battles" yet "remain[s] untouched in connexion with...the conduct of war."[58] For evidence that supplication happens frequently in war, Gentili gives numerous epic examples before a

[49] Gentili, *Commentary*, 264.   [50] Gentili, *Commentary*, 252.
[51] Gentili, *Commentary*, 252.   [52] Gentili, *Commentary*, 252, 256.
[53] Gentili, *Commentary*, 259.   [54] Gentili, *Commentary*, 259.
[55] Gentili, *Commentary*, 260.   [56] Gentili, *Commentary*, 259.
[57] Gentili, *De Armis Romanis*, 2.12.
[58] Gentili, *De Jure Belli Libri Tres*, 2.20, 401; Walter Stephens, "Reading Tasso Reading Vergil Reading Homer: An Archeology of Andromache," *Comparative Literature Studies* 32, no. 2 (1995): 297; Derridians might call supplication the distinctive "mark" of the epic genre. See Jacques Derrida, "The Law of Genre," in *Modern Genre Theory*, ed. David Duff (Harlow: Longman, 2000), 219–31.

lengthy discussion of Vergil's Aeneas. Gentili then devotes considerable space to defending Aeneas from the charge that Vergil's purportedly pious hero had impiously failed to spare suppliants. At first glance, Gentili's worry over acknowledged "invented deeds and fictitious actions" may seem surprising, but Aeneas' actions in war had troubled Christian commentators at least since the Church father Lactantius (*c.* 240–320 CE), who influentially berated Vergil for presenting a hero who, epithet notwithstanding, was "not pious...no way: he killed not only those who yielded without resistance [*non repugnantes*] but even those who prayed to him [*precantes*]."[59] Vergil's much-repeated *pietas* could translate either as piety or pity, and the philological question of how either of these words could apply to Aeneas provoked much subsequent thinking about the *Aeneid*.[60]

A brief glance at Vergil will cast some light on why Gentili dedicated such space to Aeneas in *De Jure Belli*. Although most Renaissance commentators praised Aeneas' actions, charges against Vergil were leveled repeatedly throughout the Renaissance, and central to them—and clearly important to Gentili—was the poignant conclusion of the *Aeneid*, in which Aeneas, unmoved by his enemy's supplication, slays the pleading enemy at his feet (see Figure 2.1).[61] The Italian king Turnus had in conventional epic fashion invited Aeneas into a union of pitying sons concerned for their fathers. Turnus begs: "If any thought of a parent's grief can touch you, I beg you—you too had such a father in Anchises—pity [my father's] old age, and give me...back to my kin. You are the victor...Lavinia is your wife; do not press your hatred further."[62] Vergil notes that Turnus' words "began to sway [Aeneas] more and more," and, suggesting for many readers that Aeneas is prepared to spare Turnus, Aeneas hesitates [*cunctantem*] before the story takes an important emotional turn (12.939–941). What apparently compels Aeneas to kill Turnus is that Aeneas notices Turnus "clad in the spoils [*spoliis*]" of Aeneas' slain friend Pallas, the noticing of which sets Aeneas "ablaze with fury and terrible in his wrath" [*furiis accensus et ira / terribilis*]. Vergil's Aeneas, "in burning rage," then "buries his sword full in Turnus' breast," despite Aeneas' father's earlier enjoinment that Aeneas "spare the vanquished" (6.853). The epic ends with Vergil's haunting description of Turnus' "limbs [growing] slack and chill...his life fle[eing] resentfully to the Shades below." In a certain reading, one that in the twentieth century has come to be known as the Harvard School reading, Vergil provided a chilling glimpse of the dark heart of Augustan imperialism.[63] In Aeneas' merciless slaughter of Turnus,

[59] Lactantius, *Divine Institutes*, trans. Anthony Bowen and Peter Garnsey (Liverpool: Liverpool University Press, 2003), 5.10.1.9.
[60] James D. Garrison, "War: Turnus and 'Pietas' in the Later Renaissance," in *Pietas from Vergil to Dryden* (University Park, PA: Pennsylvania State University Press, 1992), 161–204.
[61] Craig Kallendorf, *In Praise of Aeneas: Virgil and Epideictic Rhetoric in the Early Italian Renaissance* (Hanover, NH: University Press of New England, 1989); Craig Kallendorf, *The Other Virgil: "Pessimistic" Readings of the Aeneid in Early Modern Culture* (Oxford: Oxford University Press, 2007), 38–50.
[62] Virgil, *Virgil*, ed. G.P. Goold, trans. H. Rushton Fairclough, rev. edn. with new introduction (Cambridge, MA: Harvard University Press, 1999), 12.932–937 All Latin and English references are to this text.
[63] S. J. Harrison, "Some Views of the Aeneid in the Twentieth Century," in *Oxford Readings in Vergil's Aeneid*, ed. S. J. Harrison (Oxford: Oxford University Press, 1990), 1–20.

Fig. 2.1. *The Fight between Aeneas and King Turnus, from Vergil's Aeneid.*
Giacomo del Po (Italy, Naples, 1652–1726) Italy, circa 1700, Oil on Copper. Public domain image made available by the Los Angeles County Museum of Art.

in other words, Rome's most important literary work concluded with a notorious war crime, cloaked in the language of piety.

Although not absent in the Renaissance, this reading of the *Aeneid* hardly pre-vailed, for generally, as Timothy Hampton has observed, "the task of the Renais-sance reader who is well schooled in ancient history and poetry" is not to find fault with someone like Aeneas but "to unpack ... great deeds from the mere appearance of the name."[64] Craig Kallendorf has shown that the most prevalent reading of the *Aeneid* in the Renaissance not only exculpated Aeneas but, in the schoolroom tra-dition of epideictic rhetoric of praise and blame, praised him.[65] Even if few in the Italian Renaissance resisted this practice and adopted what's now known as the "pessimistic" Harvard School reading, we can be certain that Gentili himself was familiar with it, for he himself employed a version of it in *De iniustitia bellica Romanorum actio*, his fascinating 1590 denunciation of Roman imperialism. Aeneas is hardly the only important figure in Roman historiography to be subject to with-ering assault in this important, if little studied, declamation, yet Aeneas in this work is a parody of justice. Citing Lactantius' *Divinarum Institutionum Libri VII*,

---

[64] Hampton, *Writing from History*, 25.   [65] Kallendorf, *In Praise of Aeneas*.

Gentili calls Aeneas a "traitor" who has "sprung from [a] fratricide."[66] If Aeneas is virtuous, it is only if "virtue" is wrested to mean "avarice, deposition of rulers, [and] oath-breaking."[67] When, nine years later, Gentili published a second declamation arguing the opposite case to *De iniustitia bellica Romanorum actio*, Aeneas was unsurprisingly described in a new light, as he became a "great and lofty spirit," an "exemplar of heroic fortitude."[68] It is to this second book that Gentili's discussion in *De Jure Belli* bears more similarity.

Gentili's lawyerly defense of Aeneas in *De Jure Belli* could only have been offered by a man who had considered the opposing charges, and it is notable that Gentili expanded his defense of Aeneas for his second edition of *De Jure Belli*, having in the meantime composed *De iniustitia bellica Romanorum actio*.[69] "[N]o base deed was ever done by the Romans, no matter how publicly performed it may have been," Gentili wrote in the meantime, "which the writers did not turn upside down with their lies and twist about through every sort of contrivance."[70] If this was Gentili's view, Gentili himself may have taken a cue from the Roman encomiasts, whose rhetorical arsenals included a key device known as *paradiastole*, a practice in which vices were strategically re-described as virtues.[71] Despite the fact that Aeneas "was trying to get possession of what belonged to another," Gentili concluded that "the attempts of Aeneas were lawful."[72] Aware, however, that Aeneas' killing of Turnus potentially eroded Aeneas' moral example for princes, Gentili gave several reasons why Aeneas' killing of the suppliant Turnus was also lawful, reasons that are worth expanding upon for the insight they offer into how literary criticism helped Gentili formulate his laws of war and Philip Sidney fashion his *New Arcadia*.

A paradox important to note is that Gentili and other late sixteenth-century readers treated the *Aeneid* as a repository of "facts" despite the poem's self-evident fiction.[73] While Sidney's fiction, too, could be read in this way—indeed, Sidney's characters themselves weave (fictional) facts and into judicial narratives—the key point for now is the extent of Gentili's forensic defense.[74] Some of his proofs are more convincing to modern ears than others. Gentili's first defense of Aeneas, picking up in lexically punctilious fashion on Vergil's verb *immolat*, is that Aeneas did not "merely slay [*interficit*] Turnus, but he offered him up [*immolat*]."[75] A second argument made explicit core epic assumptions of mimetic violence on behalf of

---

[66] Gentili, *De Armis Romanis*, 1.13, 119.   [67] Gentili, *De Armis Romanis*, 1.13, 119.

[68] Gentili, *De Armis Romanis*, 2.12, 319.

[69] Compare Alberico Gentili, *De Iure Belli Commentatio Secunda* (London: Iohannes Wolfius, 1588), 13v–14v; *De Jure Belli Libri Tres*, 2.20, 401–9.

[70] Gentili, *De Armis Romanis*, 1.2, 21.

[71] On the device of rhetorical re-description, paradiastole, see Quentin Skinner, "Moral Ambiguity and the Renaissance Art of Eloquence," in *Visions of Politics* (Cambridge: Cambridge University Press, 2002), vol. II, 264–85.

[72] Gentili, *De Jure Belli Libri Tres*, 1.5, 47.

[73] Kristine Louise Haugen, "A French Jesuit's Lectures on Vergil, 1582–1583: Jacques Sirmond between Literature, History, and Myth," *The Sixteenth Century Journal* 30, no. 4 (1999): 985.

[74] Hutson, *The Invention of Suspicion*, 131–4.   [75] Gentili, *De Jure Belli Libri Tres*, 2.20, 402.

kin. Much in the way that an ambassador by a "Sort of Fiction" could be "taken for" his or her sovereign in a foreign court, for Gentili, Aeneas' violence could "represent" his slain friend's.[76] It was not Aeneas who sacrificed Turnus, he claimed, but Pallas himself, as could clearly be seen in Aeneas' irate words, "Pallas it is, Pallas who sacrifices you with this stroke."[77] These arguments, together with the proposition that "the deed [was] in accord with … Greek religion," help Gentili make his enthymematic third argument that at the same time highlights the problem of the historical custom in epic: "Pallas … sacrificed Turnus … in accord with Greek religion."[78] To summarize then: it was sacrifice, it was Pallas, and it was allowed in ancient Greek religion.

Taking a slightly different approach, Gentili then turns to pay special attention to the role of pacts and treaties in the poem. Gentili's apparent method is to scan the *Aeneid* for agreements and, where applicable, their contravention. Turnus was "undeserving of mercy," Gentili submits, because "he broke [*turbauit*] the treaty [*foedus*] which was made by the kings [*regibus*]" earlier in the poem.[79] Noteworthy about Gentili's legalistic reading of Vergil is again not necessarily its originality but rather its similarity with other humanist readings of the age. Gentili goes on to endorse Julius Caesar Scaliger's reading of the morally fraught hesitation Vergil inserts before Aeneas kills Turnus. Like Colin Burrow, who has written of this hesitation that it provokes "a sense that something new, something less deadly … might be on the brink of emerging," Scaliger had subtly inquired into Aeneas' ethical turn.[80] Scaliger's reading, which Gentili adopted without qualification, was that Aeneas "does not kill Turnus as he begged for mercy until he considers another phase of courage more potent, namely the avenging of friends. Therefore [Aeneas] does not wish to make himself responsible, as he does elsewhere … but he charges it to the account of friendship."[81] Gentili thought this argument for revenge worthy of reproducing, but he does not stop here in defending Aeneas. He proposes both that Pallas' father Evander had obliged Aeneas to kill Turnus and even suggests that Turnus' "insulting words" justified Aeneas' act. Finally, Gentili argues that "the law did not require that Turnus should be spared at a time when … the victory which was sought would be rendered uncertain. It is proper for a warrior when engaged with an enemy to lay aside all pity and clemency [*clementia*] and show no mercy [*mansuetudine*]."[82] It is only "when victory is assured" that "the question of suppliants arises," according to Gentili. In such ways did Gentili's laws of war emerge from his engagements with the epic genre.

---

[76] Hugo Grotius, *De Jure Belli Ac Pacis Libri Tres*, ed. Richard Tuck (Indianapolis, IN: Liberty Fund, 2005), 912.

[77] Gentili, *De Jure Belli Libri Tres*, 2.20, 404.   [78] Gentili, *De Jure Belli Libri Tres*, 2.20, 404.

[79] Gentili, *De Jure Belli Libri Tres*, 2.20, 403. For another late sixteenth-century reader who took "an intensive, almost single-minded" interest in "the making and breaking of the 'foedus' or pact between the Trojans and the Latins," see Haugen, "A French Jesuit's Lectures on Vergil," 982–5.

[80] Colin Burrow, *Epic Romance: Homer to Milton* (Oxford: Clarendon Press, 1993), 49.

[81] Gentili, *De Jure Belli Libri Tres*, 2.20, 404.   [82] Gentili, *De Jure Belli Libri Tres*, 2.20, 404f.

"IT IS VERY LATE TO DIG A WELL WHEN ONE IS THIRSTY": SIDNEY'S *NEW ARCADIA*, HUMANISM, AND INTERNATIONAL LEGAL HERMENEUTICS

In his *Arcadia*, which Philip Sidney revised considerably over the period in the early 1580s when he and Gentili were closest, Sidney explored many of the same legal issues as Gentili explored, particularly where classical texts like the *Aeneid* were concerned. According to Gentili's own account, it was Sidney himself who prompted Gentili to write about the laws of diplomacy. Sidney's famous *Defence of Poesy*, which called Vergil's Aeneas an "excellent man [in] every way" and "a virtuous man in all fortunes," begins by reminding readers of Sidney's own diplomatic mission as an urbane twenty-two-year-old to the Holy Roman Emperor, Rudolf II, and it proceeds to set out a theory of poetic representation that, as Joanna Craigwood has recently noted, proceeds analogously with the mimetic structure of diplomatic representation.[83] In the analysis of the *New Arcadia* that follows, I want to add to existing work by emphasizing how epic allows Sidney to represent the doubtful cases in the law of nations. Epic tradition offered Sidney and his Elizabethan readers a unique yet crucial space for working through the many moral and legal aspects of what Aristotle in his *Nicomachean Ethics* had long before called "ultimate particulars."[84]

Central to Sidney's emphasis on international legal issues is the way episodes in Sidney's text develop from a humanist stress on elite reading and preparedness. Gentili's *De Legationibus*, along with similar works such as Hotman's *The Ambassador* (which was dedicated to Sidney's nephew, William Herbert, third Earl of Pembroke, when it was published in English in 1603), functioned as conduct manuals for an elite proto-diplomatic corps. Books like these set reading programs for potential ambassadors that "envisage[d] action as the *outcome* of reading—not simply reading as active, but reading as trigger for action."[85] Hotman, for example, argued

---

[83] Philip Sidney, *The Countess of Pembroke's Arcadia: (The Old Arcadia)*, ed. Katherine Duncan-Jones (Oxford: Oxford University Press, 1999), 343, 347, 353. Craigwood, "Sidney, Gentili, and the Poetics of Embassy." Roland Greene has likewise commented upon Sidney's "ambassadorial poetics," in which Sidney's reader, upon "encountering a fictional text...enacts a diplomatic role as a visitor and mediator between the one or more worlds of that fiction and the actual world, a role that depends on perspectivism, transcultural tact, and a kind of worldliness." Knowledge of the law of nations would seem an important complement to the traits Greene identifies. Roland Greene, "Fictions of Immanence, Fictions of Embassy," in *The Project of Prose in Early Modern Europe and the New World*, ed. Elizabeth Fowler and Roland Greene (Cambridge: Cambridge University Press, 1997), 177. See further Jason Powell, "Astrophil the Orator: Diplomacy and Diplomats in Sidney's *Astrophil and Stella*," in *Authority and Diplomacy from Dante to Shakespeare*, ed. Jason Powell and William T. Rossiter (Burlington, VT: Ashgate, 2013).

[84] Aristotle, *Nicomachean Ethics*, trans. Martin Ostwald (Upper Saddle River, NJ: Prentice Hall, 1999), 160 (1142a 25).

[85] Lisa Jardine and Anthony Grafton, "'Studied for Action': How Gabriel Harvey Read His Livy," *Past & Present*, no. 129 (1990): 40. Jardine and Grafton demonstrate the circle's interest in Roman law and its extraordinary "emphasis on ambassadorial virtuosity" and "vital legation," pp. 63–4. Since Hotman's work, having circulated in manuscript for an unknown period, appeared in English translation in 1603, its publication was possibly related to Jacobean enthusiasm for a Scots–English union based on Roman law. It was originally published in French as Jean Hotman, *L'Ambassadeur, Par Le Sieur de Vill. H.*, 1603.

that among the parts of Philosophie, [the ambassador] ought to have knowledge of the Morall and Politicke: and if before he have any taste of the *Roman Civill Law*, the same would give him more insight and facilitie to the negotiation of treaty and clearing many matters that fall out in diverse places: as for example of the right of succession of Princes, of the differences of the borders, of the taking booties of Prisoners, Reprisals, and of Sea matters.[86]

Evidencing a similarly Aristotelian concern for prudence or practical wisdom (*prudentiam*) for most of the third book of *De Legationibus*, Gentili declared:

I want our ambassador... to be a legal, ethical, and, from the Peripatetic point of view, [a] political philosopher. But only to a moderate degree. I don't want him produced from the shades of the schools: I want him educated in practical politics and in the administration of high offices. I want all his literary studies, without exception, to bear on this.[87]

Because, as Hotman wrote, "it is very late to dig a well, when one is thirsty, or to make armour, when it is time to fight," anyone remotely hoping to be tapped for diplomatic duty needed preparation.[88] True, Hotman found "the knowledge of Histories...to bee more necessary...than any other study," but Sidney in his *Defence of Poesy* famously put fiction before history, and Hotman and Sidney, in any case, did not disagree too strongly, since Hotman in 1582 asked his own father to dedicate a work to Sidney.[89] Gentili obviously sympathized with Sidney's view, not only drawing from Vergil, as we have seen, but also citing on a number of occasions Tasso's writings on ambassadors (both poetry and prose). The "rapid thought," "dexterity of intellect," and "mobility of the mind" needed for embassy in his view could "be developed by art [*ab arte*]."[90] Hotman, Sidney, and Gentili all agreed that to "have visualized and all but visited the scene of [one's] duties" beforehand was the obligation of a good ambassador.[91]

For Sidney, international legal cases could supply intellectual energy to poetic worlds and even be "tuned," as he put it in the *Defence*, "to the highest key of passion" (305). While his *Arcadia*, as Arthur F. Kinney rightly observes, "translated the antique past into the present's most pressing needs through the medium of verisimilar history implying moral philosophy," Sidney in person seems to have enjoyed pressing his lawyer friends for analysis.[92] Gentili explained that he "treated the subject of the Ambassador, which [Sidney] had previously induced [him] to investigate, and had aided [him] in threshing out with every variety of

---

[86] Jean Hotman, *The Ambassador* (London: James Shawe, 1603), sig. c1v.
[87] Gentili, *De Legationibus*, 2:161.   [88] Hotman, *The Ambassador*, sig. c1r–v.
[89] Hotman, *The Ambassador*, sig. [b8r]; Posthumus Meyjes, *Jean Hotman's English Connection*, 24.
[90] Garrett Mattingly, *Renaissance Diplomacy* (Boston, MA: Houghton Mifflin, 1955), 213; Gentili, *De Legationibus*, 2:176, 201, 145–6.
[91] Gentili, *De Legationibus*, 2:155.
[92] Arthur F. Kinney, "Sir Philip Sidney and the Uses of History," in *The Historical Renaissance: New Essays on Tudor and Stuart Literature and Culture*, ed. Heather Dubrow and Richard Strier (Chicago, IL: University of Chicago Press, 1988), 304–5, 311; Brian Lockey, *Law and Empire in English Renaissance Literature* (Cambridge: Cambridge University Press, 2006), 47–79, esp. 62–4, 76; Norbrook, *Poetry and Politics in the English Renaissance*, 90.

Socratic device."[93] A legal manuscript in the British Library written "at the request of S[i]r Phillip Sidney" "by D[octor John] Hammond" investigates questions such as whether "Foreeigners [are] charcable with treason," "Ambassadors [are] punishable by deathe," and whether "Safe conduct [is] protection to offences after co[m]mitted"—preemptive immunity from later crimes.[94]

For Sidney, epic fiction itself works as a kind of Socratic device in which *topoi* of the law of nations such as these are given *enargeia* and depth. In *De Jure Belli*, Gentili would also include a relatively fleshed out theory of exemplarity. Gentili championed the educative role of actions performed by "those who are regarded as honourable and of good repute. For they too appear to have acted in accordance with nature."[95] After acknowledging the maxim that "one ought not to judge from examples," Gentili said it was nevertheless "clear that a plausible conjecture may be deduced from examples. Indeed, in cases of doubt one is obliged to judge from examples, and also when anything has become a custom."[96] Sidney's artifact, composed with such cases of doubt in mind, repeatedly joins rhetoric, politics, and the law of nations in uniquely challenging combinations for the purpose of helping his high-born readers forge the diplomatic armor needed for appropriate response. Notwithstanding deprecating remarks Sidney made about his fancies, close examination of the legal relations in the *New Arcadia*'s third book in particular reveals Sidney's sustained and artful ingenuity in preparing Elizabethan readers for "matters that fall out in diverse places."[97] To read Sidney's carefully constructed episode through sixteenth-century debates over the *ius gentium* was to encounter the thorniest issues of international law and, thereby, for delight as well as profit, to start to make one's armor before the fight.

In the third book of the *New Arcadia*, for example, Pamela and Philoclea, virtuous princesses and heirs to King Basilius' throne, are taken captive by agents of their treasonous aunt Cecropia, who hopes to match her noble son Amphialus with Philoclea so he might advance to the Arcadian throne.[98] Along with the heroic knight Pyrocles disguised as the Amazon Zelmane, the princesses are subsequently removed to a "castle . . . in the midst of a great lake, upon a high rocke . . . [which is] by all men esteemed impregnable," where they resist fulsome praise and torture in their refusal to assent to Amphialus' plea for marriage.[99] Sidney carefully distinguishes the princesses' passive resistance from active resistance, however. When some of

---

[93] Gentili, *De Legationibus*, 2:vi.

[94] BL Add MS 48027, fols. 380–97, H. R. Woudhuysen, "Leicester's Literary Patronage: A Study of the English Court, 1578–1582" (Oxford: University of Oxford, Faculty of English Language and Literature, 1981), 72; On Sidney's involvement in legal matters related to the prosecution of Mary Queen of Scots, see Blair Worden, *The Sound of Virtue: Philip Sidney's "Arcadia" and Elizabethan Politics* (New Haven, CT: Yale University Press, 1996), 181.

[95] Gentili, *De Jure Belli Libri Tres*, 11.   [96] Gentili, *De Jure Belli Libri Tres*, 11.

[97] For a related account of the function of Renaissance literature, see Kahn, *Machiavellian Rhetoric*.

[98] Martin N. Raitiere, *Faire Bitts: Sir Philip Sidney and Renaissance Political Theory* (Pittsburgh, PA: Duquesne University Press, 1984), 19–38; Richard C. McCoy, *Sir Philip Sidney: Rebellion in Arcadia* (New Brunswick, NJ: Rutgers University Press, 1979).

[99] Sidney, *The Countess of Pembroke's Arcadia (the New Arcadia)*, 316–17. Except where indicated, all references are to this edition by Skretkowicz and will be noted parenthetically in the text.

Cecropia's disgruntled agents offer the princesses a plan for escape, Pamela refuses the offer on the grounds that such resistance constitutes "treason," refusing "so horrible a wickedness" and protesting, "let the Gods dispose of me as shall please them—but sure it shall be no such way, nor way-leader, by which I will come to liberty!" (389). Philoclea, likewise, "would rather yield to perpetual imprisonment than consent" (389). Because many writers not only permitted but required a prisoner of war to try to escape captivity, the princesses' refusal to resist is striking.[100]

Sixteenth-century *ius gentium* theories involved intense considerations of what obligations were owed to whom. In such theories, the prisoner's specific rights and duties depended on the all-important question of who merited the rights of enemies. The designation of "enemy" was a privilege for *ius gentium* theorists in that it assured certain unbreachable protocols, such as the safe passage of heralds and ambassadors.[101] A relation of enmity also set the terms for the treatment and duties of prisoners of war.

Theorists differed sharply on these matters, and, inevitably, differences signaled political concerns and exigencies. In 1573, in the wake of the St. Bartholomew's Day massacre, the Huguenot jurist François Hotman set a notably low threshold for enemy status in his *Quæstionum Illustrium*, arguing that rebellious subjects had been accorded enemy status in Roman law and suggesting that internal conflicts such as the one then ongoing in France should be conducted according to the law of nations rather than municipal law.[102] If accepted, this would mean that rebels like Sidney's Cecropia and Amphialus warranted the privileged status of enemy. In support for this view, Hotman offered Caesar's *Civil Wars* among other sources. Although William Fulbecke in his *Pandectes of the Law of Nations* (1602) was only one of many to insist against François Hotman that "a Rebell may not properlie be called an enemie," François' son Jean followed his father in arguing that the law of nations "ought to prevaile...for devided subjects."[103] "The assurance that is granted unto" the heralds and ambassadors of rebels, "fugitives, outlawes, or pirates," Jean Hotman argued, "is not for [rebels'] sakes, but in consideration of the Common good."[104] Whether Sidney thought Amphialus, as a "subaltern magistrate," had the right to resist Basilius has rightly been an interest of scholars, yet

---

[100] According to the Italian jurist Pierino Belli, writing in 1559, "the man who, after being captured by the enemy, fails to return to his people when there is opportunity" is "like to the deserter." "Whosoever being taken prisoner by his enemies, dooth not seeke to eskape as often as he may[, violates his duty] except hee hath given his promise not to depart without leave," a manual for soldiers published in England in 1589 declared. Sidney's surprising use of the term "treason" to describe his own prisoners' resistance of a torturous jailor, then, suggests the benefit to be had from giving the legal status of the third book some sustained attention. Pierino Belli, *De re militari et bello tractatus*, trans. Arrigo Cavaglieri (Oxford; London: Clarendon Press, 1936), 2.224; Raimond Beccarie de Pavie, *Instructions for the Warres*, trans. Paul Ive (London: Thomas Man, 1589), 262.

[101] For detailed treatment of these issues, see Maurice Hugh Keen, *The Laws of War in the Late Middle Ages* (London: Routledge & Kegan Paul, 1965), esp. ch. 1, "The Legal Basis of the Law of Arms," pp. 7–22.

[102] François Hotman, *Quæstionum Illustrium Liber* (Paris, 1573).

[103] William Fulbecke, *The Pandectes of the Law of Nations: Contayning Severall Discourses of the Questions...of Law, Wherein the Nations of the World Doe Consent and Accord* (London: Thomas Wight, 1602), sig. 39r; Hotman, *The Ambassador*, sig. [i6r].

[104] Hotman, *The Ambassador*, sig. [i6r].

viewing the question through debates in the law of nations—from the outside in, as it were—allows us to see that the legal status to be accorded to figures like Cecropia and Amphialus once they had already resisted was itself one of the hottest issues of Sidney's day (325).[105]

Gentili, who as we have seen shared most of François Hotman's political and confessional commitments, disparaged Hotman's claim in his *De Legationibus* and *De Jure Belli*. Ironically, Gentili was in line with the Spanish position influenced by the Dutch revolt as articulated by Balthazar Ayala, a Spanish judge in the Spanish Netherlands, in 1582: "rebels ought not to be classed as enemies, the two being quite distinct, and so it is more correct to term the armed contention with rebel subjects execution of legal process, or prosecution, and not war."[106] Hotman, Gentili writes, "exposes his ignorance when in his *Famous Questions* he makes the statement that *ius gentium* holds for rebels. For the fact that we find the jurist Paulus asserting that rebels are enemies to the extent of losing their citizenship, is far from establishing the contention that they should be regarded as falling within the scope of international law [*ius gentium*]."[107] Citing the civil war in Lucan's *Pharsalia* as an example of a "war without an enemy," Gentili's parsimonious account of the rights of rebels had clearly been influenced by events in England such as the Throgmorton plot and French Catholic league resistance theories, the latter of which began circulating with Hotmans' exact arguments after the Protestant Henri Navarre had become the heir presumptive in July 1584.[108] If there was also an element of *post facto* justification for Lord Grey's 1580 massacre in Ireland in this, the more immediate problem was closing the Pandora's box the Huguenots had apparently opened. Now, the principle was simple: "subject peoples...can not acquire [the right to embassy] by revolt because rights are not acquired by offenses."[109] Far from acquiring rights, the rebel loses them. Having extracted himself from the civil order by his revolt, the rebel lapses into a juridical black hole populated only by pirates and brigands: for those "who violate all laws, no laws remain in force."[110] While Gentili acknowledged rebels might be *called* "enemy," command a "regular army," and capture cities (and, as we will see in the next chapter, he did not stick to this account), in the 1580s, none of these was sufficient to win enemy status. "The assumption of public cause" was the fundamental concern.[111]

The third book of Sidney's *New Arcadia* is thus brilliantly situated at the heart of the dispute between Hotman and Gentili, giving legal theory crucial affective

---

[105] Raitiere, *Faire Bitts* offers the best analysis of the debate.

[106] Balthazar Ayala, *De Jure et Officiis Bellicis et Disciplina Militari Libri III*, ed. John Westlake, trans. John Pawley Bate (Washington, DC: Carnegie Institution of Washington, 1912), 2.19.

[107] Gentili, *De Legationibus*, 2:77.

[108] Parmelee, *Good Newes from Fraunce*, 295; J. H. M. Salmon, "Catholic Resistance Theory, Ultramontanism, and the Royalist Response, 1580–1620," in *The Cambridge History of Political Thought, 1450–1700*, ed. J. H. Burns and Mark Goldie (Cambridge: Cambridge University Press, 1991), 247; Donald R. Kelley, *François Hotman: A Revolutionary's Ordeal* (Princeton, NJ: Princeton University Press, 1973); Gentili, *De Jure Belli Libri Tres*, 2.330.

[109] Gentili, *De Legationibus*, 2: 77.   [110] Gentili, *De Jure Belli Libri Tres*, 2.24.

[111] Gentili, *De Legationibus*, 2: 24–5.

and imaginative depth. For readers honing their international legal hermeneutics, Sidney presents through Cecropia and Amphialus the ambiguous, multi-hued legal conundrum par excellence, and the first significant episode introduces the problem of rhetoric. Whatever Amphialus' hidden motives, the central problem is that he lays rhetorical claim to a public cause. He has taken the princesses captive, he says in the "justification" "he...caused to be written," for "the good estate of so many thousands over whom Basilius reigned" (325). The "unfit and ill-guarded...place" where Basilius had "set his daughters" made them vulnerable to being "conveyed to [a] forraine country," so, in the interest of "the whole commonwealth," he says, he "brought them into this strong castle of his... [where] they should be served and honored as belonged to their greatness" (325–326). Superficially, his aim is not "to bring into subjection those not deserving of such treatment," a faulty use of military training, according to Sidney's admired Aristotle, but instead "to save [Arcadians] from becoming subject to others," deemed by Aristotle the proper use of arms.[112] Nor, according to his justification, is Amphialus the aggressor. Yet if his securing of the princesses leads Basilius to attack, "he would then for his own defence take armes, desiring all that either tendered the dangerous case of their country, or in their hearts loved justice, to defend him in this just action" (326). In an historical moment in which Dutch Protestants, French Huguenots, and English and Irish Catholics all made similar claims *vis à vis* their purported sovereigns, reaching out, similarly, to confessional allies in neighboring countries, it might be said that measuring the distance between Amphialus' public rhetoric and his private motives encapsulated the supreme challenge of Elizabethan foreign affairs.

With an apposite warning of "how few there be that can discern between truth and truthlikeness," Sidney introduces a rhetorical element into the debate between Hotman and Gentili on the rebel's rights (325). At the same time, Sidney underscores that same need for frequent, attentive reading that we have seen he and his circle prized. Sidney's authorial criticism of the "foulness of [Amphialus'] treason" temporarily aligns the *Arcadia*'s implicit arguments with Gentili's assertion that "no one improves his legal status by transgression" (325).[113] Belli used the same word "treason" in his pronouncement that "he who fortifies and holds a citadel against the will of the Emperor is liable to the penalty for treason."[114] But Sidney is nowhere near as critical of Amphialus' words as he is of his dissimulation. He allows that Amphialus argues from "true commonplaces" even if he does "fetch down most false applications" (325). The chasm between Amphialus' public-spirited rhetoric and private-minded actions therefore critiques both Hotman's argument for granting the rebel enemy's rights *avant la lettre* and Gentili's for doing so when a combatant articulates a "public cause." What epic narration allows Sidney to do is to demonstrate that the rhetoric of such a cause is always available to whomever might use it, thereby reinforcing the very premise of Sidney's literary project—the need for trained, prudent judgment. In Sidney's strategically liminal case, there is

---

[112] Aristotle, *The Politics*, trans. T. A. Sinclair (New York: Penguin Books, 1981), 435 (1333b). On Sidney and Aristotle, see especially Kathy Eden, *Poetic and Legal Fiction in the Aristotelian Tradition* (Princeton, NJ: Princeton University Press, 1986), 157–75.
[113] Gentili, *De Jure Belli Libri Tres*, 2.21.   [114] Belli, *De re militari et bello tractatus*, 220.

thus something of an epistemological and fiction-validating demurral to all general legal pronouncements on rebels' rights in the law of nations: without the aid of authorial omniscience, how is one to discern the "truth" of a public cause from the "truthlikeness" of its rhetoric? Such was the need for advanced rhetorical literacy, "already have[ing] studied the situation," and the literary example.[115]

HANNIBAL READS HOMER

Despite the fact that the law of nations has been called a "principle of beneficial mutual restraint," its benefits were not always altogether clear to *de facto* powers, since observing the law of nations seemingly implied an underlying justice beneath the rebels' cause.[116] Authors like Gentili saw granting emissaries safe passage, employing heralds, and observing specific protocols with prisoners of war as the way for adjudicating just causes between sovereigns, but "private individuals, subject peoples and petty sovereigns are never confronted with the necessity of the arbitrament of Mars," Gentili said.[117] "They can obtain their legal rights before their superiors' tribunal."[118] What sovereigns feared, therefore, was that recourse to "arbitrament of Mars," by which Gentili meant trial by battle, implicitly acknowledged either that corruption was so pervasive that justice could not be had in the superior's tribunal or, even worse, that the putative superior was not superior at all.

A moment that under such conditions becomes fruitful to analyze is the moment in the third book when Phalantus makes a surprising overture to Amphialus. Sidney tells of how "obtaining leave of Basilius, [Phalantus] caused a herald to be furnished with apparel of his office and tokens of a peaceable message, and so sent him to the town to demand audience of Amphialus" (365). In its implicit recognition of Amphialus' public legal personhood, this was a deeply symbolic gesture. As such, it is no wonder that Amphialus, according with the laws of war, entertains the herald "both safely and courteously" (365). Amphialus subsequently dispatches him "with safe convoy ... from out his City" (366). Gentili's argument against rebells' rights notwithstanding, for the rest of the third book, Amphialus has the good standing of an enemy.

Having in his sensitive treatment of diplomatic relations dramatized one sort of consensual movement out of "the first Chaos," Sidney further establishes how fragile mutual consent can be in another episode—one remarkably redolent of the so-called Mendoza affair, in which Alberico Gentili and Jean Hotman had each been enlisted to determine the legal recourse once the Spanish ambassador Mendoza had been apprehended plotting against Elizabeth. Here, Sidney limns a

---

[115] Gentili, *De Legationibus*, 2:2.154.

[116] Barbara Donagan, "Atrocity, War Crime, and Treason in the English Civil War," *The American Historical Review* 99, no. 4 (October 1, 1994): 1140. Donagan shows Charles I's wariness, for example, about granting his internal mid-seventeenth century conflict the status of war as opposed to rebellion.

[117] Gentili, *De Jure Belli Libri Tres*, 20.   [118] Gentili, *De Jure Belli Libri Tres*, 20.

certain moral economy for the *ius gentium*, suggesting that however much observing the laws of war implies equality, virtue and barbarity remain, and the virtuous still must instruct the barbarous. Having earlier taken Philanax in battle, Amphialus in this episode is "inclined...in some formal sort to cause [the Basilean] to be executed" (352). Almost all *ius gentium* theorists agreed with Belli that normally "it is savage and barbarous to do violence to prisoners."[119] Doing so violated what Gentili called the "bargain [a prisoner made] with the enemy for his life"—a bargain only invalidated by the prisoner when he "or his supporters" resist.[120] "Inclined" to kill Philanax, by implication "inclined" to savagery and barbarity, Amphialus is only dissuaded by Philoclea, who—like *Proverbs*' wife who "openeth her mouth with wisdom; and in her tongue *is* the law of kindness"—importunes him to "lay no further punishment than imprisonment upon Philanax" (352).[121] What Sidney then provides is a Hannibal who *does* read Homer: sufficiently instructed by Philoclea in the laws of war, Amphialus not only obliges but agrees, as England did Mendoza, to grant Philanax "uncorrupted liberty," thereby winning Philanax's reciprocal favor to such a remarkable extent that Philanax departs with his "favorable convoy out of the town...not having visited the Princesses, thinking it might be offensive to Amphialus" (354).[122]

In *De Legationibus*, Gentili quoted a powerful rhetorical question from Xenophon: "Who would dare approach with a herald's wand those whose heralds he has put to death?"[123] Amphialus has learned to agree. Significantly, Basilius consents to the sending of a herald to Amphialus only after Amphialus has here subjected himself to the law of nations.

Together, these three episodes—Amphialus' justification, the sending of a herald to Amphialus, and Amphialus' grant of liberty to Philanax—point toward what Sidney sees as the virtuous spiral of reading, judging, and beneficial mutual restraint that can emerge even in the violent and fragile world his political theory assumes.

EPIC KINDNESS, THE "FEIGNED EXAMPLE," AND THE LAW OF NATIONS

The foregoing discussion has argued that epic romance for Sidney worked very much as history did for Jean Hotman—as something that "will greatly help [the ambassador]; which besides the pleasure of it...will encrease in him, wisdome and judgement in the affairs of his charge. Will enable him against all chances. Will bring him to the knowledge of the origine, continuance and ruine of kingdoms, countries, and townes...Will make him that he bee not astonished at any thing

---

[119] Belli, *De re militari et bello tractatus*, 86.

[120] Gentili, *De Jure Belli Libri Tres*, 216. See Theodor Meron, "Shakespeare's Henry the Fifth and the Law of War," *The American Journal of International Law* 86, no. 1 (January 1992): 1.

[121] *KJV*, Proverbs 31:26.

[122] For clarity, I follow here the 1590 edition, Philip Sidney, *The Countesse of Pembrokes Arcadia* (London: [by John Windet] for William Ponsonbie, 1590), 277.

[123] Gentili, *De Legationibus*, 2:73.

that hee heareth read or spoeken, considering that histories [or epics] will furnish him with many examples of like accidents."[124] But Sidney's *Defence of Poesy* argued that literature could do what history in and of itself could not do—"plant goodness even in the secretest cabinet of our souls" (351). While scholars have learned to treat this sentiment with a degree of skepticism, the sway Philoclea wields with Amphialus is a strong instance of Sidney's literary ambitions, whatever its faults: barbarity transformed to virtue. The "feigned example hath as much force to teach as a true example" for Sidney and, unlike the true example, the feigned example may be composed for maximum effect—"may," in Sidney's musical metaphor, "be tuned to highest key of passion" (355).

Fiction was also superior to law for Sidney, but in a slightly different way from history. Although Sidney thought "our wickedness maketh [lawyers] necessary, and necessity maketh [them] honourable," he placed poetry above the law because unlike poetry, the law did "not endeavour to make men good" (351). He contended that lawyers cared little for "how bad a man...be" if that person's "evil hurt not others" (351). Poetry by contrast could "make many...begin to hear the sound of virtue" (353). Whereas law worked externally by capitalizing on fear of punishment, poetry worked on the heart by promoting a love of virtue. Fear of punishment did not stop Hannibal from "commit[ing] many things against the justice of war," as Gentili put it, but a love of virtue may have done.

In concluding this chapter, then, I want to turn to two final episodes in the *New Arcadia* that Sidney tunes to the highest degree of passion. The second will be the princesses' refusal to escape, to which I've alluded earlier, but to which we can now add the context of a powerful Roman example of the law of nations in action that Sidney "tunes." But first is the Vergilian supplication scene in which Lycurgus begs Pyrocles for his life at the end of the *New Arcadia*. In their ways, each of these examples tests the boundaries of law, morality, and genre through questions of *kindness* in the law of nations.

In the conclusion to Sidney's *New Arcadia*, which virtually paraphrased the conclusion of the *Aeneid*, the meaning of kindness follows epic tradition. The *New Arcadia*'s genre or kind structures the moral *praxis* acceptable within its bounds.[125] The exigencies of Sidney's plot had required his male hero Pyrocles, like Elizabethan sovereignty itself, to wear a female guise, and Sidney's Turnus figure, Lycurgus, exhibits the same "hazardous" "confidence" that for Tasso and Gentili partially exculpated Aeneas.[126] Once defeated, however, Lycurgus pleads as poignantly as Turnus had done. And recalling how Aeneas momentarily "repressed" (*repressit*) his violent hand and Tasso's Tancred halted his great heart (*magnanimo cor*), Sidney's Pyrocles (described with female pronouns while he is disguised as the female Zelmane) "repressed a while her great heart—either disdaining to be cruel, or pitiful, and therefore not cruel."[127] This is a moment tuned, in a sense, with varieties

---

[124] Hotman, *The Ambassador*, sig. c2r.
[125] For the Virgilian roots, see Colin Burrow, *Epic Romance: Homer to Milton* (Oxford: Clarendon Press, 1993), 140–1.
[126] Sidney, *The Countess of Pembroke's Arcadia: (The Old Arcadia)*, 461.
[127] Sidney, *The Countess of Pembroke's Arcadia: (The Old Arcadia)*, 462.

of kindness, for, as Gentili wrote, "supplication is made through the community of nature [*communionem naturae*], which continues to be a common bond, if men are not wild beasts."[128] Morally, the moment's relevant kind is mankind, *le genre humain.* Sidney's *Old Arcadia* had spoken of "universal civility, the law of nations (all mankind being as it were coinhabiters or world citizens together)."[129] Sidney alludes to such notions of human-kindness (the double meaning is important) as he tells how "the image of human condition began to be an orator unto [Zelmane] of compassion," a phrase that amplifies the notes of forensic oratory in Vergil's *flectere* (12.940), to sway or to persuade.

Generically, however, the kindness of epic has its borders. Like Aeneas, Sidney's hero/heroine ultimately turns a deaf ear to the suppliant's claims for the expansive kindness of species. Instead, it is the particular genre of epic that conditions Pyroces' action, the mimetic relation of epic subject and her kin outweighing any claims of universal humanity. In Gentili's moral psychology, in cases of "our most cruel enemies" especially, "the ears of the victor ought often to be closed [*occulas... debere victoris aures*] to suppliants."[130] That another humanist poet in their circle, Gabriel Harvey, even entitled a now-lost poem *Anticosmopolita* suggests the pervasiveness of this thinking in their circle. And just as Vergil's Aeneas is in Gentili's reading made by Pallas' baldric to feel a bond of kinship superseding an expansively human kindness, so too is Sidney's character brought back from the brink of cosmopolitan pity for the "suppliant" by a reminder of more narrow affections, in this case by a token of conjugal love, a "garter with a jewel" that Sidney's Pyrocles had given to his love, Philoclea.[131] "The sight of that" garter, Sidney writes, "was like a cipher signifying all the injuries which Philoclea had of [Lycurgus] suffered; and that remembrance, feeding upon wrath, trod down all conceits of mercy. And therefore, saying no more but, 'No villain, die! It is Philoclea that sends thee this token for thy love,' and with that, she made her sword drink the blood of his heart." Sidney's adaptation of Vergil's final scene was consistent with many of Gentili's arguments about Vergil. Gentili, we recall, claimed that it was not Aeneas but Pallas who slew Turnus. Here, Sidney lets "she" refer ambiguously either to Zelmane or to Philoclea, and, like Turnus in Tasso's and Gentili's readings, Sidney's Lycurgus had earlier breached the "law of arms" and "use of chivalry," thereby further justifying Zelmane's refusal to spare him.[132]

Even so, Sidney's *New Arcadia* shows the author's discomfort with Pyrocles' killing of suppliants. Like Tasso, Sidney refused to end his poem, as Vergil had done, with the slaughter of a suppliant. Tasso's poem ends not with Tancred's heroic slaughter of Argente but with Goffredo's decision to spare the pleading Altamoor. According to scholarly tradition, Sidney left his poem unfinished at his death in 1586. Recalling Gentili's insistence that the legal issue of supplication arises only

---

[128] Alberico Gentili, *De Jure Belli Libri Tres* (Oxford: Clarendon Press, 1933), 2.20, 408.
[129] Gentili, *De Jure Belli Libri Tres*, 2.20, 408; Sidney, *The Countess of Pembroke's Arcadia: (The Old Arcadia)*, 349.
[130] Gentili, *De Jure Belli Libri Tres*, 2.20, 409.
[131] Burrow, *Epic Romance: Homer to Milton*, 141.
[132] Sidney, *The Countess of Pembroke's Arcadia: (The Old Arcadia)*, 411.

when "victory is assured," it is of course possible such choices reflect their authors' prudential, reason-of-state approach to supplication. Scipio Gentili, too, declared Tasso's maxim "for faith and fatherland all things are just" "most pious and holy" (*GL* 4.26.8).[133] Yet it is difficult not to find deeper legal and moral claims in the choices to extend the epics. What Tasso and Sidney suggested by continuing their stories past the slaughter of suppliants was that Aeneas' killing was not self-justifying, nor justified within the existing structure of the *Aeneid*—in other words, that supplementary "facts" and narrative were needed to justify the act.[134] The constraints placed by the genre of epic, in other words, were not all. The gesture toward a universal humanity remained.

CONCLUSION

In 1579, Thomas Vautroullier, the same Huguenot refugee who would print Gentili's *De Legationibus*, published Thomas North's important translation of Plutarch's *Lives*, from whose preface Sidney would draw for his *Defence*.[135] North's Plutarch is relevant at the conclusion of this chapter for two stories told in Plutarch's life of Pyrrhus about the Roman ambassador and consul known as Fabricius. Both stories take place during the Romans' war against Pyrrhus. In the first story, which even among the Romans was "the stuff of exemplary anecdote and annalistic embellishment," the ambassador Fabricius rejects Pyrrhus' attempt to bribe him when Fabricius had been sent to treat with Pyrrhus about prisoners of war.[136] The second, more significant story is worth quoting at length from North:

> [A]s [Fabricius] was in his campe, there came a man to him that brought him a letter from kinge Pyrrus Phisitian, wrytten with his owne handes: in which the Phisitian offered to poyson his maister, so he would promise him a good reward, for ending the warres without further daunger. Fabricius detestinge the wickednesse of the Phisitian, and having made Q. AEmilius his colleague, and fellowe Consull also, to abhorre the same: wrote a letter unto Pyrrus, and bad him take heede, for there were that ment to poyson him.[137]

Because of his honor in these stories, Fabricius embodied Roman virtue in war and faithfulness to the law of nations. In a discussion of the "law of nations" in 1592, Francis Bacon evoked Fabricius with the comment that "there have been . . . offers of murderous and traitorous attempts against the person of a prince . . . [that] have

---

[133] Scipione Gentili, *Annotationi Di Scipio Gentili Sopra La Gierusalemme Liberata Di Torquato Tasso* (London: J. Wolfe, 1586), 59; Torquato Tasso, *Jerusalem Delivered (Gerusalemme Liberata)*, ed. Anthony M. Esolen (Baltimore, MD: Johns Hopkins University Press, 2000), 448.

[134] For continuation of the Aeneid as discomfort or critique, see the discussion of Maffeo Vegio in Kallendorf, *The Other Virgil*, 41–2.

[135] Marguerite Hearsey, "Sidney's 'Defense of Poesy' and Amyot's 'Preface' in North's 'Plutarch': A Relationship," *Studies in Philology* 30, no. 4 (October 1, 1933): 535–50.

[136] Plutarch, *Plutarch's Lives* (London; Cambridge, MA: Heinemann, 1914), vol. IX, 9.406–411 (xx); Matthew Leigh, *Comedy and the Rise of Rome* (Oxford: Oxford University Press, 2004), 66.

[137] Plutarch, *The Lives of the Noble Grecians and Romanes*, trans. Thomas North (London: Thomas Vautroullier, 1579), 439–40.

been not only rejected, but also revealed."[138] Hugo Grotius said Fabricius "succeeded in the most difficult task of preserving his innocence in war, and because he believed that some acts were utterly wrong even when committed against an enemy."[139] Summarizing the humanist consensus, a late seventeenth-century writer wrote that "Fabricius was accounted a great man... for his innocence in War": "[he] believ[ed] there was something which was no ways lawful for him to do to a very Enemy."[140]

In the Elizabethan period, the volume with which Fabricius' virtue was proclaimed grew in direct proportion to fears of plots against Elizabeth. Many felt that, "urged on by the pope, the Catholic powers were now committed to murder and treachery as instruments of their cause."[141] In March 1584, an informant, perhaps Giordano Bruno, wrote to Elizabeth with news he said he had learned in a confession from a Spaniard residing in England that justified those fears. "He told me," the informant wrote, "that he had a charge from M. de Mendoza, with four others whose names I do not know except for one called Courtois, to procure your death very shortly by arms, by poisons, bouquets, underclothes, smell, waters or by any other means."[142] Elizabeth's perceived vulnerability to such methods—culminating in the 1594 execution of Dr. Lopez—led to Gentili's resounding objection to Baldus' apparent claim that it was lawful to kill an enemy by poison. Giving an unparalleled twenty reasons why poisoning was unlawful, Gentili wished, "Farewell to Baldus in this matter. Farewell to poisons. Farewell, nay perish, those who war with poison."[143] Unsurprisingly, he then produced the example of Fabricius, this time as related by Seneca in his *Essays*:

> "when the king's physician promised he would poison Pyrrus, Fabricius warned the monarch to look out for plots. He was equally determined not to be overcome by gold, and not to overcome by poison. We admired a hero who was great and blameless, a most difficult thing in war; a man who thought that some acts were impious even when done against an enemy." Claudian in this connexion notes another crime: "Fabricius sent back to the king, upon whom he was making bitter war, the man who had promised to mix a deadly drug for his master, and he also revealed the man's treachery; and Fabricius declared that he would not win a victory in war through the impious crime of a slave."[144]

Refusing to join the plot and even alerting his enemy to it, Fabricius had gone beyond bare law to perform exemplary virtue.

---

[138] Francis Bacon, "Certain Observations Made Upon a Libel Published This Present Year, 1592," in *The Works of Francis Bacon*, ed. James Spedding, Robert Leslie, and Douglas Denon Heath (London: Longman, 1861), vol. VIII, 146.

[139] Grotius, *De Jure Belli ac Pacis*, 1752.

[140] George Dawson, *Origo Legum, Or, A Treatise of the Origin of Laws, and Their Obliging Power* (London: Richard Chiswell, 1694), 153.

[141] John Bossy, *Giordano Bruno and the Embassy Affair* (London: Vintage, 1992), 32.

[142] Quoted in Bossy, *Giordano Bruno and the Embassy Affair*, 32–3.

[143] Despite this rhetorical flourish and the twenty reasons that went along with it, Gentili's prohibition on poison was not categorical: "the use of poisons cannot be legitimate," he said chillingly, "except in wars of extermination." Gentili, *De Jure Belli Libri Tres*, 155.

[144] Gentili, *De Jure Belli Libri Tres*, 156.

Near the middle of the *New Arcadia's* third book, Cecropia's and Amphialus' servants hatch a plot to free Pamela and Philoclea by "empoison[ing] Amphialus," and it is with the figure of Fabricius in the context of Elizabethan politics, I argue, that the episode needs to be read (388). Sidney's poetic theory makes direct parallels to an historical figure like Fabricius ultimately beside the point, but, as is the case with contemporary Elizabethan figures, crucial elements of the Fabricius story peek through Sidney's feigned example.[145] In the episode, Sidney's Philoclea is approached by the plotter Clinias, whose very name is a reminder of the Cretan in Plato's *Laws* and who argues that "all men are both publicly and privately the enemies of all."[146] Having been approached by Clinias, Philoclea

> (in whose clear mind treason could find no hiding place) told [Clinias], that she would be glad if he could persuade her cousin to deliver her, and that she would never forget his service therein, but that she desired him to lay down any such way of mischief, for that, for her part, she would rather yield to perpetual imprisonment than consent to the destroying her cousin, who, she knew, loved her, though wronged her. (389)

Philoclea's "unlooked-for answer," vaunting diplomatic persuasion over traitorous poison, is precisely the answer advised by Gentili, who considers poisoning "worthy of brigands and not of princes," "the acts of infidels," and "characteristic of barbarians" (389).[147] Pamela goes a step further, and in that step approaches Fabricius' exemplary virtue. When she is approached by Artesia for the same purpose, Pamela takes exactly the approach taken by Fabricius—and the one Walsingham and the English Protestants, for obvious reasons, wanted to encourage: "betray[ing] the one who offered to do the deed."[148] With noble conviction tuned to the highest degree of passion, Pamela declares to Artesia that "it shall be no such way, nor way-leader, by which I will come to liberty!" Pamela, Sidney writes, then "spake something with a louder voice than she was wont to use, so as *Cecropia* heard the noise" and then hinted to Cecropia of Artesia's betrayal: " 'Ask of her!' said Pamela. 'And learn to know that who do falsehood to their superiors, teach falsehood to their inferiors. More she would not say' " (389).

With the whole of Sidney's narrative having been directed toward the princesses' liberation, their refusal is strikingly—frustratingly—poignant. If feigned examples were to be tuned to the highest degree of passion, Sidney's narrative momentum provides the tuning fork. In a limited way, the princesses' refusal to fight "by fraud or secret acts" replays the movement of the Philanax episode wherein a heroic princess teaches a barbarian the law of nations.[149] Yet here, the lines of instruction move even more noticeably from the Arcadian world to the Elizabethan one. If Amphialus could secure entry into the norms of the law of nations by releasing Philanax, none of the characters involved with this breach is permitted equivalent

---

[145] On examples, history, and *roman a clef*, see John M. Wallace, " 'Examples Are Best Precepts': Readers and Meanings in Seventeenth-Century Poetry," *Critical Inquiry* 1, no. 2 (December 1, 1974): 273–90.

[146] Plato, *Laws*, trans. Robert Gregg Bury (Cambridge, MA: Harvard University Press, 1984), 1.9 (626).

[147] Gentili, *De Jure Belli Libri Tres*, 156–8.   [148] Gentili, *De Jure Belli Libri Tres*, 156.

[149] Gentili, *De Jure Belli Libri Tres*, 156.

redemption. Like an Edmund Campion to Artesia's Mary Stuart, Clinias and "the rest of his corrupted mates" are "executed" while Artesia is "locked up in her chamber," benefiting from private affection (390). The opportunity to learn from Sidney's feigned example, rather than being granted to Clinias and Artesia, is offered mainly to Sidney's Elizabethan readers, who—like ordinary Romans in Fabricius' war against Pyrrhus—experience the sharply uncomfortable conflict between a narrative *telos* and the law of nations. Sidney was neither the first nor the only author to capitalize on this tension: in his *Gerusalemme Liberata*, a Latin translation of which Scipio Gentili published in parts over the 1580s and one of whose parts Scipio Gentili dedicated to Sidney, Torquato Tasso revised moments in the *Iliad* and *Aeneid* where Achilles and Aeneas refused to spare suppliants begging to ransom their lives.[150] In this tradition, when passions and interests ran otherwise, exemplary heroism consisted in conforming to the law of nations.

What Sidney's aristocratic readers could find in his *New Arcadia*, then, was not uncritical, fanatical devotion to place, party, or confession, but something approaching what Kwame Appiah calls "rooted cosmopolitanism": rooted to place, party, and confession but capable of responding to difference not with horror and violence but with diplomacy and dialogue.[151] Internationalism, where the bonds of kinship do not disappear, may be an even better term.

Gentili feared that "if it is lawful for [a prisoner] to escape from [difficulties] in *any and every* way, it will surely be allowed him to be perjured and treacherous; and why not? And thus all intercourse between enemies and every law of war will be done away with."[152] No doubt, the sentiment helped ensure Mary Queen of Scots' continued imprisonment, yet even in doing so, it sought to protect the "intercourse between enemies" from degrading into relations of a different kind, specifically that of beasts. It sought to keep warfare and relations among the bearers of conflicting public interests within the conventional space organized both by epic and the laws of war. The space of the epic law of nations was human space—a space that in maintaining an ambit for diplomacy affirmed that human speech and eloquence might still prevail rather than unopposed violent power. Such was the hope Sidney and Gentili shared, and such indeed was the hope for epic, the feigned example, and ultimately public international law.

---

[150] Quint, *Epic and Empire: Politics and Generic Form from Virgil to Milton*, 264; Barbara Brumbaugh, "Jerusalem Delivered and the Allegory of Sidney's Revised Arcadia," *Modern Philology* 101, no. 3 (February 1, 2004): 337n1.

[151] Anthony Appiah, *Cosmopolitanism: Ethics in a World of Strangers* (New York: W. W. Norton, 2006).

[152] Emphasis added. Gentili, *De Jure Belli Libri Tres*, 159.

3

Jacobean Comedy and the *Anagnorisis* of Private International Law

> Recognition [Gr. *anagnorisis*] … is a change from ignorance to knowledge, disclosing either a close relationship or enmity.[1]

In the previous chapter, we saw how epic for Philip Sidney and Alberico Gentili generated foundational thinking on key public aspects of the law of nations, such as sovereign representation, conquest, diplomacy, enmity, and the laws of war. While the canonical *topoi* of public international law grew out of engagements with reading and writing epic, I now want to argue further that our understandings of Renaissance literature and the history of international law have been constrained by overly restrictive definitions of the latter. Just as epic has enjoyed a privileged status among literary genres, so too has public international law often occluded important international legal issues deemed "private."

Recently, scholars of early modern culture have devoted needed attention to "private" transnational figures like merchants, agents, playgoers, emissaries, and exiles, and they have shown the importance of commercial ideologies to the period's dramatic forms.[2] Taken alongside the excellent recent work on juridical dimensions of Renaissance comedies, however, these strains can leave a mistaken impression. They contribute to the sense that international travel, brokerage, and commerce are one thing, law another.

This effect replicates the relative inattention to the history of private international law. As A. Claire Cutler cogently explains, "the public/private law distinction is associated most closely with the following dualisms: politics/economics, state/society,

---

[1] Aristotle, *Poetics*, trans. Malcolm Heath (London: Penguin, 1997), 18 (1152a).
[2] Robert Henke and Eric Nicholson, eds., *Transnational Exchange in Early Modern Theater* (Burlington, VT: Ashgate, 2008); Brinda Charry and Gitanjali Shahani, eds., *Emissaries in Early Modern Literature and Culture: Mediation, Transmission, Traffic, 1550–1700* (Burlington, VT: Ashgate, 2009); Marika Keblusek, "Commerce and Cultural Transfer: Merchants as Agents in the Early Modern World of Books," in *Kultureller Austausch: Bilanz Und Perspektiven Der Frühneuzeitforschung*, ed. Michael North (Cologne: Böhlau, 2009), 297–307; Valerie Forman, *Tragicomic Redemptions: Global Economics and the Early Modern English Stage* (Philadelphia, PA: University of Pennsylvania Press, 2008); Zachary Lesser, "Tragical-Comical-Pastoral-Colonial: Economic Sovereignty, Globalization, and the Form of Tragicomedy," *ELH* 74 (2007): 881–908; Barbara Sebek and Stephen Deng, eds., *Global Traffic: Discourses and Practices of Trade in English Literature and Culture from 1550 to 1700* (New York: Palgrave Macmillan, 2008).

government/economy, government/family, and subject/object."³ "In most cases," Cutler continues, "one side of the dualism signifies what is properly regarded as the subject of public authority, while the other represents a sphere carved out of the regulatory ambit of...state[s] as a privileged area of more or less individual or private authority."⁴ In order to re-enliven the sense of international exchange as a locus of law in the early modern period, this chapter turns to comedy to emphasize early modern comedies' heretofore under-acknowledged preoccupations with the canonical legal concerns of what is now called "private international law," including the emerging doctrines in "conflict of laws" concerning *lex loci contractus* (law of the place of the contract), *lex rei sitae* (law of the place where an object is situated), and *lex loci delicti commissi* (law of the place where a tort is committed).

While scholars have rightly noticed that several individual Renaissance comedies exhibit strong international interests, the genre's general orientation to international exchange has been less emphasized.⁵ I want to suggest here that comedy, a form that in Kenneth Burke's estimation "requires the maximum of forensic complexity," exhibits a distinct international jurisprudence.

As we'll see, several Jacobean comedies pointedly refused the epic ontology of allies and enemies, depicting instead—largely on Aristotelian grounds—the more ordinary worlds of travelers, merchants, immigrants, factors, and exiles. Insofar as "the comic frame," more than epic, "enable[s] people to be observers of themselves, while acting," and implicitly rejects epic's legal metaphysics of enmity, it affords us a competing legacy of international law.⁶ The epic law of nations was largely organized around the state, its territory, its grand personages, and its international legal personalities. In epic, like its privileged kin tragedy, border-crossing tends to throw up exceptions and crises, to begin and end epochs. For someone like the ex-Nazi jurist Carl Schmitt, who seemed haunted by sovereigns and exceptions, it made a subterranean kind of sense to follow his study of the *ius publicum* (1950) with studies of *Hamlet* (1956) and of the "heroic era" of European conquest, "the great epic of the discovery of the New Earth."⁷ "In the private sphere only does it make

---

³ A. Claire Cutler, "Private Authority in International Trade Relations: The Case of Maritime Transport," in *Private Authority and International Affairs*, ed. Virginia Haufler, Tony Porter, and A. Claire Cutler (Albany, NY: State University of New York Press, 1999), 287. See further A. Claire Cutler, "Artifice, Ideology and Paradox: The Public/Private Distinction in International Law," *Review of International Political Economy* 4, no. 2 (1997): 261–85.

⁴ Cutler, "Private Authority in International Trade Relations," 287.

⁵ Significant exceptions include Jean E. Howard, *Theater of a City The Places of London Comedy, 1598–1642* (Philadelphia, PA: University of Pennsylvania Press, 2007); Robert Henke, "Border-Crossing in the Commedia dell'Arte," in *Transnational Exchange in Early Modern Theater*, ed. Eric Nicholson and Robert Henke (Burlington, VT: Ashgate, 2008), 19–34; Anita Allen and Michael Seidl, "Cross-Cultural Commerce in Shakespeare's *The Merchant of Venice*," *American University International Law Review* 10, no. 2 (January 1, 1995).

⁶ Kenneth Burke, *Attitudes toward History* (Berkeley, CA: University of California Press, 1984), 42, 121; Richard Rorty, "The End of Leninism and History as Comic Frame," in *History and the Idea of Progress*, ed. Arthur M. Melzer, Jerry Weinberger, and M. Richard Zinman (Ithaca, NY: Cornell University Press, 1995), 211–26.

⁷ Carl Schmitt, *The Nomos of the Earth in the International Law of the Jus Publicum Europeaum*, trans. G. L. Ulmen (New York: Telos Press, 2003); Carl Schmitt, *Land and Sea* (Washington, DC: Plutarch Press, 1997), 20, 18.

sense to love one's enemy," he scoffed.[8] Jeremy Bentham's international law, too, was the international law of epic. In his 1780 *Principles of Morals and Legislation*, the quotidian "private" international legal concerns of individuals that had animated the Renaissance law of nations were too mundane to count as "international law." "International law," in his view, was a term that ought to be limited to "the mutual transactions *between sovereigns as such*."[9] However, Bentham's was a daring revision of earlier periods' understanding of the law of nations.[10] Mark Janis reminds us that as late as William Blackstone in the mid-eighteenth century, the law of nations still concerned dealings between individuals. Blackstone defined the law of nations as

> a system of rules, deducible by natural reason, and established by universal consent among the civilized inhabitants of the world; in order to decide all disputes, to regulate all ceremonies and civilities, and to ensure the observance of justice and good faith, in that intercourse which must frequently occur between two or more independent states, *and the individuals belonging to each*.[11]

Translated into the language of literary forms, international law in Bentham's wake rejected its comic inheritance. Concerning itself primarily with states in antagonistic relation, international law had little to say about "the individuals belonging" to them.

What I refer to as the comic law of nations, then, challenges widely held assumptions built into the heroic genres concerning the epoch-making disruptiveness of enemies in international relation. Figures who, in the genres of public international law, might be counted the "enemies of the human race" turn, in comedy's private international law worlds, into worthy partners of exchange. In comedy, "international" tends to describe lived, ordinary experience far more than overt challenges to sovereignty or to what Schmitt grandly called the "*nomos* of the earth*." As opposed to heroic genres that create "epic distance" by charging their heroes with the representative functions of sovereignty, comedy contracts epic distance in favor of affective proximity.[12] Aided by recent work from the legal scholar Karen Knop, I want to suggest that comedy, like private international law in Knop's formulation, "*begins* with the idea that there will be *individual* comings and goings across borders."[13] To a lamentable degree, we have largely forgotten

---

[8] Carl Schmitt, *The Concept of the Political*, trans. George Schwab (Chicago, IL: University of Chicago Press, 1996), 29.

[9] Jeremy Bentham, *An Introduction to the Principles of Morals and Legislation*, ed. J. H. Baker, H. L. A. Hart, and F. Rosen (Oxford: Clarendon Press, 1996), 296 (emphasis added).

[10] M. W. Janis, "Jeremy Bentham and the Fashioning of 'International Law,'" *The American Journal of International Law* 78, no. 2 (April 1, 1984): 405–18; Alex Mills, "The Private History of International Law," *International and Comparative Law Quarterly* 55 (January 1, 2006): 1–50; Philip Marshall Brown, "Private versus Public International Law," *The American Journal of International Law* 36, no. 3 (July 1, 1942): 448–50.

[11] William Blackstone, *Commentaries on the Laws of England*, vol. 4 (Oxford, 1769), 66 (emphasis added).

[12] Mikhail Bakhtin, "Epic and Novel," in *The Dialogic Imagination: Four Essays*, trans. Michael Holquist (Austin, TX: University of Texas Press, 1981), 3–40.

[13] Karen Knop, "Citizenship, Public and Private," *Law and Contemporary Problems* 71, no. 3 (July 1, 2008): 319 (emphasis added); see also Annelise Riles, "A New Agenda for the Cultural Study of Law: Taking on the Technicalities," *Buffalo Law Review* 53 (2005): 973–1033.

that such comings and goings, too, were concerns of the Renaissance law of nations. This may be because we have been too influenced by Bentham's controversially narrow definition of international law. If "recognition [Gr. *anagnorisis*]...is a change from ignorance to knowledge, disclosing either a close relationship or enmity," the *anagnorisis*, or comic recognition, to which the title of this chapter refers is, in part, a needed recognition of international law in the everyday lives of Renaissance persons.[14] However, for the comic recognition of private international law that this chapter hopes to stage, Bentham, in the end, is an easy scapegoat but an imperfect villain. The chasm that Bentham opened in international law was conditioned upon the fissures of "kinds" that already operated generically in the Renaissance. Origins of the Benthamite split between "public international law" and "private international law," in other words, can be found in the Renaissance's deep divisions between heroic genres like tragedy and epic and the genres of popular custom—comedy in particular.

Few texts could better aid in illustrating comedy's connections to private international law than *Pericles* and *The Tempest*. Anchored in the traditions of Roman comedy, each of these plays was at the same time highly relevant to topical debates in early seventeenth-century private international law. In the context of Renaissance humanism, legal topicality and classical allusion worked synergistically. Though both plays are often considered "romances," this was a nineteenth-century development, and it will be by attending precisely to those aspects of *Pericles* and *The Tempest* that draw most obviously from Plautus' comedy *Rudens* that I will try to pinpoint comedy's connections with private international law. In order to unpack such connections, I will first introduce the comic law of nations in general terms. I then want to demonstrate how the *topoi* of comedy intersected with legal *topoi* by attending in detail to a fascinating case of private international law, *Venetian Ambassador v. Brooke*, which was contested between 1607 and 1611.

Illustrating that the classical and topical were hardly opposed, *Pericles* and *The Tempest* intervened in legal controversies such as *Venetian Ambassador v. Brooke* by adapting a particular debate between two characters in Plautus. The debate had become a *locus classicus* as Renaissance readers re-thought private international law questions. Plautine comedy, as I suggest, offered a Renaissance culture voracious for Greco-Roman precedents chances to think through key problems of private international law regarding salvage, travel, and exchange, and provided *exempla* of the rhetorical moves available to those involved in topical debates over maritime legal relations, the so-called "lawyers' duels" brought on by high-stakes current events.[15] Scholars have observed how "episodes in *Pericles*...show a likeness to the *Rudens*," and "some of the leading incidents in [*Pericles*] remind us of the *Rudens*";[16] other scholars have found that *The Tempest* has "obvious affinities" with *Rudens*;

---

[14] Aristotle, *Poetics*, 18 (1152a).

[15] Edmund Gayton, "The lawyer's duel, or two sonnets composed on Grotius's Mare liberum and Selden's Mare Clausum" (London, 1655).

[16] Percy Simpson, *Studies in Elizabethan Drama* (Oxford: Clarendon Press, 1955), 19. Thomas Holt White's analysis, which appeared in Boswell's edition of Malone's Shakespeare (1821), is discussed in Arthur Sherbo, *Shakespeare's Midwives: Some Neglected Shakespeareans* (Cranbury, NJ: Associated University Presses, 1992), 97.

that *Rudens* is a "seminal subtext, frequently mediated and reconstituted" in *The Tempest*; and that in *The Tempest*, "Shakespeare appropriates and adapts from the *Rudens*...aspects of its setting, several of its most prominent motifs and central themes, and principal relationships between its main characters."[17] This chapter contends that these important traditions of comedy open, quite unexpectedly, into a more textured literary history of private international law.

THE COMIC LAW OF NATIONS

"Poetry," writes Aristotle in the *Poetics*, "bifurcated in accordance with the corresponding kinds of character: more serious minded people imitated fine actions, i.e. those of fine persons; more trivial persons imitated those of inferior persons."[18] From the former arose epic and tragedy; from the latter, comedy.

In the law of nations, a parallel bifurcation obtains. Compared to public international law, private international law is at once less grand and more common; it is less sexy, though it deals quite a lot with sex. Sometimes called "conflict of laws," private international law at its narrowest can de defined as "the part of the national law of a country that establishes rules for dealing with cases involving a foreign element."[19] Such a definition, however, can obscure much of the interest and ideological complexity in the history of private international law. Much as "private life" has often been overshadowed by "public" concerns, and comedy in large measure less highly esteemed than tragedy and epic, so too has private international law generally received less attention than its public counterpart. In gendered terms, private international law has been called "the subordinate, lesser, no-force-permitted female side" against which public international law is "defined by distinction."[20] Like epic and tragedy in the Aristotelian conception, public international law's subjects are grave, and, like those genres, public international law has to do with the heightened and the exceptional. If, as Bakhtin suggested, epic is the genre for "peak times," public international law is its law.[21] As we have seen in the previous chapter, it concerns war crimes and broken treaties; it authorizes occupation and denies sovereignty or independence. It is praised and blamed, passionately. It regulates moments of crisis. We might say that its time is *kairos*, or that it is summoned by "the event."[22]

By contrast, private international law is more closely related to the norm rather than the exception. The feminist legal scholar Catherine MacKinnon associates

[17] Charles Martindale and Michelle Martindale, *Shakespeare and the Uses of Antiquity: An Introductory Essay* (London; New York: Routledge, 1990), 15. Robert S. Miola, *Shakespeare and Classical Comedy: The Influence of Plautus and Terence* (Oxford: Oxford University Press, 1994), 155. Bruce Louden, "The Tempest, Plautus, and the Rudens," *Comparative Drama* 33, no. 2 (1999): 199.

[18] Aristotle, *Poetics*, 7 (1148b).

[19] Cf. Jonathan Law and E. A Martin, eds., *A Dictionary of Law*, 6th edn. (Oxford: Oxford University Press, 2006).

[20] Catharine A. MacKinnon, *Are Women Human?: And Other International Dialogues* (Cambridge, MA: Belknap Press of Harvard University Press, 2006), 4–5.

[21] Bakhtin, "Epic and Novel," 13.

[22] Fleur Johns, Richard Joyce, and Sundhya Pahuja, eds., *Events: The Force of International Law* (New York: Routledge, 2011).

private international law with the "everyday," particularly as experienced by women who "have no state, are no state, [and] seek no state."[23] As another scholar puts it, private international law is the law that deals with "the very texture of international relations," where the term "international relations" veers closest to "interpersonal relations."[24] It concerns whether the marriage of two people from different countries is recognized in both places—or in a third. It concerns whether an immigrant may inherit property in her country of residence or his country of birth. It concerns agreements made in London about goods incoming from Venice. Most broadly, it is the law of customary life as lived, "the daily intercourse" of persons in a world of nations, the law for *chronos*, the everyday, *droit quotidien.*[25]

Bentham's exclusion of "individuals" from the realm of the "international" was a watershed event in the history of ideas about international law. In its development, it even lends itself to description as comedic plot. Insofar as Bentham severed individuals conceptually from "international law," he can be seen as an archetypal "blocking character" whose suspension of a preferred order would only be righted, with a comic scene of recognition, when nineteenth-century lawyers introduced the term "private international law." Nevertheless, concerns regarding "individuals" and "inferior persons" rather than "sovereigns" continue to seem to some, like comedy, the domain of the "trivial"—hardly worthy of the grand descriptor "international." Many writers prefer the nationalist-inflected term "conflict of laws" to "private international law," and public international lawyers, it is said, show "reticence" in acknowledging their "private" history.[26]

But like comedy's, private international law's class and gender viewpoints can be more expansive, its social net wider, its aggregate significance, arguably, even more profound than that of public international law. As Knop has recently observed, private international law continues to offer a compelling challenge to many assumptions about citizenship in a global age. She contends that the visions of citizenship that appear most often in contemporary social and political theory assume a public international law model, one defined by the principles of sovereignty and territoriality. When contemporary citizenship theorists then point out the transnational flows of migrants and capital, they are able to "challenge...analysts to think differently about the boundaries of community and membership" and to trouble existing assumptions about citizenship and nationality that are premised (as well) on a public international law ontology. Knop observes, however, that:

> Private international law starts with a different set of assumptions about the interaction of states...The very raison d'être of private international law is that the state will

---

[23] Catharine A. MacKinnon, "Law in the Everyday Life of Women," in *Women's Lives, Men's Laws* (Cambridge, MA: Harvard University Press, 2007), 32–43; Catharine A. MacKinnon, "Women's September 11th: Rethinking the International Law of Conflict," in *Are Women Human?: And Other International Dialogues* (Cambridge, MA: Belknap Press of Harvard University Press, 2006), 259–80.
[24] Brown, "Private versus Public International Law," 448–50.
[25] Brown, "Private versus Public International Law," 448–50.
[26] Mills, "The Private History of International Law," 15.

inevitably contain foreigners of different kinds—not only those who aspire to citizenship, but also those who are de passage, traders, exiles, expatriates, transmigrants—and this will necessarily draw states into a relationship with one another.[27]

Knop's is an important insight that bears on Renaissance texts.

Like Blackstone, Renaissance writers cared little for Bentham's distinction between public and private international law: they would have found the notion of a "private law of nations" unfamiliar. Some contemporary legal scholars have even encouraged us to see in the Renaissance a period before the public/private distinction had helped "to obscure the operation of private power in the global political economy," a time before the Benthamite "devolution of authority to private actors, domestically, internationally and transnationally, [had begun to] reconfigure... political space."[28] That Isidore of Seville, in his oft-quoted account of what the law of nations included, saw no problem in listing "marriages between foreigners [*alienigenas*]" alongside "the occupation of territory, building, fortification, wars, captivities, enslavements, the right of return, treaties of peace, truces, the pledge not to molest embassies" should indicate the error of retrojecting the public/private distinction in international law too haphazardly.[29] If the "private" of "private international law" is, then, only partially satisfactory, it is nevertheless a useful way to focus on a less emphasized aspect of the Renaissance law of nations, for it is indeed very far from the case that early modern Europe had no "rules for dealing with cases involving a foreign element."

Rather, it may simply be that we have forgotten how to recognize the marks of international law in the ordinary lives of the Renaissance's "inferior persons." As one seventeenth-century lawyer observed, "It often happens that transactions entered into in one place have force and effect in a different country or are judicially decided upon in another place."[30] Influential law books like Bartolus' *Commentary* on Justinian's code and Paulus Voet's *De Statutis* answered questions like, "What if someone drafts a will in his place of domicile, while observing the formalities of the place where the property is situated?"; "Must someone who has committed a crime outside the place of his domicile be punished according to the statute of the place of the delict where he is arrested?"; "What if a foreigner enters into marriage with a young woman: will he be considered to have contracted it in terms of the statute of the bride's homeland?"[31] Such questions illustrate points that have sometimes seemed surprisingly easy for scholars to lose sight of: that traders, exiles, expatriates, and migrants were indeed facts of legal life, and that vast areas of the law were premised on such basic realities.

[27] Knop, "Citizenship, Public and Private," 319.
[28] Cutler, "Artifice, Ideology and Paradox," 279.
[29] Isidore of Seville, *The Etymologies of Isidore of Seville*, trans. Stephen A Barney (Cambridge: Cambridge University Press, 2007), (V.vi), 118. Translation of *alienigenas* slightly modified.
[30] Ulrik Huber, "De Conflictu Legum Diversarum in Diversis Imperiis," trans. Ernest G. Lorenzen, *Illinois Law Review* 13 (1918): 402.
[31] Discussions of these questions appeared in Paulus Voet's *De Statutis* (1661). See Paul Voet, *The Selective Paulus Voet: Being a Translation of Those Sections Regarded as Relevant to Modern Conflict of Laws, of De Statutis Eorumque Concursu Singularis (Amstelodami, 1661)*, trans. A. Basil Edwards (Pretoria: University of South Africa, 2007).

In England, law in the sixteenth and seventeenth centuries showed what one scholar calls a distinctive "internationalism" in areas such as family law and transmarine trade.[32] In sixteenth-century English criminal law, the juries for foreigners accused of crimes included six members of the accused's country or those who spoke the accused's language. Not only were such occurrences regular enough to require specified procedures, foreign language communities were large enough to be able to depend on such numbers for so-called "mixed juries."[33] In trade, the so-called *lex mercatoria* grew up to arbitrate disputes across national boundaries. Such "observations which Merchants maintaine[d] between themselves," wrote one writer, were so ubiquitous that "if these be separated from the Law of Nations, the remainder of the said Law will consist of but few points."[34] "Piepowder" courts, so named because of the *pieds poudrés* of traveling merchants, existed at almost every fair, and they were known for swiftly judging cases of fraud and unfair dealing. When a Frieslander fled to England in 1607 to escape a judgment on the Continent, he was detained by an English Admiralty court on the grounds that the law of nations required nations to honor one another's judgments: "it is the law of nations that the justice of one nation will aid the justice in another," Chief Justice Popham proclaimed.[35] For such reasons, "private international law" remains a helpful shorthand to identify those lived, interpersonal aspects of international law in the Renaissance that have continued to suffer scholarly neglect.

Turning to literature, we should be surprised if we did not find such "private" aspects of the law of nations in Renaissance texts. Indeed, a good example comes from Thomas Heywood's comedy *The Captives* (1624), when an English "Clown" shipwrecked in Marseille comes across a local servant, Gripus, "surveugh[ing a] pryze."[36] Gripus, a fisherman, has fished a trunk out of the sea, and Heywood's Clown discovers by its marks that the trunk had belonged to his Master's love prior to the shipwreck. Inside the trunk are key proofs of the beloved's English citizenship. Raising questions of what law ought to govern the potential salvage, the recognition scene is saturated with legal puns. The Clown has just "left a full coort behynde" him, with one character "pleadinge of the one side, [his] master on the other, and the lawyers fendinge and proovinge on boathe" (4.1.19, 1–3). The trunk from the sea is described as a "case," whereby the Clown can pun, "thy case,

---

[32] Sir Otto Kahn-Freund, *The Growth of Internationalism in English Private International Law* (Jerusalem: Hebrew University Magnes Press, 1960), 11–12.

[33] Marianne Constable, *The Law of the Other: The Mixed Jury and Changing Conceptions of Citizenship, Law, and Knowledge* (Chicago, IL: University of Chicago Press, 1994); David J. Bederman, *Custom as a Source of Law* (Cambridge: Cambridge University Press, 2010), 21.

[34] Gerard Malynes, *Consuetudo: Vel, Lex Mercatoria, Or, The Ancient Law-Merchant...Necessary for All States-Men, Judges, Magistrates, Temporall, and Civill Lawyers, Mint-Men, Merchants, Mariners, and All Others Negotiating in All Places of the World* (London: Printed by W. Hunt, for N. Bourne, 1656), 2.

[35] Quoted in Paul D. Halliday, *Habeas Corpus: From England to Empire* (Cambridge, MA: Belknap Press of Harvard University Press, 2010), 142; James Fawcett and Peter North, *Cheshire and North's Private International Law* (London: Butterworths, 2005), 21.

[36] All references to *The Captives* are to Thomas Heywood, *The Captives* (London: The Malone Society, 1953) and will be cited parenthetically in the text.

and my case" is "a most playne case, and concernes the booty in that cap-case" (4.1.73–74). Gripus ("Fisher") responds in kind, "my case must not be open'd till your case bee better lookt into" (4.1.79–80). The "fisherman's rethoricke" by which he then "prove[s]" his own case for salvage further helps reorient us to the marks of private international law in the Renaissance:

Fisher: What I catche is myne owne, my lands, my goods, my copy-hold, my fee-simple, myne to sell, myne to give, myne to lend, and myne to cast away; no man claimes part, no man share, synce fishinge is free and the sea common.
Clowne: If all bee common that the sea yields, why then is not that [case] as much myne as thyne?
Fisher: By that lawe, when we bringe our fishe to the market, if every one may freely chuse what he likes and take where hee lyst, wee should have quicly empty dorsers and cleaner stalls, but light purses (4.1.87, 86, 92–101).

The scene is a loose translation of a similar debate over salvaged property in *Rudens* (to be discussed later in this chapter) and a possible reworking of related scenes in *Pericles* that also draw on Plautus. Heywood's playful treatment of salvage thematizes what would later be called "private international law."

Another literary example, recently discussed by Andrew Zurcher, appears in Book V of *The Faerie Queene*, where Edmund Spenser incorporates those same traditions of Roman comedy into his heroic poem. Artegall, the knight of justice, passes by the seashore, and chances upon two quarreling brothers who "stood ... in readinesse . . . / To ioyne the combate with cruell intent."[37] The brothers' "greedy bickerment" reworks the same famous dispute in Plautus, and it too involves a "Sea-beaten chest" (V.iv.11). The elder brother, Bracidas, is aggrieved because "the most part" of his island "hath washt away," thereby enlarging his brother's adjacent island—to the extent that Bracidas' love Philtera takes her "great threasure" to marry the younger brother Amidas when Bracidas' "live[li]ho[o]d fayle[s]" (V.iv.8, V.iv.13, V.iv.9). Because "cruell shipwracke" has deposited Philtera's treasure on Bracidas' shore and Bracidas now claims a right to it, however, Amidas, for his part, also pleads dispossession (V.iv.13). Bracidas insists to Artegall, on "my good lucke he shall not likewise pray" (V.iv.14).

Bracidas' word "pray" suggests Spenser's investigation of the law of maritime *praeda* or prize.[38] The dispute is settled when Amidas and Bracidas, mimicking the arbitration scenes of Roman comedy, "remit [their case] to some righteous man," each "lay[ing] down his sword" "under [Artegall's] foote" and agreeing to abide by Artegall's decision, which is "pronounced" in stanza 19. Artegall adjudicates the rival claims according to the general principle—repeated in stanzas 17 and 18—"That what the sea unto you sent, your own should seeme." He reasons,

[37] Edmund Spenser, *The Faerie Queene*, ed. A. C Hamilton, Hiroshi Yamashita, and Toshiyuki Suzuki (New York: Longman, 2001), V.iv.21, V.iv.6. All further references are to this edition and will be cited parenthetically in the text.
[38] Herbert B. Nelson, "Amidas v. Bracidas," *Modern Language Quarterly* 1 (1940).

> ... equall right in equall things doth stand,
> For what the mighty Sea hath once possest,
> And plucked quite from all possessors hand,
> Whether by rage of waves, that never rest,
> Or else by wracke, that wretches hath distrest,
> He may dispose by his imperiall might,
> As thing at random left, to whom he list.
> So *Amidas*, the land was yours first hight,
> And so the threasure yours is *Bracidas* by right. (V.iv.20, V.iv.19)

As Andrew Zurcher puts it, the justice of Artegall's solution is that it "balances conflicting precepts of the *jus naturale* and the *jus gentium*."[39] Consonant with the Roman *Digest*'s specification that "what [a] river adds to our land by alluvion becomes ours by the law of nations," Artegall decides that the human institution of private property authorized by the law of nations remains contingent upon nature's "rage of waves."[40] As we turn now from *The Faerie Queene* and *The Captives* to *Pericles* and *The Tempest*, we see that the latter too are interested in the sea-borne paths of private property and are highly instructive in the context of Jacobean private international law.

PERICLES AND PRIVATE INTERNATIONAL LAW

Since *Pericles* did not appear in the first folio, its significance to the Shakespeare canon is especially vexed. Various views have been put forward, but scholars now largely agree that Shakespeare wrote *Pericles* in collaboration, probably with George Wilkins.[41] Related to the question of authorship is the question of aesthetic value. John Dryden during the Restoration denigrated *Pericles* as the product of Shakespeare's youth, and similar judgments have long hovered over the play. Jonson maligned it as a "mouldy tale" in his *Ode to Himself*, a phrase that may have needled Shakespeare for drawing too much from old sources like *Apollonius of Tyre* and Plautus' *Rudens* and which gave the play a coloring of what lawyers called "the taint inhering in a thing stolen."[42] A further difficulty lies in the many textual variants: six quartos between 1609 and 1635, many with obvious mistakes, have made establishing an acceptable text especially difficult for modern scholars. My discussion of *Pericles* adds little to the authorship and bibliographical debates, but, drawing from them, it assumes that whoever wrote *Pericles*, and however little

---

[39] Andrew Zurcher, *Spenser's Legal Language: Law and Poetry in Early Modern England* (Woodbridge: D. S. Brewer, 2007), 145.

[40] Justinian, *The Digest of Justinian*, trans. Alan Watson (Philadelphia, PA: University of Pennsylvania Press, 1985), 41.1.7.1.

[41] Brian Vickers, *Shakespeare, Co-Author: A Historical Study of Five Collaborative Plays* (Oxford: Oxford University Press, 2002), 291–332; MacDonald P. Jackson, *Defining Shakespeare: Pericles as Test Case* (Oxford: Oxford University Press, 2003).

[42] Ben Jonson, "Ode to Himself," in *Ben Jonson: The Complete Poems*, ed. George Parfitt (New York: Penguin Classics, 1975), 282–4. On "taint" see Justinian, *The Digest of Justinian*, trans. Alan Watson (Philadelphia, PA: University of Pennsylvania Press, 1985), 41.3.4.6. and below at n. 60.

acclaim it has found with later audiences, *Pericles* in its conception was attractive enough to draw multiple authors and profitable enough to draw multiple printers. In addition to its significance for Jacobean private international law, *Pericles* exhibits every evidence of having been a brilliantly timed work. It is partly for those reasons that I give it sustained attention here.

What little we know about the date of *Pericles'* first performance comes from a story about the Venetian Ambassador to London, Zorzi Giustiniano. There is a report in Venetian archives that Giustiniano paid twenty crowns to take the French Ambassador, the French Ambassador's wife, and the Secretary of Florence to *Pericles*.[43] This report usefully provides the *terminus ad quem* for the play's first performance since Giustiniano left England on 23 November 1608. But it also suggests considerable international interest in *Pericles*, a "play of the sea *par excellence*" that for all its "internationalizing" "peregrinations," adventuresome comic space, and "submerged or wrecked verse," was one of Jacobean England's most notable successes.[44]

Pericles' Mediterranean plot of a lost daughter reunited with her father—shipwreck, pimps, and opportunistic fishermen notwithstanding—is a private international law *tour de force*. In the play, as in private international law, expatriates, exiles, and persons *en passage* are the ground norms, and legal questions give many of the plot's turning points their charge. Although one scholar complains that "too much attention has been paid to the circulation and exchange of commodities" in *Pericles*, such a view inadvertently illustrates just how significant contracts and property are to its plot.[45] *Pericles* repeatedly invites audiences into positions of legal speculation, requiring judgment about how its many international exchanges might be understood in legal terms. As Joel Altman explains, "the main reorientation…that a modern reader must make to recapture the approach of a Renaissance student of the play is to think of it as a rhetorical construction revolving around a central question which…also contains within it a number of *quaestiunculae* debated along the way."[46] "Comedic scenes," he argues, should be seen as "mimetic debates, wily proofs, schemes, and suasions—all suggesting that within the bustle of comic action lay specific problems to be examined and resolved by the human wit."[47] When

[43] E. K. Chambers, *William Shakespeare: A Study of Facts and Problems.* (Oxford: Clarendon Press, 1930), 2.335.

[44] Peter Holland, "Coasting in the Mediterranean: The Journeyings of Pericles," in *Charting Shakespearean Waters: Text and Theatre*, ed. Niels Bugge Hansen and Søs Haugaard (Copenhagen: Museum Tusculanum Press, University of Copenhagen, 2005), 12; David Morrow, "Local/Global Pericles: International Storytelling, Domestic Social Relations, Capitalism," in *A Companion to the Global Renaissance: English Literature and Culture in the Era of Expansion*, ed. Jyotsna G. Singh (Chichester: John Wiley and Sons, 2009), 355–77; Terence Cave, *Recognitions: A Study in Poetics* (Oxford: Oxford University Press, 1990), 288; Raphael Lyne, "Shakespeare, Plautus, and the Discovery of New Comic Space," in *Shakespeare and the Classics*, ed. Charles Martindale and A. B. Taylor (Cambridge: Cambridge University Press, 2004); Laurie E. Maguire, *Shakespearean Suspect Texts: The "Bad" Quartos and Their Contexts* (Cambridge: Cambridge University Press, 1996), 195.

[45] Morrow, "Local/Global Pericles: International Storytelling, Domestic Social Relations, Capitalism," 356.

[46] Joel B. Altman, *The Tudor Play of Mind: Rhetorical Inquiry and the Development of Elizabethan Drama* (Berkeley, CA: University of California Press, 1978), 138.

[47] Altman, *The Tudor Play of Mind*, 9.

Pericles' armour is recovered by a foreign fisherman, for instance, by what right does Pericles recover it? After Cerimon revives Thaisa from the dead, whose are the jewels that had been stowed in her coffin—the now living Thaisa's or the life-giving magus'? Is there a law capable of preventing the trafficking in women such as occurs when Marina is sold by pirates to Bolt?[48] The play repeatedly foregrounds what Bradin Cormack calls the "proximate legal histor[ies]" of goods and chattel, ultimately illustrating how "international bonds are forged less through natural law than according to contract, whereby named parties enter into a named and stable relationship."[49] Daniel Vitkus notes that "the episodic plot of *Pericles* would have reminded Shakespeare's audience of the dangers faced by English sailors trading in the contemporary Mediterranean," and some of its formal features show evidence of "debates over the early modern economy in an age of increasing globalization."[50] What may need further emphasizing, then, isn't necessarily a resolutely local *Pericles*, as David Morrow would have it, but instead how deeply connected are the many exchanges in the "internationalizing" plot of *Pericles* to "internationalizing" legal questions, in particular those that would come to form private international law.

How a play like *Pericles* and its forebears in classical comedy relate to private international law can be understood by considering a case like *Venetian Ambassador v. Brooke*. In the thirteen months before Giustiniano's departure, the Venetian Ambassador expended considerable effort on a fascinating case that adds important political and legal context for Shakespeare's later work.[51] It involved upwards of 30,000 crowns of prize, Mediterranean piracy, arcane points of private international law, English trafficking in illicit goods, and restoration of property. "The whole London market is on tip-toe of expectation" about this dramatic case, Giustiniano wrote in early January 1608, the year that saw *Pericles* entered into the Stationer's Register (but not published) and the related publication of George Wilkins' *The Painfull Adventures of Pericles, Prince of Tyre*.[52] Reciprocally, the case "created a sensation in Venice."[53] As Alain Wijffels' essay on the affair suggests, the twists and turns in which English and Venetian merchants alike tried to regain what they saw as their lost goods are remarkable in their own regard. They are also

---

[48] Gayle Rubin, "The Traffic in Women: Notes on the 'Political Economy' of Sex," in *Toward an Anthropology of Women*, ed. Rayna Reiter (New York: Monthly Review Press, 1975), 157–209.

[49] Bradin Cormack, *A Power to Do Justice: Jurisdiction, English Literature, and the Rise of Common Law* (Chicago, IL: University of Chicago Press, 2008), 287, 283.

[50] Daniel J. Vitkus, *Turning Turk: English Theater and the Multicultural Mediterranean, 1570–1630* (New York: Palgrave Macmillan, 2003), 40 ff; Lesser, "Tragical-Comical-Pastoral-Colonial," 883. Scholars' previous observations on Marina are related. In Marina, scholars have seen "not an agent of exchange but . . . the thing itself," "the object of international masculine desire, a piece of commodified flesh that attracts all comers." Steven Mullaney, *The Place of the Stage: License, Play, and Power in Renaissance England* (Chicago, IL: University of Chicago Press, 1988), 135–52.

[51] The only full account of this international crisis of which I am aware is given by Alain Wijffels, "Sir Julius Caesar and the Merchants of Venice," in *Geschichte der Zentraljustiz in Mitteleuropa: Festschrift für Bernhard Diestelkamp zum 65. Geburtstag*, ed. Bernhard Diestelkamp, Friedrich Battenberg, and Filippo Ranieri (Weimar: Böhlau, 1994), hereafter "Merchants." My account in what follows draws broadly from his essay as well as from the Venetian Ambassador's letters home, available in *Calendar of State Papers and Manuscripts, Relating to English Affairs, Existing in the Archives and Collections of Venice, and in Other Libraries of Northern Italy, 1206–* (London: H. M. Stationery Office, 1864), hereafter "*CSPV*," vols. 9 and 10.

[52] *CSPV*, 9, no. 142.   [53] *CSPV*, 9, no. 142.

remarkable for the light they shed on some of the most prominent themes of Jacobean comedy in these years.

While English and Venetian merchants bitterly disputed the facts of the case, the broad outlines are as follows. In the spring of 1607, an English merchant ship named the *Husband*, with ties to the Levant Company, arrived in the Mediterranean and, in or near the North African port of Tunis, traded gunpowder and other goods for something near 30,000 crowns worth of wool, yarn, indigo, and cinnamon, and speedily returned to Dartmouth. At issue was the nature of the goods returning to England on the *Husband* and two other English ships, the *Seraphim* and the *Unicorne*.[54] Upon arrival in Dartmouth, the *Husband* was seized by the vice-admiral according to the Venetians' claim that the goods onboard were not English but instead Venetian goods that had been plundered a few months earlier from the Venetian argosy *Reneira a Soderina*. They claimed those goods had been stolen by the notorious English pirate John Ward. The Tunis goods were therefore stolen Venetian property, Giustiniano claimed on behalf of his countrymen. This dispute, enshrined in English court records as *Venetian Ambassador v. Brooke* and chapters of Alberico Gentili's posthumous *Hispanicae Advocationis Libri Duo* (1613) such as "Whether the purchasers of plunder [*raptorum*] may keep it for themselves," rocked international political and legal circles, taking over four years to resolve. Due to "the quantity of the goods, which [was] so great as to affect many of [London's] leading merchants," between the vice-admiral's seizure of the *Husband* in October 1607 and the new Venetian Ambassador's 18 November 1611 letter home indicating all avenues for restitution had finally been pursued, the case involved a significant cast of characters, not all of them the exalted persons of tragedy. The privy council decided that "as this was a question in which were many points relating to the law of nations it was not a fit subject to send before an ordinary [Admiralty] tribunal."[55] James' European peace policy left him sensitive to Venetian complaints, and the case prompted his delicate but not especially welcome intervention with the Admiralty judges at many points, oftentimes through Robert Cecil, Earl of Salisbury. It elicited legal opinions from Padua and depositions from Tunis, and it crisscrossed through English Admiralty courts and common law courts, thereby enflaming jurisdictional conflicts between civil and common lawyers that scholars have identified as being central to growing parliamentary opposition to the crown.[56] In an era of censorship in which current events

---

[54] Wijffels, "Merchants," 196, 199 n.17, 197 n.7.   [55] *CSPV*, 9, no. 142.

[56] Anon., "A Discourse in Defence of Admirall Jurisdiction Practised in This Kingdome," in *Hale and Fleetwood on Admiralty Jurisdiction*, ed. M. J. Prichard and D. E. C. Yale (London: Selden Society, 1993), 301. The editors suggest this work was written around 1611, but a reference to Welwood's *Abridgement of All Sea Laws* (1613) suggests that it is somewhat later. Reginald G. Marsden, *Documents Relating to Law and Custom of the Sea* (London: Printed for the Navy Records Society, 1915), 1.372, n.1. On jurisdictional conflicts, see: J. G. A Pocock, *The Ancient Constitution and the Feudal Law: A Study of English Historical Thought in the Seventeenth Century* (Cambridge: University Press, 1957); Brian Levack, *The Civil Lawyers in England, 1603–1641: A Political Study* (Oxford: Clarendon Press, 1973); Glenn Burgess, *The Politics of the Ancient Constitution: An Introduction to English Political Thought, 1603–1642* (University Park, PA: Pennsylvania State University Press, 1993); L. M. Hill, *Bench and Bureaucracy: The Public Career of Sir Julius Caesar, 1580–1636* (Stanford, CA: Stanford University Press, 1988), 26–53; Charles M. Gray, *The Writ of Prohibition: Jurisdiction in Early Modern*

were generally forbidden from the English stage, it also may have given some of the allusions to Plautus in *Pericles* and *The Tempest* deep contemporary resonance. However obliquely, the otherwise perplexing "husband... at Tunis" in *The Tempest* may even register Shakespeare's awareness of the incident explicit (5.1.212).

In December 1607, an oft-proposed *terminus a quo* for *Pericles'* first performance, Giustiniano wrote to the Venetian Doge and Senate, "The merchants who bought these goods are preparing to defend themselves by all means in their power; they declare the cargo was bought from Turks and not from Ward, and that though it may be stolen goods, it was not stolen from Venetian ships. They trust that the difficulty of proof will bury the truth."[57]

Narrative, proof, and truth were concerns that cut directly from Giustiniano and private international law, on the one hand, to trends in Jacobean comedy on the other. A fundamental ingredient of plays including *Pericles* and *The Tempest*, inartistic proof, sat at the very heart of the case: how could the goods seized at Dartmouth be genuinely identified with those goods taken from the *Soderina*?[58] In order to answer such questions, lawyers deployed all of the narrative resources of Roman law and, perhaps less expectedly, many tools of literary analysis.

Giustiniano's "though it may be stolen goods" suggests how legal discourse could create remarkable spaces for imaginative, provisional thought. It is important to recognize how Roman law's secular scripture, the *Digest*, itself opened into surprisingly imaginative possibilities. In a passage that would spur the imaginations of lawyers from Padua to London in the *Soderina/Husband* case, Pomponius in the *Digest* had written of "[a] woman condemned to the saltworks for a crime, [who] was subsequently captured by petty brigands of a foreign nation and sold under the rules of trade. She was ransomed to her proper condition. The price paid was to be restored to Cocceius Firmus, a centurion, from the imperial treasury."[59] Passages from the *Digest* like this were compact narratives with deep imaginative purchase—often as compelling for what they didn't say as what they did.

As every lawyer involved in the *Soderina* case seemed to recognize, the *Digest's* dramatic narrative of the ransomed woman had many potential implications for the case at hand. But every analogy has its limits: discerning where to clump and where to split required care. The *Digest's* centurion was reimbursed from the Roman treasury for having to re-purchase what was in effect his own property. For Alberico Gentili, who, as an Italian Protestant writing on behalf of the English merchants,

---

English Law (New York: Oceana Publications, 1994); Virginia Strain, "*The Winter's Tale* and the Oracle of the Law," *ELH* 78, no. 3 (September 10, 2011): 557–84; Robert Brenner, *Merchants and Revolution: Commercial Change, Political Conflict, and London's Overseas Traders, 1550–1653* (Princeton, NJ: Princeton University Press, 1993).

[57] *CSPV*, 9, no. 130.

[58] Wijffels, "Merchants," 200 ff. Rhetoricians defined inartistic proofs as "those things which have not been furnished by ourselves but were already in existence"—proofs, as Aristotle put it, like witnesses, oaths, or documents, that originated "outside the principles of oratory." Aristotle, *Art of Rhetoric*, trans. J. H. Freese, vol. XXII, Loeb Classical Library, 1926, 15, (1.2.2, 1355b); Quintilian, *The Orator's Education*, trans. Donald A. Russell (Cambridge, MA: Harvard University Press, 2001), 2.325 (5.1); R. W. Serjeantson, "Testimony and Proof in Early-Modern England," *Studies in the History and Philosophy of Science* 30A, no. 2 (1999): 202–8.

[59] Justinian, *The Digest of Justinian*, 49.15.6.

illustrates as well as anyone the everyday realities of migration, one point to be gleaned from the case of the restored woman was that if the Venetian merchants wanted their goods back, they could trade for them as the Roman centurion had done, and they could rightly demand reimbursement from the Venetian treasury. Shrewdly, Gentili here clumped. At Roman law, the centurion was eligible for reimbursement because the woman retained what Gentili called "the taint inhering in a thing stolen" ever since she'd been abducted from the salt mines.[60] This principle worked against Gentili's English merchants, however, for if "the taint inhering in a thing stolen" operated in this case, the Venetians retained ownership over their goods while the goods passed through all the various intervening hands, including English ones. Now it was time for Gentili to split. Gentili thus responded somewhat awkwardly that such a taint only operated when disputants belonged to a single state. As an international dispute, there was no such taint in this case. In a way that especially resonates with the plot of *Pericles*, however, Gentili clumped one final time. He used the case of the restored woman to prove, against Venetian claims to the contrary that some transactions with pirates could be legitimate. He even went as far as to quote approvingly a passage from Alciati that he had refuted in an earlier publication: "a pirate commits a less serious crime if he commits it on the high seas."[61] Whereas in *De Jure Belli*, "with pirates and brigands...no laws remain in force," now "the pirate should be deprived of no right of which he is not expressly deprived by law."[62] Gentili's approach to the case clearly demonstrated the profound narrative imagination, rhetorical flexibility, and legal inventiveness we might expect from the Oxford Professor of Civil Laws.

ROMAN COMEDY AND ROMAN LAW

How comedy transected this case and others like it requires more detail, for the standard accounts of private international law do little to prepare us for the significance of Plautus' *Rudens* and its Renaissance readers and imitators. In reality, however, private international law in the Renaissance was tightly bound up with the methods of Renaissance humanism, most pertinently in the glosses of humanists like the Bolognese scholar Giovanni Battista Pio, who bathed Plautus in learned legal commentary in the Italian Renaissance.[63] Roman comedy's significance to international law debates seems less surprising once we observe how Plautus' *Rudens* itself begins from a place very close to private international law's premises of mobility. Set on the North African shore near the town of Cyrene, the play's characters are mostly Athenians who have been exiled or shipwrecked. The

---

[60] Alberico Gentili, *Hispanicae Advocationis Libri Duo*, trans. Frank Frost Abbott (New York: Oxford University Press, 1921), 2.109.

[61] Gentili, *Hispanicae Advocationis Libri Duo*, 2.111.

[62] Alberico Gentili, *De Iure Belli Libri Tres* (Oxford: Clarendon Press, 1933), 2.24; Gentili, *Hispanicae Advocationis Libri Duo*, 2.111.

[63] Scafuro likely has Renaissance readers like Pio in mind when she refers to "the juridical and philological traditions of New Comedy scholarship." Adele C. Scafuro, *The Forensic Stage: Settling Disputes in Graeco-Roman New Comedy* (Cambridge: Cambridge University Press, 1997), 7.

anagnorisis of the comedy involves the reunification of Daemones, an elderly Athenian expatriate, and his long-lost daughter Palaestra, whom the wicked pimp Labrax had bought from pirates for prostitution. At the very core of the *Rudens* are the facts of travel, commerce, and international, interpersonal relations.

Much of the comedic energy in the *Rudens* comes, along with its title, from the slave Gripus' comedic claims to a trunk (*vidulus*) full of treasure that he has fished out of the sea. The trunk, containing both Labrax's ill-gotten gold and key proof of Palaestra's Athenian citizenship, had been dislodged in the shipwreck caused by the divine narrator Arcturus, who "raised a blustering gale" in order to "c[o]me to [Palaestra's] rescue."[64] At least one scholar of the play believes that Labrax had been moving his property offshore in order to protect it from confiscation, and that Arcturus' tempest signals divine punishment for Labrax' tax dodge.[65] Having brought (*extraxit*) the trunk ashore, the local fisherman Gripus is confronted by another slave, Trachalio, who knows the trunk's provenance and grabs hold of one of the fishing ropes Gripus had used to haul the trunk to shore, refusing to let go.

In addition to giving the comedy its title, their long exchange took on considerable significance once Plautus was rediscovered in the Italian Renaissance. In fact, it became a *locus classicus* in the Renaissance for discussions over salvage, and thereby accrued significance for broad questions of possession, ownership, and community related to the sea. Lawyers like Gentili saw the core connection between wit and property. The littoral tug-of-war between Gripus and Trachalio has its linguistic analog in their battle of wits, with the rope of the title becoming a metonym for rhetoric itself—that is, a shared tool employed, in this case, in the acquisition of property.

In addition to poets and dramatists such as Spenser, Heywood, Wilkins, and Shakespeare, legal writers including Gentili, Hugo Grotius, and John Selden would all discuss this passage, and, although the transcription may postdate Milton's life, the following exchange between Gripus and Trachalio would even eventually find its way into Milton's commonplace book as well:

> Gripus: . . . the sea's common to all, that's certain.
> Trachalio: Agreed [*adsentio*].
> Then why shouldn't I have a common right to this trunk, tell me that?
> It was found in the common sea [*in mari inventust communi*].[66]

---

[64] Titus Maccius Plautus, *Plautus: with an English translation*, trans. Paul Nixon, vol. 4, Loeb Classical Library (New York; London: G. P. Putnam's Sons; W. Heinemann, 1916), 295 (argument). All further references to *Rudens* are to this text and will be cited by line number.

[65] Matthew Leigh, "Forms of Exile in the Rudens of Plautus," *The Classical Quarterly* 60, no. 1 (2010): 117.

[66] *Gr. Mare quidem commune certost omnibus. Tr. Adsentio:*
qui minus hunc communem quaeso mi esse oportet vidulem?
in mari inventust communi. (975–977)

The entry in Milton's commonplace book at fol. 249, under the heading "De re nautica et naufragiis," appears with other poetic proof texts used by Grotius and Selden in their sea debates. William Poole in private communication has suggested the entries are in a later hand and not Milton's. But a poem like *Lycidas* (1637) potentially shows Milton's interest in questions of jurisdiction in the sea shortly following the publication of *Mare Clausum*. See John Milton, *A Common-Place Book of John Milton, and a Latin Essay and Latin Verses Presumed to Be by Milton.*, ed. Alfred J. Horwood, rev. edn.

For those eager to assert the community of the seas on historical grounds like Grotius, Trachalio's *adsentio* was critical and indisputable evidence that the sea had always been held in common. This point could be made to extend beyond Plautus' Rome to ancient Greece if one attended to the Athenian setting of the comedy or followed the comedy's prologue and recognized that Plautus had relied on lost material from the Greek comedian Diphilos for his play. (The comedy's explicit invocation of its Greek source and its consistent concern with *dominion* invite the question analogous to the Gripus–Trachalio debate over the trunk of whether literary material was illicitly "taken from" or serendipitously "found in" Diphilos.)[67] Yet even for those who allowed that the sea was common, the applications of that principle were far from clear. Could the sea, by virtue of its community, transfer property from one private holder to another, as Gripus and later Spenser suggest?

When Gentili considered the debate between Gripus and Trachalio in *De Jure Belli*, one thing that stood out was Gripus' piercing wit. There, in the course of criticizing Alciati's apparent sympathy for piracy, Gentili not only followed Gripus' argument but also emulated Gripus' brisk and efficient mockery. There exists an erroneous view that there is "no discussion of...the freedom of the seas in the writings of Gentili," but in fact, as in Plautus, the community of the seas stood in dialectical tension with the notion of *dominion* for Gentili.[68] Alciati, discussed in the previous chapter regarding legal humanism but best known to many literary scholars for his emblems, understood the sea's community to mean that "their sin is less who do wrong on the sea, where the law of nations prevails and no law beside."[69] Characterizing this view as an apology for piracy in *De Jure Belli*, Gentili delivered a Gripus-like rebuke. Accepting like Gripus the premise that the "law of nations" made the sea the "common property of all," Gentili argued that Aliciati nevertheless failed to comprehend the proper lessons from the community of the seas. It was not that the community of the seas licensed plunder or reduced piracy's malignity, as Alciati seemed to suggest. Rather, goods held communally could be appropriated, just as Gripus claimed with regard to his found trunk. The twist of the knife was when Gentili explicitly compared Alciati to Trachalio: Alciati's argument was "an argument unworthy of so great a man, recalling...the character in

(Westminster: Printed for the Camden Society, 1877), fol. 249; Ziskind briefly notes Grotius' and Selden's debate over this passage in Jonathan Ziskind, "International Law and Ancient Sources: Grotius and Selden," *The Review of Politics* 35, no. 4 (October 1, 1973): 550.

[67] For water as a metaphor for literary material in Latin poetry, see the discussion of another key poetic text in debates over the status of the seas appearing in Grotius and Selden, Ovid, *Metamorphoses* 6.313–381, James J. Clauss, "The Episode of the Lycian Farmers in Ovid's Metamorphoses," *Harvard Studies in Classical Philology* 92 (January 1, 1989): 297–314.

[68] Edward P. Cheyney, "International Law under Queen Elizabeth," *The English Historical Review* 20, no. 80 (October 1, 1905): 672; For discussions of Gentili and sea law, see K. R. Simmonds, *Alberico Gentili at the Admiralty Bar, 1605–1608* (Tubingen: J. C. B. Mohr, 1958), 4–10, 12–13; Alain A. Wijffels, *Alberico Gentili and Thomas Crompton: An Encounter between an Academic Jurist and a Legal Practitioner* (Leiden: Ius Deco Publications, 1992); Alain Wijffels, "Ius Gentium in the Practice of the Court of Admiralty around 1600," in *The Roman Law Tradition*, ed. A. D. E. Lewis and D. J. Ibbetson (Cambridge: Cambridge University Press, 1994), 119–34; Wijffels, "Merchants."

[69] Gentili, *De Jure Belli Libri Tres*, 2.24.

Plautus, who declared that it was lawful to carry off fish which had been brought to market, since they were taken in the sea, which is common property."[70] Having added his Plautine rejoinder citing Plautus himself, Gentili then went on to adapt the very next argument Gripus made—in Gripus' words, that "anything my net and hooks get hold of is mine, yes, sir, mine."[71] According to Gentili,

> as soon as the fish are caught, they unquestionably become the property of the owner into whose hands they have come. "The sea is common to all, but the fish belong to those who have bought them," said Phoenicides. Things which are taken cease to be common property, and the very water of the sea, when it is collected for the manufacture of salt, belongs to him who has collected it.[72]

Renaissance commentary on Gripus and Trachalio, as this passage illustrates, could strongly anticipate John Locke, who famously argued that "Whatsoever...he removes out of the State that nature hath provided, and left it in, he hath mixed his *labour* with, and joyned to it something that is his own, and thereby makes it his *Property*."[73] Indeed, Locke would go on to say explicitly that "what Fish any one catches in the Ocean, that great and still remaining Common of Mankind...is *by* the *Labour* that removes it...*made* his *Property* who takes that pains about it."[74] While the *Rudens* on the whole treats Gripus' claims circumspectly, Gentili here adapts Gripus' local arguments with little concern for *Rudens'* broader resolution. Gentili's debate with Alciati illustrates how Plautine comedic dialogue offered Gentili both matter and rhetorical form.

From the series of "lawyers' duels" (see Figure 3.1) that erupted in the sixteenth and seventeenth centuries—between well-known figures like Alciati and Gentili and Grotius and Selden and lesser-known figures such as Borgo and Graswinckel—it can seem as though the Gripus–Trachalio dialogue provided the early modern period's rhetorical paradigm for debates in maritime private international law disputation.[75] The fact that Plautus' Latin *vidulus* might translate as "case" only heightened the scene's juridical overtones.[76]

---

[70] Gentili, *De Jure Belli Libri Tres*, 2.24.

[71] *Meum quod rete atque hami nancti sunt, meum potissimumst* (985).

[72] Gentili, *De Jure Belli Libri Tres*, 2.24.

[73] John Locke, *Two Treatises of Government*, ed. Peter Laslett, 2nd edn. (Cambridge: Cambridge University Press, 1988), 288, 289–90. For discussion, see David Armitage, *Foundations of Modern International Thought* (Cambridge: Cambridge University Press, 2012), 82–3.

[74] Locke, *Two Treatises of Government*, 288, 289–90.

[75] Gayton, "The Lawyer's Duel, or Tvvo Sonnets Composed on Grotius's Mare Liberum and Selden's Mare Clausum." See Pietro Battista Borgo and Dominicus Marcianus, *Petri Baptistae Burgi De dominio sermae Geneuensis reip. in mari Ligustico libri II.* (Romae: Dominicus Marcianus, 1641). For Graswinckel's response see Dirk Graswinckel, *Theod. J.F. Graswinckelii j.c. maris liberi vindiciae, adversus Petrum Baptistam Burgum Ligustici maritimi dominii assertorem.* (Hagae-Comitum: Adriani Vlac, 1652), 202. Richard Tuck, *The Rights of War and Peace: Political Thought and the International Order from Grotius to Kant* (Oxford: Oxford University Press, 1999), 89–90.

[76] Using the external authority of Plautus to rebut an opponent, as all of these authors did, was an example of employing "those things which have not been furnished by ourselves but were already in existence"—inartistic proofs like witnesses, oaths, or documents. Plautus in this context was one such witness brought in from afar. Even so, he was not a wholly reliable witness, and, unsurprisingly, he could be induced to say a wide range of things. See Aristotle, *Art of Rhetoric*, XXII:15 (1.2.2, 1355b);

The Lawyer's Duel,

OR TVVO SONNETS
Compoſed on

GROTIUS'S Mare Liberum,
and

SELDEN'S Mare Clauſum.

For Mare Liberum.

I.

After a pauze of great Guns loud ſalute,
NorBrutiſh thunder,though the ſons of *Brute*
See how two Famous Lawyers from the Barr,
Can ſtate the caſe of this worlds-wonder Warr.

Theſe have their Cannon too,and their Broadſeals,
Like ſhips Broadſide,do awe ſuch Common-weales.
Theſe men of the Long Robe, *le Pryn, le Wut,*
Shall wage us warre,longer then craz'd De-*Witt.*
Chorus for Grotius,
With Laurel let His Head be Crown'd,
Who neither Church, nor the Sea bound,
Who in rich lines and lofty ſtraine,
Without the leave of King of Spaine,
Or Gift of Popes, diſparks the Sea,
Set Indian Gold at liberty.

II.

How could the Pope endow the King of Spaine
With all the wealth of the America?
And from the See of Rome a Charter give
So large? the D:v'l himſelf cannot believe;
For his Black-Holyneſs is ſometime Fryar,
And makes grand promiſes: But is a Lyar.
When Aire and Fire, and Earth, are given us Free,
Why is not Water common as thoſe Three?
Chorus.
With &c.

III.

But with a ſalve to your worth St. *Hugh,*
There's little odds 'twixt *Hobs,* the Whale, and you;
For you by uſurpt Armes, made the States Free,
And then to pleaſe your *Hogens* freed the Sea.

Burgundian Dukes were firſt your Soveraigne Lords,
Which you out Burgunded with Guns and Swords,
And have forgot,O moſt oblivious States?
At what low ebb you were, and what poor Rates;
Chorus.
With &c.

IV.

This from an Earth filtre Thamer, you take an Ell,
A trick you learn'd from the Firſt Nei her-Hell.
But if your Countrymen at length will pleaſe
As they dive Poſt to *Pluto* down the Seas,

Whether they'r bound,and have our Generals Paſs,
They'l find all Hell is govern'd like that Aſs
In France, which carry's *Lewis* Salt by Land,
For *Pluto's* Prince, of abſolute Command.
Chorus.
With &c.

V.

Now you Fatt Boores, 'twas not ſuch liberty,
Of Breaking Oathes, to ſet Rebellion Free,
Which that Grand Book defends, Men of Aſſize,
Know *Grotius* was more honeſt, and more wiſe;
He meant in Merchandize 'twas free for you,
Or Us, to Truck at Bantam, or Peru,
Or farr Suratt, Jamaicha, Mex'co,
But you *Columbus* and our *Drake* out goe.
Chorus.
With &c.

Edmund Gayton.

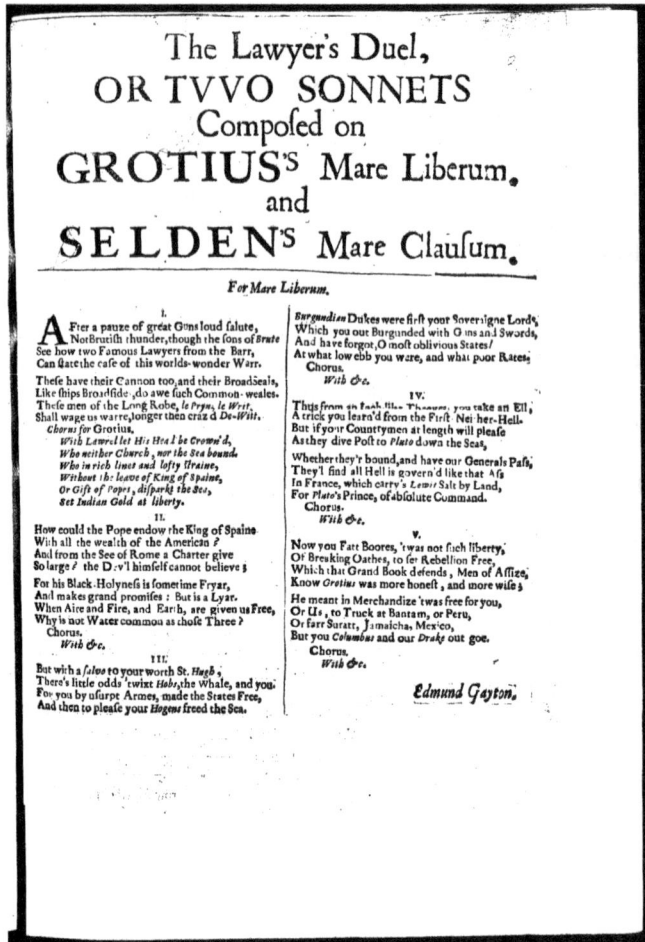

Fig. 3.1. Edmund Gayton, *The Lawyer's Duel*, BL Harl. 5936 (399).
Reproduced with kind permission from the British Library.

Comedy also offered access to historical popular custom, which could, for some writers' purposes, count as law.[77] As with Gentili, the Gripus–Trachalio exchange helped Hugo Grotius to synthesize the dialectically opposed notions of the community of the seas, on the one hand, and private property taken from them (such as fish), on the other. But Plautus for Grotius also gave important evidence for the seas' customary usage historically. The Gripus–Trachalio exchange confirmed that Grotius' conception of common seas somewhat paradoxically capable of yielding private property was "not only very common among the civilians [*jurisprudentibus*]

Quintilian, *The Orator's Education*, 2.325 (5.1); Serjeantson, "Testimony and Proof in Early-Modern England," 202–8.

[77] See Bederman, *Custom as a Source of Law*.

but also it expresseth the confession of the common people [*vulgi*]."[78] Selden in *Mare Clausum* needed all the tools of literary criticism in order to contest such claims. Pressed by Grotius to account for Trachalio's *adsentio*, Selden endeavored to analyze Trachalio's character and tone. Trachalio, he suggested, was merely a "lewd slave," *servum nequam*, and he "was but in jest with *Gripus* the Fisherman" when he agreed the seas were common.[79] Even if the sea of which the characters were speaking had been common, Selden continued brilliantly, it did not follow that all seas at all times should be considered so. Like a seventeenth-century Quentin Skinner arguing that "classic texts are concerned with their own quite alien problems" and not "our own," Selden implied that those who thought otherwise paid insufficient attention to comedy's historical context.[80] The Gripus–Trachalio debate only told us about "that place."[81] Moreover, if the sea in Plautus was indeed "common," that only meant that "the people [*populi*] either of Rome or Greece" had not exercised their rights to "prohibit" others from "fishing in that Sea."[82] Selden shows how alternative methods of literary criticism could be marshaled in topical disputes over the law of nations.

Brilliant as Selden's recourse to literary methodology was, however, it omitted a particularly damaging argument available if one read Gripus through the prism of Roman law. Gripus, Grotius wrote, "rightly objected" to Trachalio when Gripus said "anything my net and hooks get hold of is mine."[83] Such unreserved approval for Gripus is consistent with what might be described as Grotius' stance of maximal prize in *De Jure Praedae* (from which *Mare Liberum* emerged), which sought to justify the Dutch East India Company's seizure of Portuguese property as prize on the Southeast Asian seas. Yet it joined Gentili in strategically modifying a Renaissance humanist tradition that, in broad terms, saw Gripus as a gifted thief hoping clever forensic rhetoric might shield him from the rigor of the law. Pio's learned commentary glossed Plautus' debate between Gripus and Trachalio with two passages from Roman law that suggested an especially condemnatory interpretation of Gripus. One, from Ulpian in Justinian's *Digest*, suggested that, as someone illicitly attempting to appropriate goods lost by shipwreck, Gripus would be financially liable for quadruple their value.[84] The other, from Gaius in the *Digest*, said that where "things . . . are jettisoned in stress of seas to

[78] Hugo Grotius, *The Free Sea*, ed. David Armitage, trans. Richard Hakluyt (Indianapolis, IN: Liberty Fund, 2004), 26.

[79] John Selden, *Of the Dominion, Or, Ownership of the Sea*, trans. Marchamont Nedham (London: William DuGard, 1652), 145.

[80] Quentin Skinner, "Meaning and Understanding in the History of Ideas," in *Visions of Politics*, vol. 1 (Cambridge: Cambridge University Press, 2002), 50, 53.

[81] Selden, *Of the Dominion, Or, Ownership of the Sea*, 145. "[T]hat, rather than this," Nedham's translation elaborated acidly.

[82] Selden, *Of the Dominion, Or, Ownership of the Sea*, 145–6.

[83] Although Hakluyt's "it came well to hand" (26) captures Gripus' rhetorical invention especially well, I use here Magoffin's seemingly more technically accurate translation of Grotius' *recte occurrit* from Magoffin's Latin–English facing-page edition, Hugo Grotius, *The Freedom of the Seas; Or, The Right Which Belongs to the Dutch to Take Part in the East Indian Trade*, ed. James Brown Scott, trans. Ralph Van Deman Magoffin (New York: Oxford University Press, 1916), 29.

[84] Justinian, *The Digest of Justinian*, 1985, 41.1.44.

lighten the vessel[,] they remain the property of the owners."[85] Although Pio does not quote it, this section from the *Digest* concludes, "if anyone finds any such things washed up by the waves … and appropriates them with a view to gain, he is guilty of theft."[86] Gripus wasn't only an unreliable witness; he was also a possible criminal.[87]

As we shall see momentarily, the foregoing is important background for plays like *Pericles* and *The Tempest*. From *Rudens* onwards, the turns or *anagnorises* of comedies typically involved altered legal relations. The reading of Gripus as criminal—a reading that Gentili, Grotius, and Selden all abjure—required proof—not Trachalio's artistic, rhetorical proof, but the inartistic proof of the law.[88] How was one to know, for example, whether the original owners of sea-borne property were still alive? If they were alive, how could they be identified? Couldn't a greedy opportunist claiming to be the original owner easily swindle someone like Gripus out of his lawful "prize" (*praeda*, [1011, 1037])? *Pericles* and *The Tempest* would be noticeably alert to such questions, but *Rudens* already was too. This is especially so once Gripus and Trachalio agree to let Daemones arbitrate their dispute—for example, in Trachalio's request to "make [Gripus] show" the trunk to Palaestra and Ampelisca in order to validate Labrax's dominion, and in Gripus' worry in response that "once I show it, they'll instantly say they recognize it," facts notwithstanding (1095–1097). The proof of Palaestra's identity that comes from the trunk simultaneously and importantly confirms Gripus' "crime" in attempting to profit from his prize (*malefici*, [1247]). Unsurprisingly, Grotius steered well away from such a strict Roman law interpretation of *Rudens*, and Selden, the common lawyer, as we have seen, had other quibbles.

PRIZE AND PIRACY IN *PERICLES*

Having seen how the debates over Plautus intersected with international law, we are now in a better position to return to prize and piracy in *Pericles*. The prudential clumping and splitting that we saw Gentili doing in the *Soderina* case may help explain what might otherwise be seen, in the context of strong Jacobean measures against piracy, as *Pericles'* odd approbation of it. As one scholar has observed, when they appear in literary texts, pirates "more often than not … appear

[85] Titus Maccius Plautus, *Plautus integer cum interpretatione Joannis Baptistae Pii*, ed. Joannes Battista Pio (Milan: Uldericum Scinzenzeler, 1500), 711; Justinian, *The Digest of Justinian*, 1985, 41.1.9.8.

[86] Justinian, *The Digest of Justinian*, 1985, 41.1.9.8.

[87] More recently, Richard Rowland finds Gripus "aggressive and humourless" in his, "The Captives: Thomas Heywood's 'Whole Monopoly off Mischeiff,'" *The Modern Language Review* 90, no. 3 (1995): 596.

[88] For the importance of distinctions between artistic (artificial) and inartistic (inartificial) proofs to the English law of evidence, see Barbara J. Shapiro, "Classical Rhetoric and the English Law of Evidence," in *Rhetoric and Law in Early Modern Europe*, ed. Victoria Ann Kahn and Lorna Hutson (New Haven, CT: Yale University Press, 2001), 68–9 esp. For the importance of inartistic proofs to "the comic anagorisis," see Cave, *Recognitions*, 47–54.

on the sidelines… unruly, discontented figures, excluded from the main story."[89] It is true that in *Pericles* the pirates' significance to the plot corresponds poorly with their time on stage and page, but this disjunction may help us better understand the play's topical balancing act. Pirates in the play "rescue" Pericles' daughter Marina from near-certain death at the hands of the "villain" Leonine in Tarsus— yelling "a prize, a prize" (4.1.89).[90] Marina is then transported to the shady yet bustling international entrepôt of Mytilene, where the pirates sell her to Mytile-nean pimps for "a thousand pieces" (4.2.47). Having been taken under the wing of the governor of Mytilene, Lysimachus, Marina is reunited with her father Pericles through Lysimachus' good offices.

In this narrative, the pirates seem closer to sea-borne chivalric knights than *hostes humani generis*, the epic *ius gentium*'s designation of pirates as enemies of all humankind (5.1.163–165). The increasingly stringent Jacobean rhetoric against piracy made the political environment into which *Pericles* was issued much different from that of earlier plays like *Hamlet*. The transaction in Mytilene in *Pericles* between the pirates and the pander that ultimately helps to reunite Marina and her father deftly conveys the folly of ruling out all commerce with pirates *avant la lettre*. In one of Shakespeare's sources, whose 1607 reprinting could itself relate to the *Husband* case, the point is made even less subtly when the pirates are ultimately knighted, given "plenty of gold and silver, and indowed… with great possessions" in recompense.[91] While *Pericles'* accommodations to pirates are more muted, James' pre-*Soderina* promise to "cause our lawes to bee fulie executed… against Pirats, and all receavors and abettors of them and their goodes" hardly registers in *Pericles*.[92] The comic law of nations that treats pirates as worthy partners for exchange challenges the epic law of nations of sovereigns and their advocates.

Even so, the fact that contact between Pericles and the pirates is mediated through Bolt and the pander has legal and political significance. In their testimony, the English merchants contended that they had dealt lawfully with the Tunisian prefect, a man they called Crosman, and had had absolutely nothing to do with the pirate Ward, with whom, according to one of the deposed merchants, Jacob Pountis,

[89] Claire Jowitt, "Introduction," in *Pirates?: The Politics of Plunder, 1550–1650*, ed. Claire Jowitt (Basingstoke: Palgrave Macmillan, 2006), 3. Other Foucauldian readings of pirates include Anne Pérotin-Dumon, "The Pirate and the Emperor: Power and the Law on the Seas, 1450–1850," in *The Political Economy of Merchant Empires: State Power and World Trade 1350–1750*, ed. James D. Tracy (Cambridge: Cambridge University Press, 1997), 196–227; Bernhard Klein, "Staying Afloat: Literary Shipboard Encounters from Columbus to Equiano," in *Sea Changes: Historicizing the Ocean*, ed. Bernhard Klein and Gesa Mackenthun (New York: Routledge, 2004), 91–110.

[90] References are to Suzanne Gossett's *Arden* (Third Series) edition and will be cited parenthetically in the text. I have chosen this edition because it does not add long passages from other sources as Taylor and Jackson's Oxford text and texts based on it do. William Shakespeare, *Pericles*, ed. Suzanne Gossett (London: Arden Shakespeare, 2004); Christopher Harding, "'Hostis Humani Generis': The Pirate as Outlaw in the Early Modern Law of the Sea," in *Pirates?: The Politics of Plunder, 1550–1650*, ed. Claire Jowitt (Basingstoke: Palgrave Macmillan, 2006).

[91] Thomas Twyne, *The Patterne of Painefull Adventures Containing the Most Excellent, Pleasant, and Variable Historie of the Strange Accidents That Befell Unto Prince Apollonius, the Lady Lucina His Wife, and Tharsia His Daughter*, ed. Laurence Twyne (London, 1607), sig. m1r.

[92] Marsden, *Documents Relating to Law and Custom of the Sea*, 1.358.

none "of the companie of the saied ship the Husbande...did trucke, change or barter," despite the fact of Ward's undeniably having brought the *Soderina* to Tunis while the *Husband* was harbored there.[93] Moreover, one could hardly ignore the "common legal principle of taking into account the place of the contract," as Gentili insisted.[94] The appeal to *lex loci contractus* was pointed: what the Venetians alleged to be pirated goods could legitimately be seen as Tunisian goods according to local law—a law, it was said, that deemed all goods in Christian vessels not heading toward Tunis to be potentially lawful prize. There was also an epistemological argument that brought the English merchants even further into the traditional domain of comic *anagnorisis*: how could the merchants know the full history of *any* goods they bought? All that could be certain is that they had traded legally with Crosman.

Previously identified as a Turkish city and described in the play as a "mart" and again a "market," Mytilene resembles the *Husband* sailors' descriptions of Tunis, which emerges in their accounts as a loosely governed city "full of gallants," pirates, and men "of all complexions," all on the financial and sexual make (4.2.3–4, 4.2.74).[95] It is in Mytilene that Marina endures some of the most distressing travails of Shakespearean drama. "The witnesses on behalf of the London merchants confirmed that Tunis was a thriving market-place where merchants from most Christian countries came to sell and buy goods," according to Wijffels.[96] One moralizing 1609 pamphleteer who described Tunis' sexual marketplace in lurid detail complained, "Unlawfully are their goods got, and more ungodly are they consumed."[97] Or so Tunis seemed from afar, for a major part of the English claim was that in reality, they had had virtuously little to do with Tunis, having "laid anchor off the castle of Goletta commanding the approach to the city" and having dealt with the city only to the extent they dealt with Crosman, the "effective commander-in-chief at Tunis," with whom they traded legally while anchored off Goletta.[98] Thus, while those of Mytilene's lascivious merchants rubbing shoulders with the pirates in Act 4, Scene 2 of *Pericles* conspicuously include a "Transylvanian," a "Spaniard [whose] mouth watered as he went to bed to [Marina's] very description," and one Monsieur

---

[93] Quoted in Wijffels, "Merchants," 198 n15. Pountis did however admit in the same deposition that he had heard that his brother, John Pountis, had transported two hundred pounds home to the wives of Ward and another pirate.

[94] Gentili, *Hispanicae Advocationis Libri Duo*, 2.109.

[95] Constance C. Relihan, "Liminal Geography: Pericles and the Politics of Place," *Philological Quarterly* 71, no. 3 (1992): 289. Demonstrating a tendency to link Rudens with shady foreign locales, Heywood would later set his adaptation outside Marseille, a notorious pirate haven. In *The Tempest*, Gonzolo and Adrian famously debate Tunis' ancient names (II.i.80–84), on which see Jerry Brotton, "'This Tunis, Sir, Was Carthage': Contesting Colonialism in *The Tempest*," in *Post-Colonial Shakespeares*, ed. Ania Loomba and Martin Orkin (London: Routledge, 1998), 23–42.

[96] Wijffels, "Merchants," 204.

[97] See the description of Tunisian debauchery after the *Soderina* seizure in Andrew Barker, *A True and Certaine Report of the Beginning, Proceedings, Overthrowes, and Now Present Estate of Captaine Ward and Danseker, the Two Late Famous Pirates from Their First Setting Foorth to This Present Time* (London: Printed by William Hall, 1609), 15.

[98] Wijffels, "Merchants," 196, 202; Crosman appeared by name in the 1612 play *A Christian Turn'd Turk*. See Lois Potter, "Pirates and 'Turning Turk' in Renaissance Drama," in *Travel and Drama in Shakespeare's Time*, ed. Jean-Pierre Maquerlot and Michèle Willems (Cambridge: Cambridge University Press, 1996), 132.

Veroles, a "French knight," equally conspicuously, Marina's father and countrymen
are nowhere to be found (4.2.19, 92–93, 97–98). Instead, as playgoers and readers
learn from omniscient Gower, "who stand[s] i'th' gaps to teach you / The stages of
our story," Pericles and his crew turn up "at anchor" "on [Mytilene's] coast," never
setting foot on land until their business with the Crosman-like "governor of Mytilene," Lysimachus, is concluded (4.4.8–9, 5.0.15–16, 5.1.208). The play's recognition scene happens entirely onboard Pericles' ship—eliminating even the slightest
chance of Tyrian contact with pirate-infested Mytilene. The shipboard scene that
involves an exchange of Tyrian "gold" for Mytilenean "provision" is amplified by
Lysimachus' commerce-friendly approbation: "if we should deny, the most just gods
/ ...would... / ...inflict our province" (5.1.48, 51–53).[99]

Although it derives from his prose source, this "shipboard encounter" is so
important to Shakespeare that he emphasizes its location no fewer than three
times, first when "Lysimachus [their] Tyrian ship espies/... /And to [Pericles] in his
barge with fervour hies," the second when a Tyrian sailor explicitly asks Helicanus
whether Lysimachus can come aboard, and the third when Pericles recalls to Thaisa
that he was "gainst [Mytilene's] shore riding" when Marina's "fortunes brought the
maid aboard [our barque]" (5.0.18–20, 5.1.5, 5.3.10–11).[100] Whether a transaction took place on land or "within the ebb and flow of the sea" usually determined
whether a case belonged to admiralty or common law jurisdiction, and with the
Admiralty judges known to be skeptical of the Venetian claims—Giustiniano, for
example, was sure in December 1607 that "the Admiral will be against us"—
Shakespeare's play does noticeably little to suggest the case belongs under common
law, something the merchants would later suggest once the Admiralty court ruled
for the Venetians under James' influence.[101] The play instead resembles Gentili's
argument that "As everyone submits to the civil law, especially in these maritime
questions, as to a sort of law of nations, everyone will be judged according to that

[99] As indicated in Chapter 1, something deserving further attention is the biblical underpinning
of *Pericles*. Tyre and Tarsus both figure in Isaiah 23, where Tyre is described as a city whose merchants
were princes and whose traders were the most honored men on earth. Hugo Grotius, *Commentary on
the Law of Prize and Booty*, ed. Martine Julia Van Ittersum (Indianapolis, IN: Liberty Fund, 2006),
467–8.

[100] Although Klein's "shipboard encounter" is a useful phrase, Carl Schmitt's thesis that provides
his starting point may restrict our interpretations as much as it gives focus. In Klein's translation,
Schmitt contends that in sixteenth-century England, "For the first time in the history of mankind the
contrast between land and sea serves as the world-embracing foundation of a global law of nations."
Klein, "Sea Changes," 95. Yet even one of Schmitt's most evenhanded interpreters says Schmitt in
Nomos of the Earth "mixed traditional historical and legal analysis with his private mythology of the
Earth, dubious etymological claims and barely hidden resentments towards the victors of the Second
World War." That Jan-Werner Müller explicitly contrasts Schmitt's tragic vision of world order with
Alexandre Kojève's "comedy" of global law hints at a generic tension inherent in reading *Pericles*
through Schmitt. Jan-Werner Müller, *A Dangerous Mind: Carl Schmitt in Post-War European Thought*
(New Haven, CT: Yale University Press, 2003), 88, 90–8; Jürgen Habermas, "The Horrors of Auton-
omy: Carl Schmitt in English," in *The New Conservatism: Cultural Criticism and the Historians' Debate*,
trans. Shierry Weber Nicholsen (Cambridge, MA: MIT Press, 1989), 128–39.

[101] See Giustiniano's firm sense in late December 1607 and early January 1608 that an Admiralty
court decision would go against the Venetians, *CSPV*, 9, nos. 135, 141. For the eventual decision in
their favor, see Marsden, *Documents Relating to Law and Custom of the Sea*, 1.372–374.

law to his entire satisfaction."[102] The play can further be seen as plumbing the historical depths of Admiralty jurisdiction, since the civil law procedures guiding English Admiralty courts originated in Gower's lifetime under Edward III.[103] If in Lysimachus' later comment to Pericles that "when you come ashore I have another suit," it is possible to see a similar if wittier thrust of jurisdictional elbows, *Pericles'* more immediate appeal to those Londoners attuned to the case was explicit: "By you being pardoned, we commit no crime" (4.4.5, 5.1.246). Like Gower "take[ing] our imagination / From bourn to bourn, region to region," *Pericles'* plot reconstructed for Londoners a legal narrative of affairs in the Mediterranean (4.4.3–4). In rhetorical terms, it was a formidable case of forensic invention.

With its conspicuous reworking of the exchange in *Rudens*, *Pericles* set an especially exacting standard of proof. Doubt, as Giustiniano recognized, was one of the English merchants' best weapons in their attempts to have their property restored. The English merchants advanced a hyper-exacting standard of proof to their Admiralty court judges, arguing that giving to the Venetians goods that bore no marks of ever having belonged to them was profoundly unjust. As Terence Cave observes in his study of comic recognitions, "only narrative can compose identity once a severance has occurred."[104] Sharing with both *Rudens* and *Pericles* the language of "proof" [*probanda*], "identity" [*identitas*], and "recognition" [*recognitio*], Gentili is again a reliable guide to the merchants' claims:

> The Venetian...has to prove the identity of the things. Identity has to be proven by him who bases his argument thereon. Further, it has to be reconstructed [*articulanda*]...Now the proof is difficult here, where it is a question of things, which on account of their great similarity to other things of the same species, are difficult to recognize. Further, the recognition of uniform things, such as fruits or such things as are here in controversy, namely, Indian silk and similar things, is called impossible...If it is at all possible that these might be other wares surely the identity would not be proved, since proofs should lead to a necessary conclusion.[105]

Proof comes up over and over again in documents relating to the case, precisely because the courts required that identity be given narrative, rhetorical shape— that is, be reconstructed or articulated in some intellectually and aesthetically satisfying way. Venetians testified that Englishmen had defaced identifiers on the goods, and the English responded that doing so was common practice when goods changed hands.[106] In Gentili's terms, these testimonies sought to accomplish, respectively, the reconstruction and demolition of identity. Because Giustiniano was convinced, as he wrote home in cipher, that "as we are dealing with national interests everything is against us," he many times implored the Venetians to send him more and better proof in order to escape the "scandalous proceedings which

---

[102] Gentili, *Hispanicae Advocationis Libri Duo*, 2.102.

[103] Hill, *Bench and Bureaucracy*, 33–4; Gerard Malynes, *Consuetudo: Vel, Lex Mercatoria, Or, The Ancient Law-Merchant... Necessary for All States-Men, Judges, Magistrates, Temporall, and Civill Lawyers, Mint-Men, Merchants, Mariners, and All Others Negotiating in All Places of the World* (London: W. Hunt, for N. Bourne, 1656), 120.

[104] Cave, *Recognitions*, 23.   [105] Gentili, *Hispanicae Advocationis Libri Duo*, 2.111–112.

[106] Wijffels, "Merchants," 201.

in such cases take place at the Admiralty."[107] Later, buoyed by James and Cecil's personal and highly unusual interventions with the Admiralty judges, he wrote, "The affair is brought to so favourable a point that it can be ruined only by the want of those proofs which ought to be supplied by the interested parties."[108] With the Admiralty judges threatening to release the goods from sequestration if no proof of Venetian provenance emerged, again and again, he implored the Venetian merchants to furnish him with "the necessary information and proofs" but soon found in the spring of 1608 that the proofs had not arrived in time to prevent the goods from reverting to the English merchants: "every limit for the production of proof was passed."[109]

In this context, it is notable that *Pericles'* scene most reminiscent of an exchange in Plautus differs from *Rudens* most in the extent to which it foregrounds inartistic proof. In *Pericles*, as Robert Miola has pointed out, "the Plautine *vidula* becomes Pericles' rotten armour...likewise hauled on to the stage but freely and generously given away."[110] If the justice of Artegall's solution in Spenser is that it "balances conflicting precepts of the *jus naturale* and the *jus gentium*," *Rudens* had already entertained a vision in which the community of nature persists.[111] As Trachalio briefly argues, couldn't common seas mean that anything "found within the Sea" (*in mari inventum*) was also itself common? Plautus' Gripus invents an ingeniously funny *reductio ad absurdum* to this argument: "Why, if the law was like what you say, it would finish fishermen. Why, the minute fish were carried to market, no one would buy, but all crowd up and claim their share, contending they were caught in the common sea."[112]

Trachalio's argument that anything found in the common sea is itself common is a humorously absurd deduction from true principles, Gripus implies. That the key Latin word of this debate, *inventum*, straddled discourses of ownership (as a found acquisition) and rhetoric (as a found rhetorical contrivance, as in Cicero's *De Inventione*) indicates Plautus' clever exposition of both the central conflict and its dialectical, rhetorical superstratum. Plautus' Gripus and Trachalio both understand implicitly that absent some external arbiter, property is likely to be apportioned in this scenario according to the strength and wit of the *inventum*, or rhetorical proof.

This is an important dimension of Plautus that Shakespeare and Wilkins rework in *Pericles* when their fisherman reminds Pericles, "twas we that *made up* this *garment* through the *rough seams* of the waters" (2.1.144–146). The language of *making up* property anticipates Locke's labor theory of appropriation, though with a deeply rhetorical cast. The sartorial terms may plausibly glance at the wool, yarn, and silk returning on the *Husband*, but the idea of "making up" also concerns rhetorical invention. As Harlan observes, "For the fishermen, the action of claiming the

---

[107] *CSPV*, 9, nos. 229, 135.   [108] *CSPV*, 9, no, 198.
[109] *CSPV*, 9, nos. 229, 266.   [110] Miola, *Shakespeare and Classical Comedy*, 147.
[111] Zurcher, *Spenser's Legal Language*, 144.
[112] *Nam si istuc ius sit quod memoras, piscatores perierint.*
Quippe quom extemplo in macellum pisces prolati sient,
Nemo emat, suam quisque partem piscium poscant sibi,
Dicant, in mari communi captos. (978–81)

armour is a creative one, an action of '[making] up' and of making": "To claim the armour is to claim ownership of past literary forms and their present incarnations."[113] With Pericles' lost armor, however, inartistic proof notably short-circuits the forensic disputes that Plautus' Renaissance readers had learned to expect.[114] There is no comparable scene in Gower or Twine, and the scene is exceptional enough that some editors believe the 1609 quarto text to have been furnished by one of the fisherman-actors.[115] What makes the scene especially interesting is not the fishermen's "resist[ance]" to Pericles' "attempted annexation"—for that resistance was dramatized much more fully in the Gripus–Trachalio debate—but instead the opposite, the relative ease with which Pericles regains possession.[116] Where ownership of Plautus' trunk hangs in his play's balance, the restoration of Pericles' armor is expeditiously achieved in just a few lines after it briefly "hangs in the net like a poor man's right in the law" (2.1.112–113). Unlike in *Rudens*, here, the play must go on.

   If in the Gripus–Trachalio debate in Plautus, rhetoric was a rope, rhetoric in Pentapolis is a net in which Pericles skillfully enmeshes his inartistic proof. Despite the fact that the fishermen have netted the "prize" after the "rapture" of the sea—the latter word, meaning "plunder," possibly linking *Pericles* with the *Soderina*'s *raptorum*—Pericles claims the armor as "mine own" on the basis of an inartistic proof: "this brace," and again, "this mark" (2.1.151, 119, 123, 134).[117] Quintilian said that although proofs like this require "no art, it generally takes high powers of eloquence to support or to refute them."[118] Pericles quickly wraps the mark in narrative, telling how

> . . . my dead father did bequeath to me
> With this strict charge, even as he left his life:
> "Keep it, my Pericles, it hath been a shield
> 'Twixt me and death", and pointed to this brace,
> "For that it saved me, keep it . . ." (2.1.120–124)

It is this combination of inartistic proof and narrative reconstruction that persuade the fishermen to forego "the having of it" so long as Pericles "remember[s] from whence [he] had" the armor—a possible allusion to maritime law's thorny suggestion of "consideration" for salvagers according to the fuzzy remunerative criteria of

---

[113] Susan Harlan, "'Certain Condolements, Certain Vails': Staging Rusty Armour in Shakespeare's *Pericles*," *Early Theatre* 11, no. 2 (2008): 129–40.

[114] Scholars have had difficulty locating the scene of Shakespeare's seaside dispute, Pentapolis, but the *Rudens* allusion adds weight to the suggestion that Pentapolis is in North Africa since one of the North African Pentapolis' five cities was Plautus' setting, Cyrene. Suzanne Gossett, "Introduction," in *Pericles* (London: Arden Shakespeare, 2004), 129.

[115] Cf. Twyne, *The Patterne of Painefull Aduentures*, sig. c3r–v. On the theory of the fisherman-actor memorial reconstruction, see Roger Warren, "Introduction," in *A Reconstructed Text of Pericles, Prince of Tyre* (Oxford: Oxford University Press, 2003), 79.

[116] Simon Palfrey, *Late Shakespeare: A New World of Words* (Oxford: Oxford University Press, 1997), 76.

[117] "Rapture" is most editors' emendation of Q1's "rupture." "Prize" comes from the Norton editors' stage direction.

[118] Quintilian, *The Orator's Education*, 2.325 (5.1).

"right reason, a good conscience, and as justice shall appoint" (2.1.135, 147–148).[119] The meaning of "consideration" was in flux in domestic cases in Jacobean England, and Shakespeare's adding an international dimension only complicates the scene's legal questions, confirming Altman's sense that "within the bustle of comic action lay specific problems to be examined and resolved by the human wit."[120] Had Pericles and the fishermen all been Englishmen, the extent to which Pericles would be bound to them after he agrees to "pay [their] bounties, till then rest [their] debtor," would have occasioned contentious debate among lawyers (2.1.139).[121] More so where the "consideration" crossed national and linguistic boundaries, and still more so given that Admiralty law sometimes ignored promises made in distress.[122] But enmeshed in narrative, inartistic proof secures Pericles' lost goods, and he is speedily off to win his future wife.

HOW CALIBAN READ HIS PLAUTUS, OR THE PRIVATE *TEMPEST*

To turn from *Pericles* to *The Tempest* is to see *Pericles'* disputed trunk and armor transformed into an entire island. Shakespeare treats epic subjects through the affordances of comedy in *The Tempest*, and in so doing gives abstract epic characters like Amidas and Bracidas renewed comic specificity in *The Tempest*. Postcolonial writers have understood especially well that *The Tempest*, first performed at Whitehall on November 1, 1611, likely with foreign diplomats in attendance, raises grave questions of sovereignty related to public international law.[123] Yet the transition

[119] John Godolphin, *Synēgoros Thalassios. A Vievv of the Admiral Iurisdiction. Wherein the Most Material Points Concerning That Jurisdiction Are Fairly and Submissively Discussed* (London: W. Godbid for Edmund Paxton, 1661), 183; See also Malynes, *Consuetudo*, 1656, 168; Estienne Cleirac, *The Ancient Sea-Laws of Oleron, Wisby and the Hanse-Towns Still in Force: Taken out of a French Book, Intitled, Les Us & Coutumes de La Mer and Rendred into English, for Use of Navigation*, trans. Guy Miege (London: J. Redmayne for T. Basset, 1686), 10; Jordan usefully analyzes this episode in terms of common law, but civil lawyers denied common law jurisdiction in similar cases even in England, and as Shakespeare's episode occurs not in England but Pentapolis, civil, international maritime law seems at least as good an interpretive context if not better. See Constance Jordan, *Shakespeare's Monarchies: Ruler and Subject in the Romances* (Ithaca, NY: Cornell University Press, 1997), 52, n22.

[120] Altman, *The Tudor Play of Mind*, 9.

[121] David Harris Sacks, "The Promise and the Contract in Early Modern England: Slade's Case in Perspective," in *Rhetoric and Law in Early Modern Europe*, ed. Victoria Kahn and Lorna Hutson (New Haven, CT: Yale University Press, 2001), 28–53; Victoria Kahn, *Wayward Contracts: The Crisis of Political Obligation in England, 1640–1674* (Princeton, NJ: Princeton University Press, 2004), 42–8.

[122] Note Gower's apology for artificially "use[ing] one language in each sev'ral clime" (18.7). John Godolphin, *Synēgoros Thalassios. A Vievv of the Admiral Iurisdiction. Wherein the Most Material Points Concerning That Jurisdiction Are Fairly and Submissively Discussed. As Also Divers of the Laws, Customes, Rights, and Priviledges of the High Admiralty of England by Ancient Records, and Other Arguments of Law Asserted. Whereunto Is Added by Way of Appendix an Extract of the Ancient Laws of Oleron* (London: Printed by W. Godbid for Edmund Paxton, 1661), 167–8.

[123] Michael Srigley, *Images of Regeneration: A Study of Shakespeare's The Tempest and Its Cultural Background* (Uppsala: Academiae Upsaliensis, 1985); David Scott Kastan, *Shakespeare After Theory* (New York: Routledge, 1999); Patricia Seed, "'This Island's Mine': Caliban and Native Sovereignty," in *"The Tempest" and Its Travels*, ed. Peter Hulme and William Howard Sherman (Philadelphia, PA: University of Pennsylvania Press, 2000); Barbara Fuchs, "Conquering Islands: Contextualizing The

from movables to immovables, salvage to sovereign title, shows Shakespeare developing an international jurisprudence in which the forensic traditions of Roman comedy challenge heroic international law. In the reading of *The Tempest* that follows, I argue that characters in *The Tempest* apply judgments—more and less successfully—about the kinds of things (*res*) they find (*inveniunt*), those things' international histories and geographies, and the legal scenarios that could plausibly pertain. Shakespeare in the process subordinates epic legal questions to the comic law of nations and, deploying the forensic spirit of the comic law of nations, levels a critique at heroic international law.

The Tempest's subordination of epic to comedy is consonant with contemporaneous legal developments at the time. Historians of international law have observed that disputes over colonial territories led early modern thinkers to seek resources in the body of private Roman law.[124] The notions that promises must be kept (*pacta sunt servanda*), that empty land could be appropriated (*terra nullius*), and that *de facto* possessors might under certain circumstances retain possession (*uti possidetis*), all derived from private Roman law and were applied to international concerns. "Analogies from Roman private law such as *pacta sunt servanda*, *terra nullius*, and *uti possidetis* [were all] utilized to create new [international] rules for the changing circumstances of the early modern era."[125] If the argument is correct that particular genres argued in effect for the salience of certain legal questions and approaches, the early modern transposition of Roman private law to the relations between sovereigns should also have found expression at the level of literary form. And indeed, *The Tempest* shows how an argument made with increasing frequency—that the Roman *Corpus Juris Civilis* "holds for sovereigns…though it was established by Justinian for private individuals"—cashes out generically.[126] Instead of accommodating private law to epic form—something Milton will do to interesting effect in *Paradise Lost*, for instance— Shakespeare treats epic questions in the conventionally private light of comedy.

Many of *The Tempest*'s reflections on the grandest questions of sovereignty can indeed be traced to Shakespeare's important borrowings from epic, in particular Vergil's *Aeneid*.[127] Shakespeare's Prospero, Donna Hamilton observes, "embodies

Tempest," *Shakespeare Quarterly* 48, no. 1 (Spring 1997): 45–62; Antony Anghie, "The Heart of My Home: Colonialism, Environmental Damage, and the Nauru Case," *Harvard International Law Journal* 34 (1993): 445.

[124] Arthur Nussbaum, "The Significance of Roman Law in the History of International Law," *University of Pennsylvania Law Review* 100, no. 5 (March 1, 1952): 678–87; Lauren Benton and Benjamin Straumann, "Acquiring Empire by Law: From Roman Doctrine to Early Modern European Practice," *Law and History Review* 28, no. 1 (2010): 1–38; Benjamin Straumann, "The Corpus Juris as a Source of Law Between Sovereigns in Alberico Gentili's Thought," in *The Roman Foundations of the Law of Nations: Alberico Gentili and the Justice of Empire*, ed. Benedict Kingsbury and Benjamin Straumann (Oxford: Oxford University Press, 2011), 101–25; Kaius Tuori, "The Reception of Ancient Legal Thought in Early Modern International Law," in *The Oxford Handbook of the History of International Law*, ed. Bardo Fassbender and Anne Peters (Oxford: Oxford University Press, 2012), 1012–33, <http://www.oxfordhandbooks.com/view/10.1093/law/9780199599752.001.0001/law-9780199599752-e-1>.

[125] Tuori, "The Reception of Ancient Legal Thought in Early Modern International Law," 1015.

[126] Gentili, *De Iure Belli Libri Tres*, 2.17.

[127] Donna B. Hamilton, *Virgil and The Tempest: The Politics of Imitation* (Columbus: Ohio State University Press, 1990); Aimé Césaire, *A Tempest: Based on Shakespeare's The Tempest, Adaptation for a Black Theatre*, trans. Richard Miller (New York: TCG Translations, 2002).

the idea of rule associated with Aeneas," while Caliban's conspiracy with Trinculo and Stephano threatens to topple Prospero's new Troy as had the Trojan Horse.[128] But Shakespeare ultimately subordinates such borrowings to comic tropes. When Shakespeare's Caliban contends against Prospero that "This island's mine" (1.2.334), he operates as a kind of Turnus or Argante, restaging epic, public international law contests over territory, yet the dynamic between Prospero and Caliban most closely resembles comic disputes between Gripus and Trachalio, and, especially, between Pericles and the fisherman, where the disputed property "hangs in the net like a poor man's right in the law."

We can see the epic law of nations subordinated to comedy most clearly at the end of the play when, following the sprite Ariel's supplicating appeal to "kindness," Shakspeare's Vergilian Prospero opts for comedic tenderness over epic revenge.[129] With Prospero's "enemies" Antonio, Sebastian, and Alonso kept "prisoner" by Ariel's spell, Ariel tells Prospero "if you now beheld them, your affections / Would become tender," adding "Mine would, sir, were I human" (4.1.259, 5.1.9, 5.1.18–20). The common humanity that Aeneas rejects with the slaughter of Turnus here sways Shakespeare's magus, who acknowledges himself "one of their kind" before forgiving Antonio, Sebastian, and Alonso (5.1.23). "Epic distance" is contracted by comic kind-ness. Ariel's word "tender" reminds us that such kind-ness is rarely far from *tender*'s juridical and commercial associations; but the Latin etymology of *tendere*, to stretch, also discloses a morally expansive outlook embedded in the comic law of nations. The comic law of nations recognizes the so-called "enemy" as kindred with oneself. Following Act 4, "enemy" does not appear in the play again.

Insofar as *The Tempest*'s epic hero rejects enmity and its most prominent private figure wages what looks in many respects like an epic campaign, Shakespeare creates unstable scenes of "inferior persons" of comedy and their sovereign "betters" in discursive international relation. The instability reflects changing early modern legal arrangements. Scholars of Roman law explain that in private legal relations, "the parties were equals and the state the referee."[130] By contrast, "in public legal relations the state was a party, and as representative of the public interest . . . it was a party superior to the individual."[131] The introduction of private law introduced formal equality into what nevertheless remained a hierarchical world. Canonical distinctions in the law, such as between salvage and sovereignty, became in the process as fungible as the traditionally rigid borders between the clowns of comedy and the heroes of epic.

The comedic resources of improvised forensic wit became all the more significant in this newly fluid environment. Lauren Benton points out that pirates, for instance, learned to argue with the language of private law.[132] Rhetorically trained

---

[128] Hamilton, *Virgil and The Tempest*, 124, 87.   [129] Hamilton, *Virgil and The Tempest*, 123–4.
[130] John Henry Merryman and Rogelio Pérez-Perdomo, *The Civil Law Tradition: An Introduction to the Legal Systems of Europe and Latin America*, 3rd edn. (Stanford, CA: Stanford University Press, 2007), 94.
[131] Merryman and Pérez-Perdomo, *The Civil Law Tradition*, 94.
[132] Lauren Benton, *A Search for Sovereignty: Law and Geography in European Empires, 1400–1900* (Cambridge: Cambridge University Press, 2009), 112–20.

humanists like Alberico Gentili and Hugo Grotius thrived.[133] Grotius, for one, argued that "people[s] in respect of all mankind have the place of private men," and he proceeded to thrust and cut through the verbal landscape like a character from Plautus.[134]

Shakespeare for his part laid emphasis on the vestigial hierarchies that persisted within formal equality. Much like the poor fishermen in *Pericles*, Caliban confronts a powerful opponent practiced in legal invention, and indeed Caliban, in this "mixed" encounter, fares even worse than *Pericles'* fisherman. Prospero's legal invention is of a piece with his magical powers.

Though Caliban's legal invention on the topic of sovereignty is outmatched by Prospero's, what we might call Caliban's "private" wit bests even the Europeans Trinculo and Stephano—who, it turns out, have failed to study Plautus' private juris-prudence as carefully as Caliban has done. Earlier, we saw in the story of the woman abducted from the salt mines how the *Corpus Juris Civilis* had bequeathed an archive of short narratives not altogether unlike the six-word gem attributed to Hemingway, "For sale, baby shoes, never worn."[135] The *Digest* also explained that legitimate legal title could be had "by the law of nations" in cases of "An island arising in the sea"—"a rare occurrence," it adds, for such islands were akin to fish or wild animals in that they had been no one's property, *res nullius*.[136] In addition to rich imaginative tab-leaux like the rare island arising in the sea, private Roman law also had important strains of humility and provisionality. Historically, two formally equal private people quarreling presented their grievances to a magistrate, whose role it was to transform the dispute into a concise linguistic artifact, a single-sentence summary of the issue. Equipped with such an artifact, the disputants could then empower any ordinary citizen to decide their case using a simple speech-act: "Let A be judge." The next sentences packed extraordinary imaginative purchase. Despite the goal of conci-sion, the formula was often peppered with conditional "if" and "unless" clauses that coalesced into something that was at once a baroque logical puzzle and a pow-erful imaginative spur. Every such formula contained within itself multiple fictional worlds. A formula concerning possession of a ring might read:

> Let Gaius be judge. If Aulus Agerius had for one year possessed the ring which he bought in good faith and which was delivered to him, then if that ring which is at issue would have belonged to him at civil law, unless the ring which is at issue belongs at civil law to Numerius Negidius, and Numerius Negidius did not sell and deliver the

---

[133] Benjamin Straumann, "'Ancient Caesarian Lawyers' in a State of Nature: Roman Tradition and Natural Rights in Hugo Grotius' *De Iure Praedae*," *Political Theory* 34, no. 3 (2006): 328–50.

[134] Grotius, *The Free Sea*, 31.

[135] Vico even considered Roman law itself "a serious poem." Giambattista Vico, *New Science: Prin-ciples of the New Science Concerning the Common Nature of Nations*, trans. David Marsh (New York: Penguin Books, 1999), 455.

[136] "An island arising in the sea (a rare occurrence) belongs to the first taker, for it is held to belong to no one" (*Insula quae in mari nascitur (quod raro accidit) occupantis fit: nullius enim esse creditor*, 41.1.7.3). Shakespeare's Caliban, we recall, is described as a fish. For readings that usefully emphasize the play's fishing interests, see Paul Franssen, "Canute or Neptune? The Dominion of the Seas and Two Versions of *The Tempest*," *Cahiers Élisabéthains* 57 (April 2000): 79–94; Edward M. Test, "*The Tempest* and the Newfoundland Cod Fishery," in *Global Traffic: Discourses and Practices of Trade in English Literature and Culture from 1550 to 1700*, ed. Barbara Sebek and Stephen Deng (New York: Palgrave Macmillan, 2008), 201–19.

ring at issue to Aulus Agerius, and it has not in the opinion of the judge been restored to Aulus Agerius, whatever its value shall be let the judge condemn Numerius Negidius to pay that to Aulus Agerius; if it does not so appear, let him absolve.[137]

Contingencies of plot proliferate through the language of private Roman law. "If it does not so appear," "whatever its value shall be," "unless it belongs": the provisionality of things inside the increasingly dominant discourse of Renaissance international argument orients us to a more modest, curious mode of legal inquiry than the heroic law of nations might lead us to expect.

While *The Tempest* exhibits strong marks of Roman law's narrative provisionality in its generally speculative mode, the play also casts Caliban's public law arguments as inexpert results of a legal apprenticeship cut short. While Prospero successfully deploys criminal law to claim the island—Caliban's alleged attempt on Miranda, in particular—Caliban's unsuccessful claim relies on matrilineal descent. Sycorax, we're told, had been banished to the uninhabited island from her home in Algiers, saved from execution only by her pregnancy with Caliban. As with the story of Caliban's mother Sycorax in Algiers, the audience knows little about Caliban's alleged prior crime, only that Caliban does not deny it. Even assuming its accuracy, Shakespeare gives us no reason to assume that criminal conviction invalidates inheritance. A formula derived from the plot of *The Tempest* might include "If such a crime occurred," "unless inheritance supersedes or is independent of crime." After all, Caliban continues to claim from matrilineal descent—"This island's mine by Sycorax my mother"—years after his alleged rape of Miranda. The complex of issues requires invention, Altman's "schemes and suasions."

In a celebrated essay, "Prospero's Wife," Stephen Orgel once pointed out that Caliban had little need to rely on matrilineal claims: since he was there first, claims from prior possession could have served.[138] This is precisely where Prospero's superior legal invention shows. The dark side of the fusion of epic and comedy, we might say, comes when international legal personalities like Prospero wage unequal battles with private law. Shakespeare suggests Caliban's stunted legal wit by yoking it to his stunted pupilage in language, particularly his formal proficiency as a sonneteer. Like the sonnet that begins with the line "This island's mine, by Sycorax my mother," the legal argument is recognizable as such, but also inexpert. Shakespeare stages the question of how to adjudicate contested property as Plautus had, but he also powerfully demonstrates the elevated stakes in the context of colonialism, the spoils of context-appropriate legal invention, and the influential distinctions in power across international lines even when parties are formally equal *per* private Roman law.[139]

---

[137] Adapted from David Johnston, *Roman Law in Context* (Cambridge: Cambridge University Press, 1999), 115. Johnston's own example concerns an arresting case of a dispute over a slave. See further the examples and excellent overview of Roman law procedure in Ditlev Tamm, *Roman Law and European Legal History* (Copenhagen: DJØF Pub., 1997), 49–68.

[138] Stephen Orgel, "Prospero's Wife," *Representations*, no. 8 (October 1984): 1–13.

[139] Offering insight into the debate's private international law contexts, Patricia Seed wisely observes, "anyone familiar with the bilateral inheritance systems of Spain and Portugal would find the claim to inherit the island through Sycorax, his mother, to be totally unexceptional." At English law, however, Caliban's matrilineal claims would not hold. Seed, "'This Island's Mine': Caliban and Native Sovereignty," 210.

Overmatched though he may be in the grand debates of epic international law, Caliban's socio-legal wisdom shines in comparison with Trinculo and Stephano, whose biggest misstep may have been in paying too little attention to Plautus' lessons of private international law. As the play ends with the drunk Trinculo and Stephano arraigned for theft, it is because the reappearance of the nobles had altered the very wine that had lubricated their subplot—not transubstantiating the wine, exactly, but transforming its legal nature from property found to property stolen. As we have seen, Renaissance commentators had glossed the Gripus–Trachalio dispute with passages from the *Digest* regarding salvage and theft. While the play leaves open whether Caliban too might be liable for drinking the salvaged wine, he alone of his trio apprehends the true meaning of Plautine *praeda* or "prize." When the co-conspirators approach Prospero's cave, Trinculo and Stephano are successfully baited by the apparently unclaimed "glistering apparel" set out for them by Ariel, but Caliban is rightly wary of goods no better than those to be found in a Plautine *vidulus*. "What do you mean / to dote thus on such *luggage*?," says Caliban, foregoing the more frequent translations of "trunk" or "case" (4.1.228–229, emphasis added). Such "trumpery" is "trash" in comparison to "The prize I'll bring thee to," prods Caliban (4.1.186, 222, 204). The comments illustrate Caliban's thoughtful engagement with the private international law tropes of comedy: Plautus too could be "studied for action."[140] Even as Trinculo and Stephano pun on the "line" from which their newfound clothes hang, Caliban alone apprehends its danger, something communicated to the audience just a few lines earlier when the "rope" of *Rudens* had become Prospero's menacingly equivocal directive to Ariel: "Hang them on this line" (4.1.193).[141] When Alonso sends Trinculo and Stephano "Hence," telling them to "bestow your luggage where you found it," and Sebastian adds, "Or stole it, rather," the two servants exit the play for good under the cloud of this error (5.1.302–303). Far from duplicating epic international law's sovereign metaphysics of enmity, then, Shakespeare's invented island becomes legible instead as a locus of private international law, dominated by things (*res*) and invention (*invenio*), both in the sense of finding and of making up.

CONCLUSION

Reading *Pericles* and *The Tempest* in the context of the "private" law of nations illustrates what might be gained by moving beyond the restrictive Benthamite definition of "international law." Because the Renaissance law of nations concerned not only the grand personages of what would become "public international law" but also the "inferior persons" of private international law, the chapter has looked to comedy in order to restore a fuller understanding of literature and the law of nations in the context of Renaissance humanism. In reconnecting texts as varied as Heywood's *The*

---

[140] Lisa Jardine and Anthony Grafton, "'Studied for Action': How Gabriel Harvey Read His Livy," *Past & Present* 129, no. 1 (1990): 30–78.

[141] Editors have long debated whether "line" or "lime" is correct here. The likely Plautine allusion leads me to depart from the Norton here and favor the former.

Captives, Spenser's *Faerie Queene*, Shakespeare and Wilkins' *Pericles*, and Shakespeare's *The Tempest* to the "private" law of nations tradition that strongly developed through Renaissance readings of Plautus' *Rudens*, the chapter has focused less on doctrine than on a comedic tradition that was highly self-conscious about the role of rhetoric in debates over private international law. Proof and invention, as we have seen, were central both to Renaissance comedy and to Renaissance private international law. As the case of *Venetian Ambassador v. Brooke* reminds us, literary invention could resonate deeply with topical debates, and proofs were as central to the outcomes of literary plots as to the lifeplots of "inferior persons" living in a world regulated by private international law. Renaissance comedy shares with private international law the starting assumption that individuals will be drawn for reasons of love, necessity, pleasure, or commerce into international relation with one another. When Trinculo, Stephano, and Caliban reappear at the end of *The Tempest* in their "stolen apparel," Prospero advises the other nobles around him to "Mark but the badges of these men, my lords, / Then say if they be true" (5.1.270–271). In order to appreciate fully the Renaissance law of nations, we need to be able to connect such moments to cases like that of the *Husband* and the *Soderina*, for the "badges," or marks of identity to which Prospero here draws attention were precisely the kinds of marks on which judgments in private international law regularly turned.

In a tragicomic reversal, it would be their own failure to provide inartistic proof that ultimately sank the English merchants in the case of the *Husband*.[142] As the English merchants originally expected, the Venetians indeed failed to produce the necessary proofs, the "badges," as Prospero puts it, by which crime could be confirmed. The allegations remained "baseless fabric" (4.1.151). Yet this very failure prohibited the Admiralty judges from following James' express desire that they decide for the Venetian merchants. In late 1608, James pressured the judges into reversing the burden of proof. Whereas the Venetians had heretofore been asked to produce proof that the *Husband* goods were the same as the *Soderina* goods, now the burden rested with the English merchants, and they met with equivalent difficulty. Could Trinculo and Stephano, after all, "prove" native origins for their wine? Required to tender sureties for the property now presumed to be Venetian, the English merchants then repaid the Venetians in pieces over the next few years, and the matter was effectively concluded in November 1611, the month of *The Tempest*'s first performance, at Whitehall.

We don't know exactly when either of the two 1609 quartos of *Pericles* was published. It is possible that one or both was late 1608, as was common practice. How directly *Pericles* and *The Tempest* related to *Venetian Ambassador v. Brooke* can probably never be ascertained for certain: "some oracle / Must rectify our knowledge" (5.1.247–248). However, I've suggested in this chapter that Renaissance comedy helps reorient us to the private side of the law of nations in the early seventeenth century, and that we misrecognize both the period's law and its literature if we ignore the hierarchies of status inscribed into Renaissance genres. Those same hierarchies were, I have suggested, enabling conditions for the Benthamite split that has left private international law in the historiographical shadows.

---

[142] Wijffels, "Merchants."

4

The Tragicomic Law of Nations

The Winter's Tale and the Union

There is in any commonwealth a certain power above the laws, that can abolish them and make them anew . . . It is a perpetual law that no civil law is perpetual.

Francis Bacon, *Aphorismi de Jure Gentium* (unpublished manuscript)[1]

Time: . . . it is in my power
To o'erthrow law, and in one self-born hour
To plant and o'erwhelm custom . . .

William Shakespeare, *The Winter's Tale*, 4.1.7–9

Time in regarde of Eternitie, is but a winters day.

William Fulbecke, *The Pandects of the Law of Nations* (1602)[2]

Through epic and comedy, we have already seen how aspects of the law of nations were regularly understood in the Renaissance in conjunction with particular literary forms and how keeping literary form and the law of nations in the same frame can enrich our accounts of both. Tragicomedy, we observed in the Introduction, could stage the conflicts between the new jurisgenetive claims made by a rising merchant class, historically characterized as "private," and the traditional claims to "public" law made under sovereign authority. In this chapter, I propose to explore a different jurisgenetive dimension of the tragicomic law of nations through Shakespeare's *The Winter's Tale* (1611). A compelling way to understand the distinctive form of *The Winter's Tale*, I want to suggest now, can be found in the questions of mixing, belonging, and joining that were at the heart of the law of nations and the debates over the Anglo-Scottish Union in the early years of James' reign.[3]

---

[1] *quaedam potestas supra leges quae easdem abrogare, et novas corxiere possit . . . perpetua lex est, nullam civilem legem perpetuam esse.* Francis Bacon, "Aphorismi de Jure Gentium Majore Sive de Fontibus Justiciae et Juris," in *The Making of the Instauration: Science, Politics, and Law in the Career of Francis Bacon*, ed. and trans. Mark S. Neustadt (Ph.D. dissertation, The Johns Hopkins University, 1987), 281. I thank Mark Neustadt for permission to quote his edition and translation.

[2] William Fulbecke, *The Pandectes of the Law of Nations: Contayning Severall Discourses of the Questions . . . of Law, Wherein the Nations of the World Doe Consent and Accord. Giving Great Light to the Understanding and Opening of the Principall Objects . . . of the Civill Law, and Common Law of His Realme of England* (London: Thomas Wight, 1602), 1.

[3] This analysis builds on Donna B. Hamilton, "The Winter's Tale and the Language of Union, 1604–1610," *Shakespeare Studies* 21 (1993), 228–52 though Hamilton is less concerned with questions of genre in relation to the Union debates and is at pains to account for the persistence of Union discourse in a play as late as 1611. For a taut discussion showing Shakespeare using genre for "political thinking" about Britain as early *1 Henry IV*, however, see Matthew Greenfield, "1 Henry IV: Metatheatrical Britain," in *British Identities and English Renaissance Literature*, ed. David J. Baker and Willy

In the last fifty years, we have become accustomed to thinking about tragedies of the commons.[4] But long before we came to think in terms of tragedies—or even comedies—of the commons, Renaissance dramatic forms were already locations inscribed with highly politicized theories of union.[5] The anonymous writer of *A Treatise About the Union of England and Scotland* (1604), for example, pointed to the "perpetuall hostilitie between the devided nations of this island," and the many "tragicall events, caused by the ambitious humours and mistrusting jalosies of the devided kingdoms in this island."[6] Similar to the generic transformation found in *The Winter's Tale*, the Union in his estimation would effect a desired progression from "tragicall events" to comedy. Using genre similarly, the Scots writer John Russell worried about the Union "beginning at ane comedie and ending in ane tragedie."[7] Union needed to be "trew" and no "pretext of freindship."[8] In cases of the latter, comedy easily turns to tragedy, such as when "the traffiquin merchant begyinnis at the uord societie, but quen in comes '*ad pronominal possesiva meum, tuum, suum* [to the possessive pronouns of mine, thine, and his]' fallis furth in ane heich contentioun."[9] That relations between Leontes and Polixenes began literally in "the word societie"— so says Camillo at 1.1.19–27—before falling into contention, illustrates the close relations between debates over the Union, the form and events of *The Winter's Tale*, and what I consider Shakespeare's generic jurisprudence of the law of nations.

Previous chapters have of course discussed epic and comedic dimensions of the law of nations. But for many Renaissance thinkers, the Roman *Digest*, in conjunction with the Genesis narrative, told a story of the law of nations that can best be described as "tragicomic." According to the picture of natural law developed by Ulpian and adopted in slightly modified Christian form by thinkers from Vitoria to Milton, men first existed unconstrained by human laws or external government. In this *status naturae*, it made little sense to differentiate between men and beasts since there existed none of the human laws or institutions that fell broadly under the term of civilization. It was only "As a consequence of [the law of nations that] wars were introduced, nations differentiated, kingdoms founded, properties individuated, estate boundaries settled, buildings set up, and commerce established,

Maley (Cambridge: Cambridge University Press, 2002), 71–80. For key discussions of *King Lear* and the Union, see Annabel M. Patterson, *Censorship and Interpretation: The Conditions of Writing and Reading in Early Modern England* (Madison, WI: University of Wisconsin Press, 1984), 58–73; Glynne Wickham, "From Tragedy to Tragi-Comedy: 'King Lear' as Prologue," in *Shakespeare Survey*, ed. Kenneth Muir (Cambridge: Cambridge University Press, 1973), 33–48.

[4] Garrett Hardin, "The Tragedy of the Commons," *Science*, December 13, 1968, 1243–8.

[5] Carol Rose, "The Comedy of the Commons: Custom, Commerce, and Inherently Public Property," *The University of Chicago Law Review* 53, no. 3 (Summer 1986): 711–81; Bruce L. Levine, "The Tragedy of the Commons and the Comedy of Community: The Commons in History," *Journal of Community Psychology* 14, no. 1 (1986): 81–99; Patricia Yaeger, "Sea Trash, Dark Pools, and the Tragedy of the Commons," *PMLA* 125, no. 3 (2010): 523–45.

[6] Anon., "A Treatise about the Union of England and Scotland," in *The Jacobean Union: Six Tracts of 1604*, ed. Bruce Galloway and Brian P. Levack (Edinburgh: Scottish History Society, 1985), 49.

[7] John Russell, "A Treatise of The Happie and Blissed Unioun," in *The Jacobean Union Six Tracts of 1604*, ed. Bruce Galloway and Brian P. Levack (Edinburgh: Scottish History Society by C. Constable, 1985), 85.

[8] Russell, "A Treatise of The Happie and Blissed Unioun," 85.

[9] Russell, "A Treatise of The Happie and Blissed Unioun," 85–6.

including contracts of buying and selling and letting and hiring."[10] For Christian readers, the disjunction between natural law and the law of nations offered an underdeveloped narrative for which Genesis could be a supplement. Whereas *ius naturae* named the radical innocence recalled by Gonzalo's speech on "no sovereignty," the law of nations was the legal order for fallen man. As Martii Koseniemi explains, "the pre-lapsarian *ius naturae*…was adjusted in the world of real human beings by a consensual and historical *ius gentium*."[11] Francis Bacon, in Calvin's Case, considered the law of nations an abridgment to natural law.[12] In his unpublished *Aphorismi de Jure Gentium*, Bacon lamented that natural fountains of justice had been "tinged and stained" by historical circumstances, distinguishing between a "greater law of nations" and a "lesser law of nations," *majore* and *minore*.[13] Even Alberico Gentili, who preferred to equate the *ius naturae* and *ius gentium,* though giving both a strongly historical character, could not help but call the law of nations "a portion of the divine law which God left with us after our sin."[14] Among the things that tended to make the law of nations tragicomic for a number of important writers, then, was its mixed and makeshift character, its simultaneous accommodations to sin and its origins in human inventiveness.

One of the most thoughtful and explicit investigations of the tragicomic law of nations in the English Renaissance, as we shall see in more detail in Chapters 6 and 7, was Milton's. The law of nations became most relevant to Milton in the context of his writings on divorce. Whereas Milton's Adam and Eve wed before the Fall in *Paradise Lost*, divorce was part of the law of nations. Divorce, like the law of nations on the whole, was needed "because the hardness of another's heart might…inflict all things upon an innocent person, whom far other ends brought into a league of love."[15] Milton went on to refer to the "restraint of divorce."[16] The institutions of the law of nations were regularly justified in just this ameliorative and pragmatic way—as protection from even further harm. Insofar as humanity was capable of mitigating the damage caused by the Fall, "law of nations" named the catalogue of devices for doing so. Like the stability that so often re-emerged at the end of a tragicomedy, the law of nations brought a kind of order even as it could never fully repair the breach.

For such reasons, a tragicomedy like *The Winter's Tale* (1611) offers surprising insight into how Renaissance thinkers understood the law of nations theoretically.[17]

[10] Justinian, *The Digest of Justinian*, trans. Alan Watson, 4 vols. (Philadelphia, PA: University of Pennsylvania Press, 1985), 1.2.

[11] Martti Koskenniemi, "International Law and Raison D'état: Rethinking the Prehistory of International Law," in *The Roman Foundations of the Law of Nations: Alberico Gentili and the Justice of Empire*, ed. Benedict Kingsbury and Benjamin Straumann (Oxford: Oxford University Press, 2011), 303.

[12] "The Case of the Postnati, or of the Union of the Realm of Scotland with England," in *Cobbett's State Trials*, vol. 2 (R. Bagshaw, 1809), 559–696.

[13] Bacon, "Aphorismi de Jure Gentium," 273.

[14] Alberico Gentili, *De Iure Belli Libri Tres* (Oxford: The Clarendon Press, 1933), 2.7–8.

[15] John Milton, *Complete Prose Works*, ed. Don M. Wolfe (New Haven, CT: Yale University Press, 1953), 2.662.

[16] Milton, *CPW*, 2.662.

[17] I opt for period's term "tragicomedy" over the later term "romance" for reasons that will become evident throughout this chapter. Most particularly, however, I wish to emphasize the aspects of union enacted by "tragicomedy."

While critics like Felperin have noted that the play's first acts stage a "loss of verbal innocence," the drama also becomes a fable of legal ingenuity in relation to domestic and international political orders.[18] *The Winter's Tale* gives us a tragic encounter with Otherness, as James Knapp emphasizes, but it does not stop there.[19] Instead, like certain versions of the law of nations, it offers Leontes and his audiences a path through fully realized darkness. The dead Mamillius, Antigonus, and mariners will never be recovered, but nor, at the end of the play, have the relations between husband and wife or sovereign and sovereign settled in the darkest depths made possible by human depravity. Reconciling what *The Winter's Tale* calls the "noble combat... twixt joy and sorrow," the law of nations was itself human art, and what made it "art / [as] Lawful as eating," to use Leontes' famous terms, was its relation to the kind of life it kept at bay and the kind of life it sustained (5.2.66–67, 5.3.110–111).[20]

The 1611 historical situation of the play suggests even more detailed engagements with the law of nations in *The Winter's Tale*, however. The play's first known performance was at court in November of that year, and, as is well known, the 1603 accession of James VI of Scotland to the crown of England had created a powerful momentum toward Anglo-Scottish Union in the first decade of the seventeenth century, one with significant legal, cultural, and geographical consequences.[21] The Union was, as a parliamentary committee charged with considering it understood, a "Matter of common law, [a] Matter of civil law, [a] Matter of *ius gentium*, [a] Matter of State, [and a] Matter of Story."[22] It is often suggested that the Union debates ceased in about 1610, when parliamentary support for the Union had dried up, but the Union's awkward contingency on the bodily continuation of the Stuart line nevertheless provided continuing motivation for supporters of the Union to develop more durable bonds. One English speaker in Parliament had worried, "If the King should die without Issue, the Law of Nations giveth it to the Heir of the Father's Side; which is a Scottish Man."[23] In *The Winter's Tale*, the

---

[18] Howard Felperin, "'Tongue-Tied Our Queen?': The Deconstruction of Presence in The Winter's Tale," in *Shakespeare and the Question of Theory*, ed. Patricia Parker and Geoffrey Hartman (London: Methuen, 1985), 10. Richard Strier offers a pointed critique of Felperin's deconstructionist method in Richard Strier, *Resistant Structures: Particularity, Radicalism, and Renaissance Texts* (Berkeley, CA: University of California Press, 1995), 44–5. While Strier rightly argues that Leontes' interpretations are "crazy," I suggest below that tyrannous interpretations like Leontes' were seen as a threat to the Anglo-Scottish Union.

[19] James A. Knapp, "Visual and Ethical Truth in The Winter's Tale," *Shakespeare Quarterly* 55, no. 3 (2004): 253–78.

[20] All references to *The Winter's Tale* are to the Norton edition (1997) and will be cited in the text.

[21] Jenny Wormald, "James VI and I: Two Kings or One?," *History* 68, no. 223 (1983): 187–209; Martin Butler, *The Stuart Court Masque and Political Culture* (Cambridge: Cambridge University Press, 2008); Bruce Galloway, *The Union of England and Scotland, 1603–1608* (Edinburgh: J. Donald, 1986); Bruce Galloway and Brian P Levack, eds., *The Jacobean Union: Six Tracts of 1604* (Edinburgh: Scottish History Society, 1985).

[22] British History Online, "House of Commons Journal Volume 1: 24 February 1607 (2nd Scribe)," *Journal of the House of Commons: Volume 1*, June 22, 2003, <http://www.british-history.ac.uk/report.aspx?compid=9806>.

[23] "House of Commons Journal Volume 1: 26 April 1604 (2nd Scribe)," *Journal of the House of Commons: Volume 1*, June 22, 2003, <http://www.british-history.ac.uk/report.aspx?compid=5631>. Conrad Russell emphasizes that "the death of four people would have been enough to end the union."

lost Mamillius and the found Perdita resonate with anxieties regarding the Union and the Stuart line. Given the Union's vulnerable contingency on Stuart regeneration, law and story in 1611 remained among the most widely applicable methods for developing more durable bonds.

The lawyer and natural philosopher Francis Bacon understood as well as anyone the symbolic and constitutive role of legal forms in Britain's international self-fashioning. For Bacon, "new forms" undergirded by the greater law of nations could serve as the legal underpinning for the Unionists' ambitious project. Shakespeare, for his part, was unsurprisingly more alert to the "matter of story," in particular the constitutive power of new literary forms. In its title, *The Winter's Tale* conjures what Robert Cover calls a "folktale of justice" through the bardic tradition of storytelling, but just as such tales are not simply backward looking but also have "the capacity... to project a new legal meaning into the future" in Cover's understanding, so too does *The Winter's Tale* link legal conventions with literary conventions and join Bacon on the side of the novel.[24] As Bacon himself observed in his *Aphorismi de Jure Gentium*, the single known manuscript of which is collected alongside Bacon's *The Beginning of the History of Great Britain* and *Certain Articles or Consideration Touching the Union of England and Scotland*, "He who holds fast to custom [*consuetudinem*] and retains the appearance of antiquity in the face of change is in fact embracing a novelty [*novitatem*], since what seems in itself to be old becomes novel [*novum*] in its incongruity [*incongruetate*] to the present."[25] I argue that in the context of the Union debates, the "incongruous" generic form of *The Winter's Tale* is related to the proposed "new forms" of law that would bind English and Scots citizens together. Bacon's emphasis on new forms of law, to be situated neither in London nor Edinburgh, offers an illuminating analog to Shakespeare's matter of story, which amounts to a kind of generic jurisprudence for its much-remarked self-consciousness about its own constitutive processes. For both Shakespeare and Bacon, the need for new forms concerned the power of old forms. What became clear in the Union debates was that legal conventions, like literary conventions, could become occasions of unthinking or illicit allegiance. In Lord Chancellor Ellesmere's view, opponents of Union had inexplicably adopted an "imaginary locall allegiance."[26] New forms, by contrast, challenged customary patterns of

---

See Conrad Russell, "1603: The End of English National Sovereignty," in *The Accession of James I: Historical and Cultural Consequences*, ed. Glenn Burgess, Rowland Wymer, and Jason Lawrence (Basingstoke: Palgrave Macmillan, 2006), 5.

[24] Robert M. Cover, "The Folktales of Justice: Tales of Jurisdiction," in *Narrative, Violence, and the Law: The Essays of Robert Cover*, ed. Martha Minow, Michael Ryan, and Austin Sarat (Ann Arbor, MI: University of Michigan Press, 1992), 196–7.

[25] *Nam qui consuetudinem mutata rerum facie mordicus tenet speciem antiquitatis prensat, re vera novitatem amplectitur nam quad per se antiquum videri possit ad incongruetate coepit esse novum* Bacon, "Aphorismi de Jure Gentium," 240, 254, 281. Connecting the legal genre of *novellae leges* to the history of international law, see Chenxi Tang, "The Transformation of the Law of Nations and the Reinvention of the Novella: Legal History and Literary Innovation from Boccaccio's Decameron to Goethe's Unterhaltungen Deutscher Ausgewanderten," *Goethe Yearbook: Publications of the Goethe Society of North America* 19 (2012): 67–92.

[26] Louis A. Knafla, *Law and Politics in Jacobean England: The Tracts of Lord Chancellor Ellesmere* (Cambridge: Cambridge University Press, 1977), 247.

identification and, even more, provoked vibrant new bonds. The tragicomic *Winter's Tale* in my reading not only illustrates but also instantiates the catalyzing force ascribed by Bacon and others in the early seventeenth century to literary form and to the law of nations. A consequence—at once literary, political, legal, and geographic—is to show the law of nations' transformative efficacy on middles. Geography and persons alike are transformed by Shakespeare's generic jurisprudence in the movement from international tragedy to transnational tragicomedy.

In what follows, I flesh out this argument with further attention to law and art in *The Winter's Tale* and the debates over the Union. Having discussed the Union issue itself, its relation to the "mixed" form of *The Winter's Tale*, and what I'll call the play's "rhetorical geography," I'll then show how Shakespeare uses what Quintilian called the figure of *antinomia* to theorize legal relations between the play's two locales, which correspond broadly to differences between English and Scottish laws. With specific attention to Bacon's "new forms," I'll then turn to the play's figures of tyranny and separation, on the one hand, and openness and Union on the other before concluding with further reflections on tragicomedy, the Union, and international law.

Like epic and comedy, tragicomedy was its own jurisprudential engine with specific analytic purchase. Extending points from the previous chapters, we'll examine here tragicomedy's formal capacity to theorize relations between public and private international law. Before tragicomedy, certain kinds of questions had long been difficult to ask in literature, owing to overly sharp distinctions between the heroic genres of the law of nations and genres of customary international law. Tragicomedy made it newly possible to ask how private laws—disharmonious import duties, bastardy laws, or criminal procedures, for instance—intersected with the public questions of war and peace. As *The Winter's Tale* illustrates, tragicomedy highlighted ways that conciliatory peace projects founded in the heroic paradigm of public international law remained stubbornly dependent upon harmonious agreement of private laws. Against the backdrop of earlier chapters' epic law of nations and comic law of nations, the tragicomic law of nations ultimately foregrounds both the temporally constituted moral compromises of international law and also the artistry—indeed, the aesthetics—of "o'erwhelm[ing] custom" so fully that tragic and comedic jurisdictions might speak as one.

BORDERS, HINGES, AND DEBATABLE LANDS: RHETORICAL GEOGRAPHIES

In the Union debates, legal forms and literary conventions were called upon to turn the barren but contested middle spaces of genre and geography into the rich and festive spaces of community. Since, according to Guarini's important argument for tragicomedy in the preface to *Il Pastor Fido* (1602), "he who makes a tragicomedy does not intend to compose separately either a tragedy or a comedy, but from the two a third thing that will be perfect of its kind," tragicomedy was already understood as an engine of transformation, often with economic

dimensions.[27] Also at stake in tragicomedy, however, were questions of law, jurisdiction, and the very idea of Britain, itself a "third thing" that was not, in the eyes
of Union proponents, reducible arithmetically to England plus Scotland. Guarini
spoke explicitly of the "jurisdictions" of tragedy and comedy as though they were
sovereign domains, conceding that "one may not enter into the jurisdiction of the
other."[28] But, "will it follow from this that, since they are diverse species, they
cannot be united to make up a third poem?"[29] Although Philip Sidney, along
with much of the Aristotelian tradition, scorned tragicomedy, Guarini saw no
problem in the union of comedy and tragedy. Tragicomedy was instead like the
law of nations in providing the framework for making one from two. As the historian of Scottish law John Cairns explains, "It was the foundation of law in... the
law of nations that helped underpin claims... that Scots law and English law were
basically rather alike."[30] Nevertheless, union also required art. "[H]ow cunningly
soever a painter layeth on his colours to make two bordes seeme one, yet if they
be not made firme in the ioynts, they will alwaies remaine, and in short time
appeare to be two," wrote John Hayward in his *Treatise of Union*.[31] "[W]hatsoever
appearances are used to make two states seeme one, if they have not one commu-
nitie of lawes, they remaine notwithstanding, and upon small occasions will shew
themselves disjoynted, even in the noblest and strongest limmes of government,"
he argued.[32]

Importantly, the joints and middles found so often in the Union debates had
both literary consequences and material, geographic referents (see Figure 4.1). Geographically, the Union's contested middle spaces included those lands in the Border
region known as "debatable lands," and also what might be called, analogously,
"debatable waters"—maritime and riverine regions around the British archipelago
where rights of fishing and whaling had become especially contentious.[33] Although
a sixteenth-century Scottish legal treatise includes a section on "Sea Lawes, betwixt

---

[27] Valerie Forman, *Tragicomic Redemptions: Global Economics and the Early Modern English Stage*
(Philadelphia, PA: University of Pennsylvania Press, 2008), 7.
[28] Giambattista Guarini, "The Compendium of Tragicomic Poetry," in *Literary Criticism: Plato to
Dryden*, ed. and trans. Allan H. Gilbert (Detroit, MI: Wayne State University Press, 1962), 509.
[29] Guarini, "The Compendium of Tragicomic Poetry," 509.
[30] John W. Cairns, "Scottish Law, Scottish Lawyers and the Status of the Union," in *A Union for
Empire: Political Thought and the British Union of 1707*, ed. John Robertson (Cambridge: Cambridge
University Press, 1995), 250.
[31] John Hayward, *A Treatise of Union of the Two Realmes of England and Scotland* (London: F[elix]
K[ingston] for C[uthbert] B[urby], 1604), 9.
[32] Hayward, *A Treatise of Union of the Two Realmes of England and Scotland*, 9.
[33] William Nicolson, ed., *Leges Marchiarum, or Border-Laws: Containing Several Original Articles
and Treaties, Made and Agreed upon by the Commissioners of the Respective Kings of England and Scotland,
for the Better Preservation of Peace and Commerce upon the Marches of Both Kingdoms* (London: Tim
Goodwin, 1705), 145; T. J. Carlyle, "The Debateable Land," *Transactions of the Dumfriesshire and
Galloway Natural History and Antiquarian Society*, 1, 4 (1865): 19–50; W. Mackay MacKenzie,
"The Debateable Land," *The Scottish Historical Review* 30, no. 110 (October 1, 1951): 109–25;
Thomas Wemyss Fulton, *The Sovereignty of the Sea: An Historical Account of the Claims of England to
the Dominion of the British Seas, and of the Evolution of the Territorial Waters* (London: W. Black-
wood, 1911); Martine Julia van Ittersum, "Mare Liberum Versus the Propriety of the Seas? The
Debate between Hugo Grotius (1583–1645) and William Welwood (1552–1624) and Its Impact
on Anglo-Scotto-Dutch Fishery Disputes in the Second Decade of the Seventeenth Century," *Edinburgh
Law Review* 10, no. 2 (2006): 239–76.

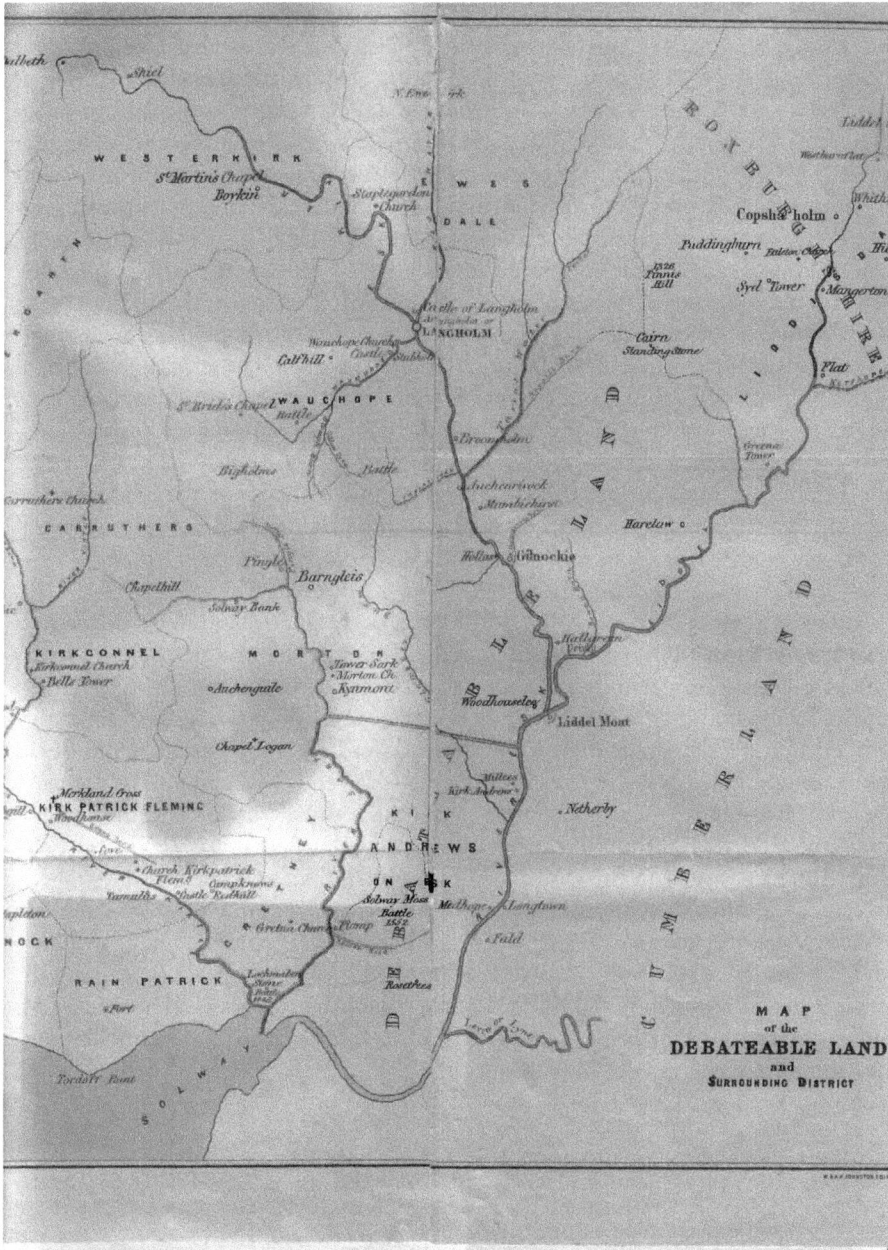

Fig. 4.1. From T. J. Carlyle, "The Debateable Land," *Transactions of the Dumfriesshire and Galloway Natural History and Antiquarian Society*, 1, 4 (1865): 19.

Scotland and England," fishing in the border rivers went largely unchecked due to the "breach [that had] opened between the English and Scottish legal systems" and the resulting contested jurisdiction.[34] Legislation acknowledged that overfishing in the Tweed and Annan rivers went unregulated due to a classic coordination problem: Scots foregoing "the slaughter of salmon in forbidden time and of kipper smolts and black fish at all times would not have made salmon any more to abound in these waters if the like order had not been then observed upon the English side."[35] As Leontes treats his alleged cuckolding as having "his pond fished by his next neighbor," *The Winter's Tale* recreates a rhetorical geography marred by acquisitive international strife, *meum* and *tuum* (1.2.196). As a result, we might say the play's dominant rhetorical figure, and a key component of Shakespeare's tragicomic jurisprudence, is what Quintilian called *antinomia*, the juxtaposition of contradictory laws.[36] Just as *antinomia* remains invested in the solutions to legal riddles even as it draws out law's contrasts, the play's harmonious resolution transforms "the lands and waters 'twixt [Leontes'] throne and [Polixenes']" (5.1.143). The legally inflected jurisdictions of tragedy and comedy in the play thereby become "matters of *ius gentium*" at the same time that they become "matters of story," narratable according to the generic conventions of tragedy, comedy, or— that "third thing"—tragicomedy.

Britain's rhetorical geography of Borders, debatable lands, and debatable waters is developed most prominently as a matter of story in the middle of *The Winter's Tale* in Shakespeare's artfully debatable third act. Leontes, King of Sicily has of course accused his wife Hermione of treason and adultery, and peremptorily decided that his daughter, soon to be dubbed Perdita, is the bastard child of his former friend Polixenes, the King of Bohemia. He sends his servant Antigonus to "bear it / To some remote and desert place, quite out / Of our dominions; and there [to] leave it, / Without more mercy, to its own protection" (3.2.81, 2.3.175–178). The play, which to this point looks very much like an *Othello*-esque tragedy of jealousy, shortly thereafter finds at once pathos and macabre humor in the fate of Antigonus, the loyal servant who famously falls victim to the demands of tragedy after his fateful yet serio-comic "Exit pursued by a bear" (3.3.57). Among the scene's many admirers is W. H. Auden, who, calling attention to the dramatic points and counterpoints that Shakespeare here sets up for the "music of reconciliation," described the scene as "the most beautiful scene in Shakespeare."[37] Formally, the

[34] Kirsty Hood, "Roots and Context of the Conflict of Laws Within the UK," in *The Conflict of Laws Within the UK*, 1st edn. (Oxford: Oxford University Press, 2007), 22, quotations pps. 10, 17; John Ford, "The Law of the Sea and the Two Unions," in *Anglo-Scottish Relations from 1603 to 1900*, ed. T.C. Smout (Oxford: Oxford University Press, 2005), 127–41.

[35] *Act Regarding the Rivers of Tweed and Annan*, 1606, <http://www.rps.ac.uk/trans/1605/6/33>.

[36] Quintilian, *The Orator's Education*, trans. D. A. Russell (Cambridge, MA: Harvard University Press, 2001), 8.7. Of Kant's important later uses of antinomy, scholars have long observed that Kant proceeds in the wake of a robust seventeenth-century legal literature on "differences between laws arising from clashes between legal jurisdictions." See, for example, Howard Caygill, *A Kant Dictionary* (Malden, MA: Blackwell Pub., 1995), 75.

[37] W. H. Auden, *Lectures on Shakespeare*, ed. Arthur C. Kirsch (Princeton, NJ: Princeton University Press, 2000), 23.

scene marks the transition from the enclosed and emotionally repressed world of the Sicilian court to the airy festivity of Bohemia's common places: in short, the transition from the tragic to the comic. Unfolding temporally, the play's memorable "middle" is a middle in relation to a temporal scale initiated by the play's tragic beginning and concluded by its comic ending.

Yet, as Auden understood, the formal, generic achievements of *The Winter's Tale* involved space as much as time. Act 3, Scene 3 of *The Winter's Tale* was "the most beautiful scene in Shakespeare... not in actual words, but in its situation," Auden wrote.[38] "Situation" for Auden was spatial. What Auden admired particularly in the scene's "situation" was at once a matter of the "dream"-like locale conjured by Shakespeare on the famous coast of Bohemia and also of what Hayden White, in his classic work on historiography, *Metahistory*, called "emplotment."[39] The scene is beautiful because of the way Shakespeare had emplotted it within the play. It was because Auden implicitly understood the play *in toto* in chorographical terms that a scene could be "situated" within its bounds. Scene again answers to the spatial coordinates of proximity and distance for Auden, as he goes on to describe the "storm and... beasts of prey, hunters hunting bears and bears hunting hunters... an innocent baby, a weak and too obedient servant who has become Leontes' accomplice, the careless youth of hunters, the good poor—the shepherd and his son," "situated," "in the middle of the desert near the scene."[40] What Auden noticed, I would argue, was an effect of the topical legal context of the Union debates. Through his emplotment of Act 3, Shakespeare raises deep questions of citizenship and allegiance both at the level of plot and at the level of genre as Shakespeare's experimentation with generic borders develops the possibilities of new forms of generic belonging.

Several of the most striking legal dimensions of *The Winter's Tale* have of course been highlighted by critics. In her analysis of legal procedures in Leontes' Sicily, Virginia Lee Strain, for instance, finds that the oracle to which Leontes turns in assessing Hermione's fidelity represents English common law judges' pattern of "suppressing, and thus mystifying, deliberative practices" that lead to judicial decisions.[41] The Sicilian context of "the play thereby resonates with the explosive tension between the judiciary and the sovereign in early seventeenth-century England."[42]

However, even though the comic space of Bohemia and the tragicomic form of *The Winter's Tale* suggest an international dimension to such observations, little commentary has developed the play's concerns with the law of nations and the Union. This is surprising, given that, as McEachern explains, "the debate over the relation of England to Britain concerns that of the local to the total[,] ... of common law to

---

[38] Auden, *Lectures on Shakespeare*, 23.

[39] Hayden White, *Metahistory: The Historical Imagination in Nineteenth-Century Europe* (Baltimore, MD: Johns Hopkins University Press, 1973).

[40] Auden, *Lectures on Shakespeare*, 23. See also Robert Henke, *Pastoral Transformations: Italian Tragicomedy and Shakespeare's Late Plays* (Newark, DE: University of Delaware Press, 1997), 151.

[41] Virginia Strain, "*The Winter's Tale* and the Oracle of the Law," *ELH* 78, no. 3 (September 10, 2011): 561.

[42] Strain, "*The Winter's Tale* and the Oracle of the Law," 557–8.

the *jus gentium*"; and that, in Hamilton's words, "the oppositions that structure the play, the chief of which are Sicily-Bohemia and Leontes-Polixenes," have been seen to "stand in homologous relationship to the English-Scottish oppositions of 1604–1610."[43] Nor is it new to observe that Shakespeare's third act operates like a hinge on his tragicomic diptych. As one critic puts it, "The first half, generically, is unquestionably 'tragic'. Equally clearly, the last notes, the language of Act 3 which introduce the second half move us towards the comic and the pastoral."[44] Shakespeare himself, however, conceived the scene, explicitly, in terms of a kind of strange justice. Languages of strangeness and justice coincide in Leontes' precise command to Antigonus in Act 2: "As by *strange* fortune / [the child, Perdita] came to us, I do in *justice* charge thee, / On thy soul's peril and thy body's torture, / That thou commend it *strangely* to some place / Where chance may nurse or end it…" (2.3.179–183, emphasis added). The repetitions of "strange" and "strangely," while referring on the one hand to narrative probability, also push Leontes' command to Antigonus into legal significance through the embedded reminder that, in a location described as "out / Of our dominions," (2.3.176–177), both Perdita and Antigonus will be, in legal terms, strangers—that is, non-citizen aliens, "strangers," according to both lawyerly and colloquial usage, being legally other, belonging to some other realm. As Paulina has earlier put it, speaking of Perdita in particular, Perdita and Antigonus become subjects of the "law and process of great nature" (2.2.63).

The doubled jurisdictions of Sicily and Bohemia, tragedy and comedy, parallel what Bradin Cormack calls "a doubleness in the play's conceptualization of…time…split[ting] the play in two."[45] Cormack shows the play's distinct preference for the legal politics of duration over against the instantaneity of the sovereign decision.[46] It remains possible, moreover, to emphasize notes of Jacobean legal topicality, for expansive temporalities ("law *and* process") regularly accompanied Union advocates' interest in the law of nations. Time in Bacon's *Aphorismi De Jure Gentium* operates as a "power above the laws," ensuring that "no civil law is perpetual," very much as Shakespeare's Time announces his "power / To o'erthrow law, and in one self-born hour / To plant and o'erwhelm custom" (4.1.7–9). Whether in Sicily and Bohemia or England and Scotland, attention to time's "process" relativized local laws, prying citizens from ill-considered formal attachments while "planting" new forms. When Leontes turns to "chance" "out / Of our dominions"

[43] "The 'real' sides in the union debates were less pro or contra King, or pro or contra constitution," she continues, "than whether the universal overrode the local, or the local the universal, when it came to the question of laws." Claire McEachern, *The Poetics of English Nationhood, 1590–1612* (Cambridge: Cambridge University Press, 1996), 155; Hamilton, "The Winter's Tale and the Language of Union, 1604–1610," 230.
[44] Charles Mosley, "The Literary and Dramatic Contexts of the Last Plays," in *The Cambridge Companion to Shakespeare's Last Plays*, ed. Catherine M. S. Alexander (Cambridge: Cambridge University Press, 2009), 56.
[45] Bradin Cormack, "Decision, Possession: The Time of Law in The Winter's Tale and the Sonnets," in *Shakespeare and the Law: A Conversation Among Disciplines and Professions*, ed. Bradin Cormack, Martha Nussbaum, and Richard Strier (Chicago, IL: University of Chicago Press, 2013), 53.
[46] Cormack, "Decision, Possession: The Time of Law in The Winter's Tale and the Sonnets," 53.

to decide Perdita's fate—this despite Antigonus' suggestion that "a present death / Had been more merciful"—Leontes begrudgingly issues the child into the temporal flow of international, rather than national, history. The play thus introduces a spatio-temporal jurisdiction superior to Leontes' own (2.3.184–185).

UNION EMPLOTMENTS

In *Metahistory*, Hayden White drew powerfully from Northrop Frye's *Anatomy of Criticism* in order to observe how historiography often takes one of a number of narrative forms. Just as playwrights like Shakespeare emplot their dramas within generic forms, so too do historians—I would include literary historians—emplot their facts within recognizable narrative structures. Some historians compose their stories as comedies, others as tragedies, and still others according to the narrative structures of what Frye called romance, but which, following early modern theater usage, I have been calling tragicomedy. In recent criticism, the Union's gains have been less emphasized than its losses. Tragedy, we might say, has become the customary generic frame. A shift to tragicomedy, I contend, may offer advantages of further nuance. Narratives of tragedy, as we shall observe in more detail in Chapter 6, help communities understand what they need by dramatizing lack, and over what James and other Union advocates articulated as a civilizing mission in the Middle Shires, the Highlands, and coastal Gaelic regions, scholars have understandably expressed worries.[47] Some have discerned presentiments of the imperial civilizing missions soon to be undertaken outside of Britain in the Americas and the East Indies. By the same token, scholarship informed by English or Scots nationalism has occasionally tended to mourn the "end of sovereignty" represented by the Union of the Crowns.[48] Nor must one be a Foucauldian critic of all "governmentality" in order to feel somewhat wistful about the localized customary practices that the Union jeopardized under the banner of legal uniformity and regularity. Impressive improvised customs had emerged in the Borders, including highly practical measures such as regular truce days and recourse to a "higher court of international standing," for everything from murder to illegal fishing and pasturing.[49] The area exhibited legal pluralism, and while this led (as we shall see) to certain irregularities, such irregularities provoked valuable confrontations with legal otherness. Uncritical valorization of union and/or uniformity indeed risks closing us off to important engagements with alterity, "erasing," as Paul Stevens puts it, "the possibility of a plurality of ways of being in the world."[50] Because of

[47] J. Peter Euben, *The Tragedy of Political Theory: The Road Not Taken* (Princeton, NJ: Princeton University Press, 1990).

[48] Russell, "1603: The End of English National Sovereignty"; Tom Nairn, "Internationalism: A Critique," in *Faces of Nationalism: Janus Revisited* (London: Verso, 1998), 25–46.

[49] David M. Walker, *A Legal History of Scotland: The Sixteenth Century*, vol. 3 (Edinburgh: W. Green, 1995), 176.

[50] Paul Stevens, "Heterogenizing Imagination: Globalization, The Merchant of Venice, and the Work of Literary Criticism," *New Literary History* 36, no. 3 (2005): 431; Paul Schiff Berman, *Global*

James' particular investment in the Union, many published sources exhibit a royalist, pro-Union bias, such that scholarship has rightly tried to counterbalance what Leah Marcus influentially called "the Jacobean line."[51] A number of communitarian, anti-imperialist, and republican values, in other words, inform many of the tragic narratives of the Union.

Nevertheless, Unionism and imperialism were not the same thing, however much they occasionally overlapped.[52] Certain strands of Unionism stood quite apart from, and even distinctly opposed to, imperialism: at the heart of much Unionist political thought was a radical sense of Anglo-Scots equality.[53] As early as 1563, "Commissioners, Orators, Embassadors and Special Messengers" for Queen Elizabeth I and her cousin Mary, Queen of Scots negotiated a treaty for the benefit of "True and Obedient Subjects" along the Borders who were regularly despoiled of "peace and quietness."[54] The "great Disorders of their Subjects of all the Marches and Frontiers of both the Realms" led to new guidelines for the Wardens of each country charged with keeping peace.[55] The commissioners were tasked to "proceed not as Parties for the one Realm, but all to join indifferently together as Persons equally chosen for both Realms, fearing God, and having Scope to reduce their Borders to some good Orders."[56] Historians of empire and bureaucratic centralization have certainly taught us to hear the ominous valence in the language of "reduction," yet we should also remain attuned to the allied view proffered by writers with quite different politics. For at least one prominent scholar, bearing (as of this writing) the title of BB&T Bank Professor for the Study of Capitalism at George Mason University, the Marches were a self-regulating libertarian utopia snuffed out by overreaching government intervention.[57] Would-be regulators of the modern capitalist system are invited in such accounts to take heed.

My point here in drawing attention to the role of contemporary libertarianism in the historiography of the Union is to suggest that literary scholars need to remain sensitive to the ways the putative tragedy of the Union has become a stick with which to ward off imaginative new legal-political forms, of which Great Britain

Legal Pluralism: A Jurisprudence of Law beyond Borders (Cambridge: Cambridge University Press, 2012).

[51] Leah S. Marcus, *Puzzling Shakespeare: Local Reading and Its Discontents* (Berkeley, CA: University of California Press, 1988).

[52] For especially subtle recent accounts, see John Kerrigan, *Archipelagic English: Literature, History, and Politics, 1603–1707* (Oxford: Oxford University Press, 2008); Colin Kidd, *Union and Unionisms: Political Thought in Scotland, 1500–2000* (Cambridge: Cambridge University Press, 2008).

[53] Arthur Williamson, "Radical Britain: David Hume of Godscroft and the Challenge to the Jacobean British Vision," in *The Accession of James I: Historical and Cultural Consequences*, ed. Glenn Burgess, Rowland Wymer, and Jason Lawrence (Basingstoke: Palgrave Macmillan, 2006), 48–68; Marie Theresa O'Connor, "A British People: Cymbeline and the Anglo-Scottish Union Issue," in *Shakespeare and the Law: A Conversation Among Disciplines and Professions*, ed. Bradin Cormack, Martha Nussbaum, and Richard Strier (Chicago, IL: University of Chicago Press, 2013), 231–55. I am grateful to Marisa O'Connor for sharing this essay with me prior to its publication.

[54] Nicolson, *Leges Marchiarum, or Border-Laws*, 120.

[55] Nicolson, *Leges Marchiarum, or Border-Laws*, 120.

[56] Nicolson, *Leges Marchiarum, or Border-Laws*, 121.

[57] Peter T. Leeson, "The Laws of Lawlessness," *The Journal of Legal Studies* 38, no. 2 (June 1, 2009): 471–503.

was once one. Culturally, the concern for education and literature that James would later shorthand as "civilitie" wasn't simply a stalking horse for royal power, accusations to the contrary notwithstanding. It was a sincere goal for many Union advocates eager to share their fervor for classical and biblical texts. As historians and critics have shown, many Unionists were motivated by an internationalist Buchananite civic humanism, which had less to do with a project of expanding royal control into the provinces than with commitments to the emancipatory power of learning.[58]

The crime and violence that were so often emphasized in Unionist discourse, moreover, were not merely mythical problems. Situated as they were at the furthest remove from their capitals, the Borders between England and Scotland eluded the tight control of either Edinburgh or London, and the region's distinct culture and legal system, while capable of eliciting a certain libertarian nostalgia, was itself in many ways a response to large-scale family feuds and criminals exploiting the jurisdictional ambiguity.[59] It is true that cries of disorder from the capitals could be used to impose outwardly burdensome new measures of conformity, but the reality of widespread and sometimes terrifying clan violence should stay any easy valorization of local customs.[60] As Rae observes, "In England, as in Scotland, there were irresponsible clans such as the Grahams, whose raiding activities caused continuous trouble both internally and internationally, and who were far from being amenable to any form of government pressure."[61] Raiding parties raised by one clan or another could reach as many as 3,000 men, such that the Borders, in David J. Baker's words, were "in a more or less constant state of low-grade warfare."[62] Allegiance to a crown normally meant less in terms of identity than did kinship to those bands of "reivers," "borderers" or "steel bonnets" who found profit and utility in choosing to be, according to one contemporary observer, "Scottishe when they will, and English at their pleasure."[63] "Debatable lands" became havens for clans who regularly raided and spoiled one another. At sea, rich herring and cod resources in the North Sea and around the Shetland Islands were regularly raided by Dutch fishing fleets, whose mariners—like the reivers, borderers, and steel

[58] Williamson, "Radical Britain: David Hume of Godscroft and the Challenge to the Jacobean British Vision"; O'Connor, "A British People: *Cymbeline* and the Anglo-Scottish Union Issue"; David Norbrook, "*Macbeth* and the Politics of Historiography," in *Politics of Discourse: The Literature and History of Seventeenth-Century England*, ed. Kevin Sharpe and Steven N. Zwicker (Berkeley, CA: University of California Press, 1987), 78–116.

[59] Cynthia J. Neville, "Remembering the Legal Past: Anglo-Scottish Border Law and Practice in the Later Middle Ages," in *North-East England in the Later Middle Ages*, ed. Christian D. Liddy and Richard H. Britnell (Woodbridge: Boydell Press, 2005), 43–55.

[60] Jane Ohlmeyer, "'Civilizinge of Those Rude Partes': Colonization within Britain and Ireland, 1580s–1640s," in *The Oxford History of the British Empire*, vol. 1, ed. Nicholas Canny (Oxford: Oxford University Press, 1998), 124–47; Mark Netzloff, *England's Internal Colonies: Class, Capital, and the Literature of Early Modern English Colonialism* (New York: Palgrave Macmillan, 2003).

[61] Thomas I. Rae, *The Administration of the Scottish Frontier, 1513–1603* (Edinburgh: Edinburgh University Press, 1966), 227.

[62] David J. Baker, "'Stands Scotland Where It Did?': Shakespeare on the March," in *Shakespeare and Scotland*, ed. Willy Maley and Andrew Murphy (Manchester: Manchester University Press, 2004), 21.

[63] Quoted in Ohlmeyer, "'Civilizinge of Those Rude Partes': Colonization within Britain and Ireland, 1580s–1640s," 126.

bonnets—capitalized on the jurisdictional ambiguity made possible by disunion.[64] Anglo-Scottish piracy further threatened relations between the two countries.[65]

The Union could also be a solution in the sense that fractious Anglo-Scottish relations took their toll on the Borders in less than obvious ways. While few borderers put much stake in national bonds and boundaries, crime and violence could be exacerbated by official Anglo-Scottish hostility nevertheless. Those richly developed customary "Marche laws" that in peace time offered mechanisms for resolving private international disputes and prosecuting cross-border crimes—for example by empanelling juries that included both English and Scots—largely languished in wartime. Anglo-Scottish hostility following Edward I's attempted conquest of Scotland in the thirteenth century repressed longstanding practices of customary international law. Thus, however labile the borderers' national identities and difficult it was even to define borders, Anglo-Scottish antagonism taxed their welfare in direct and indirect ways. The sixteenth century did see closer dynastic ties emerging between England and Scotland, yet even as relations were improving, the two countries kept wary eyes on one another. Henry V's recollection in Shakespeare's eponymous play that "my great-grandfather / Never went with his forces into France / But that the Scot on his unfurnished kingdom / Came pouring like the tide into a breach," still had bite in Elizabethan England (1.2.146–149). Early modern Scotland continued to foster its longstanding cultural, dynastic, and military ties with France partly in order to discourage any renewed temptations the English might have had toward aggrandizement. Friendly Franco-Scots relations, meanwhile, were understandably met with persistent suspicion in London, where eyes continued to dart from north to south and back again. Given certain strains of scholarship in which the Union becomes merely the harbinger of empire and repressive state control, the point here is not to rewrite the history of the Union as comedy. Rather, as we turn in the next section to the problems of contradictory laws, we should do so open to a mixed, even tragicomic narrative more closely associated with the Janus-faced character of the early law of nations through which its proponents sought to bring it about.

ANTINOMY AND JURISPRUDENCE ON THE COAST OF BOHEMIA

Bacon reported that "the Athenians had a custom of appointing six men to examine every year the contradictory titles of their laws (which they called *Antinomies*) and to report to the people such as could not be reconciled, that a definite resolution might be passed concerning them."[66] "Let the legislators of every state...as

---

[64] Fulton, *The Sovereignty of the Sea*, 139.

[65] Steve Murdoch, *The Terror of the Seas?: Scottish Maritime Warfare, 1513–1713* (Leiden: Brill, 2010), 113–20.

[66] Francis Bacon, "Of the Dignity and Advancement of Learning," in *The Works of Francis Bacon*, ed. James Spedding, Robert Leslie, and Douglas Denon Heath, trans. Francis Headlam, vol. 5 (London: Longman, 1861), 99.

often as appears good," he advised, "review their Antinomies."[67] As we turn in more detail now to *The Winter's Tale*, I am arguing that Shakespeare's own tragicomic approach proceeds, as I suggested earlier, via antinomy. At a number of crucial points, the play dramatizes divergences between laws and creates legal riddles out of the stuff of disharmonious legal orders. As such, the play's antinomian structure throws up legal problems whose solutions lie in the law of nations. Its identifiable moves toward abstraction at the same time place the play's commitments alongside those of pro-Union advocates seeking to ground the Union in new forms built out of the rational material of natural law and the law of nations.

To see how Shakespeare's antinomian approach works, we can begin by considering the crime of murder under trust, which had been dramatized poignantly by Shakespeare in *Macbeth* after having been introduced in Scottish criminal law in 1587.[68] In *The Winter's Tale*, the possibility of such a crime is raised when Leontes instructs Camillo to murder his houseguest, Polixenes. In the localized settings of Scotland and England, murder versus murder under trust was hardly a distinction without a difference, for it meant weighty alternatives in jurisdiction and punishment. As a crime of treason in Scotland, murder under trust was tried in the High Court of Justiciary, as opposed to inferior courts for regular murder. While conviction for murder brought with it the forfeiture of life, lands, and goods, criminals convicted of treason were additionally penalized by ignominious treatment of the corpse; families suffered escheat of heritage.[69] In such a context, Shakespeare's fantastic world that included the non-existent Coast of Bohemia operates in a way many now associate with Rawls' famous veil of ignorance, abstracted from any identifiable locale. Staging an antinomian confrontation, Shakespeare emplots a crime that would be a clear case of "murder under trust" in Scotland, but murder alone in England. The jurisprudential result is to hold the category of murder under trust aloft and evaluate it according to standards of right reason associated not with any particular jurisdiction but with the broader law of nations.

Just as the comparative, antinomian structure of tragicomedy enables evaluation in non-localized terms in the case of murder under trust, so too does the coast of Bohemia charge Perdita's legitimacy with signal importance. Scholars have long puzzled over the cause of Leontes' jealousy. While some have suggested that his jealousy is even more baseless than Iago's, the play primes its audiences as early as Act 1, Scene 2 with terms of sex and pregnancy, this suggestive language giving Leontes' jealousy its (limited) narrative sense.[70] Polixenes' first words refer to the "Nine changes of the watery star"—precisely the period of gestation—and terms associated with pregnancy like "burden," "breed," and "filled up" follow quickly thereafter (1.2.1–4, 12). The enjambment of lines 7–8 allows Polixenes' "standing in rich place, I multiply" to linger like a brash confession before the next line ostensibly relieves the tension in tropes of courtesy: "multiply / With one 'we thank you'

---

[67] Bacon, "Of the Dignity and Advancement of Learning," 99.

[68] Arthur Melville Clark, *Murder under Trust, Or, The Topical Macbeth and Other Jacobean Matters* (Edinburgh: Scottish Academic Press, 1981).

[69] Clark, *Murder under Trust, Or, The Topical Macbeth and Other Jacobean Matters*, 46.

[70] Felperin, "'Tongue-Tied Our Queen?': The Deconstruction of Presence in *The Winter's Tale*."

many thousands more." That the poetry encourages audiences to attend to whether Perdita is in fact the child of Polixenes' and Hermione's adulterous union opens space for Shakespeare to supply his tragicomedy with differing standards of legitimacy between Scotland and England.

In line with the play's debatable lands and debatable waters, Perdita's debatable parentage generates at once a powerful case for a union of laws and a new space for theorizing the content of that law. As Shakespeare seems to have understood, private law bastardy cases were precisely the type of case that could stop up "perfect union."[71] The two laws diverged in their treatment of a child who was the issue of an adulterous union but whose mother was nevertheless married to another man. Shakespeare may hint at the conundrum when he has Florizel, whose parentage is itself interestingly underspecified, say, "Should I now meet my father / He would not call me son" (4.4.640–641). In the plot, this statement refers to Florizel's apparent filial disobedience, but it also points to the play's more general interest in serio-comic legal riddles that arise with disharmonious laws.

According to the *ius commune* rules deriving from canon law that governed in Scotland, paternity and biology played the decisive roles. A child of an adulterous union was deemed illegitimate so long as the biological father and the mother were unmarried to one another. The *ius commune* took no cognizance of whether the mother might be married to another man. At English common law, on the other hand, such a case came to answer to a legal fiction. By that fiction, the child was treated as legitimate issue so long as the mother was married to any man whomsoever; the biological father was irrelevant. This meant that a child born out of wedlock whose parents subsequently married would face radically different fates in England and Scotland. According to English common law, such a child was a bastard and barred from inheritance; according to Scots law, following civil and canon law, however, she was legitimized by subsequent marriage and fully capable of inheriting.

Seen potentially as Polixenes' issue, Perdita, then, comes to signify at once a legal riddle and to enact a legal critique in the context of the Union debates.[72] The antinomy in which a child who obviously had a biological father could belong to no one in Scotland and to a fictional father in England was a matter the Union would seemingly need to address. Even if the two procedures were allowed to co-exist in the event of the Union, as many suggested they should, what law would govern if the biological parents were, like Hermione and Polixenes, themselves of different countries? The continuing presence of such legal discrepancies illustrates why Union supporters hoped for "new forms."

This is hardly to say that such discrepancies were not regularly downplayed by Union advocates. Hayward's *Treatise of the Union* contended that "to reduce the lawes of England and Scotland into one bodie, it seemeth the change will not bee

---

[71] In *A Power to Do Justice: Jurisdiction, English Literature, and the Rise of Common Law* (Chicago, IL: University of Chicago Press, 2008), 292–3, Cormack shows cuckoldry to be an important site where common and canon law diverged, and also how writers like Webster, Rowley, and Heywood exploited this divergence to fascinating effect in *A Cure for a Cuckold*.

[72] Cormack, *A Power to Do Justice*, 308–10, 384–5.

great ... the fundametall lawes (as they are termed) of both kingdomes and Crownes doe well agree. In other lawes of government they hold good conformities, as having heretofore bin under one scepter; but now by long severance the lawes of either nation are like a shooe worne long upon one foote, and thereby made rather unseemely than unserviceable for the other ... these lawes ... are divers but not contrarie."[73] Nevertheless, English and Scots laws indisputably treated citizens of the neighboring country as strangers, and also, in many cases, enemies; therefore, the task, as James himself averred, was one of making borders disappear. As a start, what were termed "hostile laws" needed to be removed. Furthermore, even if "all laws, customs and treaties of borders between Scotland and England" were to "be in all time coming abrogated and abolished," the Union project was not merely a negative one of removing hostile laws.[74] Positively, the Borders of Northumberland, Cumberland, Westmoreland, Durham, Roxburgh, Selkirk, Peebles, Dumfries, Kirkcudbright, Annandale, and the maritime region of the Solway Firth and the riverine Tweed, would have to be reinscribed as the common, vital geographic center of a new Britain rather than the independent, ungovernable, and unruly extremities of Scotland and England. James even sought to re-Christen the Borders as the "Middle Shires." "Those which were the Borders ... [were] now [to] become the Navell or unbilick of both Kingdomes, planted and peopled with Civilitie and riches," James told Parliament.[75] In terms that can help shed light on Shakespeare's treatment of a figure like Autolycus, Unionist writers imagined a time when "the borderer theiff and traitour, the seditious and uickit persoun" might finally be "redicited to peace and obedience, having na bak dure for his refuge."[76] Definitions of crimes and criminal procedures also required harmonization for "perfect union." Procedures for "remanding" accused criminals ascended the parliamentary agenda. "If an Englishman doth offend in Scotland and returneth into England (not taken in fresh suit) what course shalbe taken with him and so via versa," politicians wondered?[77] Although Union skeptics feared that proposed procedures amounted to encroachments on national sovereignty, its advocates argued that remanding "hath congruitie with the Lawe of Nacions, as it is in Artois and Picardy which are only in league and contract with other, and there the offendors are transmitted."[78] If remanding was fitting even when territories were "several," it would be even more appropriate where there was "One Fountain of Justice."[79]

While Union advocates like Hayward tried to downplay conflicts of laws, the difficult-to-deny differences were insuperable for Union skeptics like Sir Roger

---

[73] Hayward, *A Treatise of Union of the Two Realmes of England and Scotland*, 14.

[74] *Act Regarding the Union of Scotland and England*, 1607, <http://www.rps.ac.uk/trans/1607/3/12>.

[75] James VI and I, *King James VI and I: Political Writings*, ed. Johann P. Sommerville (Cambridge: Cambridge University Press, 1995), 169.

[76] Russell, "A Treatise of The Happie and Blissed Unioun," 116–17; Hamilton, "The Winter's Tale and the Language of Union, 1604–1610."

[77] Robert Bowyer, *The Parliamentary Diary of Robert Bowyer, 1606–1607*, ed. David Harris Willson (Minneapolis, MN: University of Minnesota Press, 1931), 301.

[78] Bowyer, *The Parliamentary Diary of Robert Bowyer, 1606–1607*, 301.

[79] "House of Commons Journal Volume 1: 28 May 1607 (2nd Scribe)," *Journal of the House of Commons: Volume 1*, June 22, 2003, <http://www.british-history.ac.uk/report.aspx?compid=8954>.

Owen, who were deeply sensitive to questions like whether juries would follow the English custom of twelve members or the Scots custom of fifteen. The proposed mixing with Scottish laws opened Englishmen to threats from a criminal procedure system Owen cast as more arbitrary and severe than that of England's.[80] In Scotland, there was no presenting grand jury, prisoners could not peremptorily challenge jurors, accessories to crimes could be tried before principals, and there was no benefit of clergy.[81] All of these, it was argued, were unfavorable to those accused of crimes, though there were distinct benefits for the accused in the Scottish system as well, particularly in that poor prisoners were furnished with advocates to plead for them and accused criminals could challenge the judge. In a Sicily that resembles England in its wealth and sophistication, it is possible to see Leontes' trial of Hermione as characterized by precisely the lack of such judicial protections.

Beyond questions of criminal procedure and crimes unknown to English law such as "murder under trust," naturalization laws also differed. In England, only children born after someone had been naturalized could succeed. Scotland retroactively naturalized those born prior to their parents' naturalization. How close to his death a man could make a valid will varied according to the two laws. As Thomas Craig observed, "In England a man may even on his death-bed devise by will property acquired by himself, whereas in Scotland that course is not lawful: for a will executed at such a time is open to grave suspicion of influence, nor is it proper that the rights of the heirs should be endangered by such a practice."[82] In the context of such antinomies, removing *The Winter's Tale* from the identifiable jurisdictions of England and Scotland offered opportunities to open legal fact to legal philosophy, legislation to jurisprudence, common law to the laws of nature and nations.

It remains important to remember that such comparativizing abstraction was already to tilt the field toward the pro-Union position as the critical possibilities of drama push Shakespeare's play from one concerned exclusively with local law to the rational "mixing" of the law of nations. Craig's argument for union, for example, insisted that "legal causes be determined...without appeal from the courts of one kingdom to those of the other, a procedure intolerable to both," and the principles by which English and Scottish law could be harmonized were to be found in Roman law's law of nature and law of nations. Craig wrote of the law of nations as "that which ought chiefly to be observed after the reasoning and understanding of the just and the good naturally inborn in us. Whatever all nations observed ought to prevail among us whenever not against civil or municipal law."[83] In England too, pro-Union voices associated with the community of civilians and canonists

[80] Brian Levack, "English Law, Scots Law and the Union, 1603–1707," in *Law-Making and Law-Makers in British History*, ed. A. Harding (London: Royal Historical Society, 1980), 113; Brian Levack, "The Proposed Union of English Law and Scots Law in the Seventeenth Century," *Juridical Review* 20 (1975): 97–115.

[81] "House of Commons Journal Volume 1: 28 May 1607 (2nd Scribe)," *Journal of the House of Commons: Volume 1*, June 22, 2003, <http://www.british-history.ac.uk/report.aspx?compid=8954>.

[82] Thomas Craig, *De Unione Regnorum Britanniae Tractatus* (Edinburgh: Scottish History Society, 1909), 316. A note on p. 317 defines deathbed wills as those made "during a sickness which ended fatally within sixty days of the date of the deed."

[83] Quoted in Cairns, "Scottish Law, Scottish Lawyers and the Status of the Union," 254.

centered at Doctors Commons pointed out that the law of nations and the *ius commune* could potentially provide the formal legal grounds needed for union.[84] England's Admiralty and Ecclesiastical courts, the civilians emphasized, followed the *ius commune*, and there was nothing in the nature of the Chancery courts of conscience and equity that made such courts hostile to it. Since the *ius commune* was used in diplomacy and church courts, this meant that however limited its influence was in comparison to common law, it was also valued in uncommonly powerful quarters. We can recall Gentili's argument, quoted in Chapter 3, that "As everyone submits to the civil law, especially in these maritime questions, as to a sort of law of nations, everyone will be judged according to that law to his entire satisfaction."[85] The only law taught in Oxford or Cambridge, civil law was also far more familiar to the Scottish king than was common law. As James told Parliament in 1607, "I can professe no great knowledge [of common law], but in the Civill law...I am a little better versed."[86] In the light of the potential union, the powerful common law took on a new and strange provinciality. It was not common law but civil law that was "the point of Coniunction of Nations," the very "Law of Nations," in James' view.[87] Civil law became to English jurisprudence what the Borders were to Britain, rapidly repositioned from the margins to the center with the changed perspective afforded by the prospect of Union. Also like the Borders, it could be the "Navell or unbilick of both Kingdomes." Indeed, as a play like *Cymbeline* suggests especially strongly, Roman law was where James and other supporters hoped grounds for union might be found.[88] To Scottish lawyers, natural law and the law of nations were reasons to be open to mixing their law with English law. English opponents of the Union, especially those with livelihoods tied to common law, feared much the same.

Since I have been arguing that such legal questions had significant if underappreciated formal dimensions, I note that both recur in the famous pastoral exchange between Perdita and the disguised Polixenes about gillyvors as "nature's bastards" (4.4.82–83). Set amidst the Bohemian sheep-shearing festival, the dialogue cut across a wide range of Renaissance concerns, but two were unavoidably topical in 1611: first, the relation between the laws of nature and of nations, which had erupted in the debates over the Union and the *postnati*; and second, the relation of tragicomedy to its purported parents of tragedy and comedy. If these seem like separate concerns, however, they quickly resolve into one, for tragicomedy itself crucially theorized

[84] Alain Wijffels, "A British Ius Commune? A Debate on the Union of the Laws of Scotland and England during the First Years of James VI/I's English Reign," *Edinburgh Law Review* 6 (2002): 315–55.

[85] Alberico Gentili, *Hispanicae Advocationis Libri Duo*, trans. Frank Frost Abbott (New York: Oxford University Press, 1921), 2.102.

[86] *King James VI and I: Political Writings*, 171.

[87] *King James VI and I: Political Writings*, 171. Even before James, his mother Mary Queen of Scots and her defenders had grounded Mary's legitimacy in the law of nations. See Constance Jordan, "Woman's Rule in Sixteenth-Century British Political Thought," *Renaissance Quarterly* 40, no. 3 (1987): 421–51.

[88] Marcus, *Puzzling Shakespeare*, 136; Willy Maley, "Postcolonial Shakespeare: British Identity Formation and Cymbeline," in *Shakespeare's Late Plays: New Readings*, ed. Jennifer Richards and James Knowles (Edinburgh: Edinburgh University Press, 1999), 145–57.

the legitimacy of contingent, historical additions to the natural laws of poetry while arguments about Union and the *postnati* took place in a tragicomic register.

In the case of the *postnati*, Bacon advanced a view in which "all men in the world are naturalized one towards another" by the law of nature, it being only the human art of the law of nations and civil law that limited the affective brotherhood of man by setting the boundaries of the city.[89] Bacon's appeal to an historically prior nature can be seen as a qualified affirmation of comic kindness against heroic genres' metaphysics of enmity. Deploying Ulpian's tripartite division among the law of nature, the law of nations (which Bacon called "national laws") and civil law, Bacon argued that Robert Calvin and the other *postnati* should not be barred from inheriting property in England as though they were "bastards" because,

> It was civil and national laws [i.e., the law of nations] that brought in these words and differences of 'civis' and 'exterus,' alien and native. And therefore because they [i.e., civil law and the law of nations] tend to abridge the law of nature, the law favoureth not them, but takes them strictly; even as our law [common law] hath an excellent rule, that customs of towns and boroughs shall be taken and construed strictly and precisely, because they do abridge and derogate from the law of the land.[90]

Bacon's appeal to an unabridged legal order follows a logic similar to Plautine comedies where natural phenomena like tempests conditionally return abandoned property to the natural community of the seas. But even if the *postnati* in James' wake in effect became *res nullius* like so much Plautine *flotsam* and *jetsam*, the *-ization* of Bacon's "naturalization" marks a troubled analogy with natural phenomena understood to release things from the institutions of *meum* and *tuum*. Naturalization implied mutability and change, a contingent order of history and nations doing the naturalizing. The category of the "natural subject" on which Bacon founded his argument, then, was no easier to arrive at than the category of "natural property," for subjection and property were commonly understood not as expressions of nature, but as contingent remedies devised by temporally situated men. Was "England" also natural? To ask that question of an obviously historical artifact is to see what made Bacon's "natural subject" a tragicomic hybrid. Bacon did not argue, after all, that the *antenati* were themselves naturalized in England.[91] Once "brought in," *civis* and *exterus* could not be returned to Pandora's box. Bacon therefore joined comedy and tragedy, using comedy's community of nature to mend, though not extinguish, the tragic logic of exclusion.

In the gillyvor exchange, Polixenes advises Perdita that there "is an art / Which does mend nature—change it rather—but / The art itself is nature" (4.4.95–97). The lines thread much the same needle as Bacon's "natural subject," drawing historical processes under the "law … of great nature." With offspring in the play

---

[89] "The Case of the Postnati, or of the Union of the Realm of Scotland with England," 594.

[90] "The Case of the Postnati, or of the Union of the Realm of Scotland with England," 595. McEachern, I think, conflates "civil and national laws" in her reading of this passage in McEachern, *The Poetics of English Nationhood, 1590–1612*, 155.

[91] Polly J. Price, "Natural Law and Birthright Citizenship in Calvin's Case (1608)," *Yale Journal of Law & the Humanities* 9 (1997): esp. 108–18.

potentially representing a kind of natural property, the debatable lands of repro-
ductive biology—the gillyvors, Perdita, even briefly Mamillius ("Mamillius, / Art
thou my boy?")—help Shakespeare theorize the border regions between nature
and nations where potentially strange hybrid categories like natural property and
natural subjection might reside (1.2.118–119).

The gillyvors exchange also restages early modern debates over tragicomedy
itself, even if the debates over tragicomedy were themselves jurisprudentially laden.
Guarini's controversial defense of tragicomedy distinguished between poetic "rules
of nature…which must always be obeyed" and more contingent "secondary
rules."[92] The "poetic mixtures" of tragicomedy followed from "the skill of the
worker," and as such added to nature without altering or violating its fundamental
laws.[93] Tragicomedy thus had one foot in the contingent history of inventions, and
the other in the enduring order of nature.[94]

Like the grafted gillyvor, tragicomedy was legitimate—no "bastard"—but its
origins in human history meant even proponents had difficulty clearing the per-
ception that the form had possibly been conceived in error or sin—that it was
corrupted, or at least corruptible. Guarini wrote anxiously that "poetry mingled of
tragic and comic parts is composed not merely according to the universal rules of
Aristotle, but is so like one of the particular species he mentions that tragicomedy
is not merely its daughter, as we have proved, but its legitimate daughter."[95]

The sense in which the gillyvor and tragicomedy both obeyed natural precepts
even though they emerged in the course of human events made them similar to
certain versions of the law of nations, most particularly the law of nations as used
in the Union debates, which was sometimes strategically lax about differentiating
the law of nations from the historical "process" of natural law. In his work of tragicomic jurisprudence, *A Brief Discourse Touching the Happy Union of the Kingdoms
of England and Scotland*, Bacon emphasized, like Polixenes and *The Winter's Tale*
more broadly, how time blurred the boundaries between nature and art. Works of
art and works of nature each contributed to the kind of union Bacon advocated, as
man's art-work of *compositio* would be perfected by the natural work (*opus naturae*)
of time. Time, so central to the re-emerging harmony of *The Winter's Tale*, was well
understood to be both a legal phenomenon and a natural one. Few in the Union
debates, for instance, could fail to notice the gap of nearly three winter months
between the beginning of the Scottish year on 1 January and the beginning of the
English year on 25 March.[96] The first chapter of William Fulbecke's *Pandectes of*

---

[92] Matthew Treherne, "The Difficult Emergence of Pastoral Tragicomedy: Guarini's Il Pastor Fido
and Its Critical Reception in Italy, 1586–1601," in *Early Modern Tragicomedy*, ed. Subha Mukherji and
Raphael Lyne (Woodbridge: D. S. Brewer, 2007), 39.

[93] Guarini, "The Compendium of Tragicomic Poetry," 510.

[94] On the Renaissance histories of inventions at the thresholds of art and nature, see Anthony
Grafton, *Worlds Made by Words: Scholarship and Community in the Modern West* (Cambridge, MA:
Harvard University Press, 2009), 79–97.

[95] Guarini, "The Compendium of Tragicomic Poetry," 527.

[96] Robert Poole, *Time's Alteration: Calendar Reform in Early Modern England* (London: UCL Press,
1998), 72; G. J. Whitrow, *Time in History: The Evolution of Our General Awareness of Time and Temporal Perspective* (Oxford: Oxford University Press, 1988), 119.

the Law of Nations (1602), dedicated entirely to time, described differing legal definitions of years, seasons, civil days, and natural days, and not without first quoting the maxim introducing this chapter, "Time in regarde of Eternitie, is but a winters day."[97] For Bacon and the Union, it was "the duty of man to make a fit application of bodies together, but the perfect fermentation and incorporation of them must be left to Time and Nature." He wrote, "[u]nnatural hasting thereof doth disturb the work, and not dispatch it. So we see, after the graft is put into the stock and bound, it must be left to Nature and Time to make that *continuum*, which was at first but *contiguum*."[98] Union was therefore a product of nature *and* art, or as Polixenes says, nature's art.

In Act 3, Scene 3 playful legal connotations—mostly associated with Roman law's language of the *ius commune*—freight the scene, beginning in the first exchange. Recall Dickens' observation that civil law had an "ancient monopoly in suits about people's wills and people's marriage, and disputes among ships and boats."[99] The useful albeit incomplete collection of probate, marriages, and Admiralty law helps us to read the *ius commune* in Shakespeare's Coast of Bohemia, which Shakespeare composes as a site made especially legible by the legal vocabulary of civil law. "Thou art perfect then our ship hath touched upon / The deserts of Bohemia?" Antigonus asks the unnamed Mariner (3.3.1–2). "Ay, my lord, and fear / We have landed in ill time. The skies look grimly / And threaten present blusters. In my conscience, / The heavens with that we have in hand are angry, and frown upon's" (3.3.2–6). Antigonus replies, "Their sacred wills be done" (3.2.6). Even as Antigonus' death looms, readers and theatergoers might hear in the exchange new notes of playfulness around the terms of contract beyond the seas, equity courts ("conscience"), and probate ("sacred wills"). What the scene makes available, then, is a kind of legal prolepsis that anticipates the more obvious turn to comedy announced by the bear later in the scene. Fundamentally, the law of nations—seen in Lord Chancellor Ellesmere's sense as the "most universall and generall Lawe in the world"—enables the transition from tragedy to comedy, and is the constituting matter for Shakespeare's new generic form.[100] Insofar as the formal transformation appears to be deliberately constructed out of the *ius commune*'s mediating *topoi* and language, then, it becomes possible to see the extent to which genre-like law could be co-partner to the constitution of the Union.[101]

Shakespeare, I contend, uses the language of *ius commune* in Act 3 to prime Jacobean audiences for a less localized legal self-consciousness, much as he uses

---

[97] Fulbecke, *The Pandectes of the Law of Nations*, 1. Fulbecke attributes the maxim to the Roman grammarian Censorinus.

[98] Francis Bacon, "A Brief Discourse Touching the Happy Union of the Kingdoms of England and Scotland," in *The Works of Francis Bacon*, ed. James Spedding, vol. 10 (London: Longman, 1861), 98. Spedding prints "grift" where Bacon clearly means "graft."

[99] Charles Dickens, *David Copperfield*, ed. Jeremy Tambling (New York: Penguin, 2004), 352.

[100] Knafla, *Law and Politics in Jacobean England*, 226.

[101] Knafla, *Law and Politics in Jacobean England*, 226. I use mediating here in the sense elaborated in Bruno Latour, *Reassembling the Social: An Introduction to Actor-Network-Theory* (Oxford: Oxford University Press, 2005), 37–42, 58–62, 232–41.

sexual puns and hints of pregnancy to prime the view of Perdita as Polixenes' potential child. Antigonus' death—not unlike the scene's interest in legitimacy and bastardy—invites intense speculation about law and place, creating its own debatable lands. When the Clown tells the Old Shepherd, "I'll go see if the bear be gone from the gentleman, and how much he hath eate...If there be any of him left, I'll bury it," there are serio-comic legal stakes in whether Antigonus has been fully consumed by the bear (3.3.116–119). Civil and canon law were remarkably detailed on what counted as a religious place: in addition to "Temples, Hospitals, [and] Chappels[,]...that is accompted a religious place, in which a mans bodie or head is buried."[102] Nor is it a small matter whether the Coast of Bohemia has now been consecrated as religious property. The legal status of the debatable Coast then, including its availability for appropriation or alienation, could, in another grim pun on "bear," turn on burial.

COMMUNE VINCULUM: BODIES IN PLACE V. COMMON BONDS

The argument I've been making about the play's middle in relation to its generic structure is reinforced at the level of plot. Antigonus' allegiance "[O]ut / Of our dominions," for example, dramatizes a certain kind of belonging capable of traversing the legal boundaries of Sicily. Juxtaposed against a number of the play's other models of belonging—Hermione's purported "treason," Camillo's defection, and, later, Autolycus' predatory non-allegiance—Antigonus' painful and ultimately ruinous choice to abandon the vulnerable child along that infamous Coast of Bohemia exemplifies a kind of entity perhaps more valuable to Leontes than the category of Sicily itself, namely a mobile entity we might call "Sicilian."[103] But so long as "strangeness" is a matter of narrative probability and theatrical affect as well as legal significance, the third act also offers a vision at the level of genre that relates to the questions of allegiance thematized throughout Shakespeare's plot. Do the strange events and debatable geographies of the third act owe their allegiance to *The Winter's Tale*'s tragic beginning or to its comic end? To which—if either—are they stranger? By thinking about the scenes at the center of *The Winter's Tale* as situated between the sovereign poles of tragedy and comedy, it becomes possible to notice how the play reduplicates on the level of genre what it dramatizes at the level of plot. *The Winter's Tale* presents different models of citizenship in characters

---

[102] William Fulbeck, *A Parallele or Conference of the Ciuill Law, the Canon Law, and the Common Law of This Realme of England Wherein the Agreement and Disagreement of These Three Lawes, and the Causes and Reasons of the Said Agreement and Disagreement, Are Opened and Discussed* (London: [Adam Islip for] Thomas Wight, 1601) 11.

[103] For a parallel analysis of allegiance in *The Tempest*, see Elliott Visconsi, "Vinculum Fidei: The Tempest and the Law of Allegiance," *Law and Literature* 20 (2008): 1. In anticipation of the analysis of Grotius and Milton in Chapter 6, I note here that Camillo and Polixenes are briefly cast as a Joseph/Pharaoh pair in the lines: "thou, having made me businesses which none without thee can sufficiently manage" (4.2.13–15).

like Hermione, Camillo, Antigonus, and Autolycus, whose divergent forms of belonging become the templates for a quasi-legal hermeneutics of citizenship by which Shakespeare's potentially "strange" middle is to be incorporated or, alternatively, estranged.

Rather than offering inflexible allegiance to its tragic beginning, what Act 3, Scene 3 accomplishes is the creation of what Francis Bacon called, in his advocacy of the Union, a "new form" of allegiance, capable of transmuting both tragic beginning and comedic end beyond meaningful differences. This is how Shakespeare's much-noted tragicomic self-consciousness in *The Winter's Tale* offers us a somewhat unexpected way to see a highly topical Shakespearean jurisprudence in which justice, like genre, becomes newly malleable, elastic, extensible, and reconfigurable. That *The Winter's Tale* has such a vibrant and distinctly memorable middle— capable of retroactively transforming *The Winter's Tale*'s tragic beginning while at the same time inaugurating a comic conclusion to a play that can never rightly be called a comedy—illustrates how ambitions for the Union cash out at the levels of genre and plot.

If Hermione, Camillo, Antigonus, and Autolycus offer different models of citizenship against which Shakespeare's potentially "strange" Act 3 could be incorporated or, alternatively, estranged, Sidney's famous *Defence of Poesy* had of course offered one of the strongest critiques of modern "mingling." His classicizing Aristotelian approach sought to preserve the "jurisdictions" of tragedy and comedy by railing against composite genres that had elements of each. Sidney's critique of "mongrel tragic-comedy" is rightly seen as based in classical ideas of decorum, but decorum in Sidney's hands also brings with it many of the less-obvious notions of belonging, strangeness, and allegiance discussed in Chapter 3 concerning private international law. For Sidney, tragedy and comedy are in effect sovereign genres whose borders are to be guarded and from which "strangeness" is to be excluded. Sidney complains of modern playwrights,

> all their plays be neither right tragedies, nor right comedies, mingling kings and clowns, not because the matter so carrieth it, but thrust in clowns by head and shoulders, to play a part in majestical matters, with neither decency nor discretion, so as neither the admiration and commiseration, nor the right sportfulness, is by their mongrel tragic-comedy obtained... If we mark [the ancients] well, we shall find, that they never, or very daintily, match hornpipes and funerals. So falleth it out that, having indeed no right comedy, in that comical part of our tragedy, we have nothing but scurrility, unworthy of any chaste ears, or some extreme show of doltishness, indeed fit to lift up loud laughter, and nothing else: where the whole tract of a comedy should be full of delight, as the tragedy should be still maintained in a well-raised admiration.[104]

In insisting on the uniformity of a "whole tract," Sidney couples a terrestrial metaphor—the "tract of a comedy" suggesting a "tract of land"—with the language of

---

[104] Philip Sidney, *An Apology for Poetry, Or, The Defence of Poesy*, ed. Geoffrey Shepherd and R. W. Maslen, 3rd edn. (Manchester: Manchester University Press, 2002), 112.

sovereign, authorial dominium. The result is to extol a kind of authorship, possibly related to Elizabethan legal arguments about Mary, Queen of Scots, characterized by adjudication and exclusion.[105] It is because elements that suggest strangeness— clowns "thrust in," "scurrility," "doltishness," and "loud laughter"—come to resemble disorder in the "tract" that playwrights are enjoined to exclude elements potentially seen as treasonous to the classical genres and to maintain their allegiance to the safer quarters of purer forms.

If we view *The Winter's Tale* in such a way, it's possible to see Shakespeare as staging in Act 3 a contest between the play's anchoring poles of tragedy and comedy for generic sovereignty. To do so without qualification, however, would be to miss important cues in Shakespeare's text. As Paulina says to the irrationally jealous Leontes, "something savours / Of tyranny" in such analysis (2.3.119–120). Indeed, to understand the third act as exclusively a contest between the play's sovereign jurisdictions is to ignore that it is precisely such "whole tract"-thinking that the plot of *The Winter's Tale* associates with tragedy and indeed critiques in the form of Leontes' irrational jealousy. That which Leontes perceives as a contest for Hermione is only a contest according to what Paulina terms Leontes' "weak-hinged fancy" and what Strain calls Leontes' "tyrannical form of historical jurisprudence" (2.3.119).[106] Leontes responds to Paulina's confrontations with renewed recourse to a now well-worn logic of belonging. "On your allegiance, / Out of the chamber with her," is his command to Paulina's husband, Antigonus, which he offers shortly before suggesting that Antigonus too is a "traitor" for "set[ting]" Paulina on (1.3.121–122, 2.3.131). These are symptoms of what Julia Reinhard Lupton refers to in her psychoanalytic reading of Leontes as a sovereign "paranoia [that] contracts and deforms the public sphere of the court itself."[107]

Seen also as a kind of "hermeneutics of suspicion," the tyrannical interpretive mode Leontes deploys was itself topical in the Union debates. While Bacon argued that "abridgements" to the law of nature represented by the law of nations should be interpreted strictly, caviling interpretive minds could also do great damage to the Union, as proponents recognized. Union opponents warned that opportunistic princes might use the occasion of the Union to squirm out of existing treaties with quibbles about names, although the law of nations itself offered alternative standards of interpretation. John Hayward countered, "If any Prince shall use pretence of change in name, as a leap from his contract, whether of confederation or commerce, hee exposeth himselfe thereby both to the hatred and revenge of other Princes, as one that violateth the law of nations."[108] And yet it wasn't just "pretense" that the law of nations disallowed; it was an approach to interpretation

---

[105] On Sidney's involvement in legal debates over the trial of Mary Queen of Scots, see Blair Worden, *The Sound of Virtue: Philip Sidney's Arcadia and Elizabethan Politics* (New Haven, CT: Yale University Press, 1996), 181.

[106] Strain, "*The Winter's Tale* and the Oracle of the Law," 566.

[107] Julia Reinhard Lupton, *Thinking with Shakespeare: Essays on Politics and Life* (Chicago, IL: University of Chicago Press, 2011), 169.

[108] Hayward, *A Treatise of Union of the Two Realmes of England and Scotland*, 43.

characterized by "rigorous or strict termes." Writers on the "law of Nations" such as Baldus and Alciati, Hayward argued,

> do altogether reject scrupulous interpretations, and are not to bee taken, either in rigorous or strict termes, or els in subtill sense of positive law, (under which colour wee doe often erre) but according to the law of Nations… according to plaine and direct meaning, according to right and upright iudgement: that they are farre from all fine fetches and streines, much more from malice and plaine deceit: that they intend no subtletie, but simplicitie, which Baldus saith, is the best interpreter of the law of nations.[109]

Seen alongside the Union politics of geopolitical interpretation, Shakespeare's plot casts grave doubts on the contracting and deforming "fetches and streines" required to keep either scenes or subjects under a single, jealous sovereign allegiance. This is to say that viewing Act 3 as the "hinge" between tragedy and comedy is already to have decided a contested and politicized hermeneutic point, as Paulina's language of "weak-hinged" fancy suggests.

The way in which Shakespeare turned to "new forms" to theorize nature, history, and union meant he shared much with Bacon. Whereas Sidney had criticized the "mingling" of forms, and writers like Russell and the author of *A Treatise About the Union of England and Scotland* analyzed the Union through comedy and tragedy as such, Shakespeare and Bacon stood alongside Guarini as one of those explicitly recuperating "mingling" as authoritative and authorized practice. Bacon redirected the antipathy that followers of Sidney reserved for "mingling" to a different type from which mixed forms were to be distinguished—composite forms. In his *A Brief Discourse Touching the Happy Union of the Kingdoms of England and Scotland*, he wrote, "The difference is excellent which the best observers in nature do take between *compositio* and *mistio*, putting together and mingling: the one being but a conjunction of bodies in place, the other in quality and consent: the one the mother of sedition and alteration, the other of peace and continuance."[110] The "peace and continuance" enabled in Bacon's eyes by mingling and mixed forms was, in his account, scientific wisdom, developed inductively from keen observation of "simple bodies."[111] "We see those three bodies, of Earth, Water, and Oil," he wrote, "when they are joined in a vegetable or a mineral, they are so united, as without great subtlety of art and force of extraction they cannot be separated and reduced into the same simple bodies again."[112] Bacon's highly political science was also forthright about the political instrumentality of new forms. Old forms joined together—composites—would remain grounds for contestation because they retained recognizable objects of earlier loyalties and affections. By contrast, mixed

---

[109] Hayward, *A Treatise of Union of the Two Realmes of England and Scotland*, 43.

[110] Bacon, "A Brief Discourse Touching the Happy Union of the Kingdoms of England and Scotland," 93–4.

[111] Bacon, "A Brief Discourse Touching the Happy Union of the Kingdoms of England and Scotland," 94.

[112] Bacon, "A Brief Discourse Touching the Happy Union of the Kingdoms of England and Scotland," 94.

forms such as those seen in vegetables and minerals outgrew the "simple bodies" of which they were composed: no one looked at an onion and got thirsty, despite its makeup from water; the elements in minerals like gold and silver were so thoroughly mixed that the identities of such minerals transcended their parts. The arguments prefigure the discussion of the gillyvors in *The Winter's Tale* and also recall passages in Justinian's *Institutes* positing "if materials owned by two people are deliberately blended together, the resultant mass becomes the common property of both."[113] Beyond its compatibility with Roman law, Bacon's tragicomic science of mingling was also a jurisgenetive politics of novelty: new, mixed forms did unparalleled work in constituting a durable new politics. This was because "the new form is *commune vinculum* [a common bond], and without that the old forms will be at strife and discord."[114] Bacon's point was to suggest that while composite forms could continue to stoke customary attachments to their elements, new, truly mixed forms both required and developed hitherto impossible attachments.

Seen alongside Guarini's argument for tragicomedy and a text like *The Winter's Tale*, Bacon's *Articles Touching the Union of the Kingdoms* suggests how new literary forms might themselves offer new common bonds for a new Britain. Bacon's thoughtful though sketchy proposals for new legal forms addressed the concrete problem of how to secure new allegiances from the tragic possibilities of discord. Bacon wrote to James, "It may be a good question, whether, as *commune vinculum* of the justice of both nations, your Majesty should not erect some court about your person, in the nature of the Grand Council of France: to which court you might, by way of evocation, draw causes from the ordinary judges of both nations."[115] Blending English and Scots law, the new court would be mixed, not just composite. James' person here stood as the locus for Bacon's key distinction between *compositio* and *mistio*. In proposals to keep the two legal systems separate, Bacon saw the dangers of settling for mere "conjunction of bodies in place." A Britain in which the "ordinary judges of both nations" continued to operate according to English and Scots law without any means to adjudicate between them was one subject to the possibilities of strife. According to Bacon's proposal, by contrast, causes arising in the two nations would not find separate decisions according to the separate laws of the two kingdoms but instead they would "mingle" "about [James'] person," the preposition "about" suggesting vitality and circulation; the verb "draw" figuring a kind of legal-political making equally indebted to art and science.

---

[113] Justinian, *Justinian's Institutes*, trans. Peter Birks and Grant McLeod (Ithaca, NY: Cornell University Press, 1987), 2.1.27. Examples cited include "where two people blend together their wine, or melt together their ingots of silver or of gold. The same applies where the materials are different and their fusion produces a new substance, for instance mead from wine and honey, or electrum from gold and silver. Even if the blend occurs by chance and not by design, the same rule applies where the materials are different and where they are the same."

[114] Bacon, "A Brief Discourse Touching the Happy Union of the Kingdoms of England and Scotland," 94.

[115] Francis Bacon, "Certain Articles or Considerations Touching the Union of the Kingdoms of England and Scotland," in *The Works of Francis Bacon*, ed. James Spedding, Robert Leslie, and Douglas Denon Heath, vol. 10 (London: Longman, 1861), 233.

New forms were paradoxical imaginative endeavors seemingly capable in Bacon's eyes of "the utter and perpetual confounding of those imaginary bounds."[116] A court of justice at Carlisle or Berwick, for instance, could have jurisdiction in both England and Scotland—"with a commission not to proceed precisely or merely according to the laws and customs either of England or Scotland, but mixtly." Here again was the critical distinction between *compositio* and *mistio*; English and Scottish laws would not simply co-exist in this new court, following English law here and Scottish law there, but instead they would be mixed to create something new that could serve as a common bond among the Borderers. "While nature alters the parts after they are united, art alters them before they are joined in order that they may be able to exist together and, though mixed, produce a single form," Guarini had written.[117] Bacon's metaphors similarly illustrated continuities between political art and political science: courts in the "middle shires" were something to "plant and erect"; they were "device[s]" for "healing and consolidating."[118]

HOW LONG IS THE COAST OF BOHEMIA?

In turning to the relation between "the matter of story" and the "matter of the *ius gentium*" in the context of the Union debates, this chapter has offered an analysis of some of the remarkable formal features of *The Winter's Tale*. In my reading, the play argues for a Union less contingent on the mortal bodies of the Stuarts, and it shows how story, "new forms," and the law of nations might be mixed to underpin a more durable union. Insofar as the play's initial relations between Sicilia and Bohemia and Leontes and Polixenes remain vulnerable to the disquieting claims of *meum* and *tuum*, the "new form" of tragicomedy illustrates the transformation over time from international tragedy into a "new form" of nation. Beyond merely illustrating that transformation, it also enacts it. Like the statue of Hermione, which appears at first as a mere representation but is revealed instead as an acting body, Shakespeare's *The Winter's Tale* does what it represents. Shakespeare in *The Winter's Tale* is a playwright whose well-known generic self-consciousness is not only matched by a legal self-consciousness in keeping with his moment, but is also deeply and fundamentally related to it. As Robert Cover writes, "law ... is a bridge from reality to a new world."[119] In the sense that Shakespeare's tragicomedy emerges out of his play's autochthonous legal language, it is like the legal foundation of the Union itself. The Union was a political project premised on the notion that a natural Britain contained within itself the latent legal principles that time

---

[116] Bacon, "Certain Articles or Considerations Touching the Union of the Kingdoms of England and Scotland," 221.

[117] Guarini, "The Compendium of Tragicomic Poetry," 512.

[118] Bacon, "Certain Articles or Considerations Touching the Union of the Kingdoms of England and Scotland," 221; David M. Walker, *A Legal History of Scotland Vol. IV, The Seventeenth Century.* (Edinburgh: T&T Clark, 1996), 33–8.

[119] Cover, "The Folktales of Justice: Tales of Jurisdiction," 187.

could transmute into a flourishing Union. My reading suggests the need to attend to the desolate Coast of Bohemia in the middle of *The Winter's Tale* as a site of borders that gets transformed by language, law, and genre into a newly, richly governed common space.

This argument has implications for various emplotments of the Union story, the Renaissance law of nations, and even for contemporary projects, like the European Union, which require reimagining international law. Bacon and Shakespeare allow us to see ways that narrowly tragic stories may require a few countervailing cautions. Without discounting the worries, it is also true that the Union offers a chance to study a project whose aspirations at least involved developing equitable modes and methods for governing shared spaces and institutions, and for protecting debatable lands and waters from the neglect of indeterminacy. Such attempts to forge common, credible new institutions of justice that were adapted to changing geographic and cultural circumstances can temper ideologically inflected nostalgia. Nor need those attempts be dismissed too readily as proto-imperialism or exclusively be mourned as the homogenization of legal difference—at least as long as we in the present century face environmental and economic challenges of similar or greater significance. "Telling new stories about nature," says Steve Mentz, "necessitates making new choices about generic forms."[120] At its best, the Union project involved aspirations of transforming contested spaces of dearth, violence, and predatory economic actors into a practicable commons.

It is true that the overlapping categories of Union and the law of nations asked for trust in a less-localized legal order. But what made both the Union and the law of nations tragicomic rather than simply tragic for their advocates were the remedies they could provide, even in the context of acknowledged loss. Union found supporters beyond James himself not because James imposed his will and propaganda on an unthinking populous, but because Union offered defensible potential solutions to real problems.

As we have seen, figures like Shakespeare and Bacon assumed that any such transformations would unfold temporally, and insofar as it remained true, as Fulbecke's maxim put it, that "Time in regarde of Eternitie, is but a winters day," that transformation would always have to be considered as a matter of temporal scale.[121] In the north Atlantic archipelago, as in *The Winter's Tale*, whether one saw *continuum* or *contiguum*, union or disunion, *mistio* or *compositio*, depended upon when and from what distance one looked. In contemporary politics, the recent prominence of the Scottish National Party illustrates that the temporal scale needed to evaluate the Union could be even longer still than Shakespeare and Bacon imagined; or alternatively, that the tragedy of Great Britain presently on stage may simply be the Sicilian half of the national comedy of Scotland.[122]

---

[120] Steven Mentz, "Tongues in the Storm: Shakespeare, Ecological Crisis, and the Resources of Genre," in *Ecocritical Shakespeare*, ed. Lynne Bruckner and Dan Brayton (Ashgate, 2011), 159.

[121] Fulbecke, *The Pandectes of the Law of Nations*, 1.

[122] Frye writes, "all comedy contains a potential tragedy within itself." See Northrop Frye, *Narrative Dynamics: Essays on Time, Plot, Closure, and Frames*, ed. Brian Richardson (Columbus, OH: Ohio State University Press, 2002), 106.

In a celebrated essay called "How Long is the Coast of Britain?" (1967) the polymath Benoît Mandelbrot called attention to the apparent curiosity that there is no satisfactory answer to the question of the paper's title. It wasn't that Britain itself was an imaginary construct; it was that everything depends on the scale of measurement. The shorter the unit of measurement, the longer the coast of Britain will be, since each shorter unit of measurement will register more of the peninsulas, crevasses and other topographical features of the coastline that cannot be captured with larger units of measurement.[123] Recalling Hayward's notion that "[H]ow cunningly soever a painter layeth on his colours to make two bordes seeme one, yet if they be not made firme in the ioynts, they will alwaies remaine, and in short time appeare to be two," we can see that *The Winter's Tale* offers a similar lesson about scale, notwithstanding Shakespeare's hope that Britain would in time appear as a harmonious unity. Even with the 1707 Treaty of the Union, there occurred no union of English and Scottish private laws. No new court at Berwick was introduced. So, while *The Winter's Tale* and the law of nations together offered ways to think about Union and to imagine new geopolitical forms, in today's Britain, as in *The Winter's Tale*, it still remains possible—at this point in time, from this distance—to see the join.[124]

---

[123] For another use of Mandelbrot's essay in literary studies, see Wai-chee Dimock, *Through Other Continents: American Literature across Deep Time* (Princeton, NJ: Princeton University Press, 2006), 76–7.

[124] Hayward, *A Treatise of Union of the Two Realmes of England and Scotland*, 9.

5

From Imperial History to International Law

Thucydides, Hobbes, and the Law of Nations

> The first page of Thucydides, as Hume puts it, is the only beginning of all true history.
>
> Kant, *Idea for a Universal History with a Cosmopolitan Purpose*[1]

In *Pericles*, Shakespeare finds the names of a number of his characters in Plutarch and Sidney, but passages from the Greek historian Thucydides, narrating some of the most intractable problems of maritime alliance and colonial administration, may lurk behind Shakespeare's locale of Mytilene and the character of "savage Cleon" (21.202).[2] Shakespeare's allusions to Mytilene and Cleon point toward some of the most morally dubious events of Greek imperial history. Cleon in Book III of Thucydides powerfully exhorts the Athenian assembly to execute the subjects of their former client city in response to Mytilene's revolt from under Athenian dominion, a response subsequently deemed unnecessarily brutal by the Athenian assembly. Cleon's brutality in Thucydides follows from his unwillingness to grant that the Mytileneans had a lawful right to revolt. "If these have justly revolted," Cleon admonished those of his compatriots proposing moderation, "you must unjustly have had dominion over them."[3]

When, in the early modern period, "the waves ruled Britannia," the examples of Greek maritime empire became standards against which British rights and

[1] Immanuel Kant, *Political Writings*, ed. Hans Siegbert Reiss, trans. Hugh Nisbet, 2nd edn. (Cambridge: Cambridge University Press, 1991), 52.

[2] Arthur F. Kinney, "Sir Philip Sidney and the Uses of History," in *The Historical Renaissance: New Essays on Tudor and Stuart Literature and Culture*, ed. Heather Dubrow and Richard Strier (Chicago, IL: University of Chicago Press, 1988), 293–314; Simon Palfrey, *Late Shakespeare: A New World of Words* (Oxford: Oxford University Press, 1997), 52–6.

[3] David Grene, ed., *The Peloponnesian War: The Complete Thomas Hobbes Translation*, trans. Thomas Hobbes (Chicago, IL: University of Chicago Press, 1989), 179. I quote in this chapter both from Grene's edition and from Hobbes' original 1629 (really 1628) edition, the latter of which prints marginal notes by Hobbes not included in Grene. To distinguish the two, I cite Hobbes' seventeenth-century edition as *Eight Bookes of the Peloponesian Warres*. Hobbes later defined war "not as actual fighting; but…the known disposition thereto"; See Thomas Hobbes, *Leviathan*, ed. C. B. MacPherson (Harmondsworth: Penguin Classics, 1968), 186. Quotations from *Leviathan* are from MacPherson's edition unless otherwise noted.

obligations in the world could be measured.[4] "In that [earlier] age almost every city... was a distinct commonwealth," Thomas Hobbes tells readers in his 1628 translation of Thucydides, the text at the center of this chapter.[5] Cleon's ferocity prompted Hobbes to tar Cleon in a marginal note as the "most popular and most violent" of Athenians.[6] Cleon's insistence on punishing the Mytileneans with death had the capacity to goad English Renaissance readers into contemplating the darkest implications of imperial enterprises. No reader could encounter Cleon without asking, starkly, what was "just" dominion over another people, and to what lengths—moral, geographical, financial—might a commonwealth go in its preservation?

At a general level, classical international histories like Thucydides' *History of the Peloponnesian War* provoked many of the same challenges concerning history, custom, and exemplarity in the law of nations as did texts discussed earlier by Homer, Vergil, and Plautus. Most readers encountering Cleon's bloody-mindedness in the wars of the fifth century BCE had already encountered Homer's Achilles, for instance, desecrating Hector's corpse. The difficulties of moral valuation and judgment were indeed kindred. But the experience of history in the sixteenth and seventeenth centuries had slowly been shifting. It was in the mid-seventeenth century that Christians, according to Daniel Shore, began to ask not "What *did* Jesus do?" but "What *would* Jesus do?" The modal shift, Shore argues, bespoke a new appreciation of "discontinuity between past and present."[7] This was a far cry from Petrarch writing to Cicero in the present tense. Whereas early humanists had turned to Greek and Roman history to find examples to emulate—*historia magistra vitae*—later humanists, many influenced by the so-called *mos gallicus* school of juridical philology, stumbled over the challenges of accommodating historical particularities to present needs.[8] In *Henry V* (1599), Shakespeare satirizes an earlier generation that had cheerfully collapsed historical differences, giving audiences the laughable character of Fluellen who finds in Henry a new Alexander the Great on the grounds that salmon swam in both of their native rivers.[9]

---

[4] Jonathan Scott, *When the Waves Ruled Britannia: Geography and Political Identities, 1500–1800* (Cambridge; New York: Cambridge University Press, 2011); Lauren Benton, *A Search for Sovereignty: Law and Geography in European Empires, 1400–1900* (Cambridge: Cambridge University Press, 2009); David Armitage, *Foundations of Modern International Thought* (Cambridge: Cambridge University Press, 2012). I have been influenced as well by Jonathan Scott, "Maritime Orientalism, or the Political Theory of Water," *History of Political Thought* 35, no. 1 (2014): 70–90, generously shared with me by the author before publication.

[5] Grene, *The Peloponnesian War: The Complete Thomas Hobbes Translation*, xxiii.

[6] Thomas Hobbes, trans., *Eight Bookes of the Peloponnesian Warre* (London, 1629), 163.

[7] Daniel Shore, "WWJD? The Genealogy of a Syntactic Form," *Critical Inquiry* 37, no. 1 (2010): 17.

[8] Anthony Grafton, *What Was History?: The Art of History in Early Modern Europe* (Cambridge: Cambridge University Press, 2007), 62–122; Donald R. Kelley, *Foundations of Modern Historical Scholarship: Language, Law, and History in the French Renaissance* (New York: Columbia University Press, 1970); Donald R. Kelley, "Law," in *The Cambridge History of Political Thought, 1450–1700* (Cambridge: Cambridge University Press, 1991), 66–94; Reinhart Koselleck, "Historia Magistra Vitae: The Dissolution of the Topos into the Perspective of a Modernized Historical Process," in *Futures Past: On the Semantics of Historical Time*, trans. Keith Tribe (New York: Columbia University Press, 2004), 26–42.

[9] David Quint, "'Alexander the Pig': Shakespeare on History and Poetry," *Boundary 2* 10, no. 3 (1982): 49–67.

Increasingly, history came to be valued less for stable prescriptions for action or what Fluellen calls "figures in all things" than for its answers to questions of sequence and chronology (4.7.26). While historical figures like Cleon still elicited moral judgments, histories more and more served cartographic ends: they helped better map the river of time.[10] Europeans' sense of their chronological place in history had of course been radically destabilized by vibrant travel, commerce, and, especially, the discovery of peoples in the new world.[11] While efforts at historical chronology could help steady newly wobbly European self-conceptions, interpretive and philological activities associated with rigorously mapping time also had formidable legal stakes. According to Bacon's *Aphorismi*, a text that Hobbes knew and almost certainly drew from, "the fountains of natural equity...flow[ed into]...the infinite variety of laws which individual legal systems have chosen for themselves."[12] Removed from the awkwardly ahistorical logic of historical imitation, international histories written by Greeks and Romans came to be re-situated slightly downstream in the "flow" of history, a bit removed from original justice on one side and but not yet within the inimitable play of municipal circumstance and custom. The new emphasis on facts—treaties, constitutions, delegations, customs of war—hardly displaced concern with norms. Loosening the tie between past events and imitation meant instead that international histories like Thucydides could now help better identify what many called the secondary law of nations and Bacon termed the *jure gentium minore*.

We have been concerned throughout this book in several ways with the interaction of texts, legal precepts, and topical circumstances. Texts and events, as we have seen, stirred legal and political thought, just as thinkers of the law of nations influenced literary texts and events. When we turn in the next chapters to Grotius' and Milton's works based on scriptural themes, we will note the ambiguously legislative role of scripture in the law of nations. The case of Hobbes' translation of Thucydides deepens earlier analyses and prepares the way for later discussions in several ways. In particular, Hobbes' Thucydides permits the exploration of productive tensions over secular international history in the early modern law of nations.

---

[10] Daniel Rosenberg and Anthony Grafton, *Cartographies of Time: A History of the Timeline* (New York: Princeton Architectural Press, 2010).

[11] Ayesha Ramachandran, "A War of Worlds: Becoming 'Early Modern' and the Challenge of Comparison," in *Comparative Early Modernities, 1100–1800*, ed. David Porter (New York: Palgrave Macmillan, 2012), 15–46; Sanjay Subrahmanyam, "On World Historians in the Sixteenth Century," *Representations* 91, no. 1 (2005): 26–57; Anthony Pagden, *The Fall of Natural Man: The American Indian and the Origins of Comparative Ethnology* (Cambridge: Cambridge University Press, 1982); S. F. Ng, "Global Renaissance: Alexander the Great and Early Modern Classicism from the British Isles to the Malay Archipelago," *Comparative Literature* 58, no. 4 (January 2006): 293–312; Jyotsna G. Singh, ed., *A Companion to the Global Renaissance: English Literature and Culture in the Era of Expansion* (Chichester: John Wiley and Sons, 2009).

[12] Francis Bacon, "Aphorismi de Jure Gentium Majore Sive de Fontibus Justiciae et Juris," in *The Making of the Instauration: Science, Politics, and Law in the Career of Francis Bacon*, ed. and trans. Mark S. Neustadt (Ph.D. dissertation, The Johns Hopkins University, 1987), 273; Andrew Huxley, "The *Aphorismi* and a *Discourse of Laws*: Bacon, Cavendish, and Hobbes 1615–1620," *The Historical Journal* 47, no. 2 (June 1, 2004): 399–412; Thomas Hobbes, Noel Reynolds, and Arlene Saxonhouse, *Three Discourses: A Critical Modern Edition of Newly Identified Work of the Young Hobbes* (Chicago, IL: University of Chicago Press, 1995).

Against the grain of much scholarship on Hobbes, both within and outside the history of international law, I wish to frame Hobbes himself as a kind of historian of the law of nations, and in so doing purposefully elevate the oft-overlooked activity of translating to the higher status of history writing. Hobbes was a thinker extremely nervous about ostentatious wit who found himself in the awkward position of having provocative things to say.[13] Analysis of Hobbes' Thucydides highlights translation as a partial solution to this problem and shows how Hobbes' translation draws in history and the law of nations.

In my reading, Hobbes' Thucydides illustrates the tension between historical custom as an evidentiary source of law, in which history is made legislative by deep strains of antiquarianism and contextualism, and history as a rhetorical storehouse, a locus—and one of many—to which disputants turned in topical controversies for authorized ideological allies. Broadly, my argument is that Hobbes achieves the latter by taking the *persona* of the former. Of early modern antiquarianism, Peter N. Miller writes, "there could be no Hayden White," and therein lay its appeal.[14] Lest law be simply the arbitrary will of self-interested actors, it needed a "pure" history, one perceived as uncontaminated by pique and prejudice. It needed objective inquirers, faithful servants of positive facts. The stuff of advocates and partisans, of embodied rhetorical actors with subjective passions and interests, could not be made law. Hobbes makes the crucial distinction in his "Life of Thucydides" when he quotes Cicero's *De Oratore* to say, "What great rhetorician ever borrowed any thing of Thucydides? Yet all men praise him, I confess it, as a wise, severe, grave relator of things done: not for a pleader of causes at the bar, but a reporter of war in history."[15] What makes the distinction illustrative of Hobbes' project is that it helped keep Thucydides safe for the present, to preserve his binding force. I contend that whereas Shakespeare in *Pericles, The Tempest*, and *The Winter's Tale*, foregrounds the artistic processes of making, Hobbes—himself deeply interested in theater—attempts to turn history into law by performing witty rhetorical agency as modest translation. The minimalist law of nations that results is a law of nations custom made for empires.

In international law's recent "historiographical turn," little of the voluminous scholarship on Hobbes prepares us to think about Hobbes, translating Thucydides with one foot in the past and one foot in the present, as a kind of historian of the law of nations.[16] Hobbes in most scholarship is a major but Janus-faced figure. Somehow at once both early modern international law's chief spokesman and also its sharpest detractor, Hobbes, for some interpreters, is the theorist of sovereignty responsible for justifying the state-centric "Westphalian" order of international

[13] Julie E. Cooper, "Vainglory, Modesty, and Political Agency in the Political Theory of Thomas Hobbes," *The Review of Politics* 72, no. 2 (2010): 241–69; Victoria Kahn, *Wayward Contracts: The Crisis of Political Obligation in England, 1640–1674* (Princeton, NJ: Princeton University Press, 2004).

[14] Peter N. Miller, "Major Trends in European Antiquarianism, from Petrarch to Peiresc," in *The Oxford History of Historical Writing*, ed. José Rabasa, Masayuki Sato, Edoardo Tortarolo, and Daniel Woolf, vol. 3: *1400–1800* (Oxford: Oxford University Press, 2011), 246.

[15] Grene, *The Peloponnesian War: The Complete Thomas Hobbes Translation*, 585.

[16] George Rodrigo Bandeira Galindo, "Martti Koskenniemi and the Historiographical Turn in International Law," *European Journal of International Law* 16, no. 3 (2005): 539–59.

law that would characterize international history until the twentieth century. For others, Hobbes, the arch-denialist, is precisely the thinker most hostile to the idea of law between states at all.

The case of Hobbes' Thucydides translation—considered *as* a translation—allows us to approach Hobbes from possibly more productive new angles, not least because it was completed prior to Hobbes' best-known works. What if, as the modern international law theorist Philip Allott argues about how our stories about international history influence contemporary relations among states, "We tend to become what we think we have been"?[17] If the question's reflexivity seems distinctly postmodern, worrisomely turning the stable lessons of history into a social instrument or a funhouse mirror, it may be salutary to recall that by the mid-seventeenth century Hobbes himself had already written the following: "Of our conceptions of the past, we make a future."[18] For Hobbes, as for Allott, the *poiesis* or making of the future remained inseparable from present perceptions of human history.

The fact that the first publication to which Hobbes gave his name was a classical translation is often noted by Hobbes scholars but rarely considered with the care devoted to later works such as *Leviathan*.[19] For many years, orthodoxy held that Hobbes started his brilliant philosophical career with a humanistic period before he encountered the Euclidean geometry that would occasion his turn from humanism to "political science"—an *anagnorisis* variously construed as comic or tragic, depending on the critic. Recent scholarship has rightly questioned such narratives, noting, for instance, that Hobbes late in his life wrote a verse autobiography and an anticlerical poem in Latin and translated Homer's epics from the Greek. Through the work of scholars like Sheldon Wolin, Quentin Skinner, Paul Davis, Victoria Kahn, Patricia Springborg, and Eric Nelson, Hobbes, we might say, has now become a kind of epic humanist, one who mobilized the full linguistic armory of humanism throughout a lifetime of intellectual campaign.[20] Hobbes' Restoration

---

[17] Philip Allott, *The Health of Nations: Society and Law Beyond the State* (New York: Cambridge University Press, 2002), 264.

[18] Thomas Hobbes, *The Elements of Law, Natural and Politic: Part I, Human Nature, Part II, De Corpore Politico; with Three Lives*, ed. J. C. A. Gaskin (Oxford: Oxford University Press, 2008), 32.

[19] But see William R. Lund, "The Use and Abuse of the Past: Hobbes on the Study of History," *Hobbes Studies* 5, no. 1 (January 1, 1992): 3–22; Robin Sowerby, "Thomas Hobbes's Translation of Thucydides," *Translation & Literature* 7, no. 2 (1998): 147–69; David Norbrook, *Writing the English Republic: Poetry, Rhetoric and Politics, 1627–1660* (Cambridge: Cambridge University Press, 1999), 59–92; Todd Butler, "Image, Rhetoric, and Politics in the Early Thomas Hobbes," *Journal of the History of Ideas* 67, no. 3 (2006): 465–87. Depending upon whether portions of the anonymous *Horae Subsecivae* (1620) are accepted as Hobbes', the Thucydides translation may in fact be Hobbes' first published work.

[20] Sheldon S. Wolin, *Hobbes and the Epic Tradition of Political Theory* (Los Angeles: William Andrews Clark Memorial Library, University of California, 1970); Quentin Skinner, *Reason and Rhetoric in the Philosophy of Thomas Hobbes* (Cambridge: Cambridge University Press, 1996); Eric Nelson, ed., *Translations of Homer*, trans. Thomas Hobbes, 2 vols. (Oxford: Clarendon Press, 2008); Patricia Springborg, "Leviathan, Mythic History, and National Historiography," in *The Historical Imagination in Early Modern Britain: History, Rhetoric, and Fiction, 1500–1800*, ed. Donald R. Kelley and David Harris Sacks (Cambridge: Cambridge University Press, 1997); Kahn, *Wayward Contracts*; Paul Davis, "Thomas Hobbes's Translations of Homer: Epic and Anticlericalism in Late Seventeenth-Century England," *The Seventeenth Century* 12 (1997): 231–55; A. P. Martinich, "Hobbes's Translations of Homer and Anticlericalism," *The Seventeenth Century* 16, no. 1 (2001): 147–57.

Homer translations, for instance, are considered by Nelson as a sort of Trojan Horse, "a continuation of *Leviathan* by other means," while Abraham Cowley's Pindaric Ode "To Mr. Hobs" (1656) had already compared Hobbes' "*Reason*" to the "shield from Heaven / To the *Trojan Heroe* given," "A shield," like Aeneas' "that gives delight / Even to the *enemies* sight."[21] But understanding Hobbes as an epic humanist who plied "the vast *Ocean*" of thought like a new Columbus, before outdoing Columbus by settling the very "*Golden Lands* of *new Philosophies*" he'd discovered, has not yet accounted for the Thucydides translation in full.[22] Now that Hobbes' Thucydides translation is seen less and less as something from which Hobbes would later turn, questions of what sort of project was signaled by the Thucydides translation come to the fore. Recent work by Jeffrey Collins and Kinch Hoekstra, taking aim, on the one hand, at the story of Hobbes' purportedly consistent royalism, and, on the other, at Hobbes' supposed turn to *de facto*-ism in *Leviathan* (it turns out it was there all the time), has made interpreting Hobbes' intentions with the Thucydides volume all the more significant.[23] In this vein, a number of diachronically conceived studies have persuasively linked Thucydides and Hobbes' later work—*Leviathan* in particular—yet they have often treated Hobbes' encounter with Thucydides as an inevitable communion of like political minds rather than as an encounter encouraged and surrounded by other texts and historical events.[24]

Deeper consideration of the humanist activity of translation can help enrich the conversation. In *Why Translation Matters*, Edith Grossman formulates the contemporary problem bracingly: "the obvious question is why any sane person would engage in a much-maligned activity that is often either discounted as menial hackwork or reviled as nothing short of criminal."[25] Drawing on earlier work by Norbrook, Springborg has observed how translated classical histories like Hobbes' Thucydides, due especially to conditions of censorship, still functioned in this period as "policy manuals," even though such works have "usually [been] overlooked by political theorists and historians because of their literary form."[26] Theorists like Lawrence Venuti have further pointed out that translation is a complex

[21] Nelson, *Translations of Homer*, xxii; Abraham Cowley, "To Mr. Hobbes," in *Seventeenth-Century Poetry: An Annotated Anthology*, ed. Robert Cummings (Oxford: Wiley-Blackwell, 2000), 377–80.

[22] Cowley, "To Mr. Hobbes."

[23] Jeffrey R. Collins, *The Allegiance of Thomas Hobbes* (Oxford: Oxford University Press, 2005); Kinch Hoekstra, "The 'De Facto' Turn in Hobbes's Political Philosophy," in *Leviathan after 350 Years*, ed. Tom Sorell and Luc Foisneau (Oxford: Oxford University Press, 2004), 33–73.

[24] Clifford W. Brown, "Thucydides, Hobbes and the Derivation of Anarchy," *History of Political Thought* 8, no. 1 (1978): 33–62; George Klosko and Daryl Rice, "Thucydides and Hobbes's State of Nature," *History of Political Thought* 6, no. 3 (1985): 405–9; Richard Schlatter, "Thomas Hobbes and Thucydides," *Journal of the History of Ideas* 6, no. 3 (1945): 350–62; G. Slomp, "Hobbes, Thucydides, and the Three Greatest Things," *History of Political Thought* 11 (1990): 565–86.

[25] Edith Grossman, *Why Translation Matters* (New Haven, CT: Yale University Press, 2010), 64.

[26] Patricia Springborg, "Classical Translation and Political Surrogacy: English Renaissance Classical Translations and Imitations as Politically Coded Texts," *Finnish Yearbook of Political Thought* 5 (2001): 20. See further Annabel Patterson, *Censorship and Interpretation: The Conditions of Writing and Reading in Early Modern England* (Madison, WI: University of Wisconsin Press, 1984); Norbrook, *Writing the English Republic*. On translation more generally, see Paul Davis, *Translation and the Poet's Life: The Ethics of Translating in English Culture, 1646–1726* (Oxford: Oxford University Press, 2008).

engagement with a foreign text, ideological but also utopian—utopian in the sense that the practice of translation is "filled with the anticipation that a community will be created around that text," ideological insofar as "communities fostered by translating...depend for their realization on the ensemble of domestic cultural constituencies among which the translation will circulate."[27] Keeping such observations in mind, we need to ask, what made translation an attractive activity to Hobbes? Which new communities did Hobbes anticipate? What were the existing 1620s Anglophone communities through which such new futures might emerge?

For all of these questions, "royalism" remains an unavoidable but partial answer. In an autobiographical poem first published in Latin in 1679, Hobbes wrote that of all the classics, "There's none that pleas'd me like Thucydides. / He says Democracy's a foolish thing, / Than a republic wiser is one king."[28] Hobbes comments similarly in his prefatory "Life and History of Thucydides" that Thucydides "least of all liked the democracy" and "best approved of the regal government."[29] Thus, with altogether clear warrant, Miriam Reik, J. P. Sommerville, Jonathan Scott, and David Norbrook all see Hobbes as impugning the divisive and potentially seditious rhetoric surrounding the 1628 Parliament whose work culminated in the Petition of Right but which Hobbes would have seen, in the words of his "Life of Thucydides," as the "contention of the demagogues for reputation and glory of wit."[30] But Norbrook also remarks upon the tension that would have accompanied such an arch-royalist position for Hobbes—a tension I will dwell upon in more detail later in order to argue for broader international contexts for Hobbes' royalism.

For now, the main problem can be summarized thus: if the parliamentary agitators are indeed Hobbes' "demagogues," then Hobbes' friend and recently deceased patron, William Cavendish, second Earl of Devonshire, would have to be counted a prime accessory to demagoguery. As Norbrook notes, Cavendish, whose secretary Hobbes proudly claimed to be on the title page of his Thucydides and whom Hobbes called in the dedicatory epistle "one whom no man was able either to draw or justle out of the straight path of Justice," had been sympathetic to the plight of the Five Knights imprisoned for their refusal to pay Charles' forced loan, a refusal that ultimately led to the Petition of Right.[31] As late as November 1627, Cavendish was still refusing to pay the very loan the five knights had been in prison since

---

[27] Lawrence Venuti, "Translation, Community, Utopia," in *Translation Changes Everything: Theory and Practice* (London: Routledge, 2013), 28.

[28] Thomas Hobbes, "Verse Autobiography," in *Leviathan: With Selected Variants from the Latin Edition of 1668*, ed. Edwin M. Curley (Indianapolis, IN: Hackett, 1994).

[29] Grene, *The Peloponnesian War: The Complete Thomas Hobbes Translation*, 572–3.

[30] Miriam M. Reik, *The Golden Lands of Thomas Hobbes* (Detroit: Wayne State University Press, 1977), 37; Jonathan Scott, "The Peace of Silence: Thucydides and the English Civil War," in *The Certainty of Doubt: Tributes to Peter Munz*, ed. Miles Fairburn and W. H. Oliver (Wellington: Victoria University Press, 1996), 90–116; Johann P. Sommerville, *Thomas Hobbes: Political Ideas in Historical Context* (Basingstoke: Palgrave Macmillan, 1992), 9–10; Norbrook, *Writing the English Republic*, 58–62; Grene, *The Peloponnesian War: The Complete Thomas Hobbes Translation*, 572.

[31] Norbrook, *Writing the English Republic*, 44; Hobbes, *Eight Bookes of the Peloponnesian Warre*, sig. a1v.

July for resisting.[32] Though Cavendish ultimately subscribed to the loan, paying by December and even using Hobbes himself to squeeze payments out of reluctant Derbyshire residents, he demonstrated his distaste for special royal measures in the subsequent Lords debates over the arbitrary imprisonment of the refusers.[33]

Cavendish's tepid opposition may come as a surprise to readers accustomed to a portrait of Cavendish as an obedient subject of the crown, whether on the loan or subsequent debates over imprisonment.[34] Yet attention to literary contexts reveals that Cavendish was the prime devotee of the period's most demonstrably republican publication, Thomas May's 1627 translation of Lucan's *Pharsalia*, and parliamentary historians such as Richard Cust and Jess Flemion follow Cavendish's contemporaries like John Holles, first Earl of Clare, in associating Cavendish with those "opposition peers" (Flemion's term) who were particularly peeved by the forced loan and who, in conference with the House of Commons in the spring of 1628, subsequently worked for a Petition of Right to protect against arbitrary imprisonment for so-called reasons of state.[35]

Here we return to Thucydides with the antinomy between antiquarianism and topical applicability in our sights. While Hobbes' folio volume included a sumptuous scholarly apparatus—foldout maps of the ancient Aegean, richly detailed diagrams of fortifications, and an index of Greek names and places (see, for example, Figure 5.1)—not even Hobbes could fix Thucydides so securely in the ancient past that Thucydides might not be deployed rhetorically for present political purposes. And it remains far from clear that he wanted to do so, as his comments about royalism and his advice that readers "draw out lessons" suggest.[36] In any case, early modern readers stood with commonplace books at the ready to record Thucydidean *sententiae*, preparing "notions in garrison" for flexible redeployment in topical controversies of many kinds.[37] Hobbes could hardly prescribe all lessons. And notwithstanding the broader trends toward chronology and antiquarianism that influenced Hobbes, toward which the material volume evidently aimed, narratives of any sort made topical resonance with contemporary events impossible to

---

[32] Richard Cust, *The Forced Loan and English Politics, 1626–1628* (Oxford: Clarendon Press, 1987), 84, 102 n. 13, 106.

[33] Skinner, *Reason and Rhetoric in the Philosophy of Thomas Hobbes*, 224; Sommerville, *Thomas Hobbes*, 9.

[34] Sommerville, *Thomas Hobbes*, 9–10, draws this portrait with the help of Hobbes' later claim that the ultraroyalist preacher Roger Manwaring "preached my doctrine" in 1627. But see Collins, *The Allegiance of Thomas Hobbes*, 59, for the counterargument that Hobbes, late in his life, should be considered a "hostile witness" on his own biography.

[35] Norbrook, *Writing the English Republic*, 44; Cust, *The Forced Loan and English Politics, 1626–1628*, 84, 102 n. 13, 6; Jess Stoddard Flemion, "The Struggle for the Petition of Right in the House of Lords: The Study of an Opposition Party Victory," *Journal of Modern History* 45, no. 2 (1973): 195 n. 10; P. R. Seddon, ed., *Letters of John Holles, 1587–1637*, vol. 2 (Nottingham: Derry and Sons for the Thoroton Society, 1975), 375–6.

[36] Grene, *The Peloponnesian War: The Complete Thomas Hobbes Translation*, xxii.

[37] Peter Beal, "Notions in Garrison: The Seventeenth-Century Commonplace Book," in *New Ways of Looking at Old Texts: Papers of the Renaissance English Text Society, 1985–1991*, ed. W. Speed Hill (Binghamton, NY: Renaissance English Text Society, 1993), 131–47; M. H. Hoeflich, "The Lawyer as Pragmatic Reader: The History of Legal Common-Placing," *Arkansas Law Review* 55, no. 87 (2002): 88–121; William H. Sherman, "Sir Julius Caesar's Search Engine," in *Used Books: Marking Readers in Renaissance England* (Philadelphia, PA: University of Pennsylvania Press, 2008), 127–48.

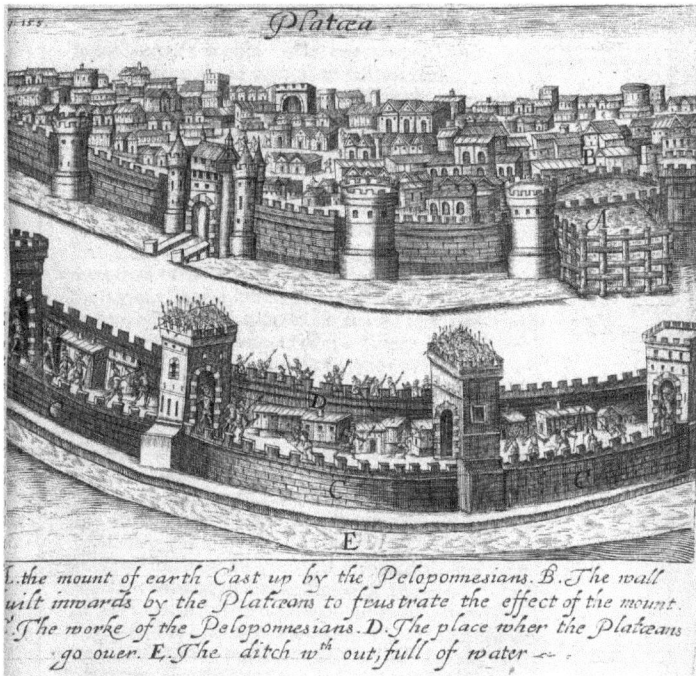

Fig. 5.1. Foldout illustration of the siege of Plataea in Hobbes' Thucydides, STC 24058. Plate before p. 155.
Reprinted with kind permission from the Folger Shakespeare Library.

avoid. Work by Zachary Lesser has shown that 1620s playbooks, for instance, aimed at pointed political commentary, and regularly achieved it: readers eagerly "applied" drama's examples to present circumstances.[38]

For English readers up in arms over certain recent "unjust, cruel and barbarous proceedings" in international affairs in the 1620s, then, Cleon's cruelty could not have failed to resonate.[39] In what popular pamphleteers, anticipating Dryden's later play on the events, termed the "Tragedy of Amboyna," representatives of the Dutch East Indies company (VOC) in Indonesia had tortured and executed ten English merchants in 1623.[40] The English East Indies merchants, the Dutch somewhat implausibly alleged, had plotted with Japanese co-conspirators to take over the Dutch fort on the island in order to secure Amboyna's lucrative spice trade, even though the Dutch outnumbered the English there by 2000 to twenty.[41] The accused

[38] Zachary Lesser, *Renaissance Drama and the Politics of Publication: Readings in the English Book Trade* (Cambridge: Cambridge University Press, 2004). See also John M. Wallace, "'Examples Are Best Precepts': Readers and Meanings in Seventeenth-Century Poetry," *Critical Inquiry* 1, no. 2 (1974): 273–90.

[39] [Dudley Digges], *A True Relation of the Unjust, Cruell, and Barbarous Proceedings against the English at Amboyna in the East-Indies, by the Neatherlandish Governour and Councel There*, Facsimile (Amsterdam 1971, 1624).

[40] Karen Chancey, "The Amboyna Massacre in English Politics, 1624–1632," *Albion* 30 (1998): 583–98.

[41] Chancey, "The Amboyna Massacre in English Politics, 1624–1632," 585.

Fig. 5.2. Title-page woodcut from *A true relation of the unjust, cruell, and barbarous proceedings against the English at Amboyna in the East-Indies* (1624), STC 7452.

Reprinted with kind permission from the Folger Shakespeare Library.

confessed to the plot under tortures that included being "cruelly burnt in divers parts of [the] body" and having "a cloth tied about [one's] neck and two men ready with their Jarres of water to be powred on [the] head," a procedure sadly now all-too familiar to the world as waterboarding (see Figure 5.2).[42]

Dutch pamphlets originally defended the "Neatherlandish governor" of Amboyna, claiming his right to punish the English plotters "according to the law

---

[42] *A True Relation of the Unjust, Cruell, and Barbarous Proceedings against the English at Amboyna in the East-Indies, by the Neatherlandish Governour and Councel There*, 7.

of *Nations*" by virtue of Dutch "dominion" over the island.[43] The Dutch, they argued, had "proceeded according to the custome of all Nations of the world," and even though the English howled of cruelly arbitrary justice "without formality," it was Dutch "dominion," secured through the "just and lawfull title of warre, according the law of *Nations*," that permitted the rightful governor of Amboyna to proceed according to Dutch form.[44]

His jurisdiction was in no way imperiled by the 1619 Anglo-Dutch treaty creating an international court at Jakarta, said one Dutch *apologia*, which an English counter-blast shortly denigrated as an "Elogie and commendation" for tyrannical justice.[45]

The international controversy that raged for several years gives interesting evidence of the law of nations being deployed in popular print: indignant friends, relatives, and associates of the English merchants fired, "Can you be so ignorant of the law of Nature and Nations" to have used torture and massacre thus?[46] Eventually a combination of popular, commercial, and diplomatic pressure prevailed and the Dutch figures responsible, including the infamous governor Harman Van Speult, were put on trial in the Low Counties in the spring of 1628. That the participants in the torture ultimately came to trial makes it tempting to invoke Jürgen Habermas' contention that it is on the "slender but robust" ground of "moral outrage" that one can conceive of a "global public sphere," thrusts in which direction might be glimpsed elsewhere in the 1620s in increasingly international audiences for news about the Thirty Years' War.[47] But the Stuarts sought diligently to maintain international affairs as *arcana imperii*, and readers familiar with the uproar over Middleton's *A Game at Chess* know well that conditions approaching anything like a public sphere were fleeting at best. John Selden's major work on the law of nations, *Mare Clausum*, had long been kept from publication due to Stuart

---

[43] "A True Declaration of the News That Came out of the East-Indies, with the Pinace Called the Hare," in *A True Relation of the Unjust, Cruell, and Barbarous Proceedings against the English at Amboyna in the East-Indies, by the Neatherlandish Governour and Councel There* (London, 1624), 10 [sig. g4v].

[44] "A True Declaration of the News That Came out of the East-Indies, with the Pinace Called the Hare," 9–10 [sig. g4r–v].

[45] "The Answer to a Dutch Pamphlet," in *A True Relation of the Unjust, Cruell, and Barbarous Proceedings against the English at Amboyna in the East-Indies, by the Neatherlandish Governour and Councel There* (London, 1624), 34 [sig. n3v]; "A True Declaration of the News That Came out of the East-Indies, with the Pinace Called the Hare," 12–13 [sigs. h1v–h2r].

[46] The author, the pastor Thomas Myriell, was friend to John Milton the elder, father of the poet. Shortly after the Amboyna massacre in 1623, Myriell would preside over the wedding of Anne Milton and Edward Phillips, the sister and brother-in-law of the poet. Thomas Myriell, "To the Right Worshipfull Mr. Maurice Abbott, Governor of the East-India Companie," in *The Stripping of Ioseph... With a Consolatorie Epistle, to the English-East-India Companie, for Their Vnsufferable Wrongs Sustayned in Amboyna, by the Dutch There* (London: W[illiam] S[tansby] for Hen. Holland and Geo. Gibbs, 1625), 15; Gordon Campbell and Thomas N. Corns, *John Milton: Life, Work, and Thought* (Oxford: Oxford University Press, 2010), 25.

[47] Jürgen Habermas, *The Divided West* (Cambridge: Polity, 2006), 142–3. As he puts it, drawing from Kant, "consonance in reactions of moral outrage toward egregious human rights violations and manifest acts of aggression" "ultimately constitute the standard for the verdicts of international courts and the political decisions of the world organization." But see also Anthony Milton, "Marketing a Massacre: Amboyna, the East Indies Company, and the Public Sphere in Early Stuart England," in *The Politics of the Public Sphere in Early Modern England*, ed. Peter Lake and Steven C. A. Pincus (Manchester: Manchester University Press, 2007), 168–90.

worries about the Dutch trade, and it was in early December 1628, the same month Hobbes' Thucydides would be published, that the Attorney General was advised of "certain printed papers" "go[ing] from hand to hand containing a relation of the proceedings of the Dutch against the English in Amboyna... set down in such manner as may breed much disaffection between the King's subjects and those of the Low Countries."[48] The wounds of furious English East Indies Company pamphleteers had been reopened by the trial, but virulent anti-Dutch outrage, thought to be infecting the public, complicated the newfound Protestant alliance Charles reluctantly deemed necessary for restoring the Protestant Palatinate.[49] Charles, the pamphleteers were made to understand, had "taken [Amboyna] into his own hands, and finds that these loose papers only exasperate misunderstandings."[50] Attorney-General Heath was "to prepare a Proclamation for the suppression of these, and all other writings and speeches not suiting with the good terms of amity between his Majesty and his allies the States General."[51] As we consider again Hobbes' Thucydides, we do so recognizing that in the absence of a viable public sphere, condemnation of Dutch cruelty could only safely be accomplished through such indirect means afforded by translation and history. Whatever else they were, translations of classical histories were tacit treaties with censors.

TIME AND LAW

In addition to being treaties with the censors, classical translations were treaties with the past. Classical translations that had one foot in the present could also be deep philological engagements with the law of nations in history's "pre-dawn light."[52] Theorists of the *ius gentium* like Gentili and Grotius were turning with increasing alacrity to Thucydides, and this I contend accounts for much of Hobbes' own interest in translating him. The law of nations, we can recall, was for many commentators distinct from natural law in that it bore the time-stamped marks of human volition. Norms of the law of nations had a characteristic temporal aspect in that they had emerged in response to human exigencies. Diplomatic customs, precise terms of treaties, causes for war—these were key features in accounts of the law of nations, but proper understanding of such things depended

---

[48] W. Noel Sainsbury, ed., "East Indies: December 1628," *Calendar of State Papers Colonial, East Indies, China and Persia*, Volume 6: 1625–1629, British History Online <http://www.british-history. ac.uk/report.aspx?compid=71289>, hereafter "CSPC." Cyndia Susan Clegg, *Press Censorship in Caroline England* (Cambridge: Cambridge University Press, 2008), 15–16.

[49] Martine Julia Van Ittersum, "'Three Moneths Observations of the Low Countreys, Especially Holland': Owen Felltham and Anglo-Dutch Relations in the Seventeenth Century," *LIAS: Sources and Documents Relating to the Early Modern History of Ideas* 27 (2000): 95–160, 161–96, 116 n. 53; Chancey, "The Amboyna Massacre in English Politics, 1624–1632."

[50] CSPC, "East Indies: December 1628."   [51] CSPC, "East Indies: December 1628."

[52] Steve Sheppard, "The Laws of War in the Pre-Dawn Light: Institutions and Obligations in Thucydides' Peloponnesian War," *Columbia Journal of Transnational Law* 43 (2004–2005): 905; George A. Sheets, "Conceptualizing International Law in Thucydides," *American Journal of Philology* 115 (1994): 51–73; David J. Bederman, *International Law and Antiquity* (Cambridge: Cambridge University Press, 2001), in passing.

on history, or—less abstractly—historians, whose own fragmentary or partisan accounts were then mediated by other agents like Renaissance scribes, translators, printers, booksellers, expositors, redactors and so on, who often had agendas of their own. Lawyers developing normative precepts for conduct forged paths through thickets of sometimes highly mediated historical exempla and precedents, often forgetting or pragmatically ignoring just how unstable were some of their historical foundations. At a basic level, Hobbes was right: making the past was indeed a way to make a future, with law being the ultimate "bridge" from history "to a new world."[53]

Hard as it may now be to imagine, in early modern England, Thucydides was something of a marginal ancient writer. Thomas More's Utopians read Thucydides, and he had been translated by Thomas Nicolls into English in 1550, yet D. R. Woolf's analysis of the inventories of Cambridge libraries between 1535 and 1609 reveals Thucydides to be just seventeenth on the list of most widely held ancient historians, with Lucan appearing in twice as many inventories, Suetonius more than three times as many, and Sallust and Caesar in nearly six times as many.[54] Somewhat later, despite the fact that Robert Burton could have read Thucydides in available editions in Greek or Latin, his library of more than 1700 titles in 1640 apparently only held Thucydides because Hobbes provided Burton with a copy of his translation.[55] Samual Pepys, likewise, held only the Hobbes translation.[56] Like most ancient historians, Thucydides was classed among the rhetoricians for most of the sixteenth century, yet, as evidenced by Gentili and Grotius, Thucydides had a special importance in the emerging genre of the *ius gentium* tract, the rise of which coincided with that of the study of history more generally: as a rough index, Oxford's first Professor of History, Degory Wheare, took

---

[53] Robert M. Cover, "The Folktales of Justice: Tales of Jurisdiction," in *Narrative, Violence, and the Law: The Essays of Robert Cover*, ed. Martha Minow, Michael Ryan, and Austin Sarat (Ann Arbor, MI: University of Michigan Press, 1992), 187. See further Anne Orford, "The Past as Law or History?: The Relevance of Imperialism for Modern International Law," *International Law and Justice Working Papers*, IILJ Working Papers, no. 2 (2012) <http://www.iilj.org>.

[54] See D. R. Woolf, *Reading History in Early Modern England* (Cambridge: Cambridge University Press, 2000), 145; confirming Peter Burke, "A Survey of the Popularity of Ancient Historians, 1450–1700," *History and Theory* 5, no. 2 (1966): 136–7. On Thucydides in the Renaissance more broadly, see Marianne Pade, "Thucydides' Renaissance Readers," in *Brill's Companion to Thucydides*, ed. Antonios Rengakos and Antonis Tsakmakis (Leiden: Brill, 2006), 779–810; Marianne Pade, "Thucydides," in *Catalogus Translationum et Commentariorum: Mediaeval and Renaissance Latin Translations and Commentaries*, ed. Virginia Brown, James Hankins, and Robert A. Kaster, vol. 8 (Washington, DC: Catholic University of America Press, 2003), 104–81.

[55] Burton's *Eight Bookes of the Peloponnesian Warre* is inscribed in Burton's hand "Ex dono Authoris." Nicolas K. Kiessling, ed., *The Library of Robert Burton* (Oxford: Oxford Bibliographical Society, 1988), 302–3. A second copy given by Hobbes survives in the collection of the Dr. Williams Library. See Peter Lindenbaum, "Dispatches from the Archives," *Times Literary Supplement*, no. 5383 (2006): 15. Besides Burton and Pepys, other owners of Hobbes' Thucydides include Sir Kenelm Digby, a friend of Hobbes' whose name and motto appear on the title page of a copy now at the Houghton Library at Harvard University, and Francis Dee, a Cambridge-educated divine who in 1629 was chaplain to the ambassador to Paris and who bequeathed his copy along with the rest of his library to St. John's College, Cambridge, where this copy now resides.

[56] Robert Latham, ed., *Catalogue of the Pepys Library at Magdalene College, Cambridge*, 7 vols., vol. 1 (Woodbridge: D. S. Brewer, 1978).

up his post in 1623, just as Grotius was writing *De Jure Belli ac Pacis*.[57] Whereas neither Augustine nor Aquinas cited Thucydides, Grotius in *De Jure Belli ac Pacis* now found a "*Saying from* Euphemus *in* Thucydides... *in every ones mouth*."[58]

Gentili and Grotius, both of whose works could be found in the library Hobbes tended in the 1620s, illustrate the unique demands the genre of the early modern Latin *ius gentium* tract made on ancient histories, which were seen to hold the potential to speak about the *ius gentium* by indicating the laws "common to all known legal systems" and "all known peoples."[59] Precisely how Hobbes conceived of the law of nations in 1628 remains difficult to say. Later in his career, Hobbes followed Gentili and the *Digest*'s Gaius in the bipartite view that equated the laws of nature and nations, notoriously assimilating the law of nations with his pessimistic law of nature; but the influence of Bacon, who as we have seen, distinguished between the greater and lesser laws of nations as part of a tripartite scheme, may still have prevailed with Hobbes in the late 1620s.[60] Thucydides regardless took on new importance as writers like Gentili and Grotius developed historically grounded responses to the *Digest*'s uncertain schemas. As Grotius put it in his 1625 *De Jure Belli ac Pacis*, theorists "are mostly very muddled and confused about which laws are natural, which divine, which are part of the law of nations, which are civil laws, and which belong to the canon law. The great deficiency in all of these writers was that they lacked the illumination provided by History."[61]

Hobbes had easy access to works by both Gentili and Grotius. He may indeed have sought them out. Alongside works including Heliodorus' classical romance *Aethiopica* and John Barclay's modern *Argenis* (Latin, 1621 and English, 1625), the Cavendishs' Hardwick library that Hobbes tended held Gentili's *De Legationibus* (1585) and Grotius' *De Antiquitate Batavica* (1610), *Apologeticus* (1622),

[57] In fact, Wheare's *De Ratione et Methodo Legendi Historias* (1625), running through the ancient historians in chronological order, quoted many of the same laudatory passages Hobbes would in his praise of Thucydides. On Wheare, see J. H. M. Salmon, "Precept, Example, and Truth: Degory Wheare and the Ars Historica," in *The Historical Imagination in Early Modern Britain: History, Rhetoric, and Fiction, 1500–1800*, ed. Donald R. Kelley and David Harris Sacks (Cambridge: Cambridge University Press, 1997), 11–36.

[58] Cian O'Driscoll, "Thucydides and the Just War Tradition: Unlikely Bedfellows?," in *A Handbook to the Reception of Thucydides*, ed. Christine Lee and Neville Morley (John Wiley & Sons, 2014), 373–90. Hugo Grotius, *The Rights of War and Peace*, ed. Richard Tuck and Jean Barbeyrac, trans. John Morrice (Indianapolis, IN: Liberty Fund, 2005), 1.76. Kinch Hoekstra describes a "a crescendo of interest in Thucydides among the intellectual and political elites of [early modern] Europe." Kinch Hoekstra, "Thucydides and the Bellicose Beginnings of Modern Political Theory," in *Thucydides and the Modern World* (Cambridge: Cambridge University Press, 2012).

[59] Thomas Hobbes, Old Catalogue, Chatsworth, MSS Hobbes E.1.A, 86, 83; Maurice Keen, *The Laws of War in the Late Middle Ages* (London: Routledge & K. Paul, 1965), 10–11; Alberico Gentili, *De Jure Belli Libri Tres*, trans. John Carew Rolfe (Oxford: Clarendon Press, 1933), 9; See also Richard Tuck, *Natural Rights Theories: Their Origin and Development* (Cambridge: Cambridge University Press, 1979), 42; For discussion of Hobbes' role in contemporary international law debates, see Kinji Akashi, "Hobbes's Relevance to the Modern Law of Nations," *Journal of the History of International Law 2*, 2000, 199–216; On Thucydides and international law, see Sheets, "Conceptualizing International Law in Thucydides."

[60] For the shift in Hobbes' thinking about the law of nations, see Armitage, *Foundations of Modern International Thought*, 62–3.

[61] Grotius, *The Rights of War and Peace*, 1755. Grotius goes on to include Gentili's as among the "attempts to supply the deficit."

and *De Jure Belli ac Pacis*.[62] Hobbes later suggested he had helped to build this collection himself.[63]

Gentili's and Grotius' influential pronouncements on the *ius gentium* were made from the stuff of classical histories, which their authors adduced as proofs of laws common to all known peoples. Dedicated as they were to uncovering common laws and customs, Grotius and Gentili cited ancient poets, dramatists, and historians with limited generic discrimination (modern writers like Guicciardini also figure prominently). Historians who wrote of wars are, however, found in greater numbers. Xenophon's *Cyropaedia*, one of the few books that could reliably be found on Hobbes' table, according to Aubrey, is cited regularly in these tracts.[64] Thucydides, likewise, is a constant presence. Even as these historians narrated conflict, they also importantly narrated those laws and customs that even adversaries agreed upon.

Ancient histories, said Grotius, carried the most authority. He valued ancient histories because they offered two classes of facts: examples of conduct, which indicated the laws of nature, and ancient historians' judgments about them, which indicated the law of nations. The considerable interest of the second should not be lost, for it meant that the law of nations had, in a certain way, been made by ancient historians. Perhaps unwittingly, and certainly retroactively, ancient historians had participated in making the law of nations. Historians' normative judgments *about facts* were themselves important facts. What made them so was that they could be accumulated and analyzed to determine legal-historical consensus. Grotius explained:

> Works of history are useful for my argument in two ways, for they provide both examples of conduct, and moral judgments upon them. Examples from the best periods and cultures [*populi*] carry the most authority, so I have selected those from the Ancient Greeks and Romans in preference to any others. Nor have I rejected their judgments, especially where everyone was in agreement: for while the law of nature (as I have said) may be determined in their ways, the law of nations is established solely by agreement.[65]

For Gentili, empirical examples from texts like Thucydides did not yield norms or precepts in precisely the same way that Grotius suggested, but they remained relevant to his laws of war. Gentili's *ius gentium* was equivalent to the *ius naturae*, and while this might imply that Gentili would have little interest in the particularities of history—in the Thomist natural law tradition, right reason was largely seen to suffice—Gentili in actuality turned the *ius naturae* toward history. "As one reads Gentili's equation of natural law and the law of nations," Jeremy Waldron observes, "it seems to bring the two concepts together on the *other* side—the empirical

---

[62] Hobbes, Old Catalogue, fols. 90 (Heliodorus), 57, 59 (Barclay), 85 (Gentili), 86 (Grotius).

[63] John Aubrey, *Brief Lives*, ed. Oliver Lawson Dick (Boston, MA: D. R. Godine, 1996), 152.

[64] Aubrey, *Brief Lives*, 152. Philip Sidney, a great admirer of Xenophon, had cited Xenophon's ability to "imitate so excellently as to give us... 'the portraiture of a just empire' under the name of Cyrus." Philip Sidney, *An Apology for Poetry, Or, The Defence of Poesy*, ed. R. W Maslen and Geoffrey Shepherd, 3rd edn. (Manchester: Manchester University Press, 2002), 87.

[65] Grotius, *The Rights of War and Peace*, 1758.

side—of the rational/empirical divide."[66] Historical examples allowed for "plausible conjectures," and they were fundamentally necessary in helping modern interpreters make judgments in "cases of doubt." And while Gentili equated the laws of nature and nations in a way Grotius did not, Gentili considered historians' "opinions" as adding "weight" to legal claims. Additionally, sometimes historical custom obliged actors in the present not because custom was just but because disrupting established custom itself imperiled justice. Gentili wrote:

> Although one ought not to judge from examples, and that principle is called Justinian's golden rule, yet it is clear that a plausible conjecture may be deduced from examples. Indeed, in cases of doubt one is obliged to judge from examples, and also when anything has become a custom. For it is not fitting to change things which have always had a fixed observance, and a decision has greater weight which is supported by the opinions of a large number of men.[67]

Because his work largely took place on the historicist, positivist side of the law of nations, Gentili, as Grotius would, went on to cite Thucydides repeatedly in his tract.

Gentili's and Grotius' variegated, at times incompatible, references to Thucydides help illustrate ancient history's uses at the time Hobbes published his translation. In *De Legationibus*, Gentili, for his part, cited Thucydides to prove that nations could forbid ambassadors as Pericles once had done; that ambassadors held no rights against peoples to which they had not been sent; that neither brigands nor pirates were entitled to the privileges of the *ius gentium*; that ambassadors should understand the language of the person with whom they were negotiating; and, that ambassadors were "wholly justified in doing many things in regard to which not a word has been said."[68] Of these, Gentili's denial of rights for brigands and pirates is especially pertinent for Hobbes. Here, Gentili derives from Thucydides evidence of man's savage natural state:

> Neither brigands nor pirates are entitled to the privileges of international law [*ius gentium*], since they themselves have utterly spurned all intercourse with their fellowmen

---

[66] Jeremy Waldron, "Ius Gentium: A Defence of Gentili's Equation of the Law of Nations and the Law of Nature," in *The Roman Foundations of the Law of Nations: Alberico Gentili and the Justice of Empire*, ed. Benedict Kingsbury and Benjamin Straumann (Oxford: Oxford University Press, 2011), 284 (emphasis added). For a similar tension in Vitoria, and an excellent discussion of Suarez in this regard, see Brian Tierney, "Vitoria and Suarez on Ius Gentium, Natural Law, and Custom," in *The Nature of Customary Law*, ed. Amanda Perreau-Saussine and James Bernard Murphy (Cambridge; New York: Cambridge University Press, 2007).

[67] Gentili, *De Jure Belli Libri Tres*, 11.

[68] Alberico Gentili, *De Legationibus Libri Tres*, trans. Gordon Jennings Laing, vol. 2, *Classics of International Law* 12 (New York: Oxford University Press, 1924), 69 (forbidding ambassadors), 62 (rights), 79 (brigands and pirates), 150 (language), 180 (role of instructions). Given that Virginia Company propaganda often cast colonists as ambassadors, Gentili's tract would likely have been a valuable source of legal and ethical guidance. *A true declaration of the estate of the colonie in Virginia*, for example, spoke of Amerindians having "violated the lawe of nations, and [having] used our Ambassadors as Ammon did the servants of David: If in him it were a just cause to warre against the Ammonites, it is lawfull, in us, to secure ourselves, against the infidels," quoted in Andrew Fitzmaurice, *Humanism and America: An Intellectual History of English Colonisation, 1500–1625* (Cambridge: Cambridge University Press, 2003), 147.

and, so far as in them lies, endeavor to drag back the world to the savagery of primitive times. In that age, as you know, men passed their lives in the manner of wild beasts, and each one carried off what fortune offered to him as prey, trained to use his strength in accordance with his own impulses and to live for himself alone. In those days, as Thucydides observes, to be a robber was an honor rather than a disgrace[.][69]

A marginal note directs readers to Book V of Lucretius' epic poem *De Rerum Natura* for further confirmation that men once lived as wild beasts.[70] Thucydides for Gentili is thus a spokesman for what Arthur Ferguson once called Tudor England's "tradition of 'hard' primitivism," the narrative of man's ascent from savagery "as distinct from the elegiac myth of a Golden Age."[71] Gentili's later work, *De Jure Belli Libri Tres*, now citing Thucydides twenty-six times, used the historian to illuminate such concerns as the jurisdiction over the seas; rights of conquest; the obligations of offensive and defensive alliances; the obligations of prisoners; the duties of captors; and the justice of defending the people of another nation against their sovereign.[72]

Grotius' *De Jure Belli ac Pacis*, which owed a number of references to Gentili, employed Thucydides similarly.[73] Here, among more than sixty citations, Thucydides testified to the proper definition of a state; the freedom of the seas and the rights to hospitality; the risks of aligning with infidels; the inevitability of sin, and even—difficult to square with some over-idealizing accounts of Grotius—the occasional legality of killing women, infants, and prisoners.[74] The story of Pericles refusing to entertain a Spartan ambassador proved, as it had in Gentili, states' rights to do so, and we also find recurring Thucydides' passage on the "old time" Greeks on which Gentili had grounded his comments on the primitive state. In Grotius, however, the passage on the old time Greeks is used to make the opposite point, emphasizing

---

[69] Gentili, *De Legationibvs Libri Tres*, 2.79; Alberico Gentili, *De Legationibus Libri Tres* (London: T[homas] Vautrollerius, 1585), sig. g3r.

[70] For recent statements of the importance of Lucretius to Hobbes, see Jon Parkin, "Hobbism in the Later 1660's: Daniel Scargill and Samuel Parker," *The Historical Journal* 42, no. 1 (1999): 85–108; Patricia Springborg, "Hobbes, Donne, and the Virginia Company: Terra Nullius and the 'Bulimia of Dominion,'" *History of Political Thought* 36, no. 1 (2015): 113–64; Patricia Springborg, "Hobbes, Heresy, and the Historia Ecclesiastica," *Journal of the History of Ideas* 55, no. 4 (1994): 553–71.

[71] Arthur B. Ferguson, *Clio Unbound: Perceptions of the Social and Cultural Past in Renaissance England* (Durham, NC: Duke University Press, 1979), 358. Ferguson traces the "hard primitivism" tradition in Tudor England through the works of Thomas Starkey and Juan Luis Vives, 356–72. Richard Tuck has speculated that Hobbes heard Gentili lecture at Oxford. Richard Tuck, *The Rights of War and Peace: Political Thought and the International Order from Grotius to Kant* (Oxford: Oxford University Press, 1999), 17.

[72] Gentili, *De Jure Belli Libri Tres*, 384 (seas), 19, 308 (conquest), 388 (alliances), 242 (hostages), 364–5 (captors), 74 (intervention); Kinch Hoesktra generously read an early version of this chapter in manuscript and he himself has subsequently reached similar conclusions. See "Gentili, Thucydides, and the Justification of Pre-Emption," in *Alberico Gentili: La Salvaguardia Dei Beni Culturali Nel Diritto Internazionale* (Milan: Giuffrè editore, 2008), 115–28; "Thucydides and the Bellicose Beginnings of Modern Political Theory."

[73] On Grotius' debts to Gentili, including discussion of a 1623 letter of Grotius' "urgently expecting" a copy of Gentili's *De Jure Belli*, see Peter Haggenmacher, "Grotius and Gentili: A Reassessment of Thomas E. Holland's Inaugural Lecture," in *Hugo Grotius and International Relations*, ed. Hedley Bull, Benedict Kinsbury, and Adam Roberts (Oxford: Clarendon Press, 1990), 133–77, esp. 152–3.

[74] Grotius, *The Rights of War and Peace*, 257 (state), 430 (seas), 446 (hospitality), 836 (infidels), 993 (sin), 1283 (women and infants), 1286 (prisoners).

the "general Corruption of Manners" that by the time narrated by Thucydides had "razed and obliterated" the "Natural Relation between all Mankind."[75] Grotius' Thucydides, as opposed to Gentili's, was thus testimony for natural sociability rather than "hard primitivism." In a remarkable 1981 article (recently reprinted), Noel Malcolm demonstrated that, like Cavendish, Hobbes both held stock and participated in the dramatic internal wrangling of the Virginia Company, siding with the prominent faction of the longtime Stuart antagonist Sir Edwin Sandys.[76] Malcolm suggested there that Hobbes must have been working on the Thucydides translation during his involvement with the Company. Germane to Hobbes' established Virginia Company interests, Grotius quoted Thucydides four times in discussions of what he called "Mother Cities," cities maintaining colonies (of which Athens was the prime example) and—undoubtedly interesting to Hobbes—Thucydides even elucidated the obligations stakeholders in a joint stock company had toward one another and the illegitimacy of their seeking recourse to external arbitration.[77] Once adventurers contracted in good faith, in Grotius' eyes, however unequal their agreement, "no action was allowed in Court against such an Inequality" nor could there be "any Redress or Constraint on that Account," a view that if accepted might have cast unwelcome doubt on Stuarts' unwarranted interventions in recent Virginia Company affairs.[78]

THE DEBATE OVER THUCYDIDES I.3–5

So far in this chapter we have seen how inter-imperial contexts stirred popular arguments about dominion, cruelty, and the law of nations and also how Stuart censorship practices encouraged the indirection afforded by historical translations. We have seen further how the allied understandings of the *History of the Peloponnesian War* as true and disinterested history—and Thucydides himself as an honorable judge of historical examples—gave Thucydides increasing authority to speak normatively to the present. In the remainder of this chapter, I want to join these two strains—topical, rhetorical, inter-imperial, on the one hand, antiquarian, disinterested, legislative on the other—to show more fully how Hobbes uses the resources of the latter to create an historical law of nations that's hardly disinterested or merely antiquarian. Historians of international law miss something fundamental about how the early modern law of nations was formulated if they fail to observe

[75] Grene, *The Peloponnesian War: The Complete Thomas Hobbes Translation*, I.5, 3; Grotius, *The Rights of War and Peace*, 904, 821–2.

[76] Noel Malcolm, "Hobbes, Sandys, and the Virginia Company," *The Historical Journal* 24, no. 02 (1981): 297–321; Noel Malcolm, *Aspects of Hobbes* (Oxford: Clarendon Press, 2002), 53–79; see further Springborg, "Hobbes, Donne, and the Virginia Company."

[77] Grotius, *The Rights of War and Peace*, 320, 326–7, 674 (colonies). Before Grotius, Bodin had also cited Thucydides in his discussion of corporations; See Jean Bodin, *The Six Bookes of a Common-Weale*, trans. Richard Knolles (London: for G. Bishop, 1606), 362, in the chapter headed "Of Corporations, and Colledges, Estates, and Communities, and what profits or incoueniences ensue thereof ynto the Commonweale."

[78] Grotius, *The Rights of War and Peace*, 763–4.

that translation of a passage like Thucydides I.3–5 provided someone like Hobbes the opportunity to influence debates. In his *Aphorismi de Jure Gentium*, Bacon coolly responded to one possible objection, "we asserted that all civil laws were changeable, [but] this was not to be taken to mean that human will can force the nature of things. For, the reckoning of good and evil is natural; the practiced wit [*solertia*] of man finds and declares [*invenit & enucleate*] justice and equity, it does not create or determine [*creat aut constituit*] it."[79] For Hobbes, the role of the translator was a way to create and determine international justice under the presumption of passively transmitting and declaring something found.

In their particulars, Gentili's and Grotius' sometimes contradictory uses of Thucydides make generalizations about the Greek historian's overall significance within the emerging *ius gentium* tradition difficult, except perhaps the generalization that Thucydides *was* significant, and increasingly so. Yet the underlying debate between Gentili and Grotius on the meaning of Thucydides I.3–5 offers a chance to see the formidable interventions a translator could make.

The ardent colonialist John Dee found in Pericles someone "wisely vnderstanding, that no other means was so easy, so ready, and so sure, for Athens to atteyn to their wished for Souerainty, among their freends and foes, dwelling about them: But if, they were Lords and Maisters of the Seas, nere and far about them."[80] Thucydides' role as the historian of empire was similarly recognized in a work published the same year in which Richard Willes concluded of attempts to recount the Spanish designs in the New World, "to drawe Geographically the places, to wryte all their battelles, victories, and conquestes, to describe the cities rased, the townes erected, to poynte out the Capitaynes personages, to shewe theyr traueyles and good hap, it would requyre an other Homere, an other Thucydides."[81] Bacon, who proposed under the heading "Doctrine Concerning the Extension of the Bounds of the Empire," that "a state...have...laws or customs which may reach forth unto them just occasions or at least pretexts for making war," turned to Thucydides in his *Considerations Touching a Warre With Spaine* (1624) to justify war against "this *Nation* of *Spaine* [that] runs a race (still) of *Empire*."[82]

Indications of Hobbes' intended contributions to this discourse about empire can be found elsewhere—in his marginal notes suggesting the Athenians' "dominion of the Seas," to take one example of many. These notes may have constituted an attempt to lay the textual groundwork for a fuller confutation of Grotius' claim on behalf of the Dutch East India Company that the seas were free, the likes of which confutation Selden would publish in his 1635 *Mare Clausum*, to Hobbes'

[79] Bacon, "Aphorismi de Jure Gentium," 289–90.

[80] John Dee, *General and Rare Memorials Pertayning to the Perfect Arte of Nauigation* (London: John Daye, 1577), 12; on which, generally, see William H. Sherman, *John Dee: The Politics of Reading and Writing in the English Renaissance* (Amherst, MA: University of Massachusetts Press, 1995).

[81] Pietro Martire D'Anghiera, Richard Eden, and Richard Willes, *The History of Trauayle in the West and East Indies, and Other Countreys Lying Eyther Way* (London: Richarde Iugge, 1577), 467.

[82] Francis Bacon, "Of the Dignity and Advancement of Learning," in *The Works of Francis Bacon*, ed. James Spedding, Robert Leslie, and Douglas Denon Heath, trans. Francis Headlam, vol. 5 (London: Longman, 1861), 85; Francis Bacon, *Considerations Touching a Warre with Spaine* ([London], 1629), 13, 24; Hoekstra, "Thucydides and the Bellicose Beginnings of Modern Political Theory."

eager expectation.[83] Hobbes' prominent associate Sir Edwin Sandys was a longtime leader in the East India Company too, even nominated to be its governor in the year of Hobbes' Thucydides.[84] The stakes of Thucydides I.3–5, however, as suggested initially in Chapter 1, included the accuracy of the Genesis story, the extent or existence of natural obligations, and the capacity of men, as one of Hobbes' marginal notes put it, to "gr[o]w...civil."[85] All of these were significant seventeenth-century debates, in large measure because of their implications for empire.

While a complete analysis of Hobbes' translation is beyond the scope of this chapter—indeed, it would take "an other Thucydides"—a brief discussion of Hobbes' rendering of Thucydides I.3–5 can suggest his translation's implications for colonial concerns. Hobbes' particular choices reveal a translator eager to confirm Gentili's account of human history, an account that appeared in modified form in Virginia Company propaganda that linked England with Athens and implicitly proposed that barbarian natives, with proper tutelage, could evolve into a civilized culture equal with England, much as England herself had purportedly evolved from savagery.[86] The ideology of "contemporary ancestors" could already be found in Thucydides, who wrote that the "old Greeks used the same form of life that is now in force amongst the barbarians of the present age," but Hobbes seems to have wanted to emphasize it further.[87] Where Grotius had stressed time's "Corruption of Manners," Hobbes' translation and notes to Thucydides I.3–5 bolster Gentili's story of growing civility. This concern is seen most clearly on two occasions.

As it is in Bacon's *New Atlantis*, navigation was for many in Stuart England a signal of scientific advancement that carried with it a strong hint of moral and spiritual superiority.[88] In Thucydides I.3, the Greek author tells of the first time Greek cities joined together to form a political community, the Trojan War. The passage garnered the attention of commentators who were concerned with the origins of political communities. The Greeks' advantageous union was made possible,

[83] Hobbes, *Eight Bookes of the Peloponnesian Warre*, 49, 324. For the significance of this debate to English colonialism, see David Armitage, *The Ideological Origins of the British Empire*, Ideas in Context 59 (Cambridge: Cambridge University Press, 2000), 109–14; Malcolm, *Aspects of Hobbes*, 63; An excellent portrait of the type of commonplacing reader Hobbes likely expected can be found in Sherman, "Sir Julius Caesar's Search Engine," 127–48; Hobbes re-asserted Athenian "dominion of the sea" in his English *Leviathan* but muted the assertion in addressing his Latin Continental audience. Compare Thomas Hobbes, *Leviathan: With Selected Variants from the Latin Edition of 1668*, ed. Edwin Curley (Indianapolis: Hackett, 1994), 455, 469.

[84] Theodore K. Rabb, "Sandys, Sir Edwin (1561–1629)," *Oxford Dictionary of National Biography* (Oxford: Oxford University Press, 2004) <http://www.oxforddnb.com.proxy.library.cmu.edu/view/article/24650>.

[85] Hobbes, *Eight Bookes of the Peloponnesian Warre*, 4.

[86] Fitzmaurice, *Humanism and America: An Intellectual History of English Colonisation, 1500–1625*, 158–9.

[87] Mary Nyquist, "Contemporary Ancestors of de Bry, Hobbes, and Milton," *University of Toronto Quarterly* 77, no. 3 (2008): 837–75; Grene, *The Peloponnesian War: The Complete Thomas Hobbes Translation*, 5; See Hobbes, *Leviathan*, 1968, 187, Ch. 13, for a similar argument substituting "the savage people in many places of America" who "live at this day in the brutish manner."

[88] Francis Bacon, "New Atlantis," in *Francis Bacon: A Critical Edition of the Major Works*, ed. Brian Vickers (Oxford: Oxford University Press, 1996), esp. 466–7.

according to Thucydides, by cities "becoming more experienced in seafaring."[89] If "experience in seafaring" provided the Greek cities the necessary means for effective political union in Thucydides' original, Hobbes' rendering subordinates the procedural value of Thucydides' "experience" in favor of a more explicitly teleological narrative. Navigation was no longer something the Greeks became "more experienced in" (David Grene suggests "they used the sea more") but, rather, something they had "now received." Noting Hobbes' departure from the original in using "now received," Grene, in an otherwise sparsely annotated edition, feels compelled to point out, "The Greek says, 'But on that expedition they came together inasmuch as now they used the sea *more*.'"[90] Positioning Thucydides along Gentilian rather than Grotian lines meant Hobbes' slight departure from Bacon, whose *New Atlantis* adopted the more Grotian narrative that "about three thousand years ago...the navigation of the world...was greater than at this day."[91] The effect of rendering navigation as something "received" rather than "experienced" was compounded by another alteration Hobbes made. Where Thucydides says the "old time" Greeks "increased their contacts by sea" (in Lattimore's translation) or "began more often to cross over" (Grene's), Hobbes renders it instead "began to cross over," omitting evidence of previous seafaring, a choice that, like "received" a few lines earlier, made Thucydides speak to the first origins of Greek navigation, rather than to its relative use.[92]

Hobbes' silent intervention here can be seen as an attempt to maintain Thucydides as a corroborator of Gentili's "hard primitivism" against the perceived threat of Grotian natural society. The stakes of this intervention would become clearest in *Leviathan,* where, in the famous paragraph describing life in the state of nature as "solitary, poore, nasty, brutish, and short," Hobbes insists that in that state, there was "no Navigation."[93]

Hobbes' marginal notes continue a quiet assault on Grotian natural society. Thucydides I.3–5, his notes suggest, is "A Digression, touching the Piracie & Robberies of old time; with other Notes of Saulvagenesse"; in old time, Hobbes instructs his readers, "Robbing had in honour" and "The continuall wearing of Armour [was] in fashion" due to the danger of daily life.[94] The original surely warranted these interpretations, but Hobbes goes out of his way to confirm Gentili's account of the Athenians' ascent from beastliness in his note upon the "golden grasshoppers, which [the newly civil Athenians] were wont to bind up in the locks of their hair." Oddly enough, it was the grasshopper that helped Hobbes solidify the intertextual relation between Thucydides I.3–5 and the passage in Lucretius V to which Gentili referred in which the Roman poet found evidence of human origins in the molting of grasshoppers. Hobbes posits, "The Athenians, holding themselves to be sprung from the ground they lived on, wore the Grasshopper for

---

[89] Steven Lattimore, ed., *The Peloponnesian War* (Indianapolis, IN: Hackett Pub Co., 1998), 5.

[90] Grene, *The Peloponnesian War: The Complete Thomas Hobbes Translation*, 3 (emphasis added).

[91] Bacon, "New Atlantis," 467.

[92] Grene also notes this omission: Grene, *The Peloponnesian War: The Complete Thomas Hobbes Translation*, 3.

[93] Hobbes, *Leviathan*, 1968, 186.   [94] Hobbes, *Eight Bookes of the Peloponnesian Warre*, 4.

a kinde of Cognizance, because that Beast is thought to be generated of the earth."[95] For Lucretius:

> All sorts of birds disclosd in that first spring
> Leaving their shells, betooke them to their wing,
> And sought foode to susteine their ranging lives,
> As grasshoppers whom the hott sum[m]er drives
> Out of their winter coats. Then in the ground
> Moysture and heate did very much abound,
> Which wheresoere earth yielded them fitt place
> Impregnated her womb with humane race[96]

Hobbes' Lucretian and Gentilian rendering of a passage already critical to the emerging *ius gentium* tradition suggests the influence Hobbes thought he might have on successive *ius gentium* historical accounts.

Similarly telling is Hobbes' rendering of the phrase in Thucydides I.5 "lived in by villages," [*kata kômas*], into "scatteringly inhabited." According to Grene, where Hobbes' Thucydides says "men ... falling upon towns unfortified and scatteringly inhabited, rifled them and made this the best means of their living," "the phrase is hardly fitly rendered 'scatteringly.'"[97] Once again, *ius gentium* debates in the context of colonialism inform Hobbes' translation here. "The key argument for the occupation of North America by the English," Richard Tuck points out, was that, in the words of John Donne's 1622 sermon to the Virginia Company, "a man [does not] become Lord of a Maine Continent, because he hath two or three cottages in the skirts therof."[98] "Filling" the land was the prime justification for "planting," and English colonialists undoubtedly welcomed confirmation of Greek precedent for "filling." As opposed to "lived in by villages," "scatteringly," therefore, opened the way for arguments built upon habitation patterns such as the one Hobbes was later to make in *Leviathan*—that settlers "are not to exterminate those they find there; but constrain them to inhabit closer together."[99] Hobbes' Thucydides I.3–5 embedded an imperialist vision of savagery and offered historical, proto-normative precedence for imperialism itself.

---

[95] Hobbes, *Eight Bookes of the Peloponnesian Warre*, 4. The reader of a heavily annotated copy now in the Huntington Library underlined this passage in the text and associated it with Anacreon's lyric on the grasshopper, the "Epicurean Animal" (in Cowley's Interregnum translation). I am grateful to Dr. Stephen Tabor of the Huntington Library for this information.

[96] Titus Lucretius Carus, *The Translation of Lucretius*, ed. Reid Barbour and David Norbrook, trans. Lucy Hutchinson, vol. 1.1, *The Works of Lucy Hutchinson* (Oxford: Oxford University Press, 2011), V.840–7. Dryden's later translation is briefer though it substitutes the more generic "insects" for "grasshoppers": "As even now, our tender Insects strive / To break their bags, get forth, and eat, and live. / Next Beasts, and thoughtful Man receiv'd their Birth."

[97] Grene, *The Peloponnesian War: The Complete Thomas Hobbes Translation*, 4.

[98] Peter Harrison, "'Fill the Earth and Subdue It': Biblical Warrants for Colonization in Seventeenth Century England," *Journal of Religious History* 29, no. 1 (2005): 3–24; Richard Tuck, "The Making and Unmaking of Boundaries from the Natural Law Perspective," in *States, Nations, and Borders: The Ethics of Making Boundaries*, ed. Allen E. Buchanan and Margaret Moore (Cambridge: Cambridge University Press, 2003), 143–70, esp. 156.

[99] Hobbes, *Leviathan*, 1968, 387; Tuck, *The Rights of War and Peace: Political Thought and the International Order from Grotius to Kant*, 138.

In the Restoration, Hobbes would take the apparently antiquarian view that it was imprudent to "derive from [histories] any Argument of Right but only Examples of Fact."[100] Yet this view was issued not as Hobbes looked back at antiquity but instead at the recent history of the English Revolution, and is a remarkable claim in any case from the seventeenth-century's most notorious *de facto*-ist.[101] Indeed, the evident consonance between Thucydidian fact and Hobbesian right belies Hobbes' disclaimer that facts have no normative purchase. Thucydidian history was imperial history, and translation made it useable for imperial law.

Thucydides is hardly naïve about the costs of maritime empire. Because of the failure of the Sicilian expedition in Book VIII Thucydides has often been read as a tragic lesson in imperial overreaching, and the figure of Cleon is just one of many examples through which Hobbes' translation tells a multihued story of imperial challenges. It has sometimes been easy to forget that for Hobbes, nature's prohibition of cruelty was one of the "natural laws whose observance does not cease even in war."[102] The overarching point, though, is that the challenges in Thucydides were challenged confronted *by an historical maritime empire*, and historical fact, especially when enhanced by an interested translator, exerted a quiet normative power of its own.

RHETORIC AND ROYALISM: THUCYDIDES AND THE VIRGINIA COMPANY

In the early 1620s, Hobbes participated in no fewer than thirty-seven meetings of the Virginia Company, whose members had had been provided access to major tracts in the emerging *ius gentium* tradition.[103] Noel Malcolm explains "that Hobbes did not have to wait till the period of his [1630s] attendance at Great Tew in order to think about the theoretical issues of jurisdiction and dominion discussed by Grotius and Selden; a decade earlier he must have heard these issues discussed [in the Virginia Company] as a matter pertinent to the practical business in which he himself had an immediate concern."[104] It will be clear that I agree completely with this assessment, and that I think Hobbes' Thucydides should be seen in precisely this light. But what then of the durable story of royalism?

Following Hobbes' patron Cavendish into the gritty details of Stuart parliamentary politics can help clear some misconceptions. Cavendish's activities in the Lords debates over the Petition of Right were subtle, and therefore easy to misinterpret.

---

[100] Thomas Hobbes, *Behemoth, the history of the causes of the civil wars of England, from 1640 to 1660* in *Tracts of Mr. Thomas Hobbs of Malmsbury* (London: W. Crooke, 1682), 125.

[101] Hoekstra, "The 'De Facto' Turn in Hobbes's Political Philosophy."

[102] Thomas Hobbes, *On the Citizen*, ed. Richard Tuck, trans. Michael Silverthorne (Cambridge: Cambridge University Press, 1998), 54; Malcolm, *Aspects of Hobbes*, 438.

[103] Malcolm, *Aspects of Hobbes*; Andrew Fitzmaurice, "Moral Uncertainty in the Dispossession of Native Americans," in *The Atlantic World and Virginia, 1550–1624*, ed. Peter C. Mancall (Chapel Hill, NC: The Omohundro Institute, 2007), 388–96.

[104] Malcolm, *Aspects of Hobbes*, 63.

He displayed nothing like the outspoken urgency of Bishop Williams of Lincoln or Viscounts Saye and Sele, the latter of whom, for example, argued passionately, "it is the due right of the subject not to be committed without cause expressed."[105] Rather, it appears that in a way similar to his response to the forced loan, Cavendish sought to resolve his objections against an overreaching crown, which was operating troublingly in the language of reason of state, and his obedience to his rightful monarch.[106] On the one hand, Cavendish specifically argued that the king's prerogative was part of "the law of the land," a statement that Sommerville suggests shows Cavendish's misgivings over the Petition.[107] But such evidence must be balanced against Cavendish's speech against discretionary imprisonment in which, quoting Magna Carta, he argued that it was "proved" that "a free man ought not to be committed nisi per legem terrae."[108] The debate was fluid enough that Northampton bewailed at one point, "I hear so many learned speeches that I am still of opinion with him that spoke last," but the tension in Cavendish's speeches need not be ascribed to excessive malleability.[109] Flemion has shown that even vehemently pro-Petition figures like John Selden, in the House of Commons, and Viscount Saye, in the Lords, used the same argument Cavendish did—that the prerogative was "tacit"—in order to keep an explicit statement of the king's prerogative out of the Petition's final wording.[110] Statements like Cavendish's accepting the prerogative can therefore be found on all sides. That Cavendish's ultimate motivation for such a statement was keeping explicit mention of the prerogative out of the Petition can be seen from his speech on 22 April 1628, about a month after Hobbes' Thucydides was entered into the Stationer's Register and less than two months before Cavendish's death (20 June 1628).[111] When inclusion of language watering down the Petition seemed imminent and Petition opponents were therefore calling for votes, Cavendish strategically intervened for further discussion with the Lower House, seeking "a way to avoid disunion with the [staunchly pro-Petition] Commons."[112] Based on surviving diaries, it appears he never questioned the prerogative outright nor even spoke particularly

[105] Mary Frear Keeler, Maija Jansson Cole, and William B. Bidwell, ed., *Proceedings in Parliament, 1628*, vol. 5 (New Haven, CT: Yale University Press, 1983), 524; Jess Flemion, "A Savings to Satisfy All: The House of Lords and the Meaning of the Petition of Right," *Parliamentary History* 10, no. 1 (1991): 27–44.

[106] Geoff Baldwin, "Reason of State and English Parliaments, 1610–1642," *History of Political Thought* 25, no. 4 (2004): 620–41; David S. Berkowitz, "Reason of State in England and the Petition of Right, 1603–1629," in *Staatsräson: Studien Zur Geschichte Eines Politischen Begriffe*, ed. Roman Schnur (Berlin: Duncker & Humblot, 1975), 165–212; Thomas Cogswell, "'In the Power of the State': Mr Anys's Project and the Tobacco Colonies, 1626–1628," *English Historical Review* CXXIII, no. 500 (February 1, 2008): 35–64, esp. 46, 60.

[107] Keeler, Cole, and Bidwell, *Proceedings in Parliament, 1628*, 5:435; Sommerville, *Thomas Hobbes*, 10 n. 18.

[108] Keeler, Cole, and Bidwell, *Proceedings in Parliament, 1628*, 5:324.

[109] Keeler, Cole, and Bidwell, *Proceedings in Parliament, 1628*, 5:323.

[110] Flemion, "A Savings to Satisfy All," 34–6.

[111] Sidney Lee and Victor Slater, "Cavendish, William, Second Earl of Devonshire (1590–1628)," *Oxford Dictionary of National Biography* (Oxford: Oxford University Press, 2004).

[112] Keeler, Cole, and Bidwell, *Proceedings in Parliament, 1628*, 5:329.

regularly; instead, his main interests appear to have been process-oriented—"avoid[ing] disunion," "conferenc[ing] for accommodation."[113] Cavendish's language of accommodation unarguably had political bite, since the "accommodation" with the Commons was accommodation with the strongest voices for the Petition, yet his particular emphasis on compromise shows evidence of a man eager to negotiate conflicts rather than to inflame them. We can discern from Cavendish's initial loan refusal and modest steps in favor of the Petition of Right that Cavendish imagined limits to royal authority, yet we can also see Cavendish's stoic reluctance to parade his disobedience or to countermand royal authority in too dramatic a fashion, if at all.

Cavendish's politics can give, at best, an imperfect picture of Hobbes'. Yet they do point us to a tension in the Thucydides volume that contemporary observers would have noted but that has yet to be adequately addressed—namely, the tension between Cavendish's strategically oppositional legacy and the voluble royalism of the Thucydides prefatory material.

Appreciating the full measure of this tension requires cognizance of the Renaissance demands of rhetoric, in particular the way that those making political proposals (the domain of deliberative rhetoric) were counseled to use to use praise and blame (epideictic rhetoric) in pursuit of their ends.[114] Positing Hobbes' specific ends, of course, presents considerable difficulties, but the endeavor is aided by considering global and international contexts for Hobbes' work during this period. As Malcolm notes, "there are almost no indications of how Hobbes was occupied after the [1624] dissolution of the Company."[115] Most scholars have therefore assumed that the crown's revocation of the Virginia Company patent marked the end of Hobbes' financial and intellectual interest in the New World. There are nevertheless reasons to question this assumption. First, even after Charles took control of the Virginia Company, Cavendish remained deeply invested in the offshoot company active in the Bermudas, the Somers Island Company—so invested, in fact, that the eminent historian of the New World companies W. F. Craven wrote that "of all those leaders who fought so valiantly, and bitterly, by the side of Sandys in 1623–1624, only Lord William Cavendish was possibly more vitally concerned with the fortunes of [the Bermudas] than [Virginia]."[116] At Cavendish's death, the Governor of Bermuda, Roger Wood, wrote a consoling letter to Cavendish's widow that also gently reminded her of

---

[113] Keeler, Cole, and Bidwell, *Proceedings in Parliament, 1628*, 5:324.

[114] See Skinner, *Reason and Rhetoric in the Philosophy of Thomas Hobbes*, 244–9, for Hobbes' rhetorical moves in his "Life of Thucydides." On the general importance of the epideictic tradition in early modern political and intellectual culture, see David Colclough, "Verse Libels and the Epideictic Tradition in Early Stuart England," *Huntington Library Quarterly* 69, no. 1 (2006): 15–30; Craig Kallendorf, *In Praise of Aeneas: Virgil and Epideictic Rhetoric in the Early Italian Renaissance* (Hanover, NH: University Press of New England, 1989); Donna B. Hamilton, *Virgil and The Tempest: The Politics of Imitation* (Columbus, OH: Ohio State University Press, 1990).

[115] Malcolm, *Aspects of Hobbes*, 73.

[116] Wesley Frank Craven, "An Introduction to the History of Bermuda: VI, the Revised Plan of Settlement," *The William and Mary Quarterly* 18, no. 1 (1938): 45–6 n.11.

the Cavendishs' "poor tenants" on their Bermuda land—still today the parish of Devonshire—who "labour almost in nakedness."[117]

It bears repeating that the only known evidence of Hobbes' involvement with the Somers Island Company comes before Charles disbanded the Virginia Company. But given the Cavendishs' involvement lasting even through the Stuart Restoration, as well as the relative dearth of surviving documentary evidence, the possibility should not be dismissed.[118] Though it has not, to my knowledge, been discussed in Hobbes scholarship, a more important factor is that even after the revocation of the Virginia Company charter (I shy from "dissolution" for reasons that will become clear), many of the Sandys faction of Virginia adventurers harbored hopes, not unrealistically, for the restoration of the Company. Charles had taken control "until such time as it could be turned over to the reorganized corporation."[119] Accordingly, there is evidence of "a serious effort to secure a renewal of the old patent" in 1625, and again in 1631—suggesting, in fact, more of a continual campaign than discrete efforts.[120] The campaign continued as late as 1640, when George Sandys, Edwin's brother and the translator of Ovid and Grotius, petitioned the House of Commons for the Company's resurrection.[121]

What part did these transatlantic interests play in Hobbes' translation? I would argue that in mid to late 1628, as Hobbes composed the prefatory materials to a volume whose title page would trumpet its origins in the Devonshire household, he judged that the aim of resurrecting the Virginia Company could best be effected by praising monarchy.

As Donna Hamilton has shown, "epideictic [rhetoric] does indeed praise, [but] it also always presents itself as praise even when the object of the writing includes significant evaluative and interventionist strategies."[122] One reason to consider resurrection of the Virginia Company as among Hobbes' objectives is the distinct echo in Hobbes' antidemocratic "Life of Thucydides" of the very language Charles used in "resum[ing]" control of the Virginia Company in 1625.[123] Remarkably, Charles used Virginia's floundering to propagandize against the evils of "popular government," emphasizing in his published proclamation that the Company was "incorporated of a multitude of persons of several dispositions" where "the affairs

---

[117] J. H. Lefroy, ed., *Memorials of the Discovery and Early Settlement of the Bermudas or Somers Islands, 1515–1685* (London: Longmans, Green, and Co., 1877), vol. 1, 532; Henry C. Wilkinson, *The Adventurers of Bermuda: A History of the Island from Its Discovery until the Dissolution of the Somers Island Company in 1684*, 2nd edn. (London: Oxford University Press, 1958), V220.

[118] Wilkinson, *The Adventurers of Bermuda: A History of the Island from Its Discovery Until the Dissolution of the Somers Island Company in 1684*, 348, 43; Lefroy, *Memorials of the Discovery and Early Settlement of the Bermudas or Somers Islands, 1515–1685*, vol. 2, 718–31.

[119] Wesley Frank Craven, *Dissolution of the Virginia Company: The Failure of a Colonial Experiment* (Oxford: Oxford University Press, 1932), 328.

[120] Craven, *Dissolution of the Virginia Company: The Failure of a Colonial Experiment*, 329.

[121] James Ellison, *George Sandys: Travel, Colonialism, and Tolerance in the Seventeenth Century* (Cambridge: D. S. Brewer, 2002), 144.

[122] Hamilton, *Virgil and The Tempest*, 7.

[123] Quotations from Charles' proclamation are taken from "Proclamation Settling the Affairs of Virginia," in W. Keith Kavenagh, ed., *Foundations of Colonial America: A Documentary History* (New York: Chelsea House, 1973), 1723.

of the greatest moment were and must be ruled by the greater number of votes and voices." The dissention of the Virginia Company, in other words, was due to its political form—a point noted by James Ellison who says "the early Stuart kings saw in the Virginia Company the monster of democracy, and sought to quash it."[124] In taking control, "his Majesty's aim," Charles wrote, "was...to reduce that government [of the Company] into such a right course as might best agree with that form which was held in the rest of his royal monarchy." He referred to the "former personal differences which have heretofore happened, the reviving and continuing whereof we utterly disallow"—which could be read both as a general rebuke and as a swipe at Cavendish's illegal 1623 attempt to duel Robert Rich, Earl of Warwick.

With the potential for a reconstituted Virginia Company hanging in the balance and Charles having indicated where praise and blame should rightly be assigned, Hobbes in his "Life of Thucydides" praises monarchy and blames democracy accordingly. In Aristotle's *Ars Rhetorica*, a 1637 English brief which is often ascribed to Hobbes, Aristotle advised just this studied mingling of epideictic and deliberative orations:

> Praise and counsels have a common aspect: for what you might suggest in counseling becomes encomium by a change in the phrase. Accordingly, when we know what we ought to do and the qualities we ought to possess, we ought to make a change in the phrase and turn it, employing this knowledge as suggestion...if you desire to praise, look what you would suggest; if you desire to suggest, look what you would praise.[125]

Hobbes evidently took to heart the lesson of the "common aspect" of praise and suggestion. Suggesting a reconstituted Virginia Company, he praised monarchy; praising monarchy, he suggested a reconstituted Virginia Company. Sensitive, politically connected readers would likely have associated a publication coming from Cavendish's household with the Virginia and Somers Island interests, and it is noteworthy that Edward Hyde's numerous extracts from the volume, for example, give no mention of Hobbes and instead describe the translator as "Secretary to the E. of Devon."[126] Hobbes' epideictic blame of democracy can therefore plausibly be seen as a rhetorical gesture of deference to Charles' Virginia Company historiography that, abstracted as it was from its immediate context, could also usefully articulate Stuart royalism in the broader world of print—all of which constituted, in effect, Hobbes' deliberative plea for a resurrected Virginia Company, reorganized if need be in a sufficiently hierarchical way to allay Charles' distaste for "popularity."

Apart from Hobbes' comments in the volume, there is little reason to think that Thucydides was a particularly apt historian to pronounce upon constitutional forms.

---

[124] Ellison, *George Sandys: Travel, Colonialism, and Tolerance in the Seventeenth Century*, 145.

[125] Aristotle, *The "Art" of Rhetoric*, trans. John Henry Freese (London; New York: W. Heinemann; G. P. Putnam's Sons, 1926), I.x.35, 101–3; Andrew Fitzmaurice also suggests Donne's indebtedness to this passage in his useful study of the oratorical and humanist facets of Virginia Company propaganda. See Fitzmaurice, *Humanism and America: An Intellectual History of English Colonisation, 1500–1625*, 103.

[126] Edward Hyde, Bodleian Library, MSS Clarendon 127, fol. 50r.

It is possible though unlikely that Hobbes knew Girolamo Cardano's contention that Thucydides was a republican not a monarchist.[127] Venetian republicans like Domenico Molino claiming Thucydides for their own are a more likely source, and Hobbes may even have noted that Grotius, in his history of the Batavian Republic, had briefly cited Thucydides to prove that kingship was a "title of honor" derived from the voluntary consent of the people, but based on Grotius' other uses of the Greek historian (not to mention Thucydides' subsequent canonization in twentieth-century international relations), the events Thucydides records were more germane to what I have been calling the epic *ius gentium*: e.g., laws of war, the rights of ambassadors, duties of captives, rights of conquest, the interpretation of treaties, and so on.[128] In fact, Hobbes' first encounter with Thucydides was apparently when the Italian author of a letter that Hobbes translated into English compared Catholic barbarity in the Thirty Years' War to Thucydides' account of primitive ancient Greece.[129]

That Thucydides was such an unlikely author to be conscripted for the cause of monarchism helps us to see Hobbes' appeal for royal attention more clearly.[130] As Kinch Hoekstra notes, passages from Thucydides had been heavily used in Charles' father's own *Basilikon Doron*, a work of royal advice James eventually passed to Charles as heir.[131] A printed marginal note beside Hobbes' translation of the infamous Corcyraean sedition even suggests Hobbes' motive. The passage has been linked by scholars to Hobbes' brutal state of nature, but at the time, as the paradigmatic narrative of a community's collapse into factionalism, Hobbes' "politic" readers would have associated the Corcyraean sedition with the fate of the Virginia Company, whose factions were elsewhere being compared to Italy's fractious Guelphs and Ghibellines.[132] Having advertised Thucydides' treatment

---

[127] Anthony Grafton, *What Was History?: The Art of History in Early Modern Europe* (Cambridge: Cambridge University Press, 2007), 183.

[128] Hoekstra, "Thucydides and the Bellicose Beginnings of Modern Political Theory," 31; Hugo Grotius, *A Treatise of the Antiquity of the Battaver, Which Is Now the Hollanders*, trans. Thomas Woods (London, 1649) sig. b2r-v, originally, *Liber De Antiquitate Reipublicae Batavicae* (Leiden, 1610).

[129] Micanzio to Cavendish 12 March 1621: "They use every where such barbaritie, as savours not of Christians, but of their ancient derivation from Gothes, and Mahometans. Leopold in Tirole and he yᵗ is governour in Carinthia have wᵗʰ severe edicts cutt of all commerce wᵗʰ us, and under pretence that Soldiers shall not passe that way, they use the most unreasonable extortion upon passengers and Merchants that ever was heard off. One may new looke to see againe that tyme whereof Thucidides maketh mention, that amongst the Graecians to be a robber was a Title of Honour, so these men will make oppression to be a secret of Empire." See Fulgenzio Micanzio, *Lettere a William Cavendish (1615–1628)*, ed. Roberto Ferrini, trans. Thomas Hobbes (Rome: Istituto storico O.S.M., 1987).

[130] Hobbes suggests that his monarchical language was composed some years after he had actually translated Thucydides. He notes in his epistle "To the Readers," "After I had finished [the translation], it lay long by mee, and other reasons taking place, my desire to communicate it ceased": Hobbes, *Eight Bookes of the Peloponnesian Warre*, sig. a4r.

[131] Hoekstra, "Thucydides and the Bellicose Beginnings of Modern Political Theory," 26.

[132] For the link between Corcyra and Hobbes' state of nature, see, for example, Brown, "Thucydides, Hobbes and the Derivation of Anarchy"; For the comparison with Italian factionalism, see Cogswell, " 'In the Power of the State,' " 37.

of the passage in his "Life," Hobbes directs readers to the Thucydidean account vividly describing the horrors of lawless Corcyra ravaged by dissention and war. In Corcyra's up-is-down dystopia, according to Hobbes' powerful translation:

> He that could outstrip another in the doing of an evil act or that could persuade another thereto that never meant it was commended. To be kin to another was not to be so near as to be of his society because these were ready to undertake anything and not to dispute it. For these societies were not made upon prescribed laws of profit but for rapine, contrary to the laws established.[133]

If Thucydides is concerned here to emphasize the destruction of rogue bands in civil conflict, Hobbes, surprisingly, takes the occasion to emphasize the historical legitimacy of joint stock corporations. Was Hobbes anxious that the example of Corcyra not be seen as an argument against a revived Virginia Company? Hobbes adds the following gloss to Thucydides' "societies" [*xunodoi*]: "The uniting of Companies under certaine Lawes, for the more profitable managing of their Trades and arts, seemeth to have beene in use then, as now."[134] "As now," likely had an ironic thrust, for it was Charles' very deviation from the ancients' "prescribed laws of profit" Hobbes ultimately wished to emphasize.

More definitive evidence that revival of the Virginia Company was at the core of Hobbes translation remains difficult to come by, but the case of George Sandys, mentioned earlier as the translator of Ovid and Grotius, provides a tantalizing parallel. While Ovid's claim to the label of "history" may today seem slight, Degory Wheare considered *Metamorphoses* a "chronicle" that "comprehended" "the *Trojan War*, the *Expedition of the Argonauts*, the Histories of *Perseus*, *Oedipus*, *Hercules*, *Theseus* and some others."[135] Sandys also translated Vergil's *Aeneid*, which, like Ovid's *Metamorphoses*, provided key matter for the *ius gentium* tracts, as we have seen. Sandys' intentions—and rewards—can therefore be suggestively considered alongside those of Hobbes and their contemporaries, not least because Sandys' 1626 Ovid and Hobbes' 1628 Thucydides each bore elaborate engraved title pages crafted by the artist beloved by colonialists, Thomas Cecil, whose work also included an imperial engraving for the famous title page of Bacon's posthumous *Sylva Sylvarum* (1627), a title page engraving for the continuation of John Smith's *History of Virginia* (1629), a map for *A Relation of Maryland* (1635), and the famous painting of Queen Elizabeth astride a horse

---

[133] Grene, *The Peloponnesian War: The Complete Thomas Hobbes Translation*, 205.

[134] Hobbes, *Eight Bookes of the Peloponnesian Warre*, 198. At least one seventeenth-century reader took special note of Hobbes' translation and annotation of this passage. A reader of British Library shelfmark Eve.b.38, perhaps the diarist and naturalist John Evelyn himself, made marginal pencil marks on most of this page. A relevant distinction is the one Hobbes makes in *Leviathan* II.22 between corporations that work as part of the body politic like muscles and corporations that infect it.

[135] Degory Wheare, *The Method and Order of Reading Both Civil and Ecclesiastical Histories in Which the Most Excellent Historians Are Reduced into the Order in Which They Are Successively to Be Read, and the Judgments of Learned Men Concerning Each of Them, Subjoin'd*, trans. Edmund Bohun (London: M. Flesher for Charles Brome, 1685), 24.

large enough to cross the Atlantic in one bound, *Truth Presents the Queen with a Lance* (1625).[136]

Sandys translated Vergil, it has been suggested, attempting to win the patronage of wealthy Virginia Company investors like the Earls of Pembroke and Southampton.[137] The resulting text suggests affinities at every turn between Englishmen and heroic, colonizing Trojans. Sandys' Ovid translation, meanwhile, completed when Sandys was in Virginia, bragged of its having been "bred in the New-Worlde, of the rude-nesse whereof it cannot but participate; especially having Warres and Tumults to bring it to light," and thus held English learning aloft against New World barbarity. In it, Sandys largely hewed closely to Ovid's original, yet, like Hobbes, Sandys occasionally suggested the barbarity of the New World by altering key phrases. To surmise Ovid's potential importance to *ius gentium* debates, Stuart England did not have to look past Grotius' *Mare Liberum* (1609). Ovid's "*usus communis aquarum est*" [the enjoyment of water is a common right] had underpinned Grotius' claim for a "free sea" in 1609, and was of enough significance that Grotius reproduced what he called this "noble passage" again in an unpublished reply to the Scotch jurist William Welwood's *An Abridgement of All Sea-Lawes* (1613) (another book, incidentally, held in the Hardwick library).[138] As with Thucydides, the commercial stakes of translation were considerable: the goal in this debate was not intellectual vindication but rather fishing rights and the control of prizes. In this context, it should not be surprising that Sandys' heavily annotated English Ovid reaped him extraordinary royal favor. On April 24, 1626, Charles took the rare step of granting Sandys a twenty-one-year patent for the exclusive printing and selling of Ovid: "the better to encourage him and others to imploie theire labours and studies in good literature."[139] If it had not been already, the word was now out that English translations of the classics, so useful for formulating the law of nations, would or could win lucrative remuneration.

---

[136] Margery Corbett and R. W. Lightbrown, *The Comely Frontispiece: The Emblematic Title-Page in England, 1550–1660* (London: Routledge & Kegan Paul, 1979), 185–6; Cecil would also engrave the title page for Grotius' anonymously translated *True Religion Explained and Defended* (1632), a work some claimed was written originally to guide Dutch sailors in converting the Indians: Hugo Grotius, *Christs Passion: A Tragedy. With Annotations*, trans. George Sandys, STC 12397.5 (London: John Letat, 1640), no sig. A3v.

[137] This paragraph is indebted to Ellison, *George Sandys: Travel, Colonialism, and Tolerance in the Seventeenth Century*, 101–60; Patricia Springborg links Sandys' Ovid with both the Virginia Company and Hobbes' Thucydides in Springborg, "Leviathan, Mythic History, and National Historiography," 267–70.

[138] Hugo Grotius, *The Free Sea*, ed. David Armitage, trans. Richard Hakluyt, Natural Law and Enlightenment Classics (Indianapolis, IN: Liberty Fund, 2004), 25, 93. Hobbes, Old Catalogue, fol. 119.

[139] George Beale Davis, *George Sandys, Poet-Adventurer: A Study in Anglo-American Culture in the Seventeenth Century* (New York: Columbia University Press, 1955), 199; Thomas Rymer, *Foedera: Conventiones, Literae, Et Cujuscunque Generis Acta Publica, Inter Reges Angliae, Et Alios Quosvis Imperatores, Reges*, vol. 18 (London: A. & J. Churchill, 1726), 676; Arnold Hunt, "Book Trade Patents, 1603–1640," in *The Book Trade & Its Customers, 1450–1900: Historical Essays for Robin Myers*, ed. Arnold Hunt, Giles Mandelbrote, and Alison Shell (Winchester: Oak Knoll Press, 1997), 27–54.

HOBBES IN THE FIELD

In a passage taken as scripture by so-called "realist" students of international relations everywhere, Hobbes wrote in *Leviathan*:

> in all times Kings, and Persons of Soveraigne authority, because of their Independency, are in continuall jealousies, and in the state and posture of Gladiators, having their weapons pointing, and their eyes fixed on one another; that is, their Forts, Garrisons, and Guns upon the Frontiers of their Kingdomes; and continuall Spyes upon their neighbours, which is a posture of War.[140]

The passage has been quoted so often that its force may have dulled, but it's nevertheless worth reminding ourselves how effectively "in all times" neutralizes the many potential agents with motive and opportunity to make international law's present and future out of its past. "In all times" reduced the fraught and historically contingent law of nations into Hobbes' minimalist, rationalist law of nature. "The Law of Nations, and the Law of nature, is the same thing," Hobbes wrote, "every Soveraign [having] the same Right, in procuring the safety of his People, that any particular man can have, in procuring the safety of his own body."[141] The field of international relations, largely taking Hobbes' (male) gladiators as normative, is only now recovering from a pervasive ahistoricism.[142]

But this need not obscure Hobbes' own prior success translating an empirical history into something with the normative force of Hobbesian self-preservation.[143] Both the Hobbesian person in the state of nature and Hobbes' "person of the state" in perpetual nature exhibit the characteristics of Thucydidean cities at war. Scholars continue to ignore or overlook that self-preserving states are told in *Leviathan* to settle colonies and secure foreign lands when they perceive threats. Hobbes, our epic humanist, can be most deadly in the quiet of night. There is grave force in his pithy suggestions that sovereigns' "augmentation of dominion" is permissible in the face of rivals of "insatiable appetite, or *Bulimia*" who pursue "acts of conquest... farther than their security requires."[144] The consequences of this doctrine only become clear when we realize insatiable appetites are most often what *other imperial bodies* have. "Augmentation of dominion over men, being necessary to a mans conservation,... ought to be allowed..."[145] This is imperial expansion justified as self-preservation.

---

[140] Hobbes, *Leviathan*, 187–8.   [141] Hobbes, *Leviathan*, 394.

[142] Hilary Charlesworth, "The Sex of the State in International Law," in *Sexing the Subject of Law*, ed. Ngaire Naffine and Rosemary J. Owens (North Ryde, NSW: LBC Information Services, 1997), 251–68; David Armitage, "'The Fifty Years' Rift': Intellectual History and International Relations," *Modern Intellectual History* 1, no. 1 (2005): 97–109; Edward Keene, *International Political Thought: A Historical Introduction* (Cambridge; Malden, MA: Polity, 2005); David Boucher, *Political Theories of International Relations: From Thucydides to the Present* (New York: Oxford University Press, 1998).

[143] Christopher N. Warren, "When Self-Preservation Bids: Approaching Milton, Hobbes, and Dissent," *English Literary Renaissance* 37, no. 1 (2007): 118–50.

[144] Hobbes, *Leviathan*, 1968, 184–5, 218.   [145] Hobbes, *Leviathan*, 1968, 185.

Several years ago, Koskenniemi noted the "Hobbesian structure of international legal discourse," by which he meant the ineradicable tension in international law between *a priori* norms and *a posteriori* justifications. "Since Hobbes," thinkers have been "unable to accept either a fully objective or fully subjective international order."[146] Koskenniemi argued that Hobbes had given states' subjective passions and interests a normative quality even as putatively objective laws and rules were, in Hobbes' work, the outgrowth of, and contingent upon, subjective self-preserving wills. International law in his wake remained caught between apology and utopia. Arguments about sovereign states' obligations made with too little acknowledgment of their subjective passions and interests were characterized as utopian. Arguments consonant with those passions and interests were *apologia* and were rejected by other states.

There is striking consonance between Koskenniemi's perspective and an incisive passage by Antony Grafton on writing history in early modern Europe:

> Writers and practitioners of the *ars historica* claimed that they knew how to walk the tightrope that stretched between practical application and pure historicism. In fact, however, they could not explain even to themselves how the modern reader was supposed to go about both setting his texts back into their own times, with all the skill of the philologist, and making them relevant to his own day, with all the bravura of a rhetorician.[147]

Hobbes, I have argued, realized that it wasn't chronicling history but translating it that could most successfully resolve the antinomies of antiquarianism and topicality, empiricism and rhetoric. It was in this way that imperial history could become imperial international law. According to Aubrey, "Before Thucydides, [Hobbes] spent two years in reading romances and plays."[148] The fashionable tragicomedies of these years, as we know, delighted in foregrounding their own wit. Hobbes, by contrast, started with imperial history, performed epic feats of humanism, and ended up victorious in a battle few even realized he'd fought.

In the introduction to his much later *Codex Iuris Gentium* (1693), a collection of treaties and documents relating to the history of the law of nations, Leibniz would come to note how the "voluntary law of nations" "changed with the passage of centuries." Leibniz cautioned, therefore, against overreliance on "unfaithful" historians motivated by "national feelings" or those "historians who habitually represent men as worse than they are in reality."[149] "Public history," had a "secret" side that included consequential particularities like whether or not "the prince has slept badly" or whether a "remark which is maliciously reported or invented strikes the

---

[146] Martti Koskenniemi, "The Hobbesian Structure of International Legal Discourse," in *Hobbes: War among Nations*, ed. Timo Airaksinen et al. (Aldershot: Avebury, 1989), 168–78. See further Martti Koskenniemi, *From Apology to Utopia: The Structure of International Legal Argument*, 2nd edn. (Cambridge: Cambridge University Press, 2005), 79–83.

[147] Grafton, *What Was History?*, 2007, 228.

[148] Aubrey, *Brief Lives*, 149. Hobbes, says Aubrey, "often repented" these years, but Aubrey was already alert to the possibility that Hobbes took more from this reading than he liked to admit ("perhaps he was mistaken").

[149] Gottfried Wilhelm Leibniz, *Political Writings*, 2nd edn. (Cambridge: Cambridge University Press, 1988), 174, 168–9.

soul of a prince...and leaves a sting."[150] The present and future of the law of nations were indeed tied to its past, but that past was remote, and it had even come to seem to Leibniz and others untrustworthy. The authority of history in the law of nations was diminishing.

The declining importance of history to the law of nations was thanks in no small measure to Hobbes' campaign. "Thy learn'd *America*," Cowley's ode to Hobbes had enthused, "is / Not onely found out first by Thee, / And rudely left to *Future Industrie*, / But thy *Eloquence* and thy *Wit*, / Has *planted, peopled, built*, and *civiliz'd* it."[151] Hobbes used Thucydides to accomplish the epic feat of establishing an imperialist law of nations before fortifying and defending the city he'd built against history itself.

[150] Leibniz, *Political Writings*, 168–9.   [151] Cowley, "To Mr. Hobbes."

6

From Biblical Tragedy to Human Rights
International Legal Personality in Grotius' *Sophompaneas*
and Milton's *Samson Agonistes*

In 1915, following the outbreak of the Great War, the great Shakespearean critic and Hegelian philosopher A. C. Bradley published a little-studied essay entitled "International Morality: The United States of Europe," in which he argued for the *prima facie* "duty of states to observe international law."[1] The author, already well known for his *Shakespearean Tragedy* (1904), did so by using the character of Hamlet to illustrate states as "moral agents" endowed with personality.[2] The present conflagration of the First World War was due to the rapid rise in Germany's military power, Germany having been "for long years, even for centuries, a 'Hamlet among the nations'; great, that is to say, in the purely spiritual spheres of religion, philosophy, music, poetry, but, to all appearance, incapable in the world of political action."[3] For Bradley, tragedy had become an organizing frame for thinking about war, sovereignty, and international law. Tragedy and war in fact depended upon one another, each having arisen from the same "great and glorious energies of the soul." As he wrote in "International Morality," "war, on the whole, may roughly be compared with tragedy...if the disappearance of either meant the disappearance, or even a lowering, of those noble and glorious energies of the soul which appear in both and are in part the cause of both, the life of perpetual peace would be a poor thing, superficially less terrible perhaps than the present life, but much less great and good."[4] While states did indeed have moral duties, those duties could theoretically include violence. The literary form of tragedy was therefore a rejoinder to overly rosy projects for perpetual peace, an acknowledgment that international morality and international law were not necessarily equivalent to pacifism. While war might be managed and tamed through law, it had not been, nor should it be, eliminated.

After Bradley, a number of more recent scholars have also emphasized the need for international legal history, international relations, and political discourse more broadly "in a tragic key."[5] When writers as diverse as Hans Morgenthau, Susan

---

[1] A. C. Bradley, "International Morality: The United States of Europe," in *The International Crisis in Its Ethical and Psychological Aspects; Lectures Delivered in February and March, 1915* (London: H. Milford, 1915), 66.

[2] Bradley, "International Morality," 66.   [3] Bradley, "International Morality," 75.

[4] Bradley, "International Morality," 64–5.

[5] T. J. Clark, "For a Left with No Future," *New Left Review* 74, March–April (2012): 59.

Marks, T. J. Clark, and David Scott invite us into their tragic frame, however, what do they mean? Pointing out that the history of human rights is often told as a "romance," Marks, following Scott, who himself follows C. L. R. James, Northrop Frye, and Hayden White, calls for more tragic "modes of emplotment" in that field, by which she means stories more alert to the "dilemmas, disappointments, ironies and uncertainties of enlightenment and liberation."[6] For Clark, whose scholarly touchstones include Bradley's *Shakespearean Tragedy* and Christopher's Hill's *The Experience of Defeat* (1984), tragedy involves above all an appreciation for life's "suffering and calamity, the constant presence of violence in human affairs, the extraordinary difficulty of reconciling that violence with a rule of law...."[7] John Mearshimer's *The Tragedy of Great Power Politics* (2001) reprises ideas made most influentially in Hans Morgenthau's *Politics Among Nations* (1948), whose tragic account of clashing states, premised on man's ostensibly "futile search for a perfection that belonged only to God," supplanted discussions like Bradley's of international law and morality with the new, more scientific discourse of "international relations."[8] For many of these writers, tragedy could be seen as that which pierces international law's blinkered, hopeful naiveté.

As Bradley may have been one of the best placed scholars to understand, however, there was little in international law as it emerged out of the Renaissance law of nations that made international law incompatible with war. In fact, the connection between war and the law of nations was so strong that Kant contrasted his own cosmopolitan project for perpetual peace with that of Grotius and others of the era whom Kant deemed "sorry comforters" for their moral compromises with early modern European warfare.[9]

For many writers, the law of nations *was* the tragedy. The early modern distinctions between *ius ad bellum*, *ius in bello*, and *ius post bellum*, strongly grounded on the moral supposition that occasions sometimes necessitated just war, had been developed *against* counselors of pacifism such as the Christian church father Lactantius. We have occasion once more to quote Isidore of Seville, this time noting explicitly how his *topoi* of the law of nations sketch a darkly tragic terrain: "the law of nations concerns the occupation of territory, building, fortification, wars, captivities, enslavements, the right of return, treaties of peace, truces, the pledge not to molest embassies, the prohibition of marriages between different races." And even though "law of nations," was often seen to name certain ameliorative obligations,

---

[6] Susan Marks, "Human Rights in Disastrous Times," in *The Cambridge Companion to International Law*, eds. James Crawford and Martti Koskenniemi (Cambridge: Cambridge University Press, 2012), 309–26; Clark, "For a Left with No Future"; J. Peter Euben, *The Tragedy of Political Theory: The Road Not Taken* (Princeton, NJ: Princeton University Press, 1990); David Scott, *Conscripts of Modernity: The Tragedy of Colonial Enlightenment* (Durham, NC: Duke University Press, 2004); Toni Erskine and Richard Ned Lebow, eds., *Tragedy and International Relations* (New York: Palgrave Macmillan, 2012).

[7] Clark, "For a Left with No Future," 58.

[8] Martti Koskenniemi, *The Gentle Civilizer of Nations: The Rise and Fall of Modern International Law, 1870–1960* (New York: Cambridge University Press, 2001), 446, 413–509. See further Nicolas Guilhot, "American Katechon: When Political Theology Became International Relations Theory," *Constellations* 17, no. 2 (2010): 224–53.

[9] Immanuel Kant, *Political Writings*, ed. Hans Siegbert Reiss, trans. Hugh Nisbet, 2nd edn. (Cambridge: Cambridge University Press, 1991), 103.

few users of the term were shortsighted enough to imagine those obligations would always be met. For such reasons, phrases like *contra juris gentium*, which anchored, for example, a work sometimes thought to show Milton's influence, the *Declaration of the Lord Protector of War against Spain* (1655), and "against the law of nature, law of nations," which Milton used in *Samson Agonistes* (1671), were standard language in any justification for war (890). Not simply a discourse of obligations, the law of nations also in moments of its putative contravention became a language of remedy, punishment, and subjective right; and this permissive sense in what was called the *ius gladii* opened into a discourse closest to what thinkers from Cicero onwards called the natural right of self-preservation. While Noam Chomsky has introduced the term "military humanism" to describe the irony of states fighting wars "in defense of humanity," seen most broadly in the light of early modern history, the irony he identifies is hardly new.[10] The question posed by Vitoria in his *Relection On the Law of War* (1539), for example, of whether it was "right to commit evil...to avoid greater evils," articulates what in more literary terms is a tragic dilemma at the heart of the Renaissance law of nations.[11] Not only were such dilemmas already well appreciated in the period, tragedy itself offered distinct modes of thinking and feeling about them. As J. Peter Euben observes in *The Tragedy of Political Theory*, "we learn what we need through suffering its lack."[12] "Dramatizing this lack," he continues, "may help us articulate the need."[13] For many early modern tragedians, lack and necessity in the international order powerfully informed the tragic project.

For certain critics of the law of nations especially, practices like warfare introduced by the law of nations *were* the irony, for the "suffering and calamity, the constant presence of violence in human affairs," had absurdly necessitated other practices founded on violence and exclusion—Isidore of Seville's "fortification, wars, captivities, enslavements...[and] the prohibition of marriages between different races." It was as though an Oedipal humanity had fled Thebes to escape its violent fate, only to return again and fulfill it through institutions of the law of nations. As a late sixteenth-century commentator on Aristotle's *Politics* put it, there were those who out of a "desire of libertie, doe absolutely condemne that forme of bondage [i.e., slavery] which is brought in by the lawe of Nations."[14] While the author deemed such writers "immoderate"—"it being a thing necessarie for the curbing and bridling of wicked ones, to have a certaine pollicie of estates and

[10] Noam Chomsky, *The New Military Humanism: Lessons from Kosovo* (Monroe, ME: Common Courage Press, 1999); Clark, "For a Left with No Future," 54; D. J. B. Trim, "'If a Prince Use Tyrannie towards His People': Interventions on Behalf of Foreign Populations in Early Modern Europe," in *Humanitarian Intervention: A History*, ed. Brendan Simms and D. J. B. Trim (Cambridge: Cambridge University Press, 2011), 29–66.

[11] Francisco de Vitoria, *Political Writings*, ed. Anthony Pagden, trans. Jeremy Lawrance (Cambridge: Cambridge University Press, 1991), 316.

[12] Euben, *The Tragedy of Political Theory*, 49.   [13] Euben, *The Tragedy of Political Theory*, 49.

[14] Aristotle, *Aristotles Politiques, or Discourses of Gouernment. Translated out of Greeke into French*, trans. J[ohn] D[ickenson] (London: Adam Islip, 1598), 33. Although this translation is sometimes attributed to John Dee, the ascription to Dickenson is in "Dickenson, John (c.1570–1635/6)," Gavin Alexander in *Oxford Dictionary of National Biography*, ed. H. C. G. Matthew and Brian Harrison (Oxford: Oxford University Press, 2004); online edn., ed. Lawrence Goldman, January 2008, <http://www.oxforddnb.com/view/article/7601>.

forme of bondage"—this tragic view of the law of nations was nevertheless premised on the notion that "all men are borne free, and that it is against reason that he
which is constrained by force, should become bondslave unto the constrainer."[15]
This latter view took on radical significance through the seventeenth century in the
works of Milton and others, eventually making its way into the early novels that
historians like Lynn Hunt and Daniel Edelstein have recently placed at the center
of their accounts of the origins of human rights.[16]

Turning our attention with Milton and Grotius directly to tragedy and the
Renaissance law of nations in this chapter with such developments in view, we can
follow Bradley's lead into the nexus of necessity, law, tragedy, and war. While violence, irony, and the dilemmas of sovereignty indeed pervade Renaissance tragedies,
these were hardly antithetical to the early modern law of nations, as I have suggested. Seen instead as tensions *within* the early modern law of nations, such constitutive elements of the law of nations could be precisely what made tragedies
attractive modes of theorizing the Renaissance *ius gentium* in relation to its conceptual sister, natural—soon to become human—rights. This chapter uses what David
Scott calls the "analytic of tragedy" in relation to the law of nations and natural
rights and seeks to bring out, in Scott's words, "tragedy's dramatic ability to contain
and represent moments of historical transformation, moments when possible
futures seem less certain than they have been, and when heroic personalities embody
both the old and the new in ways that lead to both grandeur and catastrophe."[17]

Grotius' *Sophompaneas* (1635) and Milton's *Samson Agonistes* (1671) illustrate in
very different ways how seventeenth-century biblical tragedies dramatized physical
and spiritual needs whose causes and potential solutions overflowed sovereign
boundaries. Milton's gripping poem, in which his blind Israelite strongman Samson
eventually carries out a calamitous attack on his Philistine captors in Gaza, is of
course explicitly about a hero in the *agon* of international relation, although the
international aspects have been less emphasized in the years following Hill's *Experience of Defeat* than the poem's concomitant concerns with the domestic fate of
the English Revolution, of tyranny, republicanism, and dissent.[18] Reading *Samson*
alongside the little-studied biblical tragedy centered on scripture's Joseph by
Milton's admired Grotius helps us to remain alert to a larger tradition in which

---

[15] Aristotle, *Aristotles Politiques*, 33.

[16] Lynn Hunt, *Inventing Human Rights: A History* (New York: W. W. Norton & Co, 2007); Dan
Edelstein, "War and Terror: The Law of Nations from Grotius to the French Revolution.," *French His-
torical Studies* 31, no. 2 (Spring 2008): 237–40; Matthew W. Binney, "Milton, Locke, and the Early
Modern Framework of Cosmopolitan Right," *The Modern Language Review* 105 (January 1, 2010):
31–52; Julie Stone Peters, "'Literature,' the 'Rights of Man,' and Narratives of Atrocity: Historical
Backgrounds to the Culture of Testimony," *Yale Journal of Law & the Humanities* 17, no. 2 (2005).

[17] Scott, *Conscripts of Modernity*, 136, 142.

[18] David Norbrook, "Republican Occasions in Paradise Regained and Samson Agonistes," *Milton
Studies* 42 (2003): 122; Janel Mueller, "The Figure and the Ground: Samson as a Hero of London
Nonconformity, 1662–1667," in *Milton and the Terms of Liberty*, ed. Graham Parry and Joad Raymond
(D. S. Brewer, 2002); Sharon Achinstein, *Literature and Dissent in Milton's England* (Cambridge: Cam-
bridge University Press, 2003); Christopher N. Warren, "When Self-Preservation Bids: Approaching
Milton, Hobbes, and Dissent," *English Literary Renaissance* 37, no. 1 (2007): 118–50; Daniel Shore,
Milton and the Art of Rhetoric (Cambridge: Cambridge University Press, 2012), 146–65.

Milton was participating in which biblical tragedies amassed a wide range of meanings—not only allegorizing domestic politics and dramatizing aspects of lack in the civil realm, but also theorizing the duties of tyrannized peoples or their sovereigns, clarifying who had standing to defend or enforce their rights, and dramatizing remedies and protections available to peoples or individuals under tyrannous oppression. As Joseph Wittreich has observed, Milton's tragedy participates in a literary tradition on which Grotius had already left a substantial mark.[19] If the nearly fifty pages of annotation that appeared in *Sophompaneas'* 1652 English translation are any guide, Milton probably expected the extensive humanist commentary his drama has since received, and to which this chapter modestly adds.

The violence, irony, and dilemmas of sovereignty embedded in the form of biblical tragedy do not necessarily ask that we look beyond law but instead require that we draw more thoroughgoing connections to concepts whose importance would only grow in the eighteenth century, especially, in my view, the sometimes overlapping but more often opposed concepts of international legal personality and human rights. In Protestantism, it has been argued, "man acquired an irreducible value in himself by the mere fact of his existence, of his being created by God after his own Image. One may wonder whether the doctrine of human rights, based as it is on the same concept of the irreducible value of the individual, could have developed in the way it did if the Reformers had not stressed this element of the direct and exclusive responsibility of the individual to his Creator."[20] The line between the Reformation and modern human rights is hardly a straight one, but it remains true that new talk of individual rights also brought new talk of duties for sovereigns, long argued to be the exclusive bearers of international legal personality, and responsible, in themselves, for the state of the secular world. The notorious Protestant monarchomach tract *Vindiciae contra tyrannos* argued that Protestant princes were duty-bound to defend oppressed neighboring peoples, while Quakerism and allied independent sects soon installed the individual godly conscience as a newly legitimate epistemic ground from which to contest sovereign impunity.[21] Mid-seventeenth-century Protestant thinkers like Grotius and Selden were keen, in Jason Rosenblatt's words, to "build bridges between cultures, as, for example, in the commonalities between the *praecepta Noachidarum* and the *jus gentium* of Roman law, which regard[ed] the resident alien as possessed of certain inalienable human rights."[22] Milton's powerful sonnet and letters from Cromwell after the

[19] Joseph Anthony Wittreich, *Shifting Contexts: Reinterpreting Samson Agonistes* (Pittsburgh, PA: Duquesne University Press, 2002), 25–66.

[20] P. H. Kooijmans, "Protestantism and the Development of International Law," in *Recueil Des Cours, Collected Courses of the Hague Academy of International Law*, ed. Francesco Durante, vol. IV (Sijthoff & Noordhoff, 1976), 96.

[21] Bruce Rosenstock, "Against Sovereign Impunity: The Political Theology of the ICC," in *After Secular Law*, eds. Winnifred Fallers Sullivan, Robert A. Yelle, and Mateo Taussig-Rubbo (Stanford, CA: Stanford University Press, 2011), 160–77; Trim, "'If a Prince Use Tyrannie towards His People.'"

[22] Jason Rosenblatt, *Renaissance England's Chief Rabbi: John Selden* (Oxford: Oxford University Press, 2006), 169.

1655 Massacre at Piedmont demonstrate Protestants using all means at their disposal to secure toleration for Protestants across Europe.

Oppression increasingly presented in the language of "suffering human beings, rather than only suffering co-religionists" meant that the human *qua* human took on increasing significance into the eighteenth century.[23] From the perspective of the law of nations, the emergence of human rights in the eighteenth century required a double movement. First, it required re-situating the human *qua* human as a rights- and duty-bearing subject of international law rather than an object on which recognized international legal personalities—sovereigns—merely worked. Second, the movement of the human *qua* human from the status of object to subject was achieved against the simultaneous objectification of sovereigns, who were now seen as "merely" human, or even "things," with the "people" and the "nation" wresting the privileges of international legal personality from royal genealogies.[24] Because early modern biblical tragedies were greedy, sticky forms, gobbling up meanings on as many levels as they could, few genres could better manage this double movement.

In the hands of Milton and Grotius, but also earlier Protestant authors who contributed to the genre's esteem such as Theodor Beza, George Buchanan, and Elizabeth Cary, biblical characters became gravitational centers capable of achieving remarkably complex cultural tasks. Oriented primarily toward print rather than performance, biblical tragedies organized interrelated narratives about self, community, and nation, offering durable narratives to readerly communities eager to sort out complex relations between biography, history, identity, and divine will.[25]

The exiled hero Joseph in Grotius' *Sophompaneas*, for example, was read almost immediately upon the tragedy's initial publication in 1635 as Grotius' self-depiction.[26] However, just as the story of the Dutch Arminian then being courted to serve as a Swedish diplomat in Paris could hardly be told without reference to the political conflict between Holland's Remonstrant Arminians and

---

[23] Trim, "'If a Prince Use Tyrannie towards His People,'" 38.

[24] Joad Raymond, "The King Is a Thing," in *Milton and the Terms of Liberty*, eds. Graham Parry and Joad Raymond (Cambridge: D. S. Brewer, 2002), 69–94.

[25] Elizabeth Sauer, "Closet Drama and the Case of Tyrannicall-Government Anatomized," in *The Book of the Play: Playwrights, Stationers, and Readers in Early Modern England*, ed. Marta Straznicky (Amherst, MA: University of Massachusetts Press, 2006); Marta Straznicky, *Privacy, Playreading, and Women's Closet Drama, 1550–1700* (Cambridge: Cambridge University Press, 2004); Debora Kuller Shuger, "Iphigenia in Israel," in *The Renaissance Bible: Scholarship, Sacrifice, and Subjectivity*, 2nd edn. (Waco, TX: Baylor University Press, 2010), 128–67; Gabriella Silvestrini, "With Grotius against Grotius: Jephtha's 'Appeal to Heaven' in John Locke's Two Treatises of Government," in *The Roots of International Law: Liber Amicorum for Peter Haggenmacher*, eds. Pierre-Marie Dupuy and Vincent Chetail (Leiden: Martinus Nijhoff, 2014), 59–94.

[26] "The parallel between the vicissitudes experienced by Grotius during the period 1618–1624 and the spectacular turn for the better in the life of Joseph the Patriarch over a similar period of time, while it may seem curious to modern interpreters, was crystal clear to Grotius himself," writes Arthur Eyffinger. See Hugo Grotius, *Sophompaneas, 1635*, ed. Arthur Eyffinger and B. L. Meulenbroek, trans. Arthur Eyffinger, *The Poetry of Hugo Grotius*, 4 [A–B] (Assen: Van Gorcum, 1992), 5; Madeleine Kasten, "Translation Studies—Vondel's Appropriation of Grotius's Sophompaneas (1635)," in *Joost van Den Vondel (1587–1679) Dutch Playwright in the Golden Age*, ed. Jan Bloemendal and Frans-Willem Korsten (Leiden; Boston: Brill, 2012), 249–69. Further references to Eyffinger's edition appear hereafter as *Sophompaneas [1992]*.

counter-Remonstrant Calvinists that led to Grotius' imprisonment and escape into exile, so too was the Israelite Joseph's exile and rise to public prominence in the foreign territory of Egypt part of a larger narrative of fraternal strife. Milton's sightless Samson, similarly, figures the blind Milton himself, and yet this identification hardly exhausts Samson's meanings, for Milton employs the genre of biblical tragedy to freight Samson with further representative capacity. As one eighteenth-century reader put it, Samson "and the captive state of Israel, lively represents our blind poet with the republican party after the restoration, afflicted and persecuted," to which might be added Elizabeth Sauer's reflections on "connections between [Samson's] personal and national tragedy" and Joanna Picciotto's observation that "it is Samsonian *England* that is Milton's concern, not the historical Samson of Judges."[27] Without inherently prioritizing one level over the others, authors of biblical tragedies shaped scriptural history to read as oblique autobiography, civil history, and international history all at once. Organized around a single scriptural hero, multiple levels worked together. Insofar as the autobiographical self was enmeshed in relations with neighbors and compatriots, the biblical story and the autobiographical story could both be read as a kind of auto-ethnography of a godly people in the world, a reading that in the context of its hermeneutic circle flowed back into the narratives of self and community, and around again.

Influenced by typological reading practices more generally, such features of biblical tragedy gave rise to some peculiar temporal dynamics and structures of representation. The scriptural story in a biblical tragedy both was and was not history. For while the story purported to dramatize ancient events in the history of (usually) Israel, the narrative had been chosen and shaped in accordance with the author's own experiences, needs, and desires, which is to say his or her interpenetrating narratives about self, community, and nation at the time of composition. The interpersonal in biblical tragedy both was and was not the international; autobiography was and was not auto-ethnography, or partisan account. Dramatic conflict, recognition, and reconciliation were about persons, factions, and nations all at once. A genre that in Joseph Wittreich's words could generate "double, triple, or even quadruple readings," biblical tragedy amounted to a powerful analytic Grotius and Milton used to negotiate a disruptive new antinomy pitting the concept of international legal personality based on mimetic representation against a new, unruly, non-mediated human rights.[28] "Heroic personalities embody[ing] both the old and the new in ways that lead to both grandeur and catastrophe," Milton's Samson and Grotius' Joseph illustrate biblical tragedies' distinctive concerns with representation in the international order.

Because I aim to link biblical tragedies' analogizing representative affordances to what in the seventeenth century was a growing tension between international legal

---

[27] Emphasis added. Stephen B. Dobranski and Albert C. Labriola, eds., *A Variorum Commentary on the Poems of John Milton*, vol. 3 (Pittsburgh, PA: Duquesne University Press, 2009), 39; Elizabeth Sauer, "Pious Fraud: Extralegal Heroism in Samson Agonistes," *Studies in English Literature 1500–1900* 53, no. 1 (2013): 180; Joanna Picciotto, "The Public Person and the Play of Fact," *Representations* 105, no. 1 (2009): 131 n. 134.

[28] Wittreich, *Shifting Contexts*, 66.

personality and human rights, it is necessary now to say some more about the concepts of international legal personality and human rights alongside an attendant term, "recognition." When Hegel, searching for the distinguishing characteristic of early modern tragedy in his *Aesthetics*, ultimately identified "personality" as early modern tragedy's chief difference from classical tragedy, he referred primarily to what he saw as the emergence of subjective characters no longer motivated by ethical concerns of "right" but instead by complex internal psychologies.

Historians of international law, however, have placed a slightly different account of personality at the heart of their own stories of the early modern period. In international legal scholarship, the concept of international legal personality is consistently dated to the mid-seventeenth-century world of Grotius and Milton. Having been captured most precisely in Leibniz' term *persona jure gentium*, the concept has important roots in Pufendorf's discussions of states as "moral persons," as in Hobbes' "artificial person of the state." A concept often thought to have been enshrined in the Peace of Westphalia (1648), international legal personality was also closely related to the earlier concept of the "public person," with which the English Parliament and the New Model Army, for example, legitimized their claims against the crown. As we saw in the context of the French Wars of Religion, civil war for many writers had the effect of internationalizing the legal basis for personhood. In 1640, one London minister and civil lawyer citing "rationall Grotius" assured a company of artillerymen that "When a party by power breaks the Laws of the Land...and so conclude you the State[']s Enemies, where the Laws of the Land are thus by them made too short for your security, the Laws of Nations come in for reliefe, till it can be otherwise provided."[29] International legal personhood was similarly at the heart of the crisis of late 1649 and early 1650 as the now kingless England laid claim among skeptical European neighbors to personality on the world stage.

The killings on the Continent of English ambassadors Isaac Dorislaas and Antony Ascham in 1649–1650 could be classed as private murders rather than public assassinations, for example, on the grounds that the English regicides were unrecognizable as an international legal personality. The period's fundamental "contrast between savagery and civility on the global stage," to which Pat Moloney has recently called attention, gave purchase to royalist arguments that recognition should be withheld from the English republic as systematically as it was withheld from the putative barbarians of the new world, whose own savagery (at least according to Hobbes) similarly prevented them from presenting themselves mimetically as a recognizable international legal personality.[30]

Such examples illustrate international legal personality's deep imbrication with categories from Aristotle's *Poetics* such as representation and recognition. In contemporary international law, those entities who are *recognized* are said to have *locus standi* and are seen as subjects of international law; those without standing are

---

[29] Calybute Downing, *A Sermon Preached to the Renowned Company of the Artillery, 1 September, 1640 Designed to Compose the Present Troubles by Discovering the Enemies of the Peace of the Church and State* (London: E. G. for John Rothwell, 1641), 37, 36.

[30] Pat Moloney, "Hobbes, Savagery, and International Anarchy," *American Political Science Review*, 2011, 7.

described as objects of international law. Recognition in turn follows from the legal fiction of representation, which Hobbes described as "personation," drawing attention to the theatrical origins of the word *persona*. Personation and recognition were therefore the two salient moves leading to international legal personality in seventeenth-century contract theory. A multitude personated itself in a state, and the state in turn was recognized by international legal persons as one of their own. As Lassa Oppenheim wrote in a classic account owing much to this tradition, "Through recognition only and exclusively a State becomes an International Person and a subject of International Law."[31] The classic doctrinal position that "a State becomes an International Person and a subject of international law" "only and exclusively" "through recognition" illustrates the logic of narrativized becoming that is shared, on the one hand, by international legal persons and, on the other, by the tragic heroes of Aristotelian theory.

Just as recognition or *anagnorisis* differentiates the objects of international law from its subjects, so too does it differentiate the heroic subjects of tragedy from tragedies' non-heroic objects. In Aristotelian tragedy, as in international law, in other words, persons are constituted *as* heroic "only and exclusively" through *anagnorisis* or recognition. Framed in this way, the furious European controversies following the Ascham and Dorislaas murders were in effect *literary* controversies, turning on whether Ascham and Dorislaas were tragic heroes duly bearing international legal personality. Death was hardly a sufficient condition for tragedy. The majority of early modern individuals were merely the ground on top of which proper subjects of the law of nations achieved figuration. As George Puttenham already observed in a work published in 1589, however, the allegorical structures underpinning both tragedy and international legal personality buttressed traditional, monarchical power relations. *Allegoria* for Puttenham was a "courtly figure" whose "duplicity" helped sovereigns eliminate checks on their political will.[32] Much of the appeal in tragedy's miniaturizing movement from the globe to *The Globe* was that it could reduce meaningful aspects of international law and politics like Parliament, Admiralty courts, and legal doctrine to insignificance.

This is the main reason that Carl Schmitt in his Nazi legal history *The Nomos of the Earth*, turned to Shakespearean tragedy, Hobbes, and "the allegorical tendency of the Renaissance" to stress that "in international law states live as 'moral persons' in a state of nature," a "sphere of ruthless freedom."[33] Conceived as a "great man," Schmitt's state was capable of great meta-legal "steps" that could alter the fundamental ordering (*nomos*) of the physical earth.[34] Thus, Schmitt's

[31] Lassa Oppenheim, *International Law: A Treatise* (London: Longmans, Green, 1920), 135.

[32] George Puttenham, *The Art of English Poesy*, ed. Frank Whigham and Wayne A Rebhorn (Ithaca, NY: Cornell University Press, 2007).

[33] Carl Schmitt, *The Nomos of the Earth in the International Law of the Jus Publicum Europeaum*, trans. G. L. Ulmen (New York: Telos Press, 2003), 144, 147, 293.

[34] Schmitt, *The Nomos of the Earth in the International Law of the Jus Publicum Europeaum*, 145; Carl Schmitt, "On the Barbaric Character of Shakespearean Drama: A Response to Walter Benjamin on the Origin of German Tragic Drama," trans. David Pan, *Telos* 72, June (1987): 147.

"hatred of Anglo-American universalism was mixed with admiration of English courage to enter the open seas and found a rival world order" in the early modern period.[35] Dislodging the reigning *nomos* and constituting its own, early modern England had, according to Schmitt, exercised its "full immediacy of a legal power not mediated by laws."[36] For Schmitt, English tragedies were deeply enmeshed in this story of anthropomorphic "great steps" in the extra- or meta-legal state of nature. *The Nomos of the Earth* found evidence for the state's "political personalization" in *Othello*, which purportedly allegorized Moorish Spain's threat to Venice.[37] Later, in the *Hamlet* book, Schmitt argued that "English drama...belongs entirely to the specific historical evolution of the island of England, which had then begun its elemental appropriation of the sea. This great step is both spatially and historically the intellectual background of Shakespearean drama."[38] Together, tragedy and allegory helped Schmitt move outside or beyond positive law toward what Schmitt fetishized most, the extra-legal category of the political.

One of the problems Grotius and Milton inherited from tragedy, then, was a generic tradition potentially compromised by an inherent, centralizing royalism. If, as Picciotto puts it, tragedy was already an "enemy genre," one strategy for operating in this genre that Milton employed was to use allegorical representation to multiply the number of international legal personalities, that is, to rewrite objects as subjects. Alternatively, one might level the representative field upon which both relied, reducing the gap between subject and object entirely. This potentially radical latter move is one that I associate with natural or human rights and one to which Grotius understands his biblical tragedy *Sophompaneas* as a kind of antidote.

In the context of a chapter on Grotius, Milton, and the tensions between international legal personality and human rights in Renaissance tragedies, it might briefly be noted how Milton's and Grotius' lives and legacies intertwined in the murders of Ascham and Dorislaas. Dorislaas, the commonwealth's envoy to the Low Countries, had been a friend and correspondent of Grotius.[39] Ascham, its representative in Spain, was a deep reader of Grotius and a major intellectual force behind the reception of certain of Grotius' ideas in the commonwealth years.[40]

---

[35] Jan-Werner Müller, *A Dangerous Mind: Carl Schmitt in Post-War European Thought* (New Haven, CT: Yale University Press, 2003), 46.

[36] Schmitt, *The Nomos of the Earth in the International Law of the Jus Publicum Europeaum*, 73.

[37] Schmitt, *The Nomos of the Earth in the International Law of the Jus Publicum Europeaum*, 144 n. 5.

[38] Schmitt, "On the Barbaric Character of Shakespearean Drama: A Response to Walter Benjamin on the Origin of German Tragic Drama," 147. For more on Nazi historiography of international law, see Bardo Fassbender, "Stories of War and Peace: On Writing the History of International Law in the 'Third Reich' and After," *European Journal of International Law* 13, no. 2 (2002): 479–512; Christopher N. Warren, "John Milton and the Epochs of International Law," *European Journal of International Law* 24, no. 2 (2013): 557–81.

[39] P. Alessandra Maccioni and Marco Mostert, "Isaac Dorislaus (1595–1649); the Career of a Dutch Scholar in England," *Transactions of the Cambridge Bibliographical Society* 8, no. 4 (1984): 430.

[40] Marco Barducci, "Hugo Grotius and the English Republic: The Writings of Anthony Ascham, 1648–1650," *Grotiana* 32, no. 1 (2011): 40–63; Mark Goldie, "Edmund Bohun and Jus Gentium in the Revolution Debate, 1689–1693," *The Historical Journal* 20, no. 3 (1977): 569–86.

As Secretary of Foreign Tongues, Milton had produced Ascham's letters of credence and almost certainly knew Dorislaas too. At the very least, Milton subsequently became responsible in his diplomatic letters for arguing that Dorislaas and Ascham bore the personality of the commonwealth and that the killings of Dorislaas and Ascham as bearers of international legal personality were not murders but assassinations. As we will see in more detail in Chapter 7, an attempted assassination in Portugal of Milton's successor as Secretary of Foreign Tongues, Philip Meadows, similarly occupied Milton's attention in 1655–1656. For now, however, I want to turn to Milton's diverse references to Samson in his prose and in *Paradise Lost* in order to show the range of Samson's meanings in Milton's allusions.

SAMSON AND THE "GOLDEN BEAMES OF LAW AND RIGHT"

Samson in some instances in Milton's prose figures the whole nation. In others, he is a lone, chosen warrior against tyranny who thereby defiantly resists figuration. One might think therefore that Milton's references fail the test of consistency. But the changing references will illustrate something important about *Samson Agonistes*, narrative, and international legal personality. The biblical Samson certainly for Milton symbolizes political power, but Samson in Milton's view "bears the person" of the Israelites in different ways at different times in the events of Judges, sometimes not at all. The key point is that his strength and his legitimacy as an international legal personality wax and wane with the length of his hair, the volume of God's commands, and the politics of the "occasion."[41]

Samson's heroism—his international legal personality—relies precisely on specific accounts of his life and acts. Milton's narrative approach follows from the view that Samson's international legal personality isn't an essence but instead contingent upon time, virtue, and political context. What Picciotto terms the "play" in Samson's representative capacity in *Samson Agonistes* ensures, as we shall see, the simultaneous co-constitution of a mimetically structured international realm of representative legal personalities—which I associate here with allegory, analogy, and the law of nations—alongside something logically incompatible but nevertheless made possible through the multiplicity of biblical tragedy—a flat, unmediated sphere of human rights.

In *Areopagitica* (1644), Samson would provide Milton with a stirring representation of "the noble and puissant [English] Nation," but Milton had used Samson as a figure for the state as early as his 1642 pamphlet *The Reason of Church-Government*, where he decried the prelates for deforming the state's "just power" and flattering the king into absolutism.[42] Samson was like "the

---

[41] Norbrook, "Republican Occasions in Paradise Regained and Samson Agonistes."
[42] John Milton, *Complete Prose Works*, ed. Don M. Wolfe (New Haven, CT: Yale University Press, 1953), 2.558, 1.859.

state and person of a king" whose hair symbolized the "bright and waighty tresses of his laws, and just prerogatives"; but the prelates were like Delilah, "wickedly shaving off" its "golden beames of Law and Right."[43] What made Samson a particularly brilliant personification of England for Milton to use in this case was that Samson helped Milton construct Charles' absolutism not with plenary fullness, with which royal power unconstrained by laws was too often described, but instead its opposite, lack. Since Samson without hair was no Samson at all, so a king ruling at the expense of law at the urging of the prelates was merely an ordinary man, Milton was able to suggest. Milton once again associated Samson's hair with legitimacy, sovereignty, and the law in his tract on the execution of Charles, *Eikonoklastes* (1649–1650), where Charles was explicitly disclosed as an ordinary man so long as his words were not backed by legal authority. "*The words of a King*, as they are *full of power*, in the autority and strength of Law, so like *Sampson*, without the strength of that *Nazarites* lock, they have no more power in them then the words of another man," he wrote.[44] As Charles became "another man," the impunity of international legal personality was giving way to human rights.[45]

The 1644 reference to Samson in *Areopagitica* reflects the important trends in legal and political theory mentioned earlier associated with the English civil war. In the 1640s, parliamentarians and covenant theologians were revising longstanding notions of representation and "public personhood" and thereby locating sovereignty, and by extension international legal personality, in the "people."[46] If earlier Samson had been like the "state and person of the king," Milton in *Areopagitica* would excise the king entirely from the Samson analogy, choosing instead to speak of "a noble and puissant *Nation* rousing herself like a strong man after sleep," where the feminine pronoun tilted the representative function away from the masculine person of the king toward the oft-feminized people and Parliament.[47] Finally, under the principle that "in no way can a foe of the state be its citizen," Milton in the first *Defense of the English People*, invoked Samson's just war against the Philistines as a precedent for the English execution of the gentleman Charles Stuart, who far from bearing England's legal personhood had instead become its "enemy" and was certainly "no longer king" at his death.[48] Samson, for his part, undertook just war in his own person, "single-handedly," without any other help.[49]

---

[43] Milton, *CPW*, 1.858–859.   [44] Milton, *CPW*, 3.545–546.
[45] See also Raymond, "The King Is a Thing."
[46] Christopher Hill, "Covenant Theology and the Concept of a Public Person," in *The Collected Essays of Christopher Hill*, 3 vols., Vol. 3 (Amherst, MA: University of Massachusetts Press, 1985), 300–24; Quentin Skinner, "Hobbes on Representation," *European Journal of Philosophy* 13, no. 2 (2005): 155–84; David Runciman, "What Kind of Person Is Hobbes's State? A Reply to Skinner," *Journal of Political Philosophy* 8, no. 2 (2000): 268.
[47] Emphasis added. See *Mistris Parliament Brought to Bed of a Monstrous Childe of Reformation* ([London], 1648); Sharon Achinstein, "Women on Top in the Pamphlet Literature of the English Revolution," in *Feminism and Renaissance Studies*, ed. Lorna Hutson (Oxford: Oxford University Press, 1999), 339–72.
[48] Milton, *CPW*, 4.1.402.   [49] Milton, *CPW*, 4.1.402.

TRAGEDY, THE LORE OF JUSTICE, AND GOVERNMENT IN A NEW FRAME IN *PARADISE LOST*

While Milton had already used Samson in a range of ways, then, the strong connection between Samson and tragedy emerges initially in *Paradise Lost* (1667). Milton's reference to Samson in Book 9 of the epic comes as Milton carefully narrates the birth of tragedy alongside the birth of the human law of nations. "Chang[ing]" his "notes to tragic," Milton walks his readers through the transition from human immortality to mortality, a transition that can also be described, less conventionally, as the antinomy between nature and nations (9.5–6). Even closer to Milton's own distinction, likely following Selden, it is the transition from the primary law of nature and nations to the secondary law of nature and nations. It is Adam's original sin that leads Milton to compare him to "the Danite strong, / Hercúlean Samson" who "waked / Short of his strength" "from the harlot-lap / Of Philistéan Daliláh" (9.1059–1062). In Adam and Eve's new condition of "eyes…opened" but "minds /…darkened," Milton articulates the new conditions and gloomy epistemology of the (secondary) law of nations (9.1053–1054).

Original sin, Milton wrote, "alter'd the lore of justice, and put the government of things into a new frame."[50] The notion of frames of government helpfully illuminates the encounter somewhat earlier in Book 9 between unfallen Adam and fallen Eve. Adam finds himself specifically between the legal "frames" of primary nature and secondary nations, and this antinomy provides the fundamental structure to a dilemma rightly understood as tragic.[51] Anticipating the way Samson would find himself bound in the conflict between competing Nazarite and Philistine legal orders at the temple, Adam's own tragedy develops from a kind of dual citizenship. Here, however, Adam's dual citizenship is temporal rather than national. Depicted by Milton as a citizen of nature, Adam's government is his own; his order is the order of wedded love. And yet Eve's transgression, in which Eve incorrectly "reasons that natural law supersedes the [positive] law governing the tree of knowledge," has begun to introduce the world of violence and contingency that Milton in prose tracts like *Tetrachordon* associated with divorce under the secondary law of nations.[52] Eve's willful choice to eat the fruit therefore occasions a sort of tragic riddle of frames for the still unfallen but newly vulnerable Adam through which Milton brings into sharp relief the distinction between the "prime" law of nature, from which "comes intercourse between male and female" according to Justinian's Institutes I.2, and the "secondary" law of nations, which Milton understood to authorize divorce.

---

[50] Milton, *CPW*, 2.665. Drawing attention this passage, Rosenblatt powerfully analyzes Book 9 of *Paradise Lost* in terms of what he calls the first and secondary "law of Moses." It is a testament to Milton's syncretism in combining Hebrew scripture and Roman law that "first and secondary laws of nature and nations" apply equally well. See Jason Rosenblatt, *Torah and Law in Paradise Lost* (Princeton, NJ: Princeton University Press, 1994), 51.

[51] Barbara Kiefer Lewalski, *Paradise Lost and the Rhetoric of Literary Forms* (Princeton, NJ: Princeton University Press, 1985), 220–53.

[52] Michael Komorowski, "Milton's Natural Law: Divorce and Individual Property," *Milton Studies* 53, no. 1 (2012): 92.

With Eve already having fallen, to which epoch does Adam—can Adam—belong? His bind is not unlike Antigone's. Constrained by bad alternatives, his well-meaning choice culminates in death—indeed, one of the first. Adam's tragic riddle captures many of the ambivalences writers often found in the law of nations. Its irrepressible connection with the Fall meant that images associated with the law of nations were almost always simultaneous mementos of perfection and exile, divinity and alienation therefrom. In his own early tragedy, *Adamus Exul*, Grotius wrote of God's decision to "cherish sparks of former light [*lucis antiquae*]" in human minds after the Fall (1905).[53] He elsewhere explained how the "rational faculty has been darkly beclouded by human vice yet not to such a degree but that rays of the divine light are still clearly visible, manifesting themselves especially in the mutual accord of nations."[54] Seen in such ways, it was hard to know whether the Janus-faced law of nations should make fallen humanity glad or despondent. It gathered fears as readily as it gathered hopes and dreams.

For Milton's unfallen Adam, the law of nations is a peculiar and potentially suspect locus of authority, hardly worthy of unthinking assent. This means that Adam's tragic predicament is compounded by the fact that he has difficulty understanding his situation *as* tragic. Himself unfallen and working within the original frame of nature's law, Adam remains allied to the fundamentally comic sensibility that had informed Book 4's wedding and subsequent entertainment of Raphael.[55] If we can see Adam in those earlier books as a superior Prospero, entertaining the divine Raphael rather than Prospero's less friendly visitors, we can also see how what Milton calls Adam and Eve's "property" in one another in fact creates the condition of possibility for comedies like the *Rudens* and its heirs. Miltonic marriage, as Michael Komorowski has astutely argued (quoting Milton's *Tetrachordon*), "removes both spouses 'from the community of nature' so that each becomes the exclusive possession of the other."[56] This is the key sense behind Milton's epithalamium hailing "wedded love, mysterious law, true source / Of human offspring, sole propriety / In Paradise of all things common else" (4.750–752). Earlier chapters have prepared us to see the comic logic at work. The comic law of nations, governed by the logic of *acquisition*, gives us pairs like Gripus and Trachalio, Prospero and Caliban, Stephano and Trinculo, and the shepherds in *The Winter's Tale* who appropriate fish and foundlings to themselves.[57]

But Adam's comic understanding obscures what Milton sees as the tragic link between self-preservation and alienation—the tempests that in times of "extremity"

---

[53] Hugo Grotius, "Adamus Exul," in *The Celestial Cycle; the Theme of Paradise Lost in World Literature with Translations of the Major Analogues.*, trans. Watson Kirkconnell (Toronto: University of Toronto Press, 1952).

[54] Hugo Grotius, *Commentary on the Law of Prize and Booty*, ed. Martine Julia Van Ittersum (Indianapolis, IN: Liberty Fund, 2006), 25.

[55] Lewalski, *Paradise Lost and the Rhetoric of Literary Forms*, 196–219.

[56] Komorowski, "Milton's Natural Law," 70; Milton, *CPW*, 2.665.

[57] Adam's non-tragic sensibility may mislead him, as Russell Hillier suggests, into thinking that love for Eve and obedience to God can coincide. See Russell Hillier, *Milton's Messiah: The Son of God in the Works of John Milton* (Oxford: Oxford University Press, 2011), 138–9.

necessitate throwing property back to the sea.[58] Divorce was a remedy for *tragic* times. "What cares these roarers for the name of king?" Shakespeare's boatswain hollers in *The Tempest*'s opening storm, dramatically highlighting the occasion's competing frames (1.1.15). When reminded by Gonzalo about "whom [he] hast aboard," the boatswain replies with tragic resolve, "None than I love more than myself" (1.1.17–18). Adam, by contrast, makes no such distinction, even though Milton's divorce tracts prescribed divorce when "life is in peril," literally or spiritually: "the preservation of life is worth more than the compulsory keeping of marriage."[59] Learning of Eve's transgression, Adam instead asks, "How can I live without thee, how forgo / Thy sweet converse and love so dearly joined, / To live again in these wild woods forlorn?" before confiding, "I feel / The link of nature draw me: flesh of flesh, Bone of my bone thou art, and from thy state / Mine never shall be parted, bliss or woe" (9. 908–910, 9.913–916). His "state" of marriage like *The Tempest*'s ship of state is sinking, but Adam goes down with the ship.

Milton is well aware the readers will hear in "flesh of flesh" the language of Genesis 2:23. Readers familiar with Milton's argument in *Tetrachordon* that divorce is a "remedy for intolerable wrong" brought in by the secondary law of nations, then, can hardly fail to understand Milton's intent when he avers that Adam's fall involves "submitting to what [only] *seemed* remediless" (9.919, emphasis added). However irrepressible his natural sympathy feels to Adam, however seemingly compelling is Eve's erotic "female charm," Milton's readers, I think, are meant to appreciate that Adam's predicament *is* tragic—that he must choose between two incompatible laws. In addition to the opportunity to follow natural sympathy—to hold Eve perpetually, even in death—the now unfolding secondary law of nations permits another course—namely, to shed the bond of marriage like the dead snakeskin to which it is promptly compared (9.999). In such a way does tragedy "frame" Milton's secondary law of nature and nations.

"FROM PRIVATE INTEREST TO PUBLIC CAUSE": SAMSON AND *CASUS BELLI* IN LAW OF NATIONS DISCOURSE

In Milton's *Samson Agonistes*, Milton's frame is the secondary law of nations' fallen, tragic world of warfare, captivity, mediated international politics, and divorce. Milton's decision in *Paradise Lost* and *Samson Agonistes* to associate Samson with the fallen law of nations aligns with Samson's prominence in law of nations discourse more broadly. In writers like Gentili and Grotius, Samson appeared under gloomy headings such as just war, punishments, suicide, and burial. Not unlike that of Vergil's Aeneas, who Augustine had even noted became king in Italy at exactly the time Samson became a judge in Israel, Samson's case

[58] Milton, *CPW*, 2.666.
[59] Milton, *CPW*, 2.273–274; this passage is helpfully emphasized by Stephen M. Fallon, *Milton's Peculiar Grace: Self-Representation and Authority* (Ithaca, NY: Cornell University Press, 2007), 121.

accumulated substantial forensic commentary.[60] Samson was variously cast as a singular exception to the normal laws of war and peace, but also, in keeping with the dialectic that I want to explore, as exceptionally representative—a scriptural model of becoming public in times of duress that could be available to godly persons of many sorts. Already, Augustine in *City of God* had considered Samson among those "bearing the public power in their own person" whose punishment of the wicked did not violate the commandment against killing.[61] Aware, therefore, that Samson's case could be seen as a precedent for private or "single" rebellion, early modern writers on the law of nations developed accounts of the lawfulness of Samson's warfare.[62] Alberico Gentili observed that Samson was not "roused against the Philistines without cause, but led [by God] to advance step by step from private interests to a public cause."[63] It was through having a public *casus belli* that Samson obtained the privileged status of "enemy," a name, as we have seen, signifying an international legal personality whose benefits included the rights due to enemies and the privileges of regular warfare. Such an account of Samson implied a great deal about Samson and the Israelites insofar as Gentili defined an "enemy" in *De Jure Belli* as one "who has a state, a senate, a treasury, united and harmonious citizens, and some basis for a treaty of peace, should matters so shape themselves."[64] In his *Commentary on the Law of Prize and Booty*, Grotius mused that Samson, though he had "no need of public authorization," nevertheless defended himself against the Philistines "righteous[ly] by the law of nations."[65] And yet Samson's destruction of the Philistine "house" of Judges 17:27—Milton in *Samson Agonistes* will, following Grotius, change it to a "temple"—was justified in a way that his earlier revolts had not been according to many commentators; Gentili and Grotius both emphasized that the Jews had rightly surrendered Samson to Philistine captivity because Samson's earlier attacks on the Philistines had been undertaken in the absence of legitimate public authority or what I have been calling international legal personhood.[66] Likewise, though the destruction of the house was legitimate in their eyes, it did raise questions about biblical prohibitions against suicide: here again Samson needed defending. What made his death licit according to Grotius was that "Samson...saw that the true religion was an object of derision *in his own*

[60] Augustine, *The City of God against the Pagans*, trans. Robert Dyson (Cambridge: Cambridge University Press, 1998), 845. See also Chapter 2.
[61] Augustine, *City of God*, 34.
[62] On this tradition, see R. W. Serjeantson, "Samson Agonistes and 'Single Rebellion,'" in *The Oxford Handbook of Milton*, ed. Nicholas McDowell and Nigel Smith (Oxford: Oxford University Press, 2009), 613–31.
[63] Alberico Gentili, *De Jure Belli Libri Tres*, trans. John Carew Rolfe (Oxford: Clarendon Press, 1933) 2.25.
[64] Gentili, *De Jure Belli Libri Tres*, 2.25.
[65] Grotius, *Commentary on the Law of Prize and Booty*, 134.
[66] In Russell Hillier, "Grotius's Christus Patiens and Milton's Samson Agonistes," *The Explicator* 65, no. 1 (2006): 9–13, Hillier convincingly traces the use of "temple" to Grotius' *Christius Patiens*. It might also be noted that Francis Goldsmith included a note about the "Veil of the Temple at Hierusalem" as described by Josephus in his notes to *Sophompaneas*, making the latter play a corroborating and possibly intermediary source.

person."[67] Overall, then, Samson was something of a limit case in law of nations discourse. Much as Aeneas' killing of Turnus had challenged writers on the laws of war, so too were Samson's actions and circumstances difficult enough to suggest the need for narrative supplement. This is precisely what Milton produced in *Samson Agonistes*.

MISRECOGNITION AND INTERNATIONAL LEGAL PERSONALITY IN *SAMSON AGONISTES*

Milton uses the plotted narrative frame of *Samson Agonistes* to chart what Rachel Trubowitz has perceptively described as the "international personhood that Samson must acquire in order to fulfill his divine prophecy."[68] This narrative of becoming allowed Milton to enter debates such as: which points in his life Samson bore personhood; whether his vengeance was justified; whether his death was a suicide or an accident of just war, and which, if either, God had permitted. Because of tragedy's inbuilt capacity to recognize its heroes *as* public figures, moreover, narrating Samson's life *as tragedy* encoded arguments that Samson was a public person, a just warrior, and a bearer of international legal personality. Within the resources of poetry, in other words, the specifically *tragic* frame itself argued for Samson's legal personhood, an important feature of which was the bearer's capacity for representation.

There nevertheless remained a certain tension in the forensic scrutiny given to Samson's individual and particularized actions, for the more Samson's case was reduced to its "ultimate particulars," the less Samson could be seen as a representative bearer of the personhood of Israel, the less moreover he could personate (in Hobbes' term) godly seventeenth-century English.[69] To put it in terms shared by Daniel Heinsius' *De tragoediae constitutione* (1611), to which both Milton and Grotius were indebted, and the previous chapter, the question was whether *Samson Agonistes* was more Sophocles or Thucydides, tragedy or history; for "the poet is wont to view things generically and as they are likely to be done or spoken, and that according to verisimilitude or necessity, while the historian simply shows what a particular person did or suffered. Sophocles describes Ajax one way, Thucydides describes Pericles or Alcibiades in another."[70]

---

[67] Hugo Grotius, *The Rights of War and Peace*, ed. Richard Tuck and Jean Barbeyrac, trans. [John Morris], 3 vols. (Indianapolis, IN: Liberty Fund, 2005).

[68] Rachel Trubowitz, *Nation and Nurture in Seventeenth-Century English Literature* (Oxford: Oxford University Press, 2012), 197.

[69] As scholars have shown, godly readers of scripture increasingly understood themselves in the mid-seventeenth century as "represented" by figures like Adam, the patriarchs, Samson, and Christ. This representation was often cast in explicitly legal terms. Just as action by a representative (such as an attorney) was considered as if done by him who was represented, biblical figures were increasingly being explored, often for radical political ends, as representative figures in whose ever-present actions all of the godly might participate. See Hill, "Covenant Theology and the Concept of a Public Person"; Debora Kuller Shuger, *The Renaissance Bible: Scholarship, Sacrifice, and Subjectivity*, 2nd edn. (Baylor University Press, 2010); Picciotto, "The Public Person and the Play of Fact."

[70] Daniel Heinsius, *On Plot in Tragedy*, trans. P. R. Sellin and J. McManmon (Northridge, CA: San Fernando Valley State College, 1971), 30.

As we turn now to read *Samson Agonistes* more carefully, the tension between an historical, singular Samson and a mimetic, "corporate" Samson embodying Restoration England appears in several passages.[71] Such passages contribute toward a multiplicitous poem, opening at once into the allegorical world of international legal personality and the flatter representative structure of human rights. In the course of two short lines, the chorus calls Samson both the "mirror of our fickle state" and then the "man on earth unparalleled" (164– 165). Here, Samson is both strangely particular—*sui generis*—and singularly representative, i.e., generic type. The same man who mirrors his state nevertheless refuses to be associated with "Israel's governors, and heads of tribes," of which he is categorically not one (242).

Such tension also appears in the poem, for example, in what Milton's chorus refers to as the "national obstriction" against intermarriage (312). Readers typically understand "national obstriction" to refer to the Deuteronomical law to which Samson was intermittently bound, and as such it is a particularizing term placing limits on Samson's capacity to represent any but the Jewish followers of what Samson, repeatedly, calls "our law" (1320, 1386, 1409, 1425). Pauline English Christians for whom the Christian sacrifice had inaugurated still another new legal frame would thereby be excluded. But as we have seen, "national" is Milton's habitual translation of the Latin genitive *gentium*, such that a broader reading is possible in which God's dispensation from "his own Laws" extends beyond the laws of the Jews to the broader law of nations. When the chorus remembers that God "prompted this Heroic *Nazarite*, / ... / To seek in marriage that fallacious Bride," the line indeed recalls Deuteronomy 7:3's prohibition of intermarriage, but also Isidore of Seville, for whom "the law of nations concern[end] ... the prohibition of marriages between different races." As Milton "highlights the legality of Samson's international marriage to Dalila," the question remains whether this "miracle of men" could ever be a permissive precedent or whether God's exception applied only in Samson's special case (364).[72] Samson himself seems willing to take his own exceptionality as a precedent—he says of marrying the Canaanite Dalila "I thought it lawful from my former act"—but the tragic consequences of the union with Dalila do more to complicate Samson's judgment than to confirm it (231). The effect of such tensions is to tell bifurcating stories, one compatible with allegory and international legal personality and the other with radical particularity and human rights.

Beyond mediating between these otherwise incompatible legal frames, the tragic narrative creates a forum for Milton to register doctrinal debate about international legal personality itself. Critics have rightly noted a strong presence of Roman law in the drama.[73] In Samson's exchange with Harapha, for instance, the two debate substantive legal issues long contested not only by scriptural commentators like David Pareus, as Richard Serjeantson has recently shown, but also civil lawyers

[71] Picciotto, "The Public Person and the Play of Fact."

[72] Trubowitz, *Nation and Nurture in Seventeenth-Century English Literature*, 193.

[73] Quentin Skinner, "John Milton and the Politics of Slavery," in *Visions of Politics*, vol. 2 (Cambridge: Cambridge University Press, 2002), 286–307; Rosanna Cox, "Neo-Roman Terms of Slavery in Samson Agonistes," *Milton Quarterly* 44, no. 1 (2010): 1–22.

like Gentili.[74] According to Harapha, Samson is "a league-breaker," "A murderer, a revolter, and a robber," his captivity cast as just punishment under the law of nations, first, for unauthorized breaches of the Israelite–Philistine peace and, second, theft under the pretext of taking war spoils (1184, 1180). Harapha, an apparently skilled reader of precedent and procedure, whose arguments are perhaps more subtle here than "official propaganda," finds evidence for this assessment in the fact that Samson was surrendered by the Israelites themselves.[75]

> Their magistrates confessed it, when they took thee
> As a league-breaker and delivered bound
> Into our hands: for hadst thou not committed
> Notorious murder on those thirty men
> At Ascalon, who never did thee harm,
> Then like a Robber stripdst them of thir robes? (1183–1188).

Far from bearing Israel's person, Samson in Harapha's indictment was a rogue strong man needing disciplining from Israel's "Magistrates" in conjunction with the Philistines themselves. If even the Israelites refused to recognize Samson's actions, why should their enemies the Philistines do so? According to Leibniz' summative definition of the *persona iure gentium*, "He possesses a *personality in international law* [*persona iure gentium*] who represents the public liberty, such that he is not subject to the tutelage or the power of anyone else, but has in himself the power of war and of alliances."[76] For Harapha, too, Samson's subjection to Israel's magistrates decisively illustrated that Samson had no such power "in himself."

In his discussion of the war and peacemaking capacities of private individuals, Gentili had made much the same argument as Harapha. Gentili quoted Plato's *Laws* with approbation to say that "If any one in his private capacity, without the authority of the government, makes peace or war, let him be punished with death"; he went on to affirm, in a lengthy but telling passage, "naturally, it is the function of the aforesaid supreme power to make war and peace. Therefore . . . a man who has brought on war without the order of the prince is guilty of high treason. The Romans believed that in such cases it was their duty to surrender the guilty party to those upon whom war had been made and accordingly they demanded that Hannibal be delivered into their hands. So too the Philistines asked that Samson be given up to them, and the Jews therefore surrendered him."[77] Samson's defenses against Harapha in Milton's poem therefore double as

---

[74] Serjeantson, "Samson Agonistes and 'Single Rebellion.'" Elizabeth Oldman has studied Milton's relation to Grotius, and Jason Rosenblatt has explored Milton's debts to Selden; but Samson's pervasive presence in law of nations discourse more generally has tended to go underappreciated. Elizabeth Oldman, "Milton, Grotius, and the Law of War: A Reading of Paradise Regained and Samson Agonistes," *Studies in Philology* 104, no. 3 (2007): 340–75; Rosenblatt, *Renaissance England's Chief Rabbi*; see also Julie Stone Peters, "A 'Bridge over Chaos': De Jure Belli, Paradise Lost, Terror, Sovereignty, Globalism, and the Modern Law of Nations," *Comparative Literature* 57, no. 4 (2005): 273–93.

[75] Joan S. Bennett, "'A Person Rais'd': Public and Private Cause in Samson Agonistes," *Studies in English Literature, 1500–1900* 18, no. 1 (1978): 162.

[76] Gottfried Wilhelm Leibniz, *Political Writings*, 2nd edn. (Cambridge: Cambridge University Press, 1988), 175.

[77] Gentili, *De Jure Belli Libri Tres*, 2.20.

defenses against a tradition in law of nations discourse in which Samson's destruction of the Philistine house was considered licit even as his earlier aggression had been acknowledged criminal.

Even describing himself with the technical legal label of "appellant," Milton's Samson justifies himself with a series of interrelated arguments woven within a narrative of Samson's developing international legal personhood, the recognition of which Harapha and writers like Gentili and even Grotius before him had denied (1220). Beginning with his exogamous marriage, Samson's story begins in his own account in the realm of putatively private international law before Samson is at once recognized as, and thereby transformed into, a public figure by the extra-biblical "spies" sent by "politician lords" seeking his secret (1197, 1195). By Samson's lights, Philistine agents "constrain'd" his new bride and when Samson "perceived . . . enmity," he merely reciprocated, justly killing and taking war spoils in keeping with the now public nature of the conflict (1198, 1201). He even adhered to the known doctrine in the law of nations that "conquest" is an inherently insecure title over lands and peoples (1206).[78] "Force with force / is well ejected when the conquered can" Samson argues, echoing both Grotius, whose investigation into "extreme necessity" quoted "Hebrew masters" to suggest that some might "repell by force the force of their superiours," and also Milton's own commonplace book (1206–1207).[79] Moreover, it was no good to say that Samson was merely a private person; rather, he was "a person raised" to "free [his] country," and if his countrymen failed to recognize what Dalila elsewhere refers to as "public marks" of his public persona, that hardly impinged on his legal personhood either as a matter of fact or of law (1211–1213, 992).

The debate Milton stages between Harapha and Samson was about past recognition of international legal personality. Samson in his exchange with Dalila will himself allege contravention of the "law of nature, law of nations," but as Milton introduces Samson in the beginning of the tragedy itself, Milton's Samson is "In power of others, never in my own" (78). The progression Gentili suggested in which Samson moves "step by step from private interests to a public cause" commences shortly.[80] Recognition and misrecognition both contribute to the action. At the beginning of the tragedy, this melancholic, philosophical Samson describes himself as a "sepulchre, a moving grave"—a far cry from the corporate Samson of Samson's past who was "Himself an army" and who bore the "people's safety" (102, 346, 681). At the beginning of the tragedy, Samson is what Bradley might have called a Hamlet among the nations, if not exactly "great . . . in the . . . spheres of religion, philosophy, music, poetry," surely "incapable in the world of political

---

[78] Sharon Korman, *The Right of Conquest: The Acquisition of Territory by Force in International Law and Practice* (Oxford: Oxford University Press, 1996), Ch. 1.

[79] Hugo Grotius, *The Illustrious Hugo Grotius of the Law of Warre and Peace With Annotations. III. Parts. And Memorials of the Author's Life and Death.*, trans. Clement Barksdale (London: T. Warren, for William Lee, 1654), 150–1; Serjeantson, "Samson Agonistes and 'Single Rebellion,'" 619. On Barksdale, see now Marco Barducci, "Clement Barksdale, Translator of Grotius: Erastianism and Episcopacy in the English Church, 1651–1658," *The Seventeenth Century* 25, no. 2 (2010): 265–80.

[80] Gentili, *De Jure Belli Libri Tres*, 2.25.

action."[81] Not only is Samson unrecognizable to himself, so too has the external recognition from his Father and the chorus, equally significant for Samson's "international personhood," dissolved. "Israel's governors, and heads of tribes" "Acknowledged not" Samson's deeds; they "would not seem / to count them things worth notice" (242, 245, 249–250). God's own recognition had waned. The Lord, says Samson, invoking the knowledge of *cognitio*, has "cast me off as never known" (641). No longer marked externally, by his hair, or internally, by his power, as a recognizable subject of international legal personality, he has become what Milton explicitly calls a "pitied object," "subject" only to Philistine "cruelty or scorn" (568, 645). "Just occasion[s]" to "serve/My nation, and the work from heaven imposed" appear at the start of the tragedy as things of the past (237, 564–565).

As Samson's regeneration as a *persona juris gentium* proceeds through his debates with Dalila and Harapha, irony and misrecognition become even more central to Samson's representative personhood. Heinsius had emphasized the intersubjective aspects of recognition, "for necessarily anyone who experiences recognition, recognizes someone and is recognized."[82] In the debate with Harapha, as we have seen, Harapha mistakes Samson's public persona as private. The prior debate with Dalila, as Joan Bennett points out, shows Dalila having mistaken private sin for public virtue.[83] In speeches "suing for peace," Dalila's language is suffused with the forensic diction of "pleas" "pardons," and "debate," seemingly in order to emphasize how Dalila refuses to distinguish between Samson as private husband and Samson the public enemy she was persuaded to "entrap" (855).[84] Adam's tragic choice between epochs of the law of nature and nations in *Paradise Lost* has prepared us to understand Dalila's own tragic predicament, for her error in Milton's eyes has been misrecognition of the legal frame of the law of nations. It is important here to note the key irony that results. Samson's public personhood results in good measure from Dalila misrecognizing Samson the husband. In misrecognizing the private Samson as a public person, Dalila confuses the primary law of nature and nations that authorizes marriage with the secondary law of nature and nations that authorizes war. Having been situated by the Philistine lords through little of her own doing at a tragic nexus, Dalila, in other words, helps to make Samson precisely the public enemy that she and they fear.[85] It is at this point that Samson, prompted by Dalila's legal language, becomes a judge in his own case. He begins to put on the mask of

---

[81] Bradley, "International Morality," 75.   [82] Heinsius, *On Plot in Tragedy*, 40.

[83] Bennett, "A Person Rais'd," 158.

[84] See Lynne A. Greenberg, "Dalila's 'Feminine Assaults': The Gendering and Engendering of Crime in Samson Agonistes," in *Altering Eyes: New Perspectives on "Samson Agonistes*, ed. M. R. Kelley and Joseph Wittreich (Newark, DE: University of Delaware Press, 2002), 192–219.

[85] "The thesis…that our identity is partly shaped by recognition or its absence, often by the *mis*recognition of others, and so a person or group of people can suffer real damage, real distortion, if the people or society around them mirror back to them a confining or demeaning or contemptible picture of themselves," has been explored most influentially by Charles Taylor. Insofar as Milton is here dramatizing a version of this thesis, it follows that such a view arose earlier than the late eighteenth century to which Taylor dates it. See Charles Taylor, "The Politics of Recognition," in *Multiculturalism and "The Politics of Recognition": An Essay*, ed. Charles Taylor and Amy Gutmann (Princeton, NJ: Princeton University Press, 1992), 25.

the public *persona* when he "determinist weakness for no plea" (843). Milton in fact deploys epic conventions to emphasize what thereby emerges, in effect, as Dalila's generic misprision. When Dalila approaches Samson by saying, "Let weakness then with weakness come to parl / So near related or the same of kind," her appeal to Samson's kind-ness and what she terms "love's law" treats Samson as an epic warrior, with Dalila herself supplicating like a Turnus or a Priam at Samson's feet (785–786, 811). The specific reference may even be to Tasso's *Gerusalemme Liberata*, in which a sorceress named Armida, associated like Dalila with magic and the East, is sent to penetrate the enemy camp and entrap Godfrey's Christian warriors. Guided by a maxim both praised by Tasso's translator Scipione Gentili (Alberico's brother) and strikingly similar to Dalila's own—"for faith and fatherland, all things are just"—Armida exemplifies the epic ethos of war rather than "prime" law of nature, from which "comes intercourse between male and female, which we call marriage."[86] Dalila's strikingly relativizing speech about "double-mouth'd" "fame" that "with contrary blast proclaims most deeds" (971–972) suggests a potential reader of Alberico Gentili's *Wars of the Romans* in which subsequent volumes by the same author first denounced and then defended the history of the Roman empire. For Milton, it isn't exactly that Dalila or Scipione and Alberico Gentili were wrong about such matters, it was more that Dalila badly misrecognized the legal frame. In so doing, she gave Samson a *public* grievance, whose remedy could no longer be secured by Samson the particular husband but must instead be won by Samson the regenerated international person, "who represents the public liberty,... is not subject to the tutelage or the power of anyone else, [and] has in himself the power of war and of alliances."

EGYPT, IRONY, CATASTROPHE

"In free states," Leibniz argued, "a juridical person is considered by analogy to a natural one, inasmuch as he possesses a will."[87] In *Samson Agonistes*, the dramatic momentum toward Samson's violent destruction of the temple comes as Milton articulates Samson's emergence as an international legal person as movement from a position of incapacity ("I cannot come") to volition ("I will not come" [1321, 1332]). The shift introduces a legal frame in which Samson's will matters on the world stage. When Samson ultimately goes to the temple, he does so "of [his] own accord" (1643). This is a Samson who "has *in himself* the power of war and of alliances."

Samson's growing privileges as a legally recognizable international person come alongside the Philistine "lords" devaluing their own privileged legal personality. By invading Samson's conscience, Milton suggests, the Philistines qualify their

---

[86] Torquato Tasso, *Jerusalem Delivered (Gerusalemme Liberata)*, ed. and trans. Anthony M. Esolen (Baltimore, MD: Johns Hopkins University Press, 2000), 4.19–96, p. 448.
[87] Leibniz, *Political Writings*, 174.

international legal personhood. In Samson's eyes, these lords amount to little more than an

> ...impious crew
> Of men conspiring to uphold thir state
> By worse then hostile deeds, violating the ends
> For which our country is a name so dear. (891–894)

The *ius gladii* that Samson lawfully wields in the poem's violent climax becomes in this reciprocal movement an instrument of punishment not against equal and opposite international personality but against a "crew" that has surrendered its personality by violating the consciences of the particular persons within their power. The same "crew" that, against the law of nature and nations has conscripted Dalila against her husband, finally invades Samson's "conscience and internal peace" by forcing him to participate in the idolatrous Philistine rite (1334). According to Milton himself in 1673, even Protestant England had the duty by the "Law of Nations" to allow Catholic merchants and diplomats in England to worship according to their beliefs.[88]

It thus becomes possible to see how Milton casts religious toleration as both the recognition of basic human rights and also the final threshold of the tragic. The conditions for tragic catastrophe emerge whenever something considered so fundamental is on the line. Philistine coercion banishes conscience, but tragedy teaches that "what we banish returns with...explosive power."[89] For Milton, the coercion of particular humans ironically transformed private belief into international legal personality while reducing coercers' international legal personality to the status of mere force. Representation was closely related to this double movement. Philistines who'd once enjoyed corporate personhood enjoyed no such thing once they'd violated the mind-plot of Samson's particular conscience. Samson's own representative function emerges finally when he is coerced to worship a god other than his own. It is corporate Samson, representing all Israelite believers and who has progressed step by step from private interest to public cause, who lawfully destroys the Philistine temple. For Milton, the particular human's right to worship becomes the measure by which international legal personality is won and lost.

It should be evident that I largely agree with the reading of *Samson Agonistes* that sees Milton sanctioning, rather than critiquing, Samson's recourse to violence, but it should also be evident that I see Milton's analytic of tragedy framing that violence as a sad event in the contingent history of international religious persecution. The "play" between Samson as particular individual and Samson as embodiment of nation or godly faction is hardly resolved in the drama's catastrophe. "The conscience of a nation" entailed in an allegorical reading remains as difficult a thing to fathom as an international legal person's diet (Hobbes' bulimia), "his" sleep, "his" procreation, or "his" suicide. Nevertheless, a reading of *Samson Agonistes* in which international legal personality for Milton is both contingent upon the recognition of certain human rights relating to the conscience and also capable of legitimized destruction

---

[88] Milton, *CPW*, 8.431.   [89] Euben, *The Tragedy of Political Theory*, 49.

of individual objectified humans in defense of such rights aligns with Milton's reflections on war, tragedy, toleration, and representation more broadly. Samson had just public cause and the right of punishment, and it's a regrettable thing too.

In *Eikonoklastes*, often called a "regicide tract" though it actually denies England killed its king, Charles had instead become what Dalila calls Samson, "A common enemy, who had destroy'd / Such numbers of our Nation" (856–857). Having done so, gentleman Charles Stuart lost the privileges of representation alongside the title of king. Charles' war, says Milton, had been waged through Anglican conformity, an approach Milton characterizes as tragically ironic. "Those Kings and Potentates who have strove most to ridd themselves of this feare, by cutting off or suppressing the true Church," Milton observed, "have drawn upon themselves the occasion of thir own ruin, while they thought with most policy to prevent it."[90] In the very next sentence, Milton invoked the ironic outcome of Egyptian persecution of the Israelites, whose earlier history had been the subject of Grotius' own biblical tragedy *Sophompaneas*. "Thus *Pharaoh*," Milton continued, in words that pointed both backward to Grotius' *Sophompaneas* and forward to his own multiplicitous Samson, "once he began to feare ... the Israelites, least they should multiply and fight against him, and ... his feare stirr'd him up to afflict and keep them under, as the onely remedy of what he feard, soon found that the evil which before slept, came suddenly upon him, by the preposterous way he took to shun it."[91]

GROTIUS IN EGYPT

Just as *Paradise Regained* and *Samson Agonistes* would appear back to back in a single 1671 volume, so too had Grotius' drama on an Old Testament figure appeared next to Grotius' five act meditation on Christ, *Christus Patiens*, in the volume of Grotius' poetry published in London in 1639. Milton's nephew Edward Phillips commented shortly after Milton's death, had Grotius' "extolled works in Prose, never come to Light, his extant and universally approved Latin Poems, had been sufficient to gain him a Living Name."[92] Yet for all the attention paid to Grotius' prose tracts by scholars of seventeenth-century literature and international thought, surprisingly little has been paid to his poetry. Of his corpus of nearly 25,000 lines of poetry, the 1230 lines of his 1635 biblical tragedy *Sophompaneas* may be among the most promising objects of study, not least because Grotius composed the tragedy while revising his celebrated *De Jure Belli ac Pacis*. In recent years, scholars have assumed that Milton "ardently desired to meet" Grotius in the mid-1630s due to Grotius' justly deserved reputation for *De Jure Belli ac Pacis*, but poetry likely formed part of the impetus too.[93] Indeed, poetry may have been one of few commonalities, given the evidence that their ideologies in certain respects

---

[90] Milton, *CPW*, 3.509.   [91] Milton, *CPW*, 3.509–510.
[92] Edward Phillips, *Theatrum Poetarum, Or, A Compleat Collection of the Poets Especially the Most Eminent, of All Ages* (London: Charles Smith, 1675), 74.
[93] Milton, *CPW*, 4.1.615; Wittreich, *Shifting Contexts*; Oldman, "Milton, Grotius, and the Law of War"; Peters, "A 'Bridge over Chaos.' "

diverged. Both were free-will Arminians with strong tolerationist streaks, yet the generic and thematic elements in Milton's *Samson Agonistes* closest to Grotius' *Sophompaneas* also flag disputed ideological terrain.

Sophompaneas was translated into Dutch by Vondel and subsequently performed in the Low Countries, but its Senecan neo-classicism and prefatory materials—a dedicatory letter to Gerard Vossius and a catalogue of Grotius' biblical and historical sources—indicate *Sophompaneas* was, like *Adamus Exul, Christus Patiens*, and George Buchanan's neo-Latin dramas, among other possible examples, intended more for publication than performance.[94] One audience was the European republic of letters, which was newly intrigued by the "possibility of constructing a new history of Europe that integrated the ancient Egyptian, Israelite, and Phoenician worlds of the eastern Mediterranean with the Greek and Roman civilizations of the western."[95] Grotius' dedicatory letter even gestured to the "community of students of letters all over the world" (*totum orbem literas amantium universitate commune*), but the fact that Vossius sent the tragedy to the ever-worldly Archbishop Laud upon publication suggests an extra ambition for the drama to reach the highest levels of power.[96] The subtitle Grotius briefly proposed—*A Tragedy which enlarges on the Pious Morals of a Prince*—suggests much the same.

Sophompaneas' erudite title, derived from a Coptic name that Pharaoh gave to Joseph in Genesis 41:45, perplexed even Daniel Heinsius, at the time one of Europe's most learned theologians, who discussed the drama at Leiden University soon after its publication.[97] Long before, Heinsius had suggested that the Joseph Genesis story was already a "perfectly complete" tragedy for its complex combination of *peripeteia* and *recognition*, the story "mov[ing] pity so strongly that often it wrings tears against my will... no action more suitable for tragedy can be found."[98] But what did it mean to imagine the story of Joseph, and biblical history more

---

[94] In Latin, *Sophompaneas* seems to have been staged only once, in 1660, but Vondel's Dutch translation saw over sixty performances between 1638 and 1665. See Arthur Eyffinger, "Introduction," in *Sophompaneas, 1635*, by Hugo Grotius, trans. Arthur Eyffinger, *The Poetry of Hugo Grotius*, 4 [A–B] (Assen: Van Gorcum, 1992), 112–14. For more on Vondel's translation, see Freya Sierhuis, "Therapeutic Tragedy: Compassion, Remorse, and Reconciliation in the Joseph Plays of Joost van Den Vondel (1635–1640)," *European Review of History: Revue Europeenne D'histoire* 17, no. 1 (2010): 27–51; Kasten, "Translation Studies—Vondel's Appropriation of Grotius's Sophompaneas (1635)."

[95] Peter N. Miller, *Peiresc's Europe: Learning and Virtue in the Seventeenth Century* (New Haven, CT: Yale University Press, 2000), 10.

[96] Grotius, *Sophompaneas [1992]*, 155, 70.   [97] Grotius, *Sophompaneas [1992]*, 85.

[98] "We...have both in the story of Joseph, and indeed in such a way that it excels everything in the tragic poets. For the passions are effective to a wonderful degree. The patriarchs are departing with the wheat. Although they know nothing, a search is made for Joseph's cup, with bondage the penalty for possession. At length it is found on Benjamin, the youngest. On him and him alone the spirit and life of the old Jacob had depended ever since Joseph was lost. Therefore his brothers accompany him into servitude, in which suddenly they meet with good fortune surpassing all expectation. This is the purest peripety. The other part is gracefully yoked to this as cause to effect: they indeed recognize their brother, and this is the recognition. For there can be peripety without recognition, but there can be no recognition without peripety. In this argument it moves pity so strongly that often it wrings tears against my will. Hence the story of Joseph is complex, not simple, and perfectly complex because it yokes peripety and recognition alike—and no action more suitable for tragedy can be found." See Heinsius, *On Plot in Tragedy*, 37.

broadly, from the point of view of Egypt? Grotius, a reader of Heinsius and translator of Euripides' *Phoenissae* (1630), was alert to the reciprocity of recognition. He
would point out in his published *Annotations* on the Old Testament (1644) that
"Sophompaneas" did not appear in Latin vulgate bibles, only that Pharaoh called
Joseph "in the language of Egypt" *salvatorem mundi*, savior of the world.[99] Grotius,
following rabbinic commentators and Josephus' *Jewish Antiquities*, returned to
Pharaoh a sovereign naming power that the vulgate had eclipsed. He introduced
a further meaning occluded in the vulgate version, noting that the Coptic name
also meant *arcanorum reportoreum*, revealer of secrets, which fit Joseph's dream-
interpreting well.

Vossius sent the copy to Laud in August 1635, but *Sophompaneas* was not
printed in England until an unauthorized 1639 London volume of Grotius' *Poe-
mata*. The printer was Richard Hodgkinson, the man Parliament accused of being
"Printer to the said Archbishop," and about whom it was claimed that when he was
confronted in 1638 for printing John Cowell's arch-royalist *Interpreter* against a
parliamentary order, "took [a copy of the order] up and flung it down again saying,
in a scornful manner, this came forth in a seditious and scandalous parliament
time."[100] Common textual discrepancies show that it was Hodgkinson's unauthorized volume that provided the source text for the English translation published in
1652, shortly after Milton's *Eikonoklastes*, by the high-church royalist Francis
Goldsmith.

Grotius' poetry had never veered far from the political, legal, commercial, and
theological aspects of his life. While Goldsmith's rhyming couplets sought to mark
literary Grotius as a sort of continental Cavalier, the glosses show Goldsmith
untroubled by the assumption that Grotius' theological and legal treatises were the
proper context in which to read *Sophompaneas*. Grotius' poetic tributes to Arminius had impressed high-church theologians who'd paid close attention to the disputes at Leiden and Dort, but Grotius' works also included a 1603 plea for Stuart
assistance for the Dutch revolt, coming in the form of a 614-line panegyric to
James on the occasion of James' ascent to the throne, and an epigram to Sir Francis
Vere, the famed Calvinist leader of English troops in the Netherlands, both of
which appeared in the 1639 London volume. The poems on Arminius, of course,
presented Grotius as a theological ally of the Laudians, whose movement toward
Rome helped to preclude entrance to the Thirty Years' War; the panegyric and Vere
epigram introduced him as an imploring voice for Protestant engagement on the
Continent, with typological thinking turning 1620s Bohemia into a latter day
Low Countries similarly under threat from the papal Antichrist. Grotius the Laud

[99] Hugo Grotius, *Opera Omnia Theologica*, ed. Pieter de Groot (Amsterdam, 1679), 1.23.
[100] D. F. McKenzie and Maureen Bell, eds., *A Chronology and Calendar of Documents Relating to
the London Book Trade, 1641–1700* (Oxford: Oxford University Press, 2005), 1.106. Hodgkinson's (or
"Hodskins'") reaction was reported somewhat differently in Laud's trial in the Lords: "The Proclamation was made in a schismatical and scandalous Parliament Time": "House of Lords Journal Volume
6: 13 March 1644," *Journal of the House of Lords: volume 6: 1643* (1767–1830), 467–9 <http://www.
british-history.ac.uk/report.aspx?compid=37472>.

ally is on display in a 1637 Oxford anthology dedicated to the soon-to-be-notorious Laudian clergyman William Heywood in which seventy-five of Grotius' epigrams appeared.[101] On the other hand, George Sandys' translation of Grotius' drama *Christus Patiens* (orig. 1608; trans. 1640) is a conspicuous harkening to early Grotius—the Grotius of the Dutch rebellion—and a revival of a drama whose potential anti-Laudian message is nicely captured by James Ellison's summary: "a moderate ruler... led astray by... an over-powerful persecuting priest."[102] The tolerationist, "anti-absolutist note" of the drama, as Ellison points out, is most clear in Falkland's description in a prefatory poem of Sandys as "the English Buchanan," a figure who at that point in 1639 was a tutelary figure for the Scottish covenanters.[103] In an interesting example of Grotius' complex cultural meaning, Grotius' testimony for Heywood's Laudianism may have provided the ideological cover under which Sandys could have his critique pass the scrutiny of two separate Laudian censors.[104]

Grotius' arguments on behalf of the Dutch East India Company did not go without their literary complements. Composed around the same time as *Mare Liberum* (*c.*1603; published anonymously, 1609), Grotius' discussion of the "beauteous *Nereids*, Sov'reigns of the Seas" in his nautical idyll *Myrtillus* helps to confirm the polemical stance of *Mare Liberum* that in ancient times, "the sea was so common, that it may be in the dominion of none but God alone," much as the poem's discussion of "liquid air" reinscribes Grotius' wish in *Mare Liberum* to treat the sea and air as legally comparable, "*publica juris gentium*: that is, common to all and proper to none."[105] A suggestion that readers could be well aware of these implications of Grotius' poetry even before Selden in *Mare Clausum* chastised Grotius' reliance on "old poets" comes from a pair of Scotsmen, the jurist William Welwood and the Latin poet and student of civil law with links to the Jacobean court, John Leech.[106] It is well known that Welwood replied in prose to Grotius' *Mare Liberum* conceding the general point of Grotius' argument "for the

---

[101] Abraham Wright, *Delitiae Delitiarum Sive Epigrammatum* (Oxford: Leonard Lichfield, 1637), 173–98; *The Petition and Articles Exhibited in Parliament against Doctor Heywood, Late Chaplen to the Bishop of Canterburie, by the Parishioners of S. Giles in the Fields. With Some Considerable Circumstances (worth Observing) in the Hearing of the Businesse before the Grand Committee for Religion, and of His Demeanour Since.* (London, 1641).

[102] James Ellison, *George Sandys: Travel, Colonialism, and Tolerance in the Seventeenth Century* (Cambridge: D. S. Brewer, 2002), 243, 238–46.

[103] Ellison, *George Sandys: Travel, Colonialism, and Tolerance in the Seventeenth Century*, 245. This is not to suggest that the covenanters should be considered tolerationist, only that Laud's eagerness to require the Book of Common Prayer in Scotland offended the Great Tew Circle's tolerationist impulses.

[104] Hugo Grotius, *Christs Passion a Tragedie, with Annotations.*, trans. George Sandys (London: John Legatt, 1640). STC 12397.5 bears the imprimatur of "Tho: Whykes," dated 17 September 1639 and another, on its final page, by "Ioannes Hansley" on 27 September.

[105] Hugo Grotius, "Eclogues," in *Select Translations from the Works of Sannazarius H. Grotius, Bapt. Amaltheus, D. Heinsius, G. Buchanan, and M. Hier. Vida.*, trans. John Rooke (London, 1726), 2, 7; William Welwood, "Of the Community and Propriety of the Seas," in *The Free Sea*, ed. David Armitage (Indianapolis, IN: Liberty Fund, 2004), 30, 25.

[106] D. K. Money, "Leech, John (Fl. 1610–1624)," *Oxford Dictionary of National Biography* (Oxford: Oxford University Press, 2004).

main sea or great ocean," yet at the same time asserting British jurisdiction over the North Sea in defense of Scottish fishing rights.[107] Like Selden, Welwood had objected that Grotius (though officially anonymous) "would make *mare liberum* to be a position fortified by the opinions and sayings of some old poets."[108] Appearing three years after a major collection of Grotius' poems, John Leech's *Musae Priores* (1620) featured a sympathetic speaker who complained of a "greedy Myrtilus" imperiling skiffs, nets, and hooks: fishing equipment.[109] Grotius' marshaling of poetry in the Anglo-Dutch disputes would not go unrequited.[110] The implications for North Sea fishing, of course, were for Britons the most troublesome parts of Grotius' arguments, whether verse or prose. The suggestion that the law of nations prohibited Iberian claims to the seas, however, was more than welcome. Eventually applying the same logic to the Dutch, British merchants even quoted Grotius' *Mare Liberum* against Grotius and the Dutch East India Company when their representatives conferred in London and the Hague in 1613 and 1615.[111] Even as they defended Scottish fishing rights, many Britons therefore had particular reason to applaud Grotius' *Epicedium Jacobi Heemskerkii*, a memorial of the Dutch captain that appeared in all of the major editions of Grotius' poetry and that compared van Heemskerk denying "Spanish dominion of the seas" [*Hispani regnum mare*] to the English defeat of the Armada.[112] In the poem, Heemskerk, the captain whose seizure of the Portuguese merchantman *Santa Catarina* was the impetus for Grotius' *De Jure Praedae*, gives a stirring justification

---

[107] Welwood, "Of the Community and Propriety of the Seas," 74. On the importance of this debate through the 1610s, see Martine Julia van Ittersum, "Mare Liberum Versus the Propriety of the Seas? The Debate between Hugo Grotius (1583–1645) and William Welwood (1552–1624) and Its Impact on Anglo-Scotto-Dutch Fishery Disputes in the Second Decade of the Seventeenth Century," *Edinburgh Law Review* 10, no. 2 (2006): 239–76; Bradin Cormack, *A Power to Do Justice: Jurisdiction, English Literature, and the Rise of Common Law* (Chicago, IL: University of Chicago Press, 2008), 256–75.

[108] Welwood, "Of the Community and Propriety of the Seas," 66.

[109] Henry Marion Hall, *Idylls of Fishermen: A History of the Literary Species* (New York: Columbia University Press, 1912), 140–2.

[110] Leech, whose works were regularly printed on the Continent, for his part, sought to restore *eclogae nauticae* to what the British saw as its proper place confirming Scottish fishing rights. His can be seen as a poetic complement to Welwood's complaint that: "by the near and daily approaching of the buss-fishers the shoals of fishes are broken and so far scattered away from our shores and coasts that no fish can be found worthy of any pains and travails, to the impoverishing of all the sort of our home fishers and to the great damage of all the nation." Evidently, verse arguments needed rebuttal just as prose arguments did. Perhaps this element is why one Dutch reader, adopting a suitably menacing vocabulary, opined that reading Grotius' poetry was like glimpsing the paw of a lion. J. W. Binns, *Intellectual Culture in Elizabethan and Jacobean England: The Latin Writings of the Age* (Leeds: Francis Cairns, 1990), 109. Welwood, "Of the Community and Propriety of the Seas," 74. Herbert F. Wright, "Some Less Known Works of Hugo Grotius: Consisting of a Translation of His Works on Fisheries in His Controversy with William Welwood; a Translation of Extracts from His Letters Concerning International, Natural Law and Fisheries; an Account of His Controversy with Johan De Laet on the Origin of the American Aborigines; And, a Translation of Peerlkamp's Appreciation of His Ability as a Poet," in *Bibliotheca Visseriana Dissertationum Ius Internationale Illustrantium*, vol. 7 (Leiden, 1928), 232.

[111] Peter Borschberg, "Hugo Grotius, East India Trade and the King of Johor," *Journal of Southeast Asian Studies* 30, no. 2 (September 1, 1999): 225–48.

[112] Hugo Grotius, *Original Poetry, 1604–1608*, ed. Edwin Rabbie (Assen: Van Gorcum, 1992), 383.

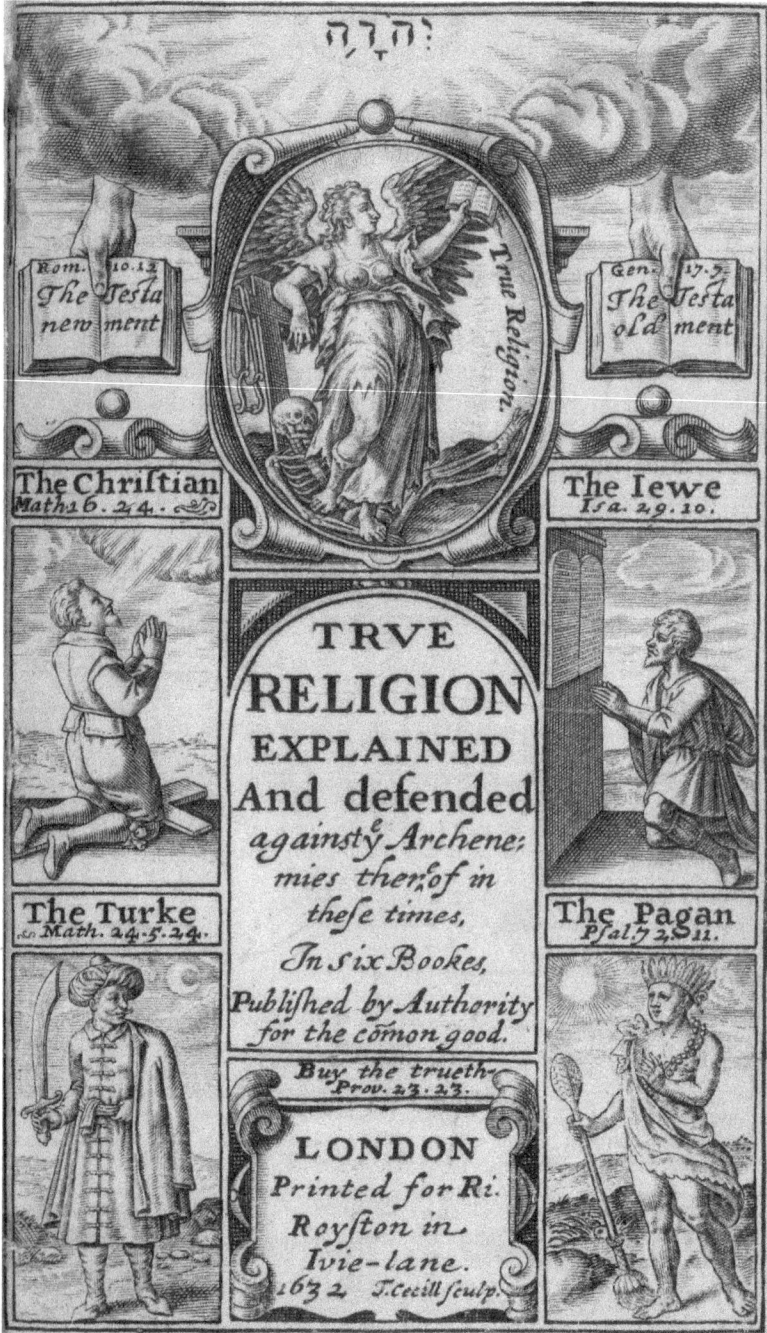

Fig. 6.1. Title-page engraving by Thomas Cecil for *True religion explained, and defended against the archenemies thereof in these times. In six bookes. Written in Latine by Hugo Grotius* (1632), STC 12400.

of the Dutch resort to arms that closely parallels the just-war arguments of Grotius' unpublished *Commentarius in theses XI* and *De Jure Praedae* and interestingly anticipates Satan's speech in Book 2 of *Paradise Lost*.[113] Andrew Marvell's poem "The Character of Holland" (1653) mentioned Grotius' *Mare Liberum* and *De Jure Belli ac Pacis* by name, and there is likely a previously unnoticed reference to Grotius in Marvell's description of Amsterdam as the multicultural home of "Turk-Christian-Pagan-Jew," a formulation indebted to the English title page of Grotius' *True Religion Explained and Defended* created by Thomas Cecil, engraver of Hobbes' Thucydides frontispiece (see Figure 6.1).[114]

While Grotius' seventeenth-century receptions in England were varied, they confirm John Owen's contemporary evaluation that Grotius was "a Gyant in all kinds of Literature."[115]

PREAMBLE TO THE LAWS

Sophompaneas, a biblical tragedy concerning "adjacent Countries" (4.91), was, like the rest of Grotius' poetry, closely related to his international legal theory. In broad outlines, Grotius' *Sophompaneas* retells Genesis 44–50, in which Joseph, operating as vicegerent of Egypt, again meets the brothers who years earlier had sold him into slavery and who have now been forced by famine to leave Canaan in search of food in Egypt. As a result of Joseph's political standing there, Pharaoh permits the distressed Israelites' relocation to Egypt. Divided into five acts, the drama employs a chorus of Ethiopian serving maids whose speeches punctuate each act and who, at the end of the drama, express a wish to take part in Christ's redemption.[116]

The list of Grotius' concerns in *Sophompaneas* is a long one. The drama was an irenic plea for Christian unification, an etiology of property, a primer on Afro-European

---

[113] This is true especially of Thesis XI, "The State [of Holland] undertook a just war in defense of a mark of sovereignty which lay within their competence." Hugo Grotius, *Hugo Grotius "Commentarius in theses XI": an early treatise on sovereignty, the just war, and the legitimacy of the Dutch revolt*, ed. and trans. Peter Borschberg (New York: P. Lang, 1994). For a recent account of the *Santa Catarina* capture, see Martine Julia Van Ittersum, "Hugo Grotius in Context: Van Heemskerck's Capture of the Santa Catarina and Its Justification in De Jure Praedae (1604–1606)," *Asian Journal of Social Science* 31, no. 3 (2003): 511–48.

[114] I quote from Andrew Marvell, *The Poems of Andrew Marvell*, ed. Nigel Smith, rev. edn. (London: Pearson Longman, 2007).

[115] John Owen, *Vindiciae Evangelicae or The Mystery of the Gospell Vindicated, and Socinianisme Examined* (Oxford: Leonard Lichfield, 1655), sig. a1r. See also Henry Hammond, *A Second Defence of the Learned Hugo Grotius* (London: J. Flesher, for Richard Royston, 1655), sig. a2.

[116] It has been suggested that Grotius tells this story of Joseph's unjust treatment followed by a rise to power in order to parallel his own imprisonment by the Orangeists and subsequent political ascent in the foreign Swedish court. The first reference Grotius makes in his correspondence to a nearly completed *Sophompaneas* in April 1634 comes just two months before he formally agreed to represent the Swedish crown. At that point, Grotius had been in talks with Oxenstierna, the Swedish vicegerent, for at least a year. Arthur Eyffinger, " 'La Plus Belle Des Histoires'. Grotius' Drama on Joseph in Egypt in the Tradition of the Theme," *Grotiana* 8, no. 1 (1987): 267; Christian Gellinek, *Hugo Grotius* (Boston, MA: Twayne Publishers, 1983), 20–4. Grotius, *Sophompaneas [1992]*, 76.

relations, a piece of biblical chronology, an argument for religious toleration, and a scholarly analysis of revealed scripture. Its appeal to Laud and other Episcopalians had to do with Genesis 47:22–26, a passage ostensibly grounding priestly benefices in the law of nations, and one that carried special weight given the perilous famine and its evidence for non-Israelite practice.[117] "How carefull was Pharaoh (a Heathen King) in the extremitie of Famine, to provide for his Priests, and preserve their Lands from Sale or Alienation?," one high-church apologist wrote.[118] Even Pharaoh, the argument went, sustained a priesthood. The Ethiopian chorus gave the drama further topicality, since Ethiopia, a strong concern of Grotius', had reverted in 1632 from Catholicism to Coptic orthodoxy, expelling Portuguese Jesuit missionaries.[119]

Much as Milton's prose sheds light on *Samson Agonistes*, Grotius' use of the Joseph story in *De Jure Belli* provides numerous reasons to read *Sophompaneas* in terms of Grotius' legal theory.[120] Grotius was interested in Egypt's political form, its mechanisms of government, and its legal jurisdiction—particularly over lands periodically covered by the overflowing Nile. Joseph's authority under Pharaoh, meanwhile, helped Grotius defend trade monopolies—the index of the 1625 edition has an entry for "Iosephi Patriarchae monopolium," for example—and the Jews' arrangements with Egypt helped to confirm Grotius' argument that conducting leagues and alliances with infidels was permissible according to divine law, Hebrew law, and Christian law alike. On the way to endorsing the proposition that "What is taken from the Enemy, by the Law of Nations, immediately becomes the Captors['']," Grotius read Genesis 48:22, Jacob's bequest to Joseph, to license future dispossession: "The Patriarch Jacob leaving an especial Legacy to Joseph above his Brethren [said], *I give to thee... one Part above thy Brethren which I took out of the Hand of the* Amorite, *with my Sword and with my Bow.*" "*The Word, I took*," Grotius

---

[117] Minsters' benefices were "justified not only by the judiciall lawe of Moses; but also by the lawe of Nations in Pharaoh['s] Priests," one clergyman explained, "who had lands and livings...which... they were not forced to sell when-as all the rest of the peo[ple] sould their landes to buy...corne...; neither would Joseph meddle with them, but they had an ordinarie allowance of Pharaoh to live uppon." See Henry Morley, *The Cleansing of the Leper Discoursed* (London: H[umphrey] L[ownes] for Clement Knight, 1609), 247.

[118] James Martin, "Epistle Dedicatory," in *Vindiciae Sacrae. A Treatise of the Honor and Maintenance due to Ecclesiasticall Persons*, by Adrien Saravia, trans. James Martin (London: T. Cotes and R. Cotes for James Boler, 1629), a6r.

[119] Grotius' letters and published writing show his keen interest in Christianity's contemporary fate in Ethiopia, as does his Ethiopian Chorus' final description of their "hearts burn[ing] with a coelestiall heat" for the "one/Channell... of pure religion." For background, see Girma Beshah and Merid Wolde Aregay, *The Question of the Union of the Churches in Luso-Ethiopian Relations, 1500–1632*, (Lisbon: Junta de Investigacões do Ultramar and Centro de Estudos Históricos Ultramarinos, 1964). Jane O. Newman, "'Race,' Religion, and the Law: Rhetorics of Sameness and Difference in the Work of Hugo Grotius," in *Rhetoric and Law in Early Modern Europe*, ed. Victoria Kahn and Lorna Hutson (New Haven, CT: Yale University Press, 2001), 42. See further John Michael Archer, *Old Worlds: Egypt, Southwest Asia, India, and Russia in Early Modern English Writing* (Stanford, CA: Stanford University Press, 2001), 34–8.

[120] Bernhard Lang, *Joseph in Egypt: A Cultural Icon from Grotius to Goethe* (New Haven, CT: Yale University Press, 2009), 195.

continues, "seems to be taken prophetically for *I shall surely take* [Quo in loco illiud *cepi* prophetico loquendo genere pro *certo capium*], and this attributed to *Jacob*, which was done after by his Posterity..."[121] In *Sophompaneas*, the character of Benjamin insists "*Abraham to Lot* / Was such an Unkle. As who did expose / His own life, that he might from savage foes / Him rescue by his sword..."[122] Grotius in *DJBP* used the example of Abraham and Lot to prove nations' "Obligation of assisting" their "Friends," whether or not the two nations were "under any formal Promise," suggesting *Sophompaneas* too belongs to the history and rhetoric of humanitarian intervention, to be explored more fully in Chapter 7.[123] The lines that follow in *Sophompaneas*—"...and back [Abraham] brings / Victoriously the spoiles home of four Kings"—further show Grotius keen, even in verse, to treat questions of war prizes and the duties of neighboring princes.[124] I argue in what follows, however, that literature—specifically biblical tragedy—is what Grotius employs to secure the international order from the potentially catastrophic rights of necessity—rights Grotius himself powerfully elaborated but refused, in *Sophompaneas*, to dramatize.

Joseph was for Grotius the model *persona juris gentium*. Above all, Joseph's story enabled thinking about the rights of necessitous humans in relation to the stability of established international order. In "the extremitie of famine," Grotius' Joseph wisely manages trade, migration, colonialism, and rights of worship. But if Milton would emphasize the irony of coercion that turned private belief into international legal personality, Grotius emphasizes the way exemplary international legal persons like Joseph artfully manage the destabilizing rights of transitory, necessitous humans. Grotius' tragedy is notably free of war and conquest, and it lacks the sad ending (*exitus infelix*) that many saw as requisite to tragedy. As Goldsmith's prefatory poem rhymed in royalist overtones, "*Here no Medea her own Children kils, / Nor Hercules the Stage with horror fils.*"[125] In a fallen world in which war and conquest were lamentably, demonstrably legal, Grotius presented a version of humane, godly statecraft protecting a fragile international arena not only from the worst excesses possible in that arena but even from the strict "rigor allowed" by the laws of nature and nations.[126]

---

[121] In his *Annotations on the Old Testament*, Grotius similarly wrote that Jacob meant, "*Cepiam per posteros meos*," "I will take with my posterity." Grotius makes clear in both places that his aim is to refute rabbinic readings of Genesis 48:22 that, however inadvertently, suggested Jacob was bequeathing impiously gotten war spoils; still, Grotius' eagerness to defend "just and religious" Jacob by moving from "I took" (*cepi*) to "I shall surely take" (*certo capium*) adds dispossession to the already numerous *ius gentium* concerns on which the Joseph story might be brought to bear. Grotius, *DJBP*, 1319, 1315. Grotius, *Opera Omnia Theologica*, 1.25.

[122] Hugo Grotius, *Hugo Grotius His Sophompaneas, or Ioseph. A Tragedy. With Annotations*, ed. and trans. Francis Goldsmith (London: W. H., 1652), 36. References to this volume appear hereafter as *Sophompaneas, or Joseph [1652]*.

[123] Grotius, *DJBP*, 1156.

[124] Grotius, *Sophompaneas, or Joseph [1652]*, 36. But see also Grotius, *Commentary on the Law of Prize and Booty*, 84–5.

[125] Grotius, *Sophompaneas, or Joseph [1652]*, sig. b3r.

[126] Grotius, *DJBP*, 1364, for *summo illo rigore*.

The dedicatory letter offers the fullest introduction to Grotius' intentions.[127] Grotius writes that Moses, as the author of Genesis,

> in the preamble of his most old lawes . . . had given us three choice patterns for a private life, the first of him [Abraham] who by the aid of the arts and excellent learning came from false gods to the true; the second [Isaac], whose birth it selfe and happy education did very much advantage him; and a third [Jacob], who besides these benefits had this also, which I by experience think the greatest, a triall by afflictions, would adde likewise a man exercised in publike government, notable, not onely for those hereditary and domestique virtues, but what were also profitable to the Common-wealth; which indeed in *Joseph* he hath so perform'd, as that he, a leader of the people, if ever any, provident for the future, unbroken in evils, a maintainer of justice, observing modera-tion in all things, may seeme to have set himselfe no other copy, next to the divine Commandements, by which to order his actions, then the life of this *Joseph*.[128]

Joseph is as different as possible from the biblical enemies who "afflict" and oppress consciences and in so doing ironically create the insurrections they fear. Grotius' pious Joseph is instead an exemplary leader whose civil wisdom helped him suc-cessfully avoid, postpone, and manage tragedy in the word's most typically violent sense. Joseph the *persona juris gentium* is Grotius' solution for an international order rendered deeply vulnerable by the violent and unsettling implications of human necessity and natural human rights. Even as the tragedy's depictions of famine, persecution, and exile unmask the pretentions of sovereign borders in his tragedy, remedies of asylum, commerce, centralization, and contract emerge as the salvific instruments of a new kind of international legal personality embodied in Joseph. Joseph's forgiveness of his brothers in the tragedy's final act may have been especially valued by Grotius' royalist admirers in the royalist campaign for clem-ency in the early 1650s, but the tragedy perhaps more centrally develops through its commercial and managerial ethos a tragic law of nations without tragedy—the obverse of Milton's and against which Milton's own tragic law of nations seems to have been formed.

As with *Samson Agonistes*, Grotius' tragedy investigates international legal per-sonality and natural rights through a single biblical figure whose story also becomes legible as autobiography and political allegory. Grotius' Joseph over the course of the tragedy becomes an international legal personality through a double recognition. Having been "made merchandise, / And to hard bondage sold" by his brothers, Joseph ultimately gains recognition by Pharaoh and the Egyptian subjects as a virtuous, meritorious "governor."[129] Later, he is recognized in what Grotius intends as a more consequential way by his brethren, as an Israelite still beholden to natural bonds of filiation, to which Goldsmith's "fils" may have been intended to allude. Linguistic identities being at the heart of both recognitions, Joseph's virtue finds

---

[127] Grotius, *Sophompaneas, or Joseph [1652]*, sig. a6r; Arthur Eyffinger, "The Fourth Man: Stoic Tradition in Grotian Drama," in *Grotius and the Stoa*, eds. Hans W. Blom and Laurens C. Winkel (Assen: Royal van Gorcum, 2004), 139–41, 145, 148. Milton in *The Reason of Church-Government* (1642) also described *Genesis* as God's "prologue to his laws." Milton, *CPW*, 1.747.

[128] Grotius, *Sophompaneas, or Joseph [1652]*, sig. a5v–a6r.

[129] Grotius, *Sophompaneas, or Joseph [1652]*, 4.

Fig. 6.2. *Joseph Distributing Grain in Egypt*, Etching by Jan de Bisschop, Dutch, 1648–1657.
Reproduced with kind permission from The Minneapolis Institute of Arts.

formal recognition in the Coptic name Pharaoh bestows upon Joseph, and with such a name does "Sophompaneas" accrue legal personality allowing him to represent the kingdom of Egypt.

The tragedy's subsequent recognition happens as the figure who bears the personhood of Egypt, "Sophompaneas," comes to be recognized as "Joseph," a bearer—in addition—of the personhood of Israel. Recognition that "Sophompaneas" is indeed "Joseph" begins in an exchange between Judah and Joseph in Act 4 in which Joseph, discussing with Judah the fate of Joseph's natural brother Benjamin, reveals knowledge of the name's Hebrew etymology. Joseph, whose Egyptian public personhood was revealed in his political acts on behalf of the commonwealth of Egypt, and affirmed in the marks given to him by Pharaoh, is subsequently also recognized as the representative of Israel. Pharaoh, affirming this international person's legitimized power to make war and alliances, then contracts a treaty with Joseph that allows the Israelites, whom Joseph is now seen to represent, to sojourn in Egypt.

RAGING HUNGER NO ALLEGIANCE KNOWS

In Grotius' tragedy, famine is the most important vehicle for investigating the interplay of international legal personality and natural or human rights of self-preservation. Necessity, as the legal maxim had it, knows no law, and it could powerfully disrupt international stability. Grotius' Joseph shrewdly observes how "the nations all around…are wont to feed on Egypt's produce" amidst the famine.[130] He muses in an opening soliloquy, "great danger to a State [*imperiis*] still growes, For raging hunger no alleagiance knows."[131]

Grotius' relatively fluid conception of borders meant that in moments of necessity like Genesis' famine, natural law permitted almost anything. "In a Case of absolute Necessity," Grotius wrote in *De Jure Belli*, "that antient Right of using Things, as if they still remained in common, must revive and be in full Force."[132] Seen through *De Jure Belli ac Pacis*, the famine justified "using" Goshen without Pharaoh's concurrence. But Grotius in *De Jure Belli* draped his discussion of natural rights with caveats that could only come from having seen the rhetoric of necessity outstrip the reality. "Precautions are to be observed"; "all other possible Means should be first used"; "Restitution shall be made when the necessity's over"; "all things being equal, the [original] Possessor has the Advantage": Grotius understood that natural rights of necessity had to be tightly hedged if they were to be protected from the abuse of opportunists.[133] With the Joseph in Egypt story having become important in discussions of colonization, Grotius recognized that both opportunists using the rhetoric of necessity and those who were legitimately in need threatened international stability.[134] When Grotius issued his admonition in *De Jure Belli*, "The Priveledges of Necessity may not be too far extended," the Latin word he used for "privileges" was *licentia*, whose negative connotation Milton made famous in his stinging line, "License they mean when they cry liberty."[135] *Circumscribere* was another word Grotius used to describe the ways natural law needed to be restrained, as if to note how important writing was in the process of hedging natural law.[136] Precisely because the *licentia* of necessity threatened the international order, it was important to help European readers visualize a case of necessity where international order was peacefully preserved. Evidence from seventeenth-century readers of *De Jure Belli* suggests they would have been alert to *Sophompaneas*' contrapuntal *ought* to the disruptive *is* of licentious natural law. The owner of a copy of Clement Barksdale's 1654 translation of *De Jure Belli* habitually underscored phrases like "circumscribe natural liberty," and "in extreme necessity," even

---

[130] Grotius, *Sophompaneas [1992]*, 229.

[131] *Periculosum semper imperiis malum,/retinere quipped nescit obsequium fames/nullosque sentit vulgus impastum metus.* Grotius, *Sophompaneas, or Joseph [1652]*, 3 (1.69–70); Grotius, *Sophompaneas [1992]*, 158–9.

[132] Grotius, *DJBP*, 434.   [133] Grotius, *DJBP*, 435, 437, 436.

[134] "[A]s…Pharaoh said to Joseph, in land of Goshen let thy father and brethren dwell, Gen. 47, 5, 6 So in Virginia King Powhatan desired the English to come from James Town, a place unwholesome, and take possession of another whole Kingdome, which he gave them." See Thomas Thorowgood, *Jewes in America, Or, Probabilities That the Americans Are of That Race* (London: W. H. for Tho. Slater, 1650), 57–8; Peter Harrison, "'Fill the Earth and Subdue It': Biblical Warrants for Colonization in Seventeenth Century England," *Journal of Religious History* 29, no. 1 (2005): 20.

[135] "On the Detraction which followed upon my Writing Certain Treatises" in John Milton, *Complete Shorter Poems*, ed. and trans. John Carey, 2nd edn. (London: Longman, 1997), 297, l. 11; Grotius, *DJBP*, 435.

[136] Hugo Grotius, *Hugonis Grotii De Jure Belli Ac Pacis Libri Tres* (Paris, 1625), 433.

adding a manicule to the underlining in the case of the "tacit exception of extreme necessitie" that, Grotius argued, applied even to the laws of God.[137]

As discussed previously in the context of Hobbes, much Northern European colonialism took place on the premise of using or "filling" unused lands, and little of the legal discussion in *De Jure Belli* dissents from the natural law and biblical warrants others used to justify colonial enterprises.[138] *De Jure Belli* allowed, for example, that "if there be any waste or barren Land [*deserti ac sterilis soli*] within our Dominions, that also is to be given to Strangers, at their Request, or may be lawfully possessed by them."[139] We know also from his *Annotations* that Grotius read Genesis 47:6—"give unto them the land Goshen"—in accordance with "the part in Manetho's history [where Manetho writes] *he gave them Abaris, then left empty* [vacuam] *by the shepherds* [pastoribus]."[140] The description of Goshen in *Sophompaneas* is therefore of considerable interest:

> A pleasant Land there lies not far
> From *Heliopolis*, where grasse still green;
> And pastures ever flourishing are seen.
> The bordering Pelusians it call
> *Goshen*. This land hath hitherto been all
> Lost to the use of men [*usibus mortalium*][141]

To someone looking for them, "Lost to the use of men" could inaugurate a cascade of derivative arguments for the Israelites' possession of Goshen in their extremity.[142] But far from amounting to an annexation of Goshen by *fiat*, these words are spoken by Joseph to Pharaoh, in a request that, even in the Israelites' moment of necessity, remains cognizant of Pharaoh's sovereign and moral agency. Grotius intends Joseph's wisdom to shine as Joseph mitigates the most dangerous aspects of the natural right of necessity. Grotius in *De Jure Belli* offered as possibilities "applying to a Magistrate, to see how far he would relieve us" and "entreating the Owner to supply us with what we stand in Need of," both of which Joseph does.[143]

Beforehand, Grotius had carefully inscribed Pharaoh's personhood and imperium, neither of which is compromised by his religion. The title of the drama can be seen as Grotius' first step in this direction. Grotius' implicit recognition of Pharaoh's authority to name Joseph was a prominent recognition both of infidels' moral

[137] Grotius, *The Illustrious Hugo Grotius of the Law of Warre and Peace With Annotations. III. Parts. And Memorials of the Author's Life and Death.*, Shelfmark UJX2093.E5 1965 in the Posner Collection at Carnegie Mellon University, 150, 206, 207. "J. Corvin" is on the flyleaf. On seventeenth-century oath-takers turning to Grotius for such matters, see Edward Vallance, "Oaths, Casuistry, and Equivocation: Anglican Responses to the Engagement Controversy," *The Historical Journal* 44, no. 01 (2001).

[138] Richard Tuck, "The Making and Unmaking of Boundaries from the Natural Law Perspective," in *States, Nations, and Borders: The Ethics of Making Boundaries*, ed. Allen E. Buchanan and Margaret Moore (Cambridge: Cambridge University Press, 2003), 156.

[139] Grotius, *DJBP*, 448.   [140] Grotius, *Opera Omnia Theologica*, 1.25.

[141] Grotius, *Sophompaneas, or Joseph [1652]*, 39–40.

[142] Richard Tuck, *The Rights of War and Peace: Political Thought and the International Order from Grotius to Kant* (Oxford: Oxford University Press, 1999), 105.

[143] Grotius, *DJBP*, 435.

agency and their legal jurisdiction, a condensed version of thoughts originally set out in Grotius' unpublished manuscript called *De Societate Publica cum Infidelibus* (*Of Public Society with Infidels*) that defended leagues with non-Christians.[144] In *De Jure Belli ac Pacis*, Grotius writes:

> Let us first consider, what the Divine Right [*iure divino*, i.e., divine law] of the Old Testament directs in this Affair…We find that inoffensive Leagues, and such as tended to no one's Injury [*fedus non nocendi*], might, before the Time of *Moses*, be contracted with People who were not of the true Religion…Let the *Aegyptians* be a Precedent, who doubtless were Idolaters, yet the *Hebrews* were strictly forbid to abhor, or have any Aversion to them.[145]

The story of the Israelites in Egypt for Grotius was a tolerationist "precedent" for "inoffensive leagues," the latter of which could be positively built on top of natural law and thereby help to "restrain [*circumscribere*] natural liberty."[146]

Grotius uses Joseph's pious leadership in a moment of necessity to contrast scripture's legitimate right of refugees with a harsher, opportunistic, and more brutal colonial program, one in which little notice is taken of native rulers and existing jurisdictions, where infidels are enemies and therefore inappropriate treaty-partners, where permissive natural law use-doctrines were all one needed to take into account—one likelier, in other words, to result both in warfare and iniquity. English and Iberian legal regimes, fairly or unfairly, would at various times be possible targets for such criticisms. Grotius' Joseph is a godly leader in a fallen world already characterized by its "Mad thirst of gold"; Joseph's virtue lies not in his abstention from avarice, but from the brakes he places upon it first through law but more through example.[147] "By laws [*lege severa*]," Joseph "makes men give o're" their "vice," Grotius writes, "but by his own example more" [*magis exemplo*].[148] Resisting utopian moralizing, the chorus finds reason to "much congratulate" an Egypt "whose crimes [*culpas*] / An excellent Governour [*dux*] restraines, [*coercet*] / And in the narrowest bounds containes."[149] Grotius thus offers a tragic international legal personality whose duty is not to exterminate iniquity, but to stanch, temper, and circumscribe it through law and example.[150] The poles Grotius explores in *Sophompaneas* are not colonialism and anti-colonialism but restrained colonialism and unrestrained colonialism. The true necessity of the refugee versus the feigned necessity of the adventurer, moreover, was a distinction worth keeping.

---

[144] Borschberg, "Hugo Grotius, East India Trade and the King of Johor." I have found John Rawls' conception of toleration for "decent" but non-liberal societies useful for considering Grotius' understanding of infidels. See John Rawls, *The Law of Peoples; With, The Idea of Public Reason Revisited* (Cambridge, MA: Harvard University Press, 1999). See further Richard Tuck, "Alliances with Infidels in the European Imperial Expansion," in *Empire and Modern Political Thought*, ed. Sankar Muthu (Cambridge: Cambridge University Press, 2012), 61–82.

[145] Grotius, *DJBP*, 828. I am grateful to Peter Borschberg for correspondence about *De Societate Publica cum Infidelibus*.

[146] Grotius, *DJBP*, 433.   [147] Grotius, *Sophompaneas, or Joseph [1652]*, 16.

[148] Grotius, *Sophompaneas, or Joseph [1652]*, 18.

[149] Grotius, *Sophompaneas, or Joseph [1652]*, 18.

[150] Grotius, *Sophompaneas, or Joseph [1652]*, 18.

The contract between Joseph and Pharaoh that Grotius ultimately dramatizes in the fifth act is painstakingly composed, but Grotius sets it up equally carefully with an important narrative in the third act of how Pharaoh came to be "Proprietor of every particular Spot of Ground in his Kingdom" in the first place, which is how Grotius described the "Kings of *Aegypt*, after the times of Joseph" in *De Jure Belli ac Pacis*.[151] Critical to Grotius' story was Genesis 47:6, in which Pharaoh grants to the Israelites Goshen, "the best of all the land of Egypt."[152] Such themes of property and necessity at the heart of *Sophompaneas* were also at the heart of the tensions between Charles and the English people in the 1630s. Charles' extra-parliamentary taxation during his Personal Rule prompted sophisticated thinking about when, if ever, the king could take his subjects' property. For their arguments that subjects held property only so far as the king allowed or desired, absolutists drew from the law of nations to argue that English subjects were equivalent to slaves or villeins and therefore subject to the arbitrary rule of Charles, their master.[153] Given that *Sophompaneas* dramatized how such slavery could, in theory, have taken place, it is partly in this context that we should see *Sophompaneas'* first English printing in 1639, issued from Richard Hodgkinson's notoriously royalist press.

In *Sophompaneas*, it is the character Simeon who recounts how Joseph traded grain for Egyptians' lands and liberties. The Egyptians' voluntary enslavement to Pharaoh via Joseph in a case of necessity echoes the argument of *De Jure Belli*, famously denounced by Rousseau, where Grotius notes,

> There may be many Causes why a People should renounce all Sovereignty in them-selves, and yield it to another: As when they are upon the Brink of Ruin, and they can find no other Means to save themselves; or being in great Want, they cannot otherwise be supported.[154]

Excepting church lands from the transfer, Grotius summarizes the result in *Sophompaneas* as follows:

> all those grounds which the great *Nile* doth see,
> Except that to the Priests allotted bee;
> And all the people by the King were bought[155]

The fact that the narrative is told retrospectively by Simeon, however, helpfully sheds light on Grotius' intentions. In Genesis, the famine in Egypt *follows* Joseph's agreement with Pharaoh regarding the Israelite settlement. In the drama, Grotius

---

[151] Grotius, *DJBP*, 300.

[152] Grotius, *Sophompaneas, or Joseph [1652]*, 40. Genesis 45:20, Geneva Bible (1587).

[153] J. P. Sommerville, *Politics and Ideology in England, 1603–1640* (London: Longman, 1986), 146–51.

[154] Grotius, *DJBP*, 262.

[155] Grotius, *Sophompaneas, or Joseph [1652]*, 28. In his *Annotations*, Grotius elaborates significantly on the *terra sacerdotali*, "which was free of this condition": "The condition of taxes, or emphyteutic. Diodorus Siculus remembers its immunity. Under the name of priests [sacerdotum], however, were comprised all who gave their work to Astrology, Medicine, the knowledge of natural matters, measure-ments, numbers and history." Grotius, *Opera Omnia Theologica*, 1.25. See also Barducci, "Clement Barksdale, Translator of Grotius."

departed from scripture to solidify Pharaoh's prior right to alienate the land of Goshen. Generally, Grotius contended in *DJBP*, "a King, who tho' he be vested with the full Sovereignty, yet...does not possess it with a full Right of Property."[156] Imperial contexts, in which Grotius continued to be involved, put the issue in sharp relief.[157] Could indigenous princes "transport [...], cede [...], and transfer [...]...land with all its jurisdiction, sovereignty and rights," as one 1638 agreement in New Sweden (present day Delaware) put it?[158] Genesis 47 offered an answer, or rather, it could, when presented in a particular way. The reversed chronology shows Grotius' labor to reconcile Pharaoh's grant of Goshen with the history of Egyptian property, for as Stephen Buckle has pointed out, Grotius' "belie[ved] that the development of property was in fact a process involving a number of distinct events."[159] The narrative that in *Sophompaneas* is historically prior to the bequest of Goshen is one of people in need successively alienating their rights and property to their ruler in exchange for their preservation.

Grotius, it has been observed, was "willing to explain relationships in terms of the transfer of *dominium*, and to treat liberty as a piece of property."[160] Accordingly, of the Egyptians racked by famine, Grotius wrote in *Sophompaneas* that, "Hunger did them compel / their slaves to sell" to Joseph "for corn."[161] This transaction was soon followed by Egyptians bringing "all their breed / Of Oxen, and...Cattell" "[w]hen the famine more / Cruelly pinch'd."[162] In a final alienation of liberties and property, "they mortgage all / Their Lands, and afterward themselves inthrall" [*At mox at agros, deinde ius etiam sui*].[163] So much, then, for the need for the peoples' consent. Chilling as this final transfer may be, it is unambiguously true necessity. The episode explains how Pharaoh gains his local authority to organize his lands and his people as he pleases—an authority that takes center stage in Act 5 when Pharaoh's agreement with the Israelites allows the Israelites to occupy Goshen. When the Israelites move to Goshen, they do so with the full permission of the land's sovereign proprietor. Grotius has carefully and creatively provided for Pharoah's right to cede the land.

---

[156] *DJBP*, 2.6.

[157] Erik Thomson, "France's Grotian Moment? Hugo Grotius and Cardinal Richelieu's Commercial Statecraft," *French History* 21, no. 4 (December 1, 2007): 377–94; Martine Julia van Ittersum, "The Long Goodbye: Hugo Grotius' Justification of Dutch Expansion Overseas, 1615–1645," *History of European Ideas* 36, no. 4 (2010): 386–411.

[158] Albert Cook Myers, ed., "Affidavit of Four Men from the Key of Calmar, 1638," in *Narratives of Early Pennsylvania, West New Jersey and Delaware, 1630–1707* (New York: C. Scribner's Sons, 1912), 88, 87; Grotius, *DJBP*, 573. This was the North American Lenni Lepate "princes[']" agreement with the Swedes. On North America, Anthony Pagden also notes of Northern European colonial ideas that "it was crucial that the Native Americans should enjoy natural rights of property in their lands since only then could they dispose of them as they wished." See Anthony Pagden, *Lords of All the World: Ideologies of Empire in Spain, Britain and France C. 1500–C. 1800* (New Haven, CT: Yale University Press, 1995), 83.

[159] Stephen Buckle, *Natural Law and the Theory of Property: Grotius to Hume* (Oxford: Oxford University Press, 1991), 43.

[160] Richard Tuck, *Natural Rights Theories: Their Origin and Development* (Cambridge: Cambridge University Press, 1979), 60.

[161] Grotius, *Sophompaneas, or Joseph [1652]*, 28.

[162] Grotius, *Sophompaneas, or Joseph [1652]*, 28.

[163] Grotius, *Sophompaneas, or Joseph [1652]*, 28; Grotius, *Sophompaneas [1992]*, 216.

Upon Joseph's appeal for Pharaoh's relief, Pharaoh does not acknowledge a natural right for the Israelites based on their physical necessity nor one based on the land's disuse. Neither does he respond directly to Joseph's "promise" that both Israel and Egypt will "profit."[164] Instead, he grants Goshen to the Israelites as a gift for Joseph's aid. It is to Joseph's "aid" that "*Aegypt* owes" "her safety," that "the fields [do] not lie" "all wast[e]," according to Pharaoh.[165] Joseph puts a similar sentiment in equally strong terms: "this Nation/Unto my care...owe[s] its preservation"; "by my gift doth *Ægypt*...live."[166] If one response to the problem of sovereignty is to insist upon sacrosanct borders, the picture that Grotius offers to European readers instead is one of fluid mutual assistance in which neither religious nor national borders are too sacrosanct to preclude mutually beneficial cooperation.[167]

Treaties and contracts become key instruments by which Joseph manages the problems associated with famine, necessity, and natural right.[168] Grotius, as we have seen, invested much energy in defending "inoffensive leagues." Exploring the content of the Israelites' league with Pharaoh in careful detail, *Sophompaneas* lets Grotius convert sacred history to sophisticated contract theory. In an addition to the biblical story, Grotius' Joseph—cast here as a cunning negotiator—adds two important stipulations to the pact that serve both to distinguish the Israelites' agreement with Pharaoh from the Egyptians' voluntary enslavement of Act 3 and to inoculate the league against the charge that it was somehow offensive. The Israelites will never be compelled to change their religion—an important precedent for religious toleration—and they will be free to depart Goshen when they so choose. Agreeing, Pharaoh pledges,

> ...I sweare
> And this my head and successors I here
> For ever bind; that their Religion free
> To th' Hebrews, their departure safe shall bee.[169]

For surety, he offers conditions including the following, which readers recognize as the coming plagues of Exodus:

> If any King hereafter break this oath
> May foaming *Nilus* with a bloody froath
> Colour the Ocean, loathsome Frogs the ground
> Cover, and in the bed-chambers abound.
> A raging Murrain on the cattell light;
> No herbs look green, the corn a tempest smite.

[164] Grotius, *Sophompaneas, or Joseph [1652]*, 40.
[165] Grotius, *Sophompaneas, or Joseph [1652]*, 39.
[166] Grotius, *Sophompaneas, or Joseph [1652]*, 3.
[167] "*Why should we not,*" Grotius quotes Cicero to say, "*when we can do without any Detriment to ourselves, let others share in those Things that may be beneficial to them who receive them, and no inconvenience to us who give them*[?]" Grotius, *DJBP*, 438.
[168] Victoria Kahn, *Wayward Contracts: The Crisis of Political Obligation in England, 1640–1674* (Princeton, NJ: Princeton University Press, 2004).
[169] Grotius, *Sophompaneas, or Joseph [1652]*, 40.

The positive, explicit stipulations for toleration and (though it anticipates Exodus 7:16's "let my people go") right of departure have no clear biblical referents, which is one way to tell their significance to Grotius. Grotius seems to be indemnifying his contentions from specific objections in some novel ways. Linking Pharaoh's pledge to maintain the Israelites' liberties with the plagues of Exodus was a way of heading off one specific counterargument. As Grotius recognized, some readers could grant that the Joseph story depicted a league with infidels but still refuse Grotius' main point, which was that such leagues were permissible by law. Far from being a warrant for leaguing with infidels, it could be objected, the Israelites' association with the Egyptians was proof of its iniquity. Simply look at the Israelites' resulting captivity in the book of Exodus, the argument would go. Although Milton, for example, in a section of his *De Doctrina Christiana* on "The duties of magistrate and people TOWARDS NEIGHBORING STATES" cites examples of lawful biblical treaties, he also cites numerous biblical examples of "forbidden" treaties that "had an unhappy outcome."[170] Needing, then, to explain the captivity of Exodus, Grotius does so with recourse to the twofold proposition that kings can bind their successors, however much earlier writers like Bodin denied it, and that Pharaoh did just that in his agreement with Joseph in Genesis. The plagues were thus cast as punishment levied against Pharaoh's Egyptian successor, who broke the familiar dictum *pacta sunt servanda* (promises must be kept) when he oppressed the Israelites in Exodus 1. This reading is confirmed by Grotius' annotations on Exodus 1:1, where Grotius notes the new Pharaoh's failure to keep Egypt's promise.[171]

The drama ends shortly after Pharaoh's pledge with a prophetic sweep through biblical history. "Again some of th' Hebrew Nation / Shall hither come and make a new plantation," Joseph prophesies, before Christ, "the Worlds Redeemer," transforms legal relations among the Israelites and the Egyptians alike.[172] Christ is depicted as a lawgiver whose "new covenant" "enjoin[s]" "a much greater holiness…than is required of us by the law of nature in itself."[173] Of Christ, "The prince of piety," Joseph says,

> …He
> The same Lawes unto my Country-men
> The Hebrews, and unto th' Egyptians then
> Shall give, and *Nile* and *Iorden* teach in one
> Channell to meet of pure Religion.

The chorus concludes with a further plea for Christian unification from the Ethiopian chorus: "Partakers of so great a good may wee / In *Aethiopia* also be."[174]

In the final chapter of *De Jure Belli ac Pacis*, at the end of three long books, Grotius ended with a plea. Princes should adhere to their contracts. The title was "The Conclusion, with Admonitions to preserve Faith and seek Peace." "The Observation of [faith] is the Bond of human life," he implored, glancing at a growing *raison d'état* literature in the "Art of Deceiving."[175] "Take away Faith," and

[170] Milton, *CPW*, 6.801–802.   [171] Grotius, *Opera Omnia Theologica*, 1.28.
[172] Grotius, *Sophompaneas, or Joseph [1652]*, 41.   [173] Grotius, *DJBP*, 1759.
[174] Grotius, *Sophompaneas, or Joseph [1652]*, 42.   [175] Grotius, *DJBP*, 1638, 1639.

"Sovereign Princes...will be like wild Beasts, whose Rage all Men dread."[176] Peace, international order, and humanity itself, for Grotius, were ultimately founded on sovereigns' faithfulness to agreements. Problematically, however, princes could offend "with more Impunity than others."[177]

In Grotius' view at least, biblical tragedies like *Sophompaneas* offered a number of possible solutions. For one thing, they offered the now familiar power of example: in his piety, Joseph refused to manipulate the international order opportunistically much as Grotius, in the midst of the Thirty Years' War, refused to follow tragedians "who when they would give us the Character of a Prince, are wont to make him a man compos'd of deceit and perfidiousnesse, and an obdurate contempt of God and all laws, as wel common as peculiar, to any people."[178] *Sophompaneas* also let Grotius introduce punishment, for if the problem in the international order was the lack of a "supreme power," "Impunity" forever tempted sovereigns to deceive. In linking Pharaoh's pledge to the plagues of Exodus, Grotius dramatized a guaranteed international order in which faithful sovereigns could share in a "just Confidence in the Protection of Heaven" and in the face of which protection, unfaithful leaders ought to tremble. One of Grotius' greatest English admirers, Richard Baxter, expressed the logic precisely enough to suggest that he himself had read *Sophompaneas*:

> Kings rule their Kingdoms, but God ruleth the world...Else there were no Governour over Soveraigns, and so no Blasphemies, no Murders (even of Millions) no Perjuries &c. were unlawful to them, nor were it possible for them to sin...Then no plagues, flames, wars or death were divine punishments, nor any to be feared here or hereafter, but men might as safely defie and blaspheme God, as Love and Honour him...Else there were no Law of Nations obliging many to mutual justice, but only interest and contract.[179]

Baxter may have shared Grotius' logic, but Grotius was concerned enough about sovereign "perfidiousness" that he did more than *describe* godly protection. Using one of Renaissance humanism's most versatile tools, the biblical tragedy, he dramatized it as well, tapping into an Aristotelian tradition that bound readers together through their common affective response.[180]

In a little-noticed addition Grotius made to the *Prolegomena* of his 1631 edition of *De Jure Belli ac Pacis*, Grotius praised "sacred history" because it "greatly excites our social feeling": "it teaches us that all men are sprung from the same first parents; so that in this sense too we can truthfully say...that there is a kinship established among us by nature: and as a consequence that it is wrong for one man to plot against another."[181] Sacred history thus helped to enact the kinship for which

---

[176] Grotius, *DJBP*, 1639.
[177] Grotius, *DJBP*, 1639.   [178] Grotius, *Sophompaneas, or Joseph [1652]*.
[179] Richard Baxter, *The Judgment of Non-Conformists about the Difference between Grace and Morality* (London, 1676), 11.
[180] Grotius, as Victoria Kahn has pointed out, was a thinker "unusually attuned...to...affective dilemmas." Kahn, *Wayward Contracts*, 64.
[181] See the translation and discussion in Tuck, *The Rights of War and Peace: Political Thought and the International Order from Grotius to Kant*, 101.

it likewise provided evidence. And whatever sacred history could do to excite social feeling, tragedy could augment it. "An institution that helped tame the wilderness," tragedy was seen as a catalyst for community.[182] In *De Jure Belli ac Pacis*, no one had to choose between piety and reason of state, between natural rights and peaceful order, or between severity and clemency, all of which choices confronted Joseph in *Sophompaneas*. *De Jure Belli* gave an ample, even eloquent, vision of how sovereigns ought to behave on the world stage, but the prayer with which it ended gave poignant expression to Grotius' sense that *De Jure Belli* in itself could not finally insure the community of sovereigns against that beast-like "rage [that] all men dread." *Sophompaneas*, on the other hand, provided affective experience of his moral vision.

In *Shakespearean Tragedy*, A. C. Bradley famously argued about Shakespeare that tragedy is fundamentally about "waste" in the "moral order" of the world. In an effort to rid themselves of evil, Shakespearean tragic worlds sacrifice their heroes and in the process lose "a part of [their] own substance—a part more dangerous and unquiet, but far more valuable and nearer to [their] heart[s] than that which remains—a Fortinbras, a Malcolm, an Octavius."[183] For Milton and Grotius, what biblical tragedy ultimately offered was access to the "dangerous and unquiet" world of natural persons in all their bodily and spiritual necessities, who pressured the putatively more rational and orderly community of *personae juris gentium* in which they were represented. What emerges from Grotius' *Sophompaneas* is both a parable about human rights in relation to international legal personality and also a normative defense of an international politics artfully mediated by legal persons. Out of the unmediated, unruly human rights associated with the *zoon politikon*, came the more mediated and orderly international politics that the law of nations funneled through the fiction of international legal personalities. If Grotius' tragic world accommodated both heroes and happy endings, it was also unstable enough to require support from biblical tragedy itself. In *Samson Agonistes*, Milton, however, was more concerned to remind audiences of the plenary rights and potentialities of the particular, vernacular human person—rights and possibilities linked to the extreme necessity that particular humans occasionally encountered and that did not close off in advance either disturbingly violent or appealingly utopian consequences. Samson's death, then, consecrated the more predictable, allegorical, and type-bound world of international legal personality, which, we might say, could only be born in mourning for those natural rights, possibilities, and particularities sacrificed by individuals to the moral person of the state. As Bradley might have said, Grotius' vision of the world was "superficially less terrible perhaps than the present life, but [also perhaps] much less great and good."[184]

[182] Euben, *The Tragedy of Political Theory*, 35; Elizabeth Sauer, "The Politics of Performance in the Inner Theater: 'Samson Agonistes' as Closet Drama," in *Milton and Heresy*, ed. Stephen B. Dobranski and John Peter Rumrich (Cambridge: Cambridge University Press, 1998).
[183] A. C. Bradley, *Shakespearean Tragedy; Lectures on Hamlet, Othello* (New York: Macmillan, 1922), 37.
[184] Bradley, "International Morality," 64–5.

7

"A Problem from Hell"
From *Paradise Lost* to the Responsibility to Protect

Up into heaven from Paradise in haste
The angelic guards ascended, mute and sad
Paradise Lost, 10.17–18

INTRODUCTION

In preparation for Chapter 6's argument about *Samson Agonistes*, I contended that in the time between Eve's fall and Adam's in *Paradise Lost*, Milton makes Adam a dual citizen in the orders of nature and nations. Eve's fall opened the tragic permissions of the secondary law of nature and nations—most significantly, divorce—but Adam refuses the lifeboat back to comedy. Before turning in this chapter more directly to Adam, and especially Eve, as emergent *personae juris gentium* in a cosmic epic, it may be worth articulating some of the main conclusions of the book to this point.

As we observed in the Introduction, and briefly again in Chapter 3 with Bentham, the eighteenth-century professionalization and institutionalization of international law dramatically narrowed the contents of the law of nations. That Milton, in *Tetrachordon*, could credibly discuss divorce in the same breath as the secondary law of nature and nations indicates at once the comparative breadth of the early modern law of nations and also its subsequent contraction. When, in the eighteenth century, the law of nations traded poetry for professorships and took on the new name of international law, it de-emphasized the nexus of so-called private concerns related to what I have called the comic law of nations—contracts, commerce, family law, criminal law, and torts. All of these kinds of law would face challenges laying claim to the privileged name of international law.

A century earlier, Milton was reframing private and public *topoi* by manipulating their generic contexts. In theorizing divorce through tragedy in *Paradise Lost* and *Samson Agonistes*, Milton in effect elevated matters potentially trivialized as "economical misfortune[s]" (from *oikos* for "home") to the level "of great and powerfull importance to the governing of mankind"—his notably expansive description of domestic life in *The Doctrine and Discipline of Divorce*.[1] Treating divorce in the

---

[1] John Milton, *Complete Prose Works*, ed. Don M. Wolfe (New Haven, CT: Yale University Press, 1953), 2.227, 2.229.

heroic genres was a deft move. Comedy's conventional distribution of subjects and objects perpetuated the very distinction between the domestic family and the public good that Milton wished to upend. "No effect of tyranny can sit more heavy on the Common-wealth," Milton wrote, "then this household unhappines on the family."[2] Unless tragedies and epics happened to involve dynastic marriages or, as in Homer and Vergil, women as war spoils, husbands and wives were largely anathema to the heroic versions of the laws of nations. Transposing the subjects and objects of the comic law of nations into the heroic landscape, Milton appropriates the heroic genres while bolstering the status, significance, and standing of the—divisible—man and wife.

In this chapter, I want to suggest that this transposition becomes part of an overarching Miltonic project in *Paradise Lost* to give pluralized humanity itself the privileged status of the epic subject—Bederman's actor, or player on the international scene—and to turn human tyranny into a legal object under human jurisdiction. In order to highlight the fundamental role of epic in Milton's jurisprudence of the law of nations, I turn to the notion of protection, a deceptively rich concept that offers uncommon purchase on Milton's oeuvre. As developed above all in Milton's *Second Defense* and *Paradise Lost*, Milton's epic jurisprudence relies on what we might call an analytic of protection, understood as Milton's interpretive strategy for evaluating the resources—political, legal, ethical, formal—that ostensibly guard the godly from abuse, predation, and harm. It is due to the way Milton used protection to interpret human experience, moreover—to subject *de facto* power to an evaluative standard outside itself—that protection should be seen as an analytic and not simply the set of material resources defending against harm. From matrimony to massacres, protection became a rule against which Milton measured events and institutions.

What the great humanist critic J. C. Scaliger described as the "sovereignty of the epic" enjoyed no exemption from Milton's analytic of protection.[3] If epic in Scaliger's view exhibited the "laws common to all" genres with the "privileges" of all subordinate genres flowing from epic's "universal controlling rules," Milton saw in epic's plenary literary power the capacity to protect but also to harm.[4] After some important preliminaries, I will contend that readers of *Paradise Lost* experience Milton's analytic of protection first through Adam and Eve's vulnerability to Satan's epic heroism, then through the characters' vulnerability to an epic God. Much of the drama of *Paradise Lost* develops from Milton's creation of a temporal and generic imbalance in which humanity exists without access to epic resources while Satan hones and augments his own epic arsenal.[5] The humans' defenses of

---

[2] Milton nevertheless remained wary of the royalist argument that the commonwealth *was* the king's household. See Milton, *CPW*, 2.229.

[3] Julius Caesar Scaliger, *Select Translations from Scaliger's Poetics*, trans. Frederick Morgan Padelford (New York: H. Holt, 1905), 54.

[4] Scaliger, *Select Translations from Scaliger's Poetics*, 54.

[5] I am influenced here by quite different recent analyses that nevertheless reach very similar conclusions about time and power: Rose Sydney Parfitt, "The Unequal Equality of Sovereigns: A Brief History of 'Peripheral Personality,'" *Jean Monnet Working Papers Series* 20, no. 13 (2013), <http://www.jeanmonnetprogram.org/papers/13/documents/Parfitt.pdf>; Pascale Casanova, *The World Republic of Letters*, trans. M. B. DeBevoise (Cambridge, MA: Harvard University Press, 2004).

reason and virtue having failed, Adam and Eve ultimately fall into epic, joining Satan in epic's standard relation of enmity. When Adam and Eve consequentially find themselves accounted God's own epic "enemies"—this after "The angelic guards ascended, mute and sad"—Adam and Eve experience the terrifying limits, but then the bounteous renewal, of God's necessary protection.

I will ultimately suggest at the end of this chapter that *Paradise Lost* should change the way contemporary thinkers understand modern international law's so-called "responsibility to protect," which, following a 2001 Canadian report to the United Nations, has put protection at the center of recent controversy about sovereign responsibilities to prevent "man-made crises" and international responsibilities to redress crises of "compelling human need."[6] However, I begin in the first part of this chapter suggesting that what Milton calls the secondary law of nations grows from the human duty to protect others from scripture's "hardness of heart." I show how Milton's analytic of protection is comprised of two inseparable aspects and should therefore be understood as a dyad. It includes a strong sense of what Paul Stevens calls Milton's "positive nationalism," but its no less significant second part is a fundamentally international orientation.[7] Since interpretive strategies like Milton's analytic of protection face their challenges in Aristotle's "ultimate particulars," the second section of this chapter suggests a heretofore unrecognized topical context for Milton's *Second Defense* and offers a reading of that tract emphasizing its epic ambitions and the two sides of Milton's dyadic notion of protection. The new context involves a 1654 case of hardness of heart: a murder in London committed by the Portuguese ambassador's brother, who was subsequently tried and executed in London over objections from royalist lawyers and international observers. I argue that Milton's *Second Defense*, on its face a justification of the anti-tyrannical ways of England to the world, is also more subtly a defense of English jurisdiction over Don Pantaleon. I contend that Milton sees the trial and execution of Don Pantaleon as a form of protection, a form inseparable from Milton's analysis of domestic tyranny. I then turn in the third section to the jurisdictional

---

[6] International Commission on Intervention and State Sovereignty et al., *The Responsibility to Protect Report of the International Commission on Intervention and State Sovereignty* (Ottawa: International Development Research Centre, 2001), xi, <http://site.ebrary.com/id/10119691>. As I suggest below, while the modern doctrine of the responsibility to protect is not irrelevant to my concerns here, I by no means wish to imply equivalence between Milton and contemporary international theorists like Michael Ignatieff, Gareth Evans, Samantha Power, or Philip Pettit, the first three of whom have been vocal advocates for the so-called "R2P" and the last of whom has recently turned to the history of republicanism to theorize international justice afresh. Milton was far too Christian and far too comfortable with an "ethos that tolerated violence, slavery, fraud, and falsehood" for any easy equivalence. See *inter alia* Samantha Power, *A Problem from Hell: America and the Age of Genocide* (New York: Basic Books, 2002); Philip Pettit, "Legitimate International Institutions: A Neo-Republican Perspective," in *The Philosophy of International Law*, ed. Samantha Besson and John Tasioulas (Oxford: Oxford University Press, 2010); Philip Pettit, "A Republican Law of Peoples," *European Journal of Political Theory* 9, no. 1 (2010): 70–94. The latter is an important engagement with John Rawls, *The Law of Peoples; With, The Idea of Public Reason Revisited* (Cambridge, MA: Harvard University Press, 1999). Quotation from Martin Dzelzainis, "The Politics of Paradise Lost," in *The Oxford Handbook of Milton*, ed. Nicholas McDowell and Nigel Smith (Oxford: Oxford University Press, 2009), 559.

[7] Paul Stevens, "How Milton's Nationalism Works: Globalization and the Possibilities of Positive Nationalism," in *Early Modern Nationalism and Milton's England*, ed. David Loewenstein and Paul Stevens (Toronto: University of Toronto Press, 2008), 273–301.

debates concerning the trial and execution of the ambassador's brother. Manuscript notes from the case, surviving in the Bodleian Nalson papers, are interesting from the purely legal perspective of diplomatic immunity (itself a form of protection), but literary scholars will be struck by the fact that the notes include the specific claim that the accused must be tried by the law of nations rather than common law because a common law indictment "implies a subjection." Notoriously, Eve's looks in *Paradise Lost* "implied / subjection."[8] In the final two sections, then, echoed language of implied subjection grounds the argument forecast a moment ago about vulnerability, responsibility, and protection in Milton's great epic. Insofar as Milton's epic jurisprudence helps him secure human jurisdiction over tyranny, we can see how Milton offers necessary literary-historical perspective on the now-ascendant legal doctrine that concerns the occasions when international actors might intrude into a sovereign state to protect people at risk—contemporary international law's "responsibility to protect."

PROTECTION IN AN INTERNATIONAL CONTEXT

As a republican polemicist, Milton of course grounded political legitimacy in sovereign states' willingness to protect their citizens. Milton's anti-tyrannical tracts famously judged Charles' kingship against a standard of protection and found it wanting. As early as *A Masque Presented at Ludlow Castle* (*Comus*), Milton had also made protection a key literary theme. He foregrounded questions of protection and responsibility for the body of Edward King in his canonical pastoral elegy, *Lycidas* (1637), and in the 1640s, drawing from Grotius' *De Jure Belli ac Pacis*, he cast divorce as a matter of protection.[9] Protection, we must not forget, had an international dimension conjoined to its domestic aspect. Insofar as "domestic" indicates both the home in opposition to the national, and the national in opposition to the foreign, *Comus'* Spenserian apocalypticism conjured a recognizable tradition of international Protestant intervention that had been bubbling since the Dutch revolt, while the notes of nautical eclogue in *Lycidas* suggested the poem's interest in Grotian themes relating to jurisdiction in the Irish Sea.[10] As in *Comus* and *Lycidas*, the domestic and the international are yoked together in Milton's *The Tenure of Kings and Magistrates*, where Milton draws the political inside and outside together under a single umbrella without wholly eviscerating the domestic category of Englishness. "He...that keeps peace with me, neer or remote, of whatsoever Nation, is to mee...an Englishman and a

---

[8] Searching Mark Davies, *The EEBO Corpus (Early English Books Online), 400 million words, 1470–1699* (2013), <http://corpus.byu.edu/eebo/> on August 6, 2013 yielded only five instances prior to 1654 of "imply" and "subjection," or their variants, used within three words of one another.

[9] Jason Rosenblatt, "Milton, Natural Law, and Toleration," in *Milton and Toleration*, ed. Sharon Achinstein and Elizabeth Sauer (New York: Oxford University Press, 2007), 126–43.

[10] David Norbrook, *Poetry and Politics in the English Renaissance*, rev. edn. (Oxford: Oxford University Press, 2002), 241–2; Steven Mentz, "Toward a Blue Cultural Studies: The Sea, Maritime Culture, and Early Modern English Literature," *Literature Compass* 6, no. 5 (2009): 997–1013. See also Chapter 6.

neighbor," Milton wrote.[11] Later in his career, as we have seen, the "impious crew / Of men conspiring to uphold thir state / By worse then hostile deeds" in *Samson Agonistes* presented religious toleration and lawful war-making as external standards against which sovereign statehood might be judged (891–893).[12]

As we shall observe more closely in the next section, a rich example of Milton's positive nationalism comes in his *Pro Populo Anglicano Defensio Secunda* (*Second Defense of the English People*, 1654). In this tract, which David Loewenstein calls Milton's "bold appropriation of the epic vision to revolutionary polemic," Milton bids England to "administer incorrupt justice to the people [*incorrupta populo judicia*], to help those cruelly harassed and oppressed, and to render to each very man promptly his own deserts."[13] But in addition to praising the protections of incorrupt justice, Milton also worries about sovereigns who under a "*show of protection*[,...]" hold a violent and incommunicable Sword over [their people], as readie to be let fall upon [their peoples'] own necks, as upon [their] Enemies."[14] This is a distinctly republican worry, one from which royalist thinkers largely did not suffer.[15]

In contrast with the period's royalist and absolutist thinkers, Milton remains on guard against a kind of protection that is mere theater—one that can transform sovereign borders into further instruments of oppression. Functionally, sovereigns' appeals to national sovereignty may help "kings ... do what they list with impunity; [as if] God has exempted them from all human jurisdiction."[16] The twin commitments entailed in Miltonic protection, then, are the domestic commitment to administering "incorrupt justice to the people" and the human, international commitment to jurisdiction over the tyrant whose corrupt justice is a failure to protect. It is for this reason that Milton, using the word "outlandish" to mean originating

---

[11] Milton, *CPW*, 3.215; R. B. J. Walker, *Inside/outside: International Relations as Political Theory* (Cambridge: Cambridge University Press, 1993).

[12] Quotations from *Samson Agonistes* and *Paradise Regained* are from John Milton, *Complete Shorter Poems*, ed. John Carey, 2nd edn. (London: Longman, 1997). On my reading, *Samson Agonistes* should help qualify Orford's suggestion that it wasn't until "the early nineteenth century [that] the law of nations began to treat statehood as a question that was not determined only internally." Anne Orford, "Jurisdiction without Territory: From the Holy Roman Empire to the Responsibility to Protect," *Michigan Journal of International Law* 30 (2008): 991; Anne Orford, *International Authority and the Responsibility to Protect* (Cambridge: Cambridge University Press, 2011), 162.

[13] David Loewenstein, "Milton and the Poetics of Defense," in *Politics, Poetics, and Hermeneutics in Milton's Prose*, ed. David Loewenstein and James Grantham Turner (Cambridge: Cambridge University Press, 1990), 187; Milton, *CPW*, 4.1.681. For the Latin, see John Milton, *The Works of John Milton*, ed. Frank Allen Patterson (New York: Columbia University Press, 1931), 8.242.

[14] Milton, *CPW*, 3.455–456 emphasis added. Elliott Visconsi analyzes Milton's critique of Charles I, whom Milton argued abused the sovereign equitable function according to his private will in his *Lines of Equity: Literature and the Origins of Law in Later Stuart England* (Ithaca, NY: Cornell University Press, 2008), 81–3.

[15] Quentin Skinner, *Liberty before Liberalism* (Cambridge: Cambridge University Press, 1998); Philip Pettit, *Republicanism: A Theory of Freedom and Government* (Oxford: Oxford University Press, 2000); Quentin Skinner, *Hobbes and Republican Liberty* (Cambridge: Cambridge University Press, 2008); Stanley Fish, "How Hobbes Works," in *Visionary Milton: Essays on Prophecy and Violence*, ed. Peter E. Medine, John T. Shawcross, and David V. Urban (Pittsburgh, PA: Duquesne University Press, 2010), 65–88.

[16] Milton, *CPW*, 4.1.681; Milton, *The Works of John Milton*, 8.242. See also Bruce Rosenstock, "Against Sovereign Impunity: The Political Theology of the ICC," in *After Secular Law*, ed. Winnifred Fallers Sullivan, Robert A. Yelle, and Mateo Taussig-Rubbo (Stanford, CA: Stanford University Press, 2011), 160–77.

from another country, contends that "To distinguish . . . of a Tyrant by outlandish, or domestic is a weak evasion."[17] Milton resists the conceptual architecture that allows national borders to become further instruments of tyranny. Having qualified any metaphysical distinction between English and non-English identities—"He . . . that keeps peace with me"—Milton ultimately deploys for the tyrant the category of the *hostis humani generis*, the epic law of nations' enemy of the whole human race.[18] While some saw kings as immune by the law of nations, tyrants were "the public enemy of virtually the entire human race," and "an enemy," as Gentili had written in his epic mode, could "justly be put to death anywhere."[19]

Recent conversation around *Paradise Lost* (1667) has included much fruitful analysis of republicanism and royalism, but these categories have too often been presented as if divisible from international concerns.[20] The execution of Charles I was advanced not simply as the execution of a single tyrant but as a monitory note to tyrants everywhere. Critics long comfortable reading *Paradise Lost* in tandem with Milton's *Areopagitica* (1644), *The Tenure of Kings and Magistrates* (1649), and *Eikonoklastes* (1649–1650), have been somewhat more reluctant to assimilate Milton's international engagements, perhaps most significantly Milton's work as Secretary of Foreign Tongues in the 1650s.[21] In adhering to the supposed divisions between the domestic and international, modern critics have arguably been more Westphalian than the Westphalia-era poet himself.[22] With more attention to Milton's role in international affairs in the 1650s, however, it becomes

---

[17] Milton, *CPW*, 3.215.

[18] Milton, *CPW*, 4.1.658; Milton, *The Works of John Milton*, 8.242.

[19] Milton, *CPW*, 4.1.341–343; Milton, *The Works of John Milton*, 8.196. Alberico Gentili, *De Jure Belli Libri Tres*, trans. John Carew Rolfe (Oxford: Clarendon Press, 1933), 2.265.

[20] Many examples could be cited here. As broadly representative, however, see Joan S. Bennett, *Reviving Liberty: Radical Christian Humanism in Milton's Great Poems* (Cambridge, MA: Harvard University Press, 1989); Blair Worden, "Milton's Republicanism and the Tyranny of Heaven," in *Machiavelli and Republicanism*, ed. Gisela Bock, Quentin Skinner, and Maurizio Viroli (Cambridge: Cambrdge University Press, 1991), 225–46.

[21] Sharon Achinstein shows how McCarthyite crackdowns on internal dissent led Milton scholarship from the 1950s onwards to foreground free speech and toleration while de-emphasizing Milton's international ambitions. See Sharon Achinstein, "Cold War Milton," *University of Toronto Quarterly* 77, no. 3 (2008): 801–36. For examples of important recent criticism that have helped us see a more international Milton, see Leo Miller, *John Milton & the Oldenburg Safeguard: New Light on Milton and His Friends in the Commonwealth from the Diaries and Letters of Hermann Mylius, Agonist in the Early History of Modern Diplomacy* (New York: Loewenthal Press, 1985); Leo Miller, *John Milton's Writings in the Anglo-Dutch Negotiations, 1651–1654* (Pittsburgh PA: Duquesne University Press, 1992); Robert Thomas Fallon, *Milton in Government* (University Park, PA: Pennsylvania State University Press, 1993); Paul Stevens, "Paradise Lost and the Colonial Imperative," *Milton Studies* 34 (1996): 3–22; Sharon Achinstein, "Imperial Dialectic: Milton and Conquered Peoples," in *Milton and the Imperial Vision*, ed. Elizabeth Sauer and Balachandra Rajan (Pittsburgh, PA: Duquesne University Press, 1999), 67–89; Julie Stone Peters, "A 'Bridge over Chaos': De Jure Belli, Paradise Lost, Terror, Sovereignty, Globalism, and the Modern Law of Nations," *Comparative Literature* 57, no. 4 (January 2005): 273–93; Dzelzainis, "The Politics of Paradise Lost"; Rosanna Cox, "'The Mountains Are in Labour, Only Mice Are Born': Milton and Republican Diplomacy," *Renaissance Studies* 24, no. 3 (June 2009): 420–36.

[22] For Newman, post-Westphalian criticism is principally post-secular. See Jane O. Newman, "Tragedy and Trauerspiel for the (Post-)Westphalian Age," *Renaissance Drama* 40, no. 1 (2012): 197–208. See further Feisal Mohamed, *Milton and the Post-Secular Present: Ethics, Politics, Terrorism* (Stanford, CA: Stanford University Press, 2011); Walker, *Inside/outside*.

easier to see how protection links several seemingly disparate aspects of Milton's commitments from his early career onwards.

In an entry of his commonplace likely dating to the 1630s, Milton wrote, "What those skilled in the law declare concerning natural, international [*gentium*], and civil law see Justinian. institute Book 1. tit[le] 2."[23] The standard Yale edition of the commonplace book translates Milton to say "international law" but Milton, of course, would not have used that phrase. He was referring to the law of nations, or perhaps more likely "national law," as he calls the law of nations in *Areopagitica*, *Colesterion*, and *The Tenure of Kings and Magistrates* ("the common National Law against murder").[24] Milton adopted the tripartite account of law even though other sections, even in the same title of Justinian's *Institutes*, characterized the law of nations as merely the general dictates of reason and thus as roughly synonymous with natural law. Giving weight to necessity, custom, and the exigencies of human experience, the three-part account, it seems, was most compatible with Milton's voluntaristic Arminian theology. "The Law of Nations," the passage in the *Institutes* reads, "is common [only] to the entire human race, for all nations have established for themselves [*constituerunt*] certain regulations exacted by custom and human necessity [*usu exigente et humanis necessitatibus*]."[25] The passage continues as pathology: "For wars have arisen, and captivity and slavery, which are contrary to natural law, have followed as a result, as, according to Natural Law, all men were originally born free; and from this law nearly all contracts, such as purchase, sale, hire, partnership, deposit, loan, and innumerable others have been derived."[26] Milton in *Tetrachordon* soon accommodated the tripartite account from Justinian's *Institutes* to biblical chronology using the Fall and what scripture called "hardness of heart." Where the passage from the *Institutes* used "law of nations" to denote a system of customary practices that diverged from something resembling a state of nature, Milton, likely following Selden, used the term "secondary law of nature and of nations" for much the same purpose. In Selden, the secondary law of nations is associated most importantly with time, historicity, and custom, its rights and duties too being functions of convention (*convenere*) or longstanding practice.[27] For Milton,

---

[23] Milton, *CPW*, 1.426. On the dating of the entries, see James Holly Hanford, "The Chronology of Milton's Private Studies," *PMLA* 36, no. 2 (1921): 277, which suggests a dating before 1643.

[24] Milton, *CPW*, 3.196.   [25] *Institutes*, 1.2.1–2.   [26] *Institutes*, 1.2.1–2.

[27] In this, Milton's account broadly follows Selden's. According to Selden, law may concern all nations, some nations, or just one nation. That which concerns all nations Selden calls the "universal law of nations" or the "common law of mankind." He identifies two main sources for this universal law of nations: divine law, whose sources are in scripture or revelation, and the primitive law of nations, or natural law, whose source, says Selden, arises "out of the nature of the thing itself" and is available to "right reason." Obliging some things and permitting others, together, the divine law and the primitive law of nations form the immutable core of this universal law of nations. Nevertheless, Selden suggests, the rights and duties associated with the universal law of nations are still to a limited degree temporally contingent. Specific rights and duties have been changed by God and man. Some things that were once permitted have been forbidden, and although obligatory laws cannot be altered as permissive laws can, says Selden, some obligatory laws have received "additions" or "enlargements" to provide more certainty and convenience of observation. Examples of positive additions to the law of nations include laws having to do with prisoners of war, embassy, hostages, leagues and covenants, proclaiming war, and commerce—practices which together form what Selden

210   *Literature and the Law of Nations, 1580–1680*

partly for this hardnesse of heart, the imperfection and decay of man from original righteousness, it was that God suffer'd not divorce onely, but all that which by Civilians is term'd the *secondary law of nature and of nations*. He suffer'd his owne people to wast and spoyle and slay by warre, to lead captives, to be som maisters, som servants, some to be princes, others to be subjects, hee suffer'd propriety to divide all things by severall possession, trade and commerce, not without usury; in his common wealth some to be undeservedly rich, others to be undeservingly poore. All which till hardnesse of heart came in, was most unjust; whenas prime Nature made us all equall, made us equall coheirs by common right and dominion over all creatures. In the same manner, and for the same cause he suffer'd divorce as well as marriage, our imperfect and degenerat condition of necessity requiring this law among the rest, as a remedy against intolerable wrong and servitude above the patience of man to beare.[28]

Milton's opponents argued divorce was prohibited in most cases other than female adultery because it sundered what God and nature had joined together. Milton characterized such arguments as failures of tragic imagination.

We can add here that the prohibition of divorce amounted for Milton to a failure to protect. Abuse for Milton did not need to be qualified by "domestic."[29] Milton's analytic of protection in fact helped him contemplate the structural connection between a vulnerable marriage partner and a vulnerable people. Like the institution of sovereignty, the institution of marriage could itself shield and prolong "intolerable" abuse. Milton's arguments for divorce ominously invoked "other violations" even worse than adultery, appealing to his readers to imagine the horrors of non-companionate marriages with their "ten thousand injuries, and bitter actions of despight too suttle and too unapparent for Law to deal with."[30] If tragedy was a genre capable of making such micro-aggressions legible to law, divorce in turn was a remedy permitted by the law of nations, and a necessary prophylactic against humans' shocking capacity to harm.

DON PANTALEON AND THE *JUDEX INTER HOMINES*

In his 1644 addition to *The Doctrine and Discipline of Divorce*, Milton contended, "he who marries, intends as little to conspire his own ruine, as he that swears Allegiance: and as a whole people is in proportion to an ill Government, so is one man to an ill marriage."[31] In the 1650s, ill government at home would, from a slightly

calls alternatively the secondary law of nations or the intervenient law of nations. See John Selden, *Of the Dominion, Or, Ownership of the Sea*, trans. Marchamont Nedham (London: William DuGard, 1652), 11–16. On Milton and Selden, see above all Jason Rosenblatt, *Renaissance England's Chief Rabbi: John Selden* (Oxford: Oxford University Press, 2006).

[28] Milton, *CPW*, 2.661.
[29] Catharine A. MacKinnon, "Women's September 11th: Rethinking the International Law of Conflict," in *Are Women Human?: And Other International Dialogues* (Cambridge, MA: Belknap Press of Harvard University Press, 2006), 259–80.
[30] Milton, *CPW*, 2.273, 2.623.   [31] Milton, *CPW*, 2.229.

different perspective, become the theme of Milton's *Defensio Pro Populo Anglicano* (1651) and *Pro Populo Anglicano Defensio Secunda* (30 May 1654). It is in the second of these tracts that we find Milton arguing for "incorrupt justice to the people." Having replied at length to his opponent, Milton near the end of the tract turns directly to the English, telling them,

> if the ability to devise the cleverest means of putting vast sums of money into the treasury, the power readily to equip land and sea forces, to deal shrewdly with ambassadors from abroad [*legatis exterorum*], and to contract judicious alliances and treaties [*societas & foedera peritê contrahere*] has seemed to any of you greater, wiser, and more useful than to administer incorrupt justice to the people [*incorrupta populo judicia*], to help those cruelly harassed and oppressed, and to render to each very man promptly his own deserts, too late will you discover how mistaken you have been.[32]

Here, in the domestic strain of Milton's dyadic conception of protection, Milton emphasizes England's responsibilities towards its own people. Reminded perhaps of Charles' specious arguments for Ship Money ("the power... to equip land and sea forces"), the English people are encouraged to forgo the theatricality of diplomacy and instead tend to their domestic garden. But the passage remains discordant in a Latin work that begins addressing "the entire assembly of... all... nations everywhere."[33] Geopolitical humility is hardly the tract's dominant tone. Milton's defense of throwing off the tyrant at home quickly becomes a soaring prose epic of the revolutionary present.[34] The tract concludes by explicitly acknowledging its own epic ambitions.

As we have observed several times throughout this study, the Renaissance epic carried judicial baggage. If certain royalists sought to highlight the tragedy of King Charles the martyr, Milton preferred an epic international legal framework declaring it "proper for a warrior when engaged with an enemy to lay aside all pity and clemency," as Gentili wrote in his chapter "Of Suppliants."[35] The *Second Defense's* direct address to the English, however, begins to recast the standard antagonisms of national epic, a genre that conventionally projects enmity onto a rival *gens*. Milton's departures from epic conventions continue with his treatment of violence and conquest. Charles may have taxed England and the world with tyranny, but his punishment has ushered in an epic of liberty quite different from the violence at the heart of most epics: conventions of war and conquest become for Milton "spoils of honor" and "captives" "conquered... by the truth."[36] The mimetic structure of the *Second Defense* epic differs too from classical models. After invoking the heroes Achilles and Aeneas, Milton audaciously goes on to describe his own hero as a pluralized corporate subject, "my countrymen [*popularium meorum*]."[37] Here distributing royalist heroism among the many—Milton earlier had praised several prominent English republicans by name—Milton shatters the conventions that

---

[32] Milton, *CPW*, 4.1.681. For the Latin, see Milton, *The Works of John Milton*, 8.242.
[33] Milton, *CPW*, 4.1.554.   [34] Loewenstein, "Milton and the Poetics of Defense," 187.
[35] Gentili, *De Jure Belli Libri Tres*, 2.248. See Chapter 2.
[36] Milton, *CPW*, 4.1.556, 4.1.555.   [37] Milton, *CPW*, 4.1.685.

create "epic distance" and instead invites the nations of the world to join in an emerging and geographically expansive freedom from tyranny.[38]

For his continental readers, Milton's call for incorrupt domestic justice mobilizes a strain of European humanism best exemplified by Erasmus, who, in his "Complaint of Peace," effectively encouraged Christian princes to mind their own business. This Erasmian strain of anti-imperial humanism, recently stamped into the Peace of Westphalia (1648), had an anti-diplomatic flavor similar to Milton's own. According to Erasmus:

> Princes ought to agree, once for all, which one will rule which region, and once the boundaries are settled not try to enlarge or diminish them by treaty or dynastic marriage. That way, each prince will enjoy that region of the earth which he is best able to render flourishing. All his energies will go into the one place, which he will try to make as opulent as possible for the benefit of his children. General prosperity can hardly fail to result. Among themselves princes should not rely on treaties or alliances, but join together in a pure and sincere sympathy, uniting in the greatest possible zeal for making the best of human affairs.[39]

Christian humanism's anti-diplomatic strain is evident too in Thomas More's *Utopia* and Milton's own late "brief epic," *Paradise Regained*. In *Utopia*, elegantly dressed foreign ambassadors are taken for fools among the host Utopians. In *Paradise Regained*, Milton's Son rejects the supposed "honour" of "embassies.../ From nations far and nigh," calling it a "tedious waste of time to sit and hear / So many hollow compliments and lies" (4.121–124). Ambassadors bring "Outlandish flatteries," flatteries from outside our lands (4.1.125). Such "Outlandish flatteries" are the verbal equivalent to the "sumptuous apparel" and "great chains of gold" that More's Utopians disdain.[40]

Previously understudied events in 1654 add further context to Milton's call for incorrupt justice and further illuminate just how seriously Milton took the responsibility to protect. Milton was Secretary of Foreign Tongues in November 1653 when the Portuguese ambassador's brother, Don Pantaleon de Sá, living in London, went with some friends and attendants to London's New Exchange. According to multiple popular accounts such as *The Grand Tryal in Westminster-Hall of the Lord Ambassadors Brother* (1654), Don Pantaleon and his associates traded unfriendly words with some people there. The group then left, but they returned the next night, armed with guns, stalking their adversaries from the night before. Amidst come confusion, Don Pantaleon's group shot and killed twenty-four-year-old Harcourt Greneway, a gentleman of Gray's Inn, who had been walking with his

---

[38] David Loewenstein makes the observation regarding Bakhtin's "epic distance" in "Milton and the Poetics of Defense," 187. See further Christopher Hill, "The English Revolution and the Brotherhood of Man," in *Puritanism and Revolution: Studies in Interpretation of the English Revolution of the Seventeenth Century* (New York: St. Martin's Press, 1997), 112–38.
[39] Desiderius Erasmus, "The Complaint of Peace," in *The Praise of Folly and Other Writings: A New Translation with Critical Commentary*, trans. Robert Martin Adams (New York: Norton, 1989), 107.
[40] Thomas More, *Utopia*, ed. David Harris Sacks, trans. Ralph Robynson (New York: Bedford/St. Martin's, 1999), 151–2.

fiancée. They then "discharged pistols" at the responding constables before retreating to the Portuguese ambassador's residence, where they claimed sanctuary under the law of nations. Beset by the implacable Commissary General, Edward Whalley, whom Milton praises in the *Second Defense*, the ambassador was compelled to yield Don Pantaleon and his followers up for justice. The charge could be leveled that the new English government had failed its most important responsibility, protecting its citizens.

In early July 1654, after lengthy wrangling, Don Pantaleon and his Portuguese accomplices were tried by a mixed jury of six Britons and six foreigners. They were convicted, Don Pantaleon attempted unsuccessfully to escape, and he was executed on July 10, 1654. The case has rarely been studied by Miltonists, and it has never, as far as I'm aware, been introduced to contextualize the *Second Defense*.[41] This "hard case" of international justice nevertheless usefully illuminates Milton's dyadic notion of protection in practice. The murder and trial were widely discussed in the news-books over which Milton had had supervisory responsibilities.[42] In the months leading up to Milton's *Second Defense*, the accused nineteen-year-old published a justification from prison; the victim's sisters published a reply; and Milton's employer, the Council of State, issued a printed Order calling Don Pantaleon's attack "a very great and notorious violation of the public peace."[43]

As Secretary of Foreign Tongues, Milton had deeper connections still. At the time of the murder—the anti-diplomatic passage of the *Second Defense* notwithstanding—Milton was assisting tense but sporadically productive discussions with the Portuguese ambassador over a stronger new alliance.[44] By the time of the *Second Defense*, the international community was invoking the law of nations to shield Don Pantaleon from punishment. And royalists, recalling the trial and

---

[41] Francis Peck in 1740 used the events as part of a whimsical attempt to attribute to Milton a May 1654 panegyric to Cromwell—one published in fact *by* the Portuguese ambassador—and Masson discussed the events in his multivolume *Life of Milton*, but it has rarely been studied since. See Francis Peck, *Memoirs of the Life and Actions of Oliver Cromwell: As Delivered in Three Panegyrics of Him, Written in Latin* (London, 1740); João Rodrigues de Sá e Meneses Penaguião, *Panegyrici Cromwello Scripti. Vnus À Legato Portugallici Regis. Alter À Quodam Iesuita.* ([Leyden]: [Louis Elzevier], 1654); David Masson, *The Life of John Milton: Narrated in Connexion with the Political, Ecclesiastical, and Literary History of His Time* (London: Macmillan and Co., 1859), 4.556–557; For a helpful introduction to work on Milton and Portugal, however, see John T. Shawcross, "John Milton and His Spanish and Portuguese Presence," *Milton Quarterly* 32, no. 2 (May 1998): 41–52.
[42] Blair Worden, *Literature and Politics in Cromwellian England: John Milton, Andrew Marvell, Marchamont Nedham* (Oxford: Oxford University Press, 2007), 195–217.
[43] Frances Clarke, *A Briefe Reply to the Narration of Don Pantaleon Sa* (London, 1653); Pantaleão Sá, *A Narration of the Late Accident in the New-Exchange, on the 21. and 22. of November, 1653.* (London, 1653); John Gerard, *The True and Perfect Speeches of Colonel John Gerhard... Likewise, the Speech of the Portugal Ambassadors Brother upon the Scaffold* (London: C. Horton, 1654); Anon., *The Grand Tryal in Westminster-Hall of the Lord Ambassadors Brother from the King of Portugal, the Knight of Malta, and the Master of His Excellencies Horse* (London: G. Horton, 1654).
[44] For full background to the treaty, see Thomas Bentley Duncan, "Uneasy Allies: Anglo-Portuguese Commercial, Diplomatic and Maritime Relations, 1642–1662" (Ph.D. dissertation, University of Chicago, 1967); Eduardo Brasão, *The Anglo-Portuguese Alliance* (London: Sylvan Press, 1957); L. M. E. Shaw, *The Anglo-Portuguese Alliance and the English Merchants in Portugal, 1654–1810* (Aldershot: Ashgate, 1998), 5–10; Edgar Prestage, "The Anglo-Portuguese Alliance," *Transactions of the Royal Historical Society*, Fourth Series, 17 (1934): 69–100; Timothy Venning, *Cromwellian Foreign Policy* (New York: St. Martin's Press, 1995), 122–4.

execution of Charles I, were using the *ius gentium* to lodge renewed accusations of Roundhead barbarism. Milton's argument for "incorruptible justice" at home in the *Second Defense*, I argue, was deployed to defend the Don Pantaleon trial. Demands from English petitioners raised the uncomfortable possibility that the English government would perform the theater of protection while letting heinous murders go unpunished. A government that did not try and punish Don Pantaleon, it was feared, would be dangerously close to the arbitrary sovereign who preyed on the protections afforded by inviolable Borders.

The Stuarts had supported Portugal's 1640 revolt from Spain, and the English Prince Rupert's welcome there seemed to indicate that Portugal's King, João IV, felt he owed the Stuarts a special debt. Spain, surprisingly enough, was the first European country to exchange ambassadors with the new English government, but Portugal by contrast was slow to recognize the Republic. When negotiations did commence in London with the Portuguese envoy João de Guimáraes over a possible Anglo-Portuguese peace treaty between February and May 1651, Milton provided vital linguistic assistance. The thorniest issues for the treaty concerned trade levies and toleration for Protestant English merchants in Lisbon who were prohibited access to Protestant bibles. Cromwell's later brag to Parliament indicates the stakes: the treaty, he boasted, had achieved something that "never [existed] since the Inquisition was set up there[:] . . . our people which trade thither have liberty of conscience."[45] This outcome, however, remained several years in the future. After initial attempts began in 1651, preliminary wording would still take a full three years to resolve. Milton, though by 1654 nearly totally blind, remained involved when a tenable (but not final) treaty was finally established that year with the subsequent ambassador, João Rodrigues de Sá a Menezes, brother of the murderer, Don Pantaleon de Sá.

Milton's state papers include a letter from Cromwell to King João IV either composed or translated by Milton that praises Rodrigues de Sá's service and communicates England's expectation of Portuguese ratification.[46] Though in keeping with Renaissance standards of decorum, the letter stands out these three-and-a-half centuries later for what it does not say. While the letter thanks João Rodrigues de Sá a Menezes for the "noble and illustrious embassy" by which he had sought "peace and friendship with the English Commonwealth" and affirms that the departing ambassador was "a gentleman not only approved by Your Majesty's opinion, but also found by us to be most distinguished for his gentleness, his character, his prudence, and his fidelity," the letter makes no mention of Don Pantaleon.[47] No more than fifteen days before, the brother of the recipient, Don Pantaleon de Sá, had been beheaded for murdering Harcourt Greneway.[48]

---

[45] Oliver Cromwell, *Speeches, 1644–1658* (H. Frowde, 1901), 143.
[46] Milton, *CPW*, 5.2.673–674.   [47] Milton, *CPW*, 5.2.673–674.
[48] Milton's letter to João IV is dated July 25, 1654 in some manuscripts; it is undated in others. Since a number of contemporary sources suggest that Rodrigues de Sá completed treaty negotiations and departed England on the very day his brother was executed, the letter may in fact have been composed as early as July 10. It remains plausible that Milton's letter was written on the very day Don Pantaleon was executed, while making absolutely no mention of the incident.

Leading up to the trial and execution, Portugal contended that not only acknowledged ambassadors but also members of a representative's household received diplomatic immunity, and prominent English lawyers concurred—in at least one case, anonymously, in print.[49] For the rapidly coalescing constituency of Portuguese, royalists, and other foreign agents in London, the law of nations afforded Don Pantaleon wide protection from prosecution in London. But Milton's government, in trying Don Pantaleon, had ultimately rejected such a view as too expansive. The case required a more parsimonious view of the laws of embassy. "*Jus Legationis*," as one lawyer put it, "is severable from [Don Pantaleon]."[50] Such was the premise too of Milton's diplomatic letter. Milton elsewhere chided Spain and the Netherlands for their failures to protect the assassinated English diplomats Ascham and Dorislaas. Working to expand English liberties abroad while limiting Portuguese liberties in England may suggest that English interests were Milton's guiding principle more than anything else. But protection of physical and spiritual lives was perhaps the most important "end.../ For which our country is a name so dear" (*SA*, 892–893). The deeper principle was the responsibility to protect.

In Milton's analytic of protection, punishment plays a key role. Book 12 of *Paradise Lost* includes a memorable passage in which Nimrod "dispossess" natural equality with tyranny and slavery (12.28).[51] The scene becomes the occasion for the archangel Michael to spell out the need for the secondary law of nature and nations and explain in the process how just punishment co-exists with sin. Michael has given Adam a proleptic vision of future history, included in which is the story of how natural fraternal equality yields to subjection through Nimrod and the Tower of Babel. The originator of human tyranny and slavery, Nimrod is the first of the "Violent lords" who "enthrall /...outward freedom" (12.93).

In response to Adam's broadly accurate but still relatively un-nuanced horror at Nimrod's rise, Michael nudges Adam away from the misprision that all expression of power is tyranny. Norbrook considers this qualification a possible accommodation to the censor, but the passage expresses a significant Miltonic distinction.[52] Fault lies too with the naturally free individual who "permits / Within himself unworthy powers to reign / Over free reason," Michael insists.

[49] [Timothy Baldwin], *The Priviledges of an Ambassadour: Written by a Civilian to a Friend Who Desired His Opinion Concerning the Portugall Ambassadour* ([London], 1654).
[50] Bodleian MS Nalson 17, fol. 417v, "His Highness Desiring to Be Advised Concerning the Demand Made by the Portugall Ambassador of His Brother Committed for Murde[r], to Have Him Returned to Him, & Being Ag[ainst] the Law of Nations, He Being of His Family to by Tryed by These Laws." CSPD gives *comes legationis* where the Nalson MS has *Jus Legationis*. Compare *Calendar of State Papers, Domestic 1653–1654* (London: H.M. Stationery Office, 1856), 361.
[51] All references to *Paradise Lost* are to Milton, *Paradise Lost*, ed. Alastair Fowler, 2nd edn. (London: Longman, 1998) and will be quoted in the text. The passage is quoted by Jeremy Rabkin, who takes it as a parable against building global institutions like the tower of Babel, but Milton is in fact unpacking the tradition, derived from Justinian's *Institutes*, in which "slavery is an institution of the law of nations, against nature, subjecting one man to the dominion of another" (1.3.2.). Jeremy A. Rabkin, *Law without Nations?: Why Constitutional Government Requires Sovereign States* (Princeton, NJ: Princeton University Press, 2007).
[52] David Norbrook, *Writing the English Republic: Poetry, Rhetoric and Politics, 1627–1660* (Cambridge: Cambridge University Press, 1998), 463–4.

Human powers can therefore be meting just punishment, though it is also true and, certainly justiciable, that "Violent lords" "oft" do so "undeservedly." Why then is there tyranny? Milton's analysis –"tyranny must be, / Though to the tyrant…no excuse"—asserts that space for tyranny is opened up by the occasional need for just vindication flowing through humans from God.

The conceptual links among protection, punishment, and tyranny are spelled out in Milton's *First Defense*, where Milton had put protection and punishment at the heart of human government. A key figure was what Milton called the *judex inter homines*. "Men first joined together," he writes, using the language of coming together (*convenere*) standard in accounts of the law of nations from the *Corpus Juris Civilis* onwards, "not that one might abuse the rest, but that if any injured another there might be no lack of law or of a judge between men to protect, or at least to avenge, the injured party [*judex inter homines…laesus aut defendatur aut…vindicator*]."[53] Milton continues, "Men who once were scattered and dispersed far and wide were led by someone of eloquence and wisdom to adopt a life in states [*vitam civalem*]."[54] To Salmasius' royalist claim that such a man then exercised *imperium*, Milton replies, "Perhaps you are thinking of Nimrod, who is said to have been the first tyrant."[55] The figure of the tyrant, in Milton's conception, preyed on "the rights [*juri*] of the people," the protection of which was "the most natural reason and cause, and…the true rise of…government."[56] Milton designated tyrants as *hostis humani generis*, the term Gentili and others used for pirates, for just this predation. Whereas geographically dispersed humans needed to trade with one another to supply what they lacked, pirates preyed on vulnerability for their own wealth. Tyrants, similarly, used human vulnerability as a vehicle for their own ambition. The description in *Paradise Lost* of Nimrod as a "mighty hunter" "Hunting…men not beasts" is chilling but appropriate to Milton's analysis of protection and predation (12.33, 30). Responsibility for curtailing such predatory harm was lodged in the *judex inter homines*, to whom Milton assigned the indispensible duty "to protect, or at least to avenge, the injured party."

JUST VINDICATION

In the legal debates over Don Pantaleon, questions of jurisdiction and punishment pitted competing domesticities against one another. Was the arrest at the Portuguese embassy a gross violation of diplomatic immunity—akin, at worst, to an invasion of Portugal's "little island…of alien sovereignty"—or had Don Pantaleon

---

[53] Milton, *CPW*, 4.1.472–473; Latin here and following from John Milton, *Pro Populo Anglicano Defensio* (London: William DuGard, 1651), 185.
[54] Milton, *CPW*, 4.1.473.
[55] Milton, *CPW*, 4.1.473, which misleadingly translates Milton's "imperium" (supreme jurisdiction) as "dominion" (property). On the distinction, see David Armitage, *The Ideological Origins of the British Empire* (Cambridge: Cambridge University Press, 2000), 122–4.
[56] Milton, *CPW*, 4.1.473.

forfeited any claims to the law of nations with the attack?[57] Could Don Pantaleon, a resident foreigner and member of the diplomatic retinue, be tried at common law? To whom was Don Pantaleon subject while in England? The ambassador Rodrigues de Sá appealed to Cromwell "for the return of his brother" "on the ground that it is against the law of nations that one of his family should be tried by these laws."[58] Faced with such questions, Cromwell referred the incident to the Council of State, which in turn appointed a committee "to ascertain the Law of Nations."[59]

In *Paradise Lost*, Eve's appearance famously, if troublingly, "implied / Subjection" (4.307–308). It is bracing to one familiar with *Paradise Lost* to find, in committee notes on Don Pantaleon and the law of nations, such similar language. The parliamentarian civilian Walter Walker took no issue with a trial of Don Pantaleon, but he did think it nonsensical that an "enemy" would be indicted at common law. The common law's terms of indictment—*felonie et contra pacem*—"implies a subjection."[60] If Don Pantaleon was subject to anyone, it was to the King of Portugal. The facts of Pantaleon's case instead determined for Walker that the ambassador's brother "must be tried as the *jus gentium* prescribes"—effectively as a captive—in order "to keep off...war."[61] Don Pantaleon himself seems to have rejected even that. Following in Charles I's footsteps, Don Pantaleon at his trial refused to take off his cap, "pretending privilege," as the news-book *Mercurius Politicus* put it, "above the jurisdiction of the Court," and refusing to utter the requisite response to the question of how he was to be tried—"By God and the Country"—until he'd been threatened with certain death.[62]

Committee notes surviving in the Bodleian Nalson papers, a manuscript among Thurloe's State Papers, and a little-noticed royalist pamphlet published on the topic flesh out the legal contexts and ultimately help us read Milton's epic through the analytic of protection. One of the common lawyers argued that Don Pantaleon, like "any other alien," "owe[d] a legal allegiance" to England and could therefore be tried at common law.[63] Don Pantaleon was no different than any other private person in England. "A Justification of the proceedings against the Portuguese for the murder of Mr. greenway, notwithstanding their relation to the embassador," a manuscript among Thurloe's papers surely written by a common lawyer, is the most hostile to the law of nations. It goes so far as to argue that "it is a maxim in our law, that no foreign law...can take place in this nation...And therefore whatsoever the civil law is, or the *ius gentium* practiced by other nations, is *not*

[57] Garrett Mattingly, *Renaissance Diplomacy* (Boston, MA: Houghton Mifflin, 1955), 244.

[58] *CSPD 1653–1654*, 360.

[59] Thomas Jones Howell, William Cobbett, and David Jardine, *Cobbett's State Trials*, vol. 5 (R. Bagshaw, 1810), 5.463; Masson, *The Life of John Milton*, 4.556.

[60] *CSPD 1653–1654*, 361.   [61] *CSPD 1653–1654*, 361.

[62] *Mercurius Politicus* (London: Robert White,1650), 29 June 1654 to 6 July 1654, 3604; *The Weekly Intelligencer of the Common-Wealth Faithfully Communicating All Affairs Both Martial and Civil* (London: R.C., 1650), 4 July to 11 July 1654, sig. P2.

[63] *CSPD 1653–1654*, 361. Bodleian MS Nalson 17, fol. 418r has "Locall" rather than "legal." The committee included common lawyers Chief Justice Rolle and Justices Jermyn and Atkins, the Admiralty judges John Godolphin and William Clerk, and two more civilians, Dr. Walter Walker and a Dr. Turner.

applicable to England."[64] Not even ambassadors themselves were privileged, according to the anonymous writer. As it was posed to another lawyer, the question wasn't *whether* Don Pantaleon would be punished but *how*. It was presumably a member of the committee who inquired with a civilian friend "How our *State* may justly vindicate the blood of our Natives shed by the train and followers of an Embassadour."[65] The anonymously published answer, drawing from figures as diverse as Cicero, Camden, Coke, Gentili, Selden, and Grotius, was that the offenders who are part of a diplomatic retinue ought to be remitted to their home country.

Denying common law jurisdiction, the likely author, Timothy Baldwin, affirmed that "The *Legate* brings with him the Lawes and rules of Nations" and this "Law of Nations exempts those that come upon publick Faith."[66] An embassy could be a single person, but, partly because "Parsimony of... Legations" was generally seen as ignominious, it could also be a "multitude."[67] It was on this principle that not just individual ambassadors but also whole diplomatic entourages were permitted to practice otherwise forbidden foreign religious rites, whether they were Catholic rites in London or Protestant rites in Lisbon. But Baldwin's opinion also employed an unmistakably royalist idiom, subtly linking Don Pantaleon's fate with that of Charles I. In calling ambassadors the "vocall and animate Images of Princes," Baldwin buttresses his legal argument by repurposing the sympathy generated for Charles I by the famous *Eikon Basileke*, or *The King's Image*. As with "Statues and Pictures of Princes," Baldwin wrote, "The Civilities and Violations done to their Embassadours [are] esteem'd by Princes as done to themselves."[68] The connection was easy to grasp: a government responsible for Milton's *Eikonoklastes*, whose title came from the Greek emperors who "broke all superstitious images to pieces," could hardly be expected to practice the "generous observation of Hospitality, and respect to strangers and Embassadours" required in Baldwin's estimation by law.[69] Since the most probable date for Baldwin's tract was June or early July 1654, Baldwin's boast that he'd not "flatter[ed his] Country-men into the usurpation of an illegal privilege," likely had Milton's epic flight in the *Second Defense* directly in view.[70]

[64] Emphasis added. *A Collection of the State Papers of John Thurloe*, ed. Thomas Birch (London: Thomas Woodward, 1742), 2.428. Evidence suggests this view was probably beyond the pale of acceptable parochialism. For the suggestion that it that ought to "be taken notice of, and publickly declared against," falling into the category of "speeches publickly made by any Judges or noted Lawyers upon the Bench, or in any publick Assemblies, against... the Law of Nations, which may give just offence to our Neighbours," see Edward Lake, *Memoranda: Touching the Oath Ex Officio, Pretended Self-Accusation, and Canonical Purgation Together with Some Notes about the Making of Some New, and Alteration and Explanation of Some Old Laws* (London: R. Royston, 1662), 127, 129.

[65] [Timothy Baldwin], *The Priviledges of an Ambassadour*, A2. For the ascription of authorship, see Stuart Handley, "Baldwin, Sir Timothy (bap. 1619, d. 1696)," in *Oxford Dictionary of National Biography*, ed. H. C. G. Matthew, Brian Harrison, and Lawrence Goldman (Oxford: Oxford University Press, 2008).

[66] [Timothy Baldwin], *The Priviledges of an Ambassadour*, 4, 8–9.

[67] [Timothy Baldwin], *The Priviledges of an Ambassadour*, 12, 9.

[68] [Timothy Baldwin], *The Priviledges of an Ambassadour*, 9.

[69] Milton, *CPW*, 3.343; [Timothy Baldwin], *The Priviledges of an Ambassadour*, 12.

[70] [Timothy Baldwin], *The Priviledges of an Ambassadour*, 12.

TERMS OF INDICTMENT

The word "protect" appears only once in *Paradise Lost*, but in Daniel Shore's argument the related ideas of care and guardianship inform Milton's entire relation to pagan religion, whose idols the poet refuses to destroy, choosing instead to preserve them in the poem and hold them up to view.[71] When Milton does use the word "protect," it comes at the critical moment in Book 9 just before Eve departs from Adam. Adam advises Eve, "leave not the faithful side / That gave thee being, still shades thee, and protects" (9.265–266). To the extent that Milton's secondary law of nations was associated with history, contingency, and change, it possibly had the most to do with Eve, who, in Milton's words, was "of man / Extracted" (8.496–497). As Gilbert and Gubar emphasize in their important feminist reading of literary history *The Madwoman in the Attic*, it is "Eve [who] is a secondary and contingent creation."[72] Troubling though it is to modern readers, Eve's "implied / Subjection" is fundamentally related to the husband's responsibility to protect his wife. Milton's epic voice tells readers that the "husband . . . / . . . guards [the wife], or with her the worst endures" (9.267–269). God later says that Eve's "gifts / Were such as under government well seemed" (10.153–154). If Milton's sexism is here impossible to avoid, questions of jurisdiction raised by the Don Pantaleon trial help us see Eve's implied subjection within a more international frame than we might otherwise do. Subjection and protection remain related to the third term in Walter Walker's opinion and the epic tradition more broadly: enmity. As a possessor of reason and a will, Eve may of course depart from Adam's protection, and this she does, but in so doing she loses the ambiguous privileges of subjection, which Milton and Walker associate with the protections of the household or common law.

Milton, blind, knows he shares much with Eve in this respect. In his *Second Defense*, Milton writes of how "shadows" of "divine law" keep the blind "not only safe from the injuries of men, but almost sacred."[73] Eve's departure from Adam's protective shadow expresses what Hobbes and later Vattel will call her "independency."[74] But it leaves her as vulnerable as a blind man in a dark alley. Though Eve is not a man, blind or otherwise, the comparison nevertheless reminds us of the way Hobbes influentially figured the gladiatorial state in masculine terms, and also that the laws of war traditionally protected women from harm.[75] For good and for bad,

---

[71] Daniel Shore, *Milton and the Art of Rhetoric* (Cambridge: Cambridge University Press, 2012), 85–104.

[72] Sandra M. Gilbert and Susan Gubar, *The Madwoman in the Attic: The Woman Writer and the Nineteenth-Century Literary Imagination* (New Haven, CT: Yale University Press, 1979), 197.

[73] Milton, *CPW*, 4.1.590.

[74] For Hobbes, see Chapter 5. Emer Vattel, *The Law of Nations: Or, Principles of the Law of Nature, Applied to the Conduct and Affairs of Nations and Sovereigns, with Three Early Essays on the Origin and Nature of Natural Law and on Luxury* (Indianapolis, IN: Liberty Fund, 2008), 2.4. Picciotto observes Eve's "self-sovereignty": Joanna Picciotto, *Labors of Innocence in Early Modern England* (Cambridge, MA: Harvard University Press, 2010), 474. For a reading of Eve as "right to react strongly to Adam's protective instinct," see Bennett, *Reviving Liberty*, 115.

[75] Hilary Charlesworth, "The Sex of the State in International Law," in *Sexing the Subject of Law*, ed. Ngaire Naffine and Rosemary J. Owens (North Ryde, NSW: LBC Information Services, 1997), 251–68.

independent Eve in legal terms becomes a *persona juris gentium* and, according to Satan's Hobbesian logic at least, a recognizable enemy in her own right. Her departure from Adam's protective shadow, then, is also an entrance, an entrance into individuated sovereignty and full participation in the poem's epic events. "Alone, without exterior help sustained"—alone, that is, on the battlefield in humanity's epic war against "the Enemy of mankind"—Eve is both temporarily free from Adam's coverture but also newly vulnerable to the laws and events of epic (9.494).

We are now in a position to appreciate the poem's investment in creating a temporal and generic imbalance in which humanity lives suspended in blind comic innocence while Satan hones his epic resources. By the time of their confrontation, Satan is more practiced in epic enmity than are the humans. His entrance into epic had occurred long before in cosmic history, when he forged the initial path from subjection/protection to enmity. Once having been a contented member of God's extended household, Satan, feeling himself unprotected, lit out for the territories of a darker, antagonistic generic world, both precursor to and predecessor of comic figures like Shakespeare's Malvolio. After the resulting war in heaven, Satan gained further experience as an epic hero by escaping from his corrupt jailors, Sin and Death, and by evading the watch of the guardian angels Uriel and Gabriel, whom God noticeably acquits from any wrongdoing, assuring the angels, "your sincerest care could not prevent" (10.37).[76] Satan's experience as an epic hero by the time he and Eve duel in Book 9, then, means it's hardly a fair fight. Eve may have been "sufficient to have stood," but Satan, "in meditated fraud and malice," has been "bent / On man's destruction" since Book 2 (3.99, 9.55–9.56). While Satan has been practicing the arts of empire, Eve has been picking flowers and frolicking with Adam, to whom alone Satan's designs were directly communicated.

Though Satan finds inspiration in several epic heroes, one of his primary models has been the Portuguese explorer Vasco da Gama.[77] Da Gama is the hero of Camões' Portuguese epic *Os Lusiads*, a ten-book poem, like the 1667 *Paradise Lost*, that Richard Fanshawe translated into English in 1655. Important to note is that the dedicatee of a 1644 Portuguese edition of the poem was none other than João Rodrigues de Sá a Menezes, Lisbon's Ambassador to London while Fanshawe was translating the epic, and brother, of course, to the executed Don Pantaleon (see Figures 7.1 and 7.2).[78] Milton's echoes of Camões and Fanshawe in *Paradise Lost*, then, were even more freighted with topicality than scholars have observed. Satan's association with da Gama is one way Milton triggers a need for protection on a global scale.

---

[76] Uriel falls victim to Satan's hypocrisy, Milton tells us, "which neither man nor angel can discern"; and Gabriel observes (rightly) that Satan may indeed have "o'earleaped these earthly bounds," it being difficult "to exclude / Spiritual substance with corporeal bar" (3.682, 4.583–585).

[77] James H. Sims, "Camoens' 'Lusiads' and Milton's 'Paradise Lost': Satan's Voyage to Eden," in *Papers on Milton*, ed. Philip Mahone Griffith and Lester F. Zimmerman (Tulsa, OK: University of Tulsa, 1969), 155–68; Balachandra Rajan, "Milton and Camões," *Portuguese Cultural and Literary Studies* 9 (2002): 177–87; David Quint, *Epic and Empire: Politics and Generic Form from Virgil to Milton* (Princeton, NJ: Princeton University Press, 1993), 253–67.

[78] Luis Camões, *Os Lusiadas* (Lisbon: Paulo Craesbeeck, 1644).

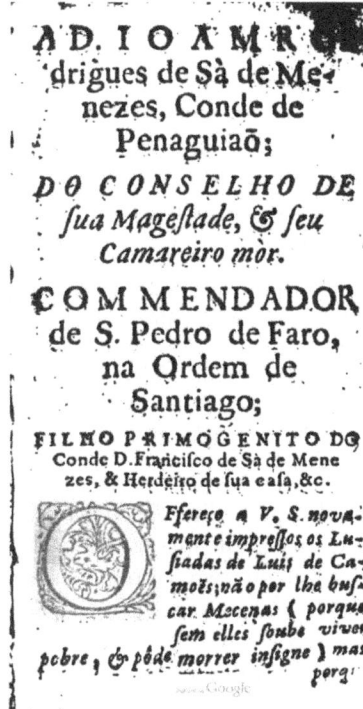

Fig. 7.1 and 7.2. Paulo Craesbeeck's 1644 dedication of *Os Lusiadas* to João Rodrigues de Sá a Menezes. Digitization by Google Books.

Reproduced with kind permission from the Bibliothèque Jésuite des Fontaines, shelfmark SJ BE 622/20.

Milton's Satan is the celestial predator, conjoined with the poet's Nimrod and Don Pantaleon in a logic of tyranny and predation. Satan may flatter Eve with the inflated epic epithet, "Sovereign of creatures, universal dame" (9.612), but Eve remains "our credulous mother" on her way to eat the fruit (9.44). Milton's adjective "credulous" communicates Eve's innocence but also, more subtly, her newly freighted mimetic character and epic vulnerability. The undercurrent is diplomatic: "credulous" evokes the diplomatic letters of credence that authorize representation, the composition of which Milton performed as Secretary of Foreign Tongues.[79]

Diplomacy, vulnerability, and predation had been linked in Milton's mind since the assassinations of Ascham and Dorislaas, and they remained so through the events around Don Pantaleon, the repercussions of which continued well into the late 1650s. In March 1655–1656, Milton had become fully blind, so Cromwell sent

---

[79] Marvell's *The First Anniversary of the Government under His Highness the Lord Protector*, a poem written roughly two years after Milton had recommended Marvell as Secretary of Foreign Tongues that draws from Milton's *Second Defense*, likewise plays on diplomacy's conventional letters of credence to describe "credulous Ambassadors." Andrew Marvell, *The Poems of Andrew Marvell*, ed. Nigel Smith, rev. edn. (London: Pearson Longman, 2007), line 348.

Philip Meadows as Ambassador to Portugal to further spur Portuguese ratification of the long-brewing Anglo-Portuguese Treaty. In May 1656, the man Milton's 1654 letter had averred was "distinguished for his gentleness, his character, his prudence, and his fidelity," and the recent dedicatee of Camões' *Os Lusiads*, Rodrigues de Sá, seems to have orchestrated an assassination attempt on Meadows in revenge for his brother's execution two years earlier. Meadows was shot in the hand and badly wounded. Thurloe's intelligencer in Lisbon noted that while the attackers had fled too quickly to be identified or apprehended,

> for divers odd discourses I suspect it a revenge for the late Pantaleon beheaded on Tower-hill: First because the conde [de Penaguiaõ, Rodrigues de Sá] in his apologie to G. Lambert suggests a suspition in excuse: Secondly because he and his brother-in-law, the conde de Torre, a man noted for bloodshed and murthers, have been marked more than usually together, both glad for the accident, and onely sorrie, as they said in private, then [sic] Mr. Meddow received a slighter wound then their brother in London.[80]

Milton's subsequent diplomatic correspondence, composed at Thurloe's behest and made necessary in the first place by Meadows' absence from London, declares that "peace between our two nations . . . can by no means remain steadfast if abominable deeds of this kind go unpunished and unavenged."[81] Sent upon "the blessed errand of peace," according to Milton's letters, Meadows had been hunted so ruthlessly that "his preservation is only to be attributed to the protection of Heaven."[82]

If Meadows sounds like Milton's "faithful" Abdiel, protected by a halo of virtue ("Though single . . . amdist" enemies, "His loyalty he kept, his love, his zeal" "nor of violence feared aught" [5.896–905]), Meadows and Abdiel both help to highlight the generic imbalance between characters like Satan and Eve. Satan, the predatory bad actor, exploits epic structures like diplomatic immunity designed for, and otherwise capable of, protection. Credulous Eve is new to epic mimesis.

Even if Satan is already prepared to treat Adam and Eve as epic representatives in Book 4, humanity has yet to join the fight. Vulnerability is central to Milton's depiction of Adam and Eve. He stresses their vulnerability in introducing them as "naked[,] . . . for they thought no ill" (4.319–320). Satan, by contrast, echoing Sidney's Amphialus, treats Paradise in epic fashion as "ill-secured," and he proceeds with his plan for "destroying the innocent" (4.370).[83] Satan's "gaze" in Book 4, as Leah Whittington points out, is the gaze of a powerful epic warrior like Achilles or Aeneas with the life of a supplicating enemy at his feet (4.356).[84] Satan "could

---

[80] Thurloe, *Thurloe Papers*, 5.114.

[81] Milton, *CPW*, 5.2.752; Fallon, *Milton in Government*, 175.

[82] John Milton, *Letters of State Written by Mr. John Milton, to Most of the Sovereign Princes and Republicks of Europe, from the Year 1649, till the Year 1659* (London, 1694), 213–14; Fallon, *Milton in Government*, 50–1.

[83] Compare Amphialus' "justification" in Philip Sidney, *The Countess of Pembroke's Arcadia (the New Arcadia)*, ed. Victor Skretkowicz (Oxford: Clarendon Press, 1987), 325 and Chapter 2. For the quotation, along with the argument that the allusions here are primarily tragic, see Barbara Kiefer Lewalski, *Paradise Lost and the Rhetoric of Literary Forms* (Princeton, NJ: Princeton University Press, 1985), 63–4.

[84] Leah Whittington, "Milton's Poetics of Supplication," *Milton Studies* 55 (forthcoming).

love" and "could pity" this "gentle pair," but Adam and Eve will instead go "unpitied" (4.364, 4.366, 4.374–375).[85] Crucially, however, the humans can't see Satan, nor do they even understand what fighting is. Satan is merely a self-appointed epic hero who uses the genre of just violence to justify his own predation. When Eve departs from Adam's protection in Book 9, she has far less in common with male epic personalities, who conventionally represent "a state, a senate, a treasury, united and harmonious citizens, and some basis for a treaty of peace," than women who "have no state, are no state, [and] seek no state."[86] Given that Satan himself knows better—"Ah gentle pair, ye little think how nigh / Your change approaches"—the word for such predatory behavior, one of the strongest in Milton's forensic arsenal, is abuse (4.366–7).

Satan's abusive character certainly invites comparison with Charles I in a domestic context but also with foreign tyrants like the Duke of Savoy, whom Milton held responsible for the massacre at Piedmont. The horror of Piedmont wasn't only that the Duke of Savoy had massacred a Protestant people under his protection. Upon the Duke's order that the Waldensians convert to Catholicism or leave his dominion on pain of death, Piedmontese suppliants had physically come to him, vulnerable to his power. However, according to Milton's letter to the Duke, "When your subjects betook themselves as suppliants to Your Royal Highness, beseeching that the edict be revoked, . . . a part of your army made an attack upon them and most cruelly massacred many, ordered others to be cast into chains, and drove the rest into desert places and mountains."[87] The Waldensians' domestic relationship with their sovereign, founded on protection and "grace," became the very occasion for their massacre.[88] Transposed into generic terms, the execution of suppliants was a limit case even in the epic law of nations; introduced into the quiet of pastoral genres, it became "intolerable."

Here we can return to the role of the *judex inter homines*, whose role is to protect against figures like the Duke of Savoy and other practitioners of Satanic abuse. Milton initially casts Satan's abuse of the innocent in Book 4 as abuse from without, but Satan makes clear there that "place[s] inviolable" will not be enough to ensure protection from such an enemy (4.843). Satan will soon be an "inmate" (9.495). Turning to the language of diplomatic alliance that Erasmus had criticized, Satan declares ". . . League with you I seek, / And mutual amity so strait, so close / That I with you must dwell" (4.375–377). Satan, in other words, appoints himself as resident ambassador. Moreover, he cannot help but abuse the privileges of hospitality and diplomatic immunity: "within him hell / He brings, and round about him" (4.20–4.21). If Satan is hell on earth, protection against Satanic tyranny falls to the *judex inter homines*.

[85] Whittington, "Milton's Poetics of Supplication."

[86] Gentili, *De Jure Belli Libri Tres*, 2.25; Catharine A. MacKinnon, "Law in the Everyday Life of Women," in *Women's Lives, Men's Laws* (Cambridge, MA: Harvard University Press, 2007), 32–43; Catharine A. MacKinnon, "Women's September 11th: Rethinking the International Law of Conflict," in *Are Women Human?: And Other International Dialogues* (Cambridge, MA: Belknap Press of Harvard University Press, 2006), 259–80.

[87] Milton, *CPW*, 5.2.685–686.   [88] Milton, *CPW*, 5.2.685–686.

GOD'S WARTIME TRIBUNAL

It is an uncomfortable fact of Milton's epic law of nations that God could justly have ended all human existence in a stroke.[89] Though imperious Satan and the Duke of Savoy preyed on innocent suppliants, God's is a different case. God sits in judgment of defendants, Adam and Eve, who confess to a crime that readers of the poem have themselves been made witness. Grotius' God in his biblical tragedy *Adamus Exul* even tells Adam and Eve directly, "I could have overwhelm'd / The pair of you with sudden gunnery of death" (*AE*, 1958–1959). But Milton for his part uses the full epic register. Like a wrathful Aeneas with a culpable humanity at his feet, God might have killed the prostrate enemies beneath him. For Tasso and Gentili, we recall, Turnus was underserving of mercy because he broke his compact with the epic hero. Nor had Milton's pluralized epic hero in the *Second Defense*, "my countrymen," shown any inappropriate pity for their guilty epic enemy, Charles.

Milton's poem, however, was not about Vergil's worldly *imperium sine fine* but instead about Christian "Love without end" (3.142). Milton uses the epic law of nations to generate the full pathos of the Christian sacrifice. God through his angels assumes the responsibility to protect Adam and Eve in Paradise, but the Fall put government into a new frame. Humanity, as Romans 5:10 averred, made themselves "enemies" to God. Milton seizes on this word, as we shall see, even though Milton's eighteenth-century editor Bentley, for one, found the term so striking that he thought it could not have been Milton's own. According to Bentley, "enemies" was "certainly of the Editor's Manufacture" on the grounds that "It's quite superfluous; it divides what's naturally connected; and it changes the Sentiment, from a *Family* under a gracious Master and *Father*, to the Condition of *Enemies*."[90] Bentley, however, was more right than he knew, for this was precisely Milton's point.

"Enemies" both evoked the wrath of the irate epic warrior and sharply implied the end of God's responsibility to protect humanity. Humanity had erred, or wandered, from underneath God's protective shade. What Milton calls humanity's "treason" entails a "forfeit[ure]" of God's angelic protection (3.207, 3.176). Accordingly, "Up into heaven from Paradise in haste / The angelic guards ascended, mute and sad" (10.17–10.18). At the moment of judgment of Book 10, Adam and Eve stand naked before a wrathful God no longer bound to protect them. The metaphor of shade is insufficient but viscerally arresting: Adam and Eve become existentially vulnerable to sunburn. Ominously, there are no other witnesses (10.79–10.80).

The Son's meritorious sacrifice, however, has pre-emptively renewed the responsibility to protect. While God's just anger will not abate until the Second Coming, the Son in offering himself performed the best diplomacy possible under epic conditions, securing "the only peace / Found out for mankind under wrath" (3.274–275).

---

[89] Famously, William Empson compared Milton's God to Stalin. See William Empson, *Milton's God*, rev. edn. (London: Chatto & Windus, 1965), 146. For a recent defense of Empson's as "the most satisfying way of reading the poem," see Tobias Gregory, *From Many Gods to One: Divine Action in Renaissance Epic* (Chicago, IL: University of Chicago Press, 2006), 197–8.

[90] Richard Bentley, ed., *Paradise Lost* (London: J. Tonson, 1732), 312.

Analysis of the judgment scene in Book 10 can be informed by Dr. Walker's opinion: "if the [offender against the law of nations] be out of custody, and being demanded is refused, it is *justa causa belli*. If in custody, he may be tried to keep off the war."[91] When the Son comes to judge Adam and Eve, the events of the epic have effectively made this a wartime tribunal. Milton writes of the Son:

> So judged he man, both Judge and Saviour sent,
> And the instant stroke of death denounced that day
> Removed far off; then pitying how they stood
> Before him naked to the air, that now
> Must suffer change, disdained not to begin
> Thenceforth the form of servant to assume:
> As when he washed his servants' feet, so now
> As father of his family he clad
> Their nakedness with skins of beasts, or slain,
> Or as the snake with youthful coat repaid:
> And thought not much to clothe his enemies (10.209–219)

What Bentley and many other readers have missed is how thoroughly the scene and its language are structured by the epic law of nations. In *De Jure Belli ac Pacis*, Grotius had commended "the exact Pattern of Christ, who laid down his Life for us, dyed for us, while we were yet Enemies to him."[92] The Son is an epic warrior who not only pities the enemies at his feet but serves them. Time itself is in the balance. The caesura before the temporal marker "then" in line 211 highlights powerfully that Adam and Eve have no entitlement to fallen time before their physical annihilation. The Son's protection is the very condition of possibility for postlapsarian time. God had promised that "The day thou eatst thereof... / ... inevitably though shalt die" (8.329–330). When the Savior postpones the "instant stroke of death" ("Removed far off"), Adam and Eve become obliged like prisoners of war spared their just deserts.[93]

Even if God might justly have ended human life in a stroke, the Son has protected Adam and Eve, and in them all of humanity. Several lines after the Son's judgment, Milton will further illuminate exactly how God's Son differs from Sin and Death, who, as emissaries of Satan, are formally analogous to the Son, but essentially cruel. They, Milton writes, enthrall—take captive or enslave—merely to "kill" (10.402). And just as Adam and Eve owe their time to the Son, so too do they owe him their bodies: when "they stood / Before him naked to the air," the Son, "pitying how they stood / Before him," "clad / their nakedness with skins of beasts" (10.2112–12, 10.216–217).

---

[91] *CSPD 1653–1654*, 361.

[92] Hugo Grotius, *The Rights of War and Peace*, ed. Richard Tuck and Jean Barbeyrac, trans. [John Morris] (Indianapolis, IN: Liberty Fund, 2005), 1122. Joseph Wittreich cites this passage in his reading of *Samson Agonistes*. Joseph Anthony Wittreich, *Shifting Contexts: Reinterpreting Samson Agonistes* (Pittsburgh, PA: Duquesne University Press, 2002), 51.

[93] Grotius' God too "preferr'd to show... clemency, and not / The rigours of my law" (*AE*, 1960–1). Hugo Grotius, "Adamus Exul," in *The Celestial Cycle; the Theme of Paradise Lost in World Literature with Translations of the Major Analogues.*, trans. Watson Kirkconnell (Toronto: University of Toronto Press, 1952).

"There is no evil in the state which God has not introduced...: hunger, disease, sedition, and public enemies," Milton writes.[94] In skins of beasts, then, we can see a final material emblem for Milton's notion of protection. If Milton's judgment scene, as Mary Nyquist suggests, "activates 'nakedness' in the sense of 'unarmed,'" skins of beasts, *spolia opima*, are arms or armour, devices for the human epic (9.1091).[95] The duty of protection remains somewhat abstract and mystical, but skins of beasts by contrast are material, quotidian—as familiar as the shame and embodied vulnerability they seek to remedy. According to Milton, humanity will have to wait until the Second Coming to find "peace assured, / And reconcilement [when] wrath shall be no more" (3.263–265). God the Father will remain like Achilles or Aeneas, at liberty to slay suppliants until "victory is assured."[96] Milton has given us what amounts to the very first humanitarian "intercess[ion]": the Son, "unimplored, unsought," secured God's grace in the meantime, and he has provided humanity with protective armor for the war of fallen existence (3.219, 10.96, 3.231).

TOWARDS THE RESPONSIBILITY TO PROTECT

God's anger, made mild by the Son's intervention, becomes the backbone of a radically international form of belonging. Milton writes in his first *Defense*, "Since...we are God's own...[,] his property alone, [we] cannot, without wickedness and extreme sacrilege, deliver ourselves as slaves to Caesar, that is to a man, and a man who is unjust, unrighteous, and a tyrant."[97] Humanity belongs to God as slaves and as servants, spared in a just war. But because the Son has become man, both judge of man and servant of man, so too do the godly participate in the dyadic responsibility to protect God's kingdom. Judgment over tyranny is participation in the mediation of God's just anger. To be a human is to be both an enemy of God, and also an instrument against God's enemies. Skins of beasts then serve a further role: to protect individual humans from the potentially redounding pain of just violence undertaken in the responsibility to protect.

I suggested at the outset of this chapter that Milton's epic jurisprudence, founded on an analytic of protection, can help us think anew about contemporary international law's "responsibility to protect," a legal doctrine that in the years since a major 2001 Canadian report to the United Nations has advanced the prevention of atrocity above state sovereignty and has sharply qualified distinctions between inside and outside or domestic and foreign. In the meantime, I have argued that Milton rejects the Westphalian division of inside and outside and instead develops an epic jurisprudence in which putatively "domestic" topics including divorce, religious liberty, civil justice, and tyranny exist on the same generic plane as international warfare, diplomatic immunity, and territorial conquest.

[94] "Is there one of these which the state will not strive with all its power to cast off?," Milton continues. See *CPW*, 4.1.387.
[95] Mary Nyquist, "Contemporary Ancestors of de Bry, Hobbes, and Milton," *University of Toronto Quarterly* 77, no. 3 (2008): 837–75.
[96] See Chapter 2 and Gentili, *De Jure Belli Libri Tres*, 2.248.
[97] Milton, *CPW*, 4.1.377.

With the understanding that Milton uses the mimetic structure of the epic law of nations, together with its *topoi* of war, conquest, and diplomacy, to develop an analytic of protection, which he applies from the domestic household to "This pendent world", we can return, finally, to the doctrine of the responsibility to protect (2.1052). Significant enough to have developed the shorthand "R2P," the responsibility to protect doctrine declares that "Sovereign States have a responsibility to protect their own citizens from avoidable catastrophe—from mass murder and rape, from starvation—but...when they are unwilling or unable to do so, that responsibility must be borne by the broader community of states."[98] As the legal warrant, or would-be warrant, for international interventions in Kosovo, East Timor, Haiti, Iraq, and Libya, "responsibility to protect" has been criticized as a troubling departure from Westphalian norms of sovereignty but also lauded by prominent intellectuals such as Michael Ignatieff and Samantha Power as a necessary remedy for genocide, influentially called by Power the "problem from hell."[99] The self-consciously modern language of "responsibility to protect" has been advanced as an improvement on the older language of "humanitarian intervention." Having been explicitly "designed to change the perspective in responding to mass atrocity from that of the prospective interveners or resisters to that of the victims of the atrocities," the language of "responsibility to protect" has successfully influenced the discussion and now rivals the "right to intervene" as the dominant conceptual frame for questions of sovereignty and catastrophe.[100] There is talk of a new norm in international law.

Whereas we are told that the responsibility to protect is a twenty-first-century doctrine, *Paradise Lost* asks us to reject contemporary R2P advocates' willful ahistoricism and instead give Milton's epic jurisprudence a foundational place in the still incomplete literary history of the international responsibility to protect. But Milton's epic analytic of protection also offers a richer model than the doctrine currently *en vogue*. One of the few scholars to have examined the responsibility to protect in historical perspective has described the concept as an episode in the "longstanding debate about the relationship between jurisdiction and territory" beginning with the Reformation.[101] According to Anne Orford,

> The linkage of sovereignty and protection...emerged alongside the modern State, as a way of distinguishing the State's *de facto* capacity to protect from *de jure* claims to authority, whether those claims were made by the peasantry (such as the revolutionary claimants to authority in seventeenth century England), the Pope, the Holy Roman Emperor, or rival claimants to territory in the new world.[102]

---

[98] International Commission on Intervention and State Sovereignty et al., *The Responsibility to Protect Report of the International Commission on Intervention and State Sovereignty*, VIII.

[99] Power, *A Problem from Hell.*

[100] Hilary Charlesworth, "Feminist Reflections on the Responsibility to Protect," *Global Responsibility to Protect* 2 (2010): 233.

[101] Orford, "Jurisdiction without Territory," 983; Orford, *International Authority and the Responsibility to Protect*, 109–64. See also Luke Glanville, *Sovereignty and the Responsibility to Protect: A New History* (Chicago, IL: University of Chicago Press, 2014).

[102] Orford, "Jurisdiction without Territory," 990. See further Glanville, *Sovereignty and the Responsibility to Protect*, 55; D. J. B. Trim, "'If a Prince Use Tyrannie towards His People': Interventions on

Drawing on work by early modern literary scholars Bradin Cormack and Victoria Kahn among others, Orford shows that the presently ascendant version of the responsibility to protect adopts absolutist assumptions from Thomas Hobbes and Carl Schmitt. Although "the idea of the 'freeborn people' as an active subject of politics that existed separately from the state emerged in England during the revolutionary period of the civil wars," she writes, "the responsibility to protect concept . . . [fails to] conceptualise the legitimacy of authority in relation to a third term, whether that be the people, the nation or the *Volk*."[103] The English Revolution's democratic gains remain absent in the modern responsibility to protect. The modern doctrine of the responsibility to protect remains beholden to the Hobbesian and Schmittian "fascist epic[s]."[104]

For such reasons, then, Milton's epic jurisprudence ultimately deserves a prominent place in our understanding of the modern responsibility to protect, not because it is equivalent to contemporary international thought about protection, but for several salient differences. Certainly, Milton's unabashed Christianity, his interest in Roman law, and his appeals to private virtue all distinguish Milton from most modern advocates of the responsibility to protect. Perhaps most importantly, however, Milton theorizes protection in ways only an epic poet could do, and his scrutiny of the theater of protection challenges absolutist assumptions still active in contemporary international law.

Behalf of Foreign Populations in Early Modern Europe," in *Humanitarian Intervention: A History*, ed. Brendan Simms and D. J. B. Trim (Cambridge: Cambridge University Press, 2011), 29–66.

   [103] Orford, *International Authority and the Responsibility to Protect*, 118, 120.
   [104] Gopal Balakrishnan, "The Geopolitics of Separation: Response to Teschke's 'Decisions and Indecisions,'" *New Left Review* 68 (April 2011): 57–72.

Conclusion

The philosopher W. V. O. Quine once observed, "A curious thing about the onto-logical problem is its simplicity. It can be put into three Anglo-Saxon monosylla-bles: 'What is there?'"[1] This book has turned to the history of international law with an eye toward amending English Renaissance literary criticism's standard answers to what there is.

I have argued throughout that when the law of nations traded poetry for profes-sorships and donned the new garb of international law, it did not erase its literary history. Early modern poetics remains present in the modern structures of interna-tional law. From the plural, overlapping landscape of early modern genres came the plural, overlapping landscape of subspecialties now identified as international law. Ultimately, the eighteenth century gave us two altars at which we might sacrifice the literary history of international law: literary aesthetics and a professionalized field of international law. We do better, however, by studying the ways early mod-ern genres continue to shape our world.

We need to recognize this literary history of international law for purely histor-ical and intellectual reasons, but the literary law of nations also has more urgent claims on our attention. It is finally time to say it: scholarship involving the history of international affairs is different from other kinds of historical scholarship. The primary reason involves Article 38 of the Statute of the International Court of Justice, the standard account of sources of international law. Among the sources of international law are "international conventions," "international custom," and "the teachings of the most highly qualified publicists of the various nations." To a degree that many find quite surprising, perhaps even unjustifiable, international law is what historians of international law say it is. Histories of customs, treaties, and laws regularly influence determinations about rules, rights, and obligations. The role of historical scholarship in international law terrifies critics like John Bolton, but Bolton correctly identifies its importance: "There is another important source of international law, which...academics refer to quite regularly: the writings of academics!"[2]

In conclusion, then, I invoke a largely unknown piece of scholarship on early modern international law that was published in 1997, a year whose highlights of early modern literary scholarship include David J. Baker's excellent monograph

---

[1] W. V. O. Quine, "On What There Is," *The Review of Metaphysics* 2, no. 5 (1948): 21.
[2] John R. Bolton, "Is There Really 'Law' in International Affairs?," *Transnational Law & Contem-porary Problems* 10 (2000): 7.

Between Nations: Shakespeare, Spenser, Marvell, and the Question of Britain and Daniel Vitkus' important article, "Turning Turk in Othello: The Conversion and Damnation of the Moor." Baker and Vitkus both examined international concerns in rich cultural detail, but law was a subordinate concern. That same year, however, a young U.S. law professor, just five years out of Yale Law School, published a twenty-one-page introduction to Alberico Gentili's *De Legationibus* (1585). As the crisply written Introduction tells it, Gentili was responsible for introducing "modern" international law. Gentili had done "more than any other thinker of his day to sweep away the theories of an international legal system dominated by the universal hegemony of the Church and the Holy Roman Empire."[3] Gentili's work had been swiftly integrated into Grotius' *De Jure Belli ac Pacis* (1625) and the Peace of Westphalia (1648), and, the Introduction suggested, therefore helped inaugurate the modern international order itself.

The young law professor's name was John Yoo. Shortly thereafter, as legal advisor to President George W. Bush, Yoo, with Jay Bybee and Robert Delahunty, would co-author the notorious "torture memos" of early 2002, which argued that international conventions on torture did not apply in the case of captured Al-Qaeda warriors fighting against the USA. While Yoo's introduction rehearses a number of received ideas about Gentili's historical role in international law, other, more idiosyncratic emphases only take on their full meaning in conjunction with Yoo's torture memos. In the Gentili introduction, Yoo insisted that in early modernity, "those who operated outside of the role of nation-states, could not receive the protections of international law."[4]

In this little-noticed introduction to an Elizabethan legal tract, Yoo sowed seeds for the policies he would later justify for the Bush Administration. Legal black holes, waterboarding, secret prisons, Guantanamo Bay: "Members of al Qaeda cannot receive the protections of POWs . . . because al Qaeda is a non-state terrorist organization," one memo averred.[5] In Yoo's hands, Gentili had become the herald of a modern international legal order whose true face would only show itself in the euphemistically described "harsh interrogation methods" of the post-September 11 world.

Because scholarship about the history of international law *is* different—because, in other words, scholars are *themselves* sources of international law—Yoo's scholarship poses serious challenges about modernity and method. Yoo's work liberated Gentili's jurisprudence for use in the war on terror. Waterboarding and other technologies of torture weren't mere vengeance, nor were they holdovers from an

---

[3] John Yoo, "Introduction," in *De Legationibus*, by Alberico Gentili (Delran, NJ: Legal Classics Library, 1997), 5.

[4] Yoo, "Introduction," 14–15.

[5] John Yoo, "Memo 14. August 1, 2002, Memorandum for Alberto R. Gonzales Counsel to the President," in *The Torture Papers: The Road to Abu Ghraib*, ed. Karen J. Greenberg and Joshua L. Dratel (New York: Cambridge University Press, 2005), 221; John Yoo and Robert J. Delahunty, "Memo 4. January 9, 2002, To: William J. Haynes II, General Counsel, Department of Defense, From: John Yoo, Deputy Assistant Attorney General, U.S. Department of Justice, Office of Legal Counsel and Robert J. Delahunty, Special Counsel, U.S. Department of Justice, Re: Application of Treaties and Laws to Al Qaeda and Taliban Detainees," in *The Torture Papers: The Road to Abu Ghraib*, ed. Karen J. Greenberg and Joshua L. Dratel (New York: Cambridge University Press, 2005), 38–79.

earlier age. Rather, they were practices of precisely that modern international order that Alberico Gentili had purportedly inaugurated in 1585.

Yoo's Gentili was both in history and outside of it. Gentili lived over 400 years ago, but he was one "us." "Medieval writers," by contrast, "could not fully conceive of the world being 'international.'"[6] Methodologically, Gentili's modernity was secured, above all, by Gentili's purportedly "modern, positivist approach to international law."[7]

This book has of course given a very different account of Renaissance humanism from the world Yoo described. Gentili, as we have seen, was as enmeshed in the literary culture of Renaissance humanism as any intellectual of his age. *De Legationibus* was dedicated to the poet and author of the famous *Defense of Poesy*, Philip Sidney. It was introduced by two prefatory poems—hardly a feature of other works in international law less-controversially deemed "modern." One of Gentili's most important sources was Vergil's *Aeneid*. Gentili cited other poets like Homer, Plautus, and Horace—even his contemporary, Torquato Tasso. Such aspects did not trouble Yoo, however. In Yoo's description, Sidney isn't a poet but a "noble."[8] Yoo gleefully narrates Gentili's education as a turn from poetry to law.

Only slightly less troubling than the language anticipating the torture memos, then, is how Yoo achieves Gentili's relevance for the present by suppressing the most alien features of Renaissance humanism. Yoo follows Carl Schmitt and others in attributing to Gentili a "revolutionary" secularism based on Gentili's now famous comment in *De Jure Belli* that theologians should keep quiet about matters beyond their ken, *silete theologi in munere alieno*.[9] But Yoo crucially fails to recognize the literary context. As literary scholars *will* recognize, the unnamed target of Gentili's comment was the Oxford Puritan theologian John Rainolds, with whom Gentili had long been sparring about the propriety of dramatic performances.[10] Yoo makes Gentili "modern" by obscuring every trace of Renaissance literary culture. He reduces the tense pluralism of the early modern law of nations into a singular epic ontology. It is undeniably true that in *De Jure Belli*, Gentili wrote that "with pirates and brigands...no laws remain in force," but Yoo fails to appreciate the contingent provisionality of this claim, to register its formal, essentially epic bounds. When Gentili turned from the epic law of nations to the comic law of nations, he declared the opposite: "the pirate should be deprived of no right of which he is not expressly deprived by law."[11] Gentili became serviceable for Yoo's

[6] Gentili's putative modernity was the flipside of the "medievalist and medievalizing discourse" that became the "paradigm for comprehending the identity, culture, and motivations of America's perceived enemy during the first few years of the War on Terror," analyzed by Bruce Holsinger in his *Neomedievalism, Neoconservatism, and the War on Terror* (Chicago, IL: Prickly Paradigm Press, 2007), v, 3–33; Yoo, "Introduction," 5.
[7] Yoo, "Introduction," 13.　　　[8] Yoo, "Introduction," 8.　　　[9] Yoo, "Introduction," 12.
[10] Alberico Gentili and John Rainolds, *Latin Correspondence by Alberico Gentili and John Rainolds on Academic Drama*, ed. and trans. Leon Markowicz (Salzburg: Institut für Englische Sprache und Literatur, Universität Salzburg, 1977).
[11] Alberico Gentili, *De Jure Belli Libri Tres*, trans. John Carew Rolfe (Oxford: Clarendon Press, 1933), 2.24; Alberico Gentili, *Hispanicae Advocationis Libri Duo*, trans. Frank Frost Abbott (New York: Oxford University Press, 1921), 2.111.

ideology through the double suppression of literary culture and the generic plurality of the early modern law of nations.

Yoo was writing at a time when the American legal academy had become sharply divided between the "law and literature" movement that was seen to focus on language and rhetoric and the "law and economics" movement and its self-proclaimed monopoly on "data" and "facts." Yoo's Gentili is wholly of the latter tribe. "Gentili's method," he writes, "is to examine actual events and practices and then by a process of reasoning and deduction infer hypotheses that he proceeds to test against other cases and evidence."[12] In a tellingly limited depiction of Renaissance humanism, Yoo goes on to claim that, "Gentili does not sprinkle his works with references to Herodotus, Thucydides, Aristotle, Polybius, Livy, Plutarch, Cicero, Dio Cassius, Diodorus Siculus, Dionysius of Halicarnassus, and so on, merely to impress. Rather, these authors have provided Gentili with the raw data from which he can identify the general principles governing conduct between nations."[13] Noticeably, Yoo omits poets like Vergil and Tasso. Erasing historical difference under the concept of "modernity," Yoo uses Gentili to validate Yoo's own approach, which is to fabricate law from historical, but not literary, artifacts.

Born partly out of an unease with John Yoo's account of early modernity, which is not Yoo's alone, this book has sought to thicken reductive narratives about the early modern law of nations by introducing writers, genres, and disciplines that international law itself has often wished to keep at arm's length. More than thickening reductive narratives, however, I have proposed a literary genealogy for modern international law. Our fragmented disciplines have given us a fragmented view of history, implausibly cutting wider cultural history from the history of international law. Histories of oppression connected with, but not identical to, the history of international law teach us that there is little reason to idealize this law of nations, little reason especially to do so in ways we wouldn't idealize other kinds of law. Nevertheless, there is excellent reason to acknowledge and study it as part of early modern culture. "All universalisms are dirty," Bruce Robbins reminds us, "and it is only dirty universalisms that will help us against the powers and the agents of still dirtier ones."[14]

When Shakespeare, Grotius, Milton and other early modern writers acknowledged that the law of nations was "built," they did not have in mind a singular, vertical structure like the biblical Tower of Babel, that lonely emblem of human folly. Their "built" law of nations was "built" instead through accumulation over time. A better emblem for the law of nations than the Tower of Babel, then, might be an ordinary cemetery: a landscape spreading horizontally, assembled as needed, in unremitting conversation with time, contingency, and the rhythms of life and death. Early modern literature and the law of nations too had their conventions for managing births, deaths, soil, and marriages, their ways of signaling—and perpetuating—wealth and status. This book has argued, fundamentally, that genres were those ways.

---

[12] Yoo, "Introduction," 12.   [13] Yoo, "Introduction," 12.
[14] Bruce Robbins, *Feeling Global: Internationalism in Distress* (New York: New York University Press, 1999), 75.

Tempting though it is to suppress the literary law of nations for the sake of legal or literary purity, we do so at our peril. Westphalia-era figures like Gentili, Bacon, Grotius, and Hobbes thought theatrically, poetically, and philologically. Exchange with figures like Shakespeare and Milton was possible because literary texts worked as veins and arteries through which law of nations theory circulated in wider literate society and from which the law of nations grew. Mediating between legal technicalities and lived experience in the world, literature of the law of nations helped frame citizenship and identity as fundamentally international. Literature contributed fresh ways to approach legal problems, to practice textual interpretation, to imagine other worlds, to hypothesize about causes and consequences, to contextualize language, and to think analogically and counterfactually. It was a locus of accessible jurisprudence, and it was a form of political participation. If we forget these lessons, we might have an early modern law of nations that's cleaner and more easily conscripted for bureaucratic doctrinal needs. But we will have lost much of what's capable of building or sustaining a more democratic international law.

Bibliography

MANUSCRIPT SOURCES

Oxford, Bodleian Library
  MS Nalson 17
  MS Clarendon 127
London, British Library
  BL Add MS 48027
Derbyshire, Chatsworth House
  MSS Hobbes E.1.A

UNPUBLISHED THESES AND DISSERTATIONS

Duncan, Thomas Bentley. "Uneasy Allies: Anglo-Portuguese Commercial, Diplomatic and Maritime Relations, 1642–1662." Ph.D., History, University of Chicago, 1967.

Neustadt, Mark S. "The Making of the Instauration: Science, Politics, and Law in the Career of Francis Bacon." Ph.D., History, The Johns Hopkins University, 1987.

Pallant, Anne. "The Printed Poems of Scipio Gentili." M.A., University of Birmingham, English, 1983.

Woudhuysen, H. R. "Leicester's Literary Patronage: A Study of the English Court, 1578–1582." D. Phil., English, University of Oxford, 1981.

PRINTED SOURCES

Achinstein, Sharon. *Milton and the Revolutionary Reader.* Princeton, NJ: Princeton University Press, 1994.

Achinstein, Sharon. "Imperial Dialectic: Milton and Conquered Peoples." In *Milton and the Imperial Vision*, edited by Elizabeth Sauer and Balachandra Rajan, 67–89. Pittsburgh, PA: Duquesne University Press, 1999.

Achinstein, Sharon. "Women on Top in the Pamphlet Literature of the English Revolution." In *Feminism and Renaissance Studies*, edited by Lorna Hutson, 339–72. Oxford: Oxford University Press, 1999.

Achinstein, Sharon. *Literature and Dissent in Milton's England.* Cambridge: Cambridge University Press, 2003.

Achinstein, Sharon. "Cold War Milton." *University of Toronto Quarterly* 77, no. 3 (2008): 801–36.

Act Regarding the Rivers of Tweed and Annan, 1606. <http://www.rps.ac.uk/trans/1605/6/33>.

Act Regarding the Union of Scotland and England, 1607. <http://www.rps.ac.uk/trans/1607/3/12>.

Adair, Edward. *The Extraterratoriality of Ambassadors in the Sixteenth and Seventeenth Centuries.* New York: Longmans Green, 1929.

Akashi, Kinji. "Hobbes's Relevance to the Modern Law of Nations." *Journal of the History of International Law* 2 (2000): 199–216.

Allen, Anita, and Michael Seidl. "Cross-Cultural Commerce in Shakespeare's *The Merchant of Venice*." *American University International Law Review* 10, no. 2 (1995).

Allott, Philip. *The Health of Nations: Society and Law Beyond the State*. New York: Cambridge University Press, 2002.

Althusser, Louis. "Ideology and Ideological State Apparatuses: Notes Toward an Investigation." In *Lenin and Philosophy, and Other Essays*, translated by Ben Brewster, 85–126. London: New Left Books, 1971.

Altman, Joel B. *The Tudor Play of Mind: Rhetorical Inquiry and the Development of Elizabethan Drama*. Berkeley, CA: University of California Press, 1978.

Anderson, Benedict. *Imagined Communities: Reflections on the Origin and Spread of Nationalism*. Rev. edn. London: Verso, 2006.

Anderson, Perry. "The Intransigent Right: Michael Oakeshott, Leo Strauss, Carl Schmitt, Friedrich Von Hayek." In *Spectrum: From Left to Right in the World of Ideas*. London: Verso, 2005.

Anghie, Antony. "The Heart of My Home: Colonialism, Environmental Damage, and the Nauru Case." *Harvard International Law Journal* 34 (1993): 445.

Anon. "A True Declaration of the News That Came out of the East-Indies, with the Pinace Called the Hare." In *A True Relation of the Vniust, Cruell, and Barbarous Proceedings against the English at Amboyna in the East-Indies, by the Neatherlandish Governour and Councel There*. London, 1624.

Anon. *The Grand Tryal in Westminster-Hall of the Lord Ambassadors Brother from the King of Portugal, the Knight of Malta, and the Master of His Excellencies Horse*. London: G. Horton, 1654.

Anon. "A Treatise about the Union of England and Scotland." In *The Jacobean Union: Six Tracts of 1604*, edited by Bruce Galloway and Brian P. Levack, 39–74. Edinburgh: Scottish History Society, 1985.

Anon. "A Discourse in Defence of Admirall Jurisdiction Practised in This Kingdome." In *Hale and Fleetwood on Admiralty Jurisdiction*, edited by M. J. Prichard and D. E. C. Yale. London: Selden Society, 1993.

Appiah, Anthony. *Cosmopolitanism: Ethics in a World of Strangers*. New York: W.W. Norton, 2006.

Archer, John Michael. *Old Worlds: Egypt, Southwest Asia, India, and Russia in Early Modern English Writing*. Stanford, CA: Stanford University Press, 2001.

Arendt, Hannah. "The Decline of the Nation-State and the End of the Rights of Man." In *The Origins of Totalitarianism*, 2nd edn., 267–302. New York: Harcourt, Brace and Co., 1958.

Arendt, Hannah. *The Human Condition*. Chicago, IL: University of Chicago Press, 1958.

Aristotle. *Aristotles Politiques, or Discourses of Gouernment. Translated out of Greeke into French*. Translated by J[ohn] D[ickenson]. London: Adam Islip, 1598.

Aristotle. *Art of Rhetoric*. Translated by J. H. Freese. Vol. XXII. Loeb Classical Library, 1926.

Aristotle. *The Politics*. Translated by T. A. Sinclair. New York: Penguin Books, 1981.

Aristotle. *Poetics*. Edited by Stephen Halliwell. Loeb Classical Library. Cambridge, MA: Harvard University Press, 1995.

Aristotle. *Poetics*. Translated by Malcolm Heath. London: Penguin, 1997.

Aristotle. *Nicomachean Ethics*. Translated by Martin Ostwald. Upper Saddle River, NJ: Prentice Hall, 1999.

Armitage, David. *The Ideological Origins of the British Empire*. Cambridge: Cambridge University Press, 2000.

Armitage, David. "Is There a Pre-History of Globalization?" In *Comparison and History*, edited by Maura O'Connor and Deborah Cohen, 165–76. London: Routledge, 2004.

Armitage, David. "'The Fifty Years' Rift, Intellectual History and International Relations." *Modern Intellectual History* 1, no. 1 (2005): 97–109.

Armitage, David. *The Declaration of Independence: A Global History*. Cambridge, MA: Harvard University Press, 2007.

Armitage, David. *Foundations of Modern International Thought*. Cambridge: Cambridge University Press, 2012.

Aubrey, John. *Brief Lives*. Edited by Oliver Lawson Dick. Boston, MA: D.R. Godine, 1996.

Auden, W. H. *Lectures on Shakespeare*. Edited by Arthur C. Kirsch. Princeton, NJ: Princeton University Press, 2000.

Augustine. *The City of God against the Pagans*. Translated by Robert Dyson. Cambridge: Cambridge University Press, 1998.

Austin, John. *The Province of Jurisprudence Determined*. Edited by Wilfrid E. Rumble. Cambridge: Cambridge University Press, 1995.

Ayala, Balthazar. *De Jure et Officiis Bellicis et Disciplina Militari Libri III*. Edited by John Westlake. Translated by John Pawley Bate. Washington, DC: Carnegie Institution of Washington, 1912.

Bacon, Francis. *Considerations Touching a Warre with Spaine*. [London], 1629.

Bacon, Francis. "A Brief Discourse Touching the Happy Union of the Kingdoms of England and Scotland." In *The Works of Francis Bacon*, edited by James Spedding, Robert Leslie, and Douglas Denon Heath, Vol. X: 90–99. London: Longman, 1861.

Bacon, Francis. "Certain Articles or Considerations Touching the Union of the Kingdoms of England and Scotland." In *The Works of Francis Bacon*, edited by James Spedding, Robert Leslie, and Douglas Denon Heath, X: 218–35. London: Longman, 1861.

Bacon, Francis. "Certain Observations Made Upon a Libel Published This Present Year, 1592." In *The Works of Francis Bacon*, edited by James Spedding, Robert Leslie, and Douglas Denon Heath, VIII:146–208. London: Longman, 1861.

Bacon, Francis. "Of the Dignity and Advancement of Learning." In *The Works of Francis Bacon*, edited by James Spedding, Robert Leslie, and Douglas Denon Heath, translated by Francis Headlam, Vol. 5. London: Longman, 1861.

Bacon, Francis. "Aphorismi de Jure Gentium Majore Sive de Fontibus Justiciae et Juris." In *The Making of the Instauration: Science, Politics, and Law in the Career of Francis Bacon*, edited and translated by Mark S. Neustadt. Ph.D. dissertation, The Johns Hopkins University, 1987.

Bacon, Francis. "New Atlantis." In *Francis Bacon: A Critical Edition of the Major Works*, edited by Brian Vickers. Oxford: Oxford University Press, 1996.

Baker, David J. "'Stands Scotland Where It Did?': Shakespeare on the March." In *Shakespeare and Scotland*, edited by Willy Maley and Andrew Murphy, 20–36. Manchester: Manchester University Press, 2004.

Bakhtin, Mikhail. "Epic and Novel." In *The Dialogic Imagination: Four Essays*, translated by Michael Holquist, 3–40. Austin, TX: University of Texas Press, 1981.

Bakhtin, Mikhail. "The Problem of Speech Genres." In *Speech Genres and Other Late Essays*, edited by Caryl Emerson and Michael Holquist, translated by Vern W. McGee, 60–102. Austin, TX: University of Texas Press, 1986.

Balakrishnan, Gopal. "The Geopolitics of Separation: Response to Teschke's 'Decisions and Indecisions.'" *New Left Review* 68 (April 2011): 57–72.

Baldwin, Geoff. "Reason of State and English Parliaments, 1610–1642." *History of Political Thought* 25, no. 4 (2004): 620–41.

[Baldwin, Timothy]. *The Priviledges of an Ambassadour: Written by a Civilian to a Friend Who Desired His Opinion Concerning the Portugall Ambassadour*. [London], 1654.

Barducci, Marco. "Clement Barksdale, Translator of Grotius: Erastianism and Episcopacy in the English Church, 1651–1658." *The Seventeenth Century* 25, no. 2 (2010): 265–80.

Barducci, Marco. "Hugo Grotius and the English Republic: The Writings of Anthony Ascham, 1648–1650." *Grotiana* 32, no. 1 (November 2011): 40–63.

Barker, Andrew. *A True and Certaine Report of the Beginning, Proceedings, Overthrowes, and Now Present Estate of Captaine Ward and Danseker, the Two Late Famous Pirates from Their First Setting Foorth to This Present Time*. London: Printed by William Hall, 1609.

Baxter, Richard. *The Judgment of Non-Conformists about the Difference between Grace and Morality*. London, 1676.

Beal, Peter. "Notions in Garrison: The Seventeenth-Century Commonplace Book." In *New Ways of Looking at Old Texts: Papers of the Renaissance English Text Society, 1985–1991*, edited by W. Speed Hill, 131–47. Binghamton, NY: Renaissance English Text Society, 1993.

Beccarie de Pavie, Raimond. *Instructions for the Warres*. Translated by Paul Ive. London: Thomas Man, 1589.

Bederman, David J. *International Law and Antiquity*. Cambridge: Cambridge University Press, 2001.

Bederman, David J. *The Spirit of International Law*. University of Georgia Press, 2002.

Bederman, David J. *Custom as a Source of Law*. Cambridge: Cambridge University Press, 2010.

Belli, Pierino. *De re militari et bello tractatus*. Translated by Arrigo Cavaglieri. Oxford; London: Clarendon Press, 1936.

Bennett, Joan S. "'A Person Rais'd': Public and Private Cause in Samson Agonistes." *Studies in English Literature, 1500–1900* 18, no. 1 (1978): 155–68.

Bennett, Joan S. *Reviving Liberty: Radical Christian Humanism in Milton's Great Poems*. Cambridge, MA: Harvard University Press, 1989.

Bentham, Jeremy. *An Introduction to the Principles of Morals and Legislation*. Edited by J. H. Baker, H. L. A. Hart, and F. Rosen. Oxford: Clarendon Press, 1996.

Bentley, Richard, ed. *Paradise Lost*. London: J. Tonson, 1732.

Benton, Lauren. *A Search for Sovereignty: Law and Geography in European Empires, 1400–1900*. Cambridge: Cambridge University Press, 2009.

Benton, Lauren, and Benjamin Straumann. "Acquiring Empire by Law: From Roman Doctrine to Early Modern European Practice." *Law and History Review* 28, no. 1 (2010): 1–38.

Berkowitz, David S. "Reason of State in England and the Petition of Right, 1603–1629." In *Staatsräson: Studien Zur Geschichte Eines Politischen Begriffe*, edited by Roman Schnur. Berlin: Duncker & Humblot, 1975.

Berlant, Lauren. "On the Case." *Critical Inquiry* 33, no. 4 (2007): 663–72.

Berman, Paul Schiff. *Global Legal Pluralism: A Jurisprudence of Law beyond Borders*. Cambridge: Cambridge University Press, 2012.

Beshah, Girma, and Merid Wolde Aregay. *The Question of the Union of the Churches in Luso-Ethiopian Relations, 1500–1632*. Lisbon: Junta de Investigacões do Ultramar and Centro de Estudos Históricos Ultramarinos, 1964.

Binney, Matthew W. "Milton, Locke, and the Early Modern Framework of Cosmopolitan Right." *The Modern Language Review* 105 (2010): 31–52.

Binns, J. W. "Alberico Gentili in Defense of Poetry and Acting." *Studies in the Renaissance* 19 (1972): 224–72.

Binns, J. W. *Intellectual Culture in Elizabethan and Jacobean England: The Latin Writings of the Age*. Leeds: Francis Cairns, 1990.

Blackstone, William. *Commentaries on the Laws of England*. 2nd edn., 2 vols. Vol. 2. Oxford, 1766.

Bodin, Jean. *The Six Bookes of a Common-Weale*. Translated by Richard Knolles. London: G. Bishop, 1606.

Bodin, Jean. *On Sovereignty: Six Books Of The Commonwealth*. Translated by M.J. Tooley. Seven Treasures, 2009.

Bolton, John R. "The Global Prosecutors: Hunting War Criminals in the Name of Utopia." *Foreign Affairs*, January 1999.

Bolton, John R. "Is There Really 'Law' in International Affairs?" *Transnational Law & Contemporary Problems* 10 (2000): 1.

Borgo, Pietro Battista, and Dominicus Marcianus. *Petri Baptistae Burgi De dominio sermae Geneuensis reip. in mari Ligustico libri II*. Rome: Dominicus Marcianus, 1641.

Borschberg, Peter. "Hugo Grotius, East India Trade and the King of Johor." *Journal of Southeast Asian Studies* 30, no. 2 (1999): 225–48.

Bossy, John. *Giordano Bruno and the Embassy Affair*. London: Vintage, 1992.

Boucher, David. *Political Theories of International Relations: From Thucydides to the Present*. Oxford: Oxford University Press, 1998.

Bourdieu, Pierre. "The Force of Law: Toward a Sociology of the Juridical Field." Translated by Richard Terdiman. *Hastings Law Journal* 38 (1987): 805–53.

Bouvé, Clement L. "Private Ownership in Airspace." *Air Law Review* 1 (1930): 232–57.

Bowyer, Robert. *The Parliamentary Diary of Robert Bowyer, 1606–1607*. Edited by David Harris Willson. Minneapolis, MN: University of Minnesota Press, 1931.

Bradley, A. C. "International Morality: The United States of Europe." In *The International Crisis in Its Ethical and Psychological Aspects; Lectures Delivered in February and March, 1915*, 46–77. London: H. Milford, 1915.

Bradley, A. C. *Shakespearean Tragedy; Lectures on Hamlet, Othello*. New York: Macmillan, 1922.

Brasão, Eduardo. *The Anglo-Portuguese Alliance*. London: Sylvan Press, 1957.

Brenner, Robert. *Merchants and Revolution: Commercial Change, Political Conflict, and London's Overseas Traders, 1550–1653*. Princeton, NJ: Princeton University Press, 1993.

Brett, Annabel. *Changes of State: Nature and the Limits of the City in Early Modern Natural Law*. Princeton, NJ: Princeton University Press, 2011.

British History Online. "House of Commons Journal Volume 1: 24 February 1607 (2nd Scribe)." *Journal of the House of Commons: Volume 1*, June 22, 2003. <http://www.british-history.ac.uk/report.aspx?compid=9806>.

British History Online. "House of Commons Journal Volume 1: 26 April 1604 (2nd Scribe)." *Journal of the House of Commons: Volume 1*, June 22, 2003. <http://www.british-history.ac.uk/report.aspx?compid=5631>.

British History Online. "House of Commons Journal Volume 1: 28 May 1607 (2nd Scribe)." *Journal of the House of Commons: Volume 1*, June 22, 2003. <http://www.british-history.ac.uk/report.aspx?compid=8954>.

Brotton, Jerry. "'This Tunis, Sir, Was Carthage': Contesting Colonialism in *The Tempest*." In *Post-Colonial Shakespeares*, edited by Ania Loomba and Martin Orkin, 23–42. London: Routledge, 1998.

Brown, Clifford W. "Thucydides, Hobbes and the Derivation of Anarchy." *History of Political Thought* 8, no. 1 (1978): 33–62.

Brown, Philip Marshall. "Private versus Public International Law." *The American Journal of International Law* 36, no. 3 (1942): 448–50.

Brumbaugh, Barbara. "Jerusalem Delivered and the Allegory of Sidney's Revised Arcadia." *Modern Philology* 101, no. 3 (2004): 337–70.

Buckle, Stephen. *Natural Law and the Theory of Property: Grotius to Hume*. Oxford: Oxford University Press, 1991.

Budden, John. *Gulielmi Patteni, Cui Waynfleti Agnomen Fuit, Wintoniensis Ecclesiae Praesulis Quondam Pientissimi, Summi Angliae Cancellari, Collegiique Beatae Mariae Magdalenae apud Oxonienses Fundatoris Celeberrimi, Vita Obitusque*. Oxford: Joseph Barnes, 1602.

Burgess, Glenn. *The Politics of the Ancient Constitution: An Introduction to English Political Thought, 1603–1642*. University Park, PA: Pennsylvania State University Press, 1993.

Burke, Kenneth. *Attitudes toward History*. Berkeley, CA: University of California Press, 1984.

Burke, Peter. "A Survey of the Popularity of Ancient Historians, 1450–1700." *History and Theory* 5, no. 2 (1966): 135–52.

Burrow, Colin. *Epic Romance: Homer to Milton*. Oxford: Clarendon Press, 1993.

Butler, Judith. *Bodies That Matter: On the Discursive Limits of "Sex."* New York: Routledge, 1993.

Butler, Judith, and Gayatri Chakravorty Spivak. *Who Sings the Nation-State?: Language, Politics, Belonging*. New York: Seagull Books, 2007.

Butler, Martin. *The Stuart Court Masque and Political Culture*. Cambridge: Cambridge University Press, 2008.

Butler, Todd. "Image, Rhetoric, and Politics in the Early Thomas Hobbes." *Journal of the History of Ideas* 67, no. 3 (2006): 465–87.

Cairns, John W. "Scottish Law, Scottish Lawyers and the Status of the Union." In *A Union for Empire: Political Thought and the British Union of 1707*, edited by John Robertson. Cambridge University Press, 1995.

Calendar of State Papers and Manuscripts, Relating to English Affairs, Existing in the Archives and Collections of Venice, and in Other Libraries of Northern Italy, 1206–. London: H. M. Stationery Office. 1864.

Calendar of State Papers, Domestic 1653–4. London: H.M. Stationery Office, 1856.

Calvin, Jean. *A Commentary upon the Prophecie of Isaiah*. Translated by Clement Cotton. London: Felix Kyngston, 1609.

Camões, Luis. *Os Lusiadas*. Lisbon: Paulo Craesbeeck, 1644.

Campbell, Gordon, and Thomas N. Corns. *John Milton: Life, Work, and Thought*. Oxford: Oxford University Press, 2010.

Carey, John. "Structure and Rhetoric in Sidney's Arcadia." In *Sir Philip Sidney: An Anthology of Modern Criticism*, edited by Dennis Kay. Oxford: Clarendon Press, 1987.

Carlyle, T. J. "The Debateable Land." *Transactions of the Dumfriesshire and Galloway Natural History and Antiquarian Society*, 1, 4 (1865): 19–50.

Casanova, Pascale. *The World Republic of Letters*. Translated by M. B. DeBevoise. Cambridge, MA: Harvard University Press, 2004.

Cave, Terence. *Recognitions: A Study in Poetics*. Oxford: Oxford University Press, 1990.

Caygill, Howard. *A Kant Dictionary*. Malden, MA: Blackwell Pub., 1995.

Césaire, Aimé. *A Tempest: Based on Shakespeare's The Tempest, Adaptation for a Black Theatre*. Translated by Richard Miller. New York: TCG Translations, 2002.

Chambers, E. K. *William Shakespeare: A Study of Facts and Problems*. 2 vols. Oxford: Clarendon Press, 1930.

Chancey, Karen. "The Amboyna Massacre in English Politics, 1624–1632." *Albion* 30 (1998): 583–98.

Charlesworth, Hilary. "The Sex of the State in International Law." In *Sexing the Subject of Law*, edited by Ngaire Naffine and Rosemary J. Owens, 251–68. North Ryde, NSW: LBC Information Services, 1997.

Charlesworth, Hilary. "Feminist Reflections on the Responsibility to Protect." *Global Responsibility to Protect* 2 (2010): 232.

Charry, Brinda and Gitanjali Shahani, eds. *Emissaries in Early Modern Literature and Culture: Mediation, Transmission, Traffic, 1550–1700*. Burlington, VT: Ashgate, 2009.

Cheyney, Edward P. "International Law under Queen Elizabeth." *The English Historical Review* 20, no. 80 (October 1, 1905): 659–72.

Chomsky, Noam. *The New Military Humanism: Lessons from Kosovo*. Monroe, ME: Common Courage Press, 1999.

Christov, Theodore. "Vattel's Rousseau: Ius Gentium and the Natural Liberty of States." In *Freedom and the Construction of Europe*, II: 167–87. Cambridge: Cambridge University Press, 2013.

Claire Jowitt. "Introduction." In *Pirates?: The Politics of Plunder, 1550–1650*. Basingstoke: Palgrave Macmillan, 2006.

Clark, Arthur Melville. *Murder under Trust, Or, The Topical Macbeth and Other Jacobean Matters*. Edinburgh: Scottish Academic Press, 1981.

Clark, T. J. "For a Left with No Future." *New Left Review* 74, March–April (2012): 53–75.

Clarke, Frances. *A Briefe Reply to the Narration of Don Pantaleon Sa*. London, 1653.

Clauss, James J. "The Episode of the Lycian Farmers in Ovid's Metamorphoses." *Harvard Studies in Classical Philology* 92 (1989): 297–314.

Clegg, Cyndia Susan. *Press Censorship in Caroline England*. Cambridge: Cambridge University Press, 2008.

Cleirac, Estienne. *The Ancient Sea-Laws of Oleron, Wisby and the Hanse-Towns Still in Force: Taken out of a French Book, Intitled, Les Us & Coutumes de La Mer and Rendred into English, for Use of Navigation*. Translated by Guy Miege. London: Printed by J. Redmayne for T. Basset, 1686.

Cobbett, William, Thomas Bayly Howell, and David Jardine, eds. "The Case of the Postnati, or of the Union of the Realm of Scotland with England." In *Cobbett's State Trials*. II: 559–696. R. Bagshaw, 1809.

Cocks, Joan. *Passion and Paradox: Intellectuals Confront the National Question*. Princeton, NJ: Princeton University Press, 2002.

Cogswell, Thomas. " 'In the Power of the State': Mr Anys's Project and the Tobacco Colonies, 1626–1628." *English Historical Review* CXXIII, no. 500 (2008): 35–64.

Coke, Edward. *The Selected Writings of Sir Edward Coke*. Edited by Steve Sheppard. 3 vols. Indianapolis, IN: Liberty Fund, 2003.

Coke, Edward, Sir. *The First Part of the Institutes of the Lawes of England. Or, A Commentarie Vpon Littleton, Not the Name of a Lawyer Onely, but of the Law It Selfe*. London: [Adam Islip] for the Societie of Stationers, 1628.

Colclough, David. "Verse Libels and the Epideictic Tradition in Early Stuart England." *Huntington Library Quarterly* 69, no. 1 (2006): 15–30.

Collings, Richard. *The Weekly Intelligencer of the Common-Wealth Faithfully Communicating All Affairs Both Martial and Civil./Collected by the Same Hand Which Drew up the Kingdoms Weekly Intelligencer*. London: R.C., 1650.

Collins, Jeffrey R. *The Allegiance of Thomas Hobbes*. Oxford: Oxford University Press, 2005.

Constable, Marianne. *The Law of the Other: The Mixed Jury and Changing Conceptions of Citizenship, Law, and Knowledge.* Chicago, IL: University of Chicago Press, 1994.

Cooper, Julie E. "Vainglory, Modesty, and Political Agency in the Political Theory of Thomas Hobbes." *The Review of Politics* 72, no. 02 (2010): 241–69.

Corbett, Margery, and R. W. Lightbrown. *The Comely Frontispiece: The Emblematic Title-Page in England, 1550–1660.* London: Routledge & Kegan Paul, 1979.

Cormack, Bradin. "Practicing Law and Literature in Early Modern Studies." *Modern Philology* 101, no. 1 (August 1, 2003): 79–91.

Cormack, Bradin. *A Power to Do Justice: Jurisdiction, English Literature, and the Rise of Common Law.* Chicago, IL: University of Chicago Press, 2008.

Cormack, Bradin. "Decision, Possession: The Time of Law in *The Winter's Tale* and the Sonnets." In *Shakespeare and the Law: A Conversation Among Disciplines and Professions*, edited by Bradin Cormack, Martha Nussbaum, and Richard Strier, 44–71. Chicago, IL: University of Chicago Press, 2013.

Cover, Robert M. "Nomos and Narrative." *Harvard Law Review* 97, no. 1 (November 1983): 4–64.

Cover, Robert M. "The Folktales of Justice: Tales of Jurisdiction." In *Narrative, Violence, and the Law: The Essays of Robert Cover*, edited by Martha Minow, Michael Ryan, and Austin Sarat, 173–201. Ann Arbor, MI: University of Michigan Press, 1992.

Cowell, John. *The Interpreter.* Amsterdam: Theatrum Orbis Terrarum, 1970.

Cowley, Abraham. "To Mr. Hobbes." In *Seventeenth-Century Poetry: An Annotated Anthology*, edited by Robert Cummings, 377–80. Oxford: Wiley-Blackwell, 2000.

Cox, Rosanna. " 'The Mountains Are in Labour, Only Mice Are Born': Milton and Republican Diplomacy." *Renaissance Studies* 24, no. 3 (2009): 420–36.

Cox, Rosanna. "Neo-Roman Terms of Slavery in Samson Agonistes." *Milton Quarterly* 44, no. 1 (2010): 1–22.

Craig, Thomas. *De Unione Regnorum Britanniae Tractatus.* Edinburgh: Scottish History Society, 1909.

Craigwood, Joanna. "Sidney, Gentili, and the Poetics of Embassy." In *Diplomacy and Early Modern Culture*, edited by Robyn Adams and Rosanna Cox, 82–100. New York: Palgrave Macmillan, 2011.

Craven, Wesley Frank. *Dissolution of the Virginia Company: The Failure of a Colonial Experiment.* Oxford: Oxford University Press, 1932.

Craven, Wesley Frank. "An Introduction to the History of Bermuda: VI, the Revised Plan of Settlement." *The William and Mary Quarterly* 18, no. 1 (1938): 13–63.

Cromwell, Oliver. *Speeches, 1644–1658.* H. Frowde, 1901.

Cust, Richard. *The Forced Loan and English Politics, 1626–1628.* Oxford: Clarendon Press, 1987.

Cutler, A. Claire. "Artifice, Ideology and Paradox: The Public/Private Distinction in International Law." *Review of International Political Economy* 4, no. 2 (1997): 261–85.

Cutler, A. Claire. "Private Authority in International Trade Relations: The Case of Maritime Transport." In *Private Authority and International Affairs*, edited by Virginia Haufler, Tony Porter, and A. Claire Cutler, 283–328. Albany, NY: State University of New York Press, 1999.

D'Anghiera, Pietro Martire, Richard Eden, and Richard Willes. *The History of Trauayle in the West and East Indies, and Other Countreys Lying Eyther Way.* London: Richarde Iugge, 1577.

Davies, Mark. *The EEBO Corpus (Early English Books Online), 400 million words, 1470–1699.* 2013 <http://corpus.byu.edu/eebo/>.

Davis, George Beale. *George Sandys, Poet-Adventurer: A Study in Anglo-American Culture in the Seventeenth Century.* New York: Columbia University Press, 1955.

Davis, Paul. "Thomas Hobbes's Translations of Homer: Epic and Anticlericalism in Late Seventeenth-Century England." *The Seventeenth Century* 12 (1997): 231–55.

Davis, Paul. *Translation and the Poet's Life: The Ethics of Translating in English Culture, 1646–1726.* Oxford: Oxford University Press, 2008.

Dawson, George. *Origo Legum, Or, A Treatise of the Origin of Laws, and Their Obliging Power.* London: Richard Chiswell, 1694.

Dee, John. *General and Rare Memorials Pertayning to the Perfect Arte of Navigation.* London: John Daye, 1577.

Del Moral, Ignacio de la Rasilla. "The Study of International Law in the Spanish Short Nineteenth Century (1808–1898)." *Chicago Kent Journal of International and Comparative Law* 13, no. 2 (2013): 121–50.

Derrida, Jacques. "The Law of Genre." In *Modern Genre Theory*, edited by David Duff, 219–31. Harlow: Longman, 2000.

Derrida, Jacques. *Rogues: Two Essays on Reason.* Translated by Pascale-Anne Brault and Michael Nass. Stanford, CA: Stanford University Press, 2005.

Dickens, Charles. *David Copperfield.* Edited by Jeremy Tambling. New York: Penguin, 2004.

[Digges, Dudley]. *A True Relation of the Vniust, Cruell, and Barbarous Proceedings against the English at Amboyna in the East-Indies, by the Neatherlandish Governour and Councel There.* Facsimile. Amsterdam 1971, 1624.

Dimock, Wai-chee. "A Theory of Resonance." *PMLA* 112, no. 5 (October 1997): 1060.

Dimock, Wai-chee. *Through Other Continents: American Literature across Deep Time.* Princeton, NJ: Princeton University Press, 2006.

Dobranski, Stephen B., and Albert C. Labriola. *A Variorum Commentary on the Poems of John Milton.* Vol. III. Pittsburgh, PA: Duquesne University Press, 2009.

Donagan, Barbara. "Atrocity, War Crime, and Treason in the English Civil War." *The American Historical Review* 99, no. 4 (1994): 1137–66.

Downing, Calybute. *A Sermon Preached to the Renowned Company of the Artillery, 1 September, 1640 Designed to Compose the Present Troubles by Discovering the Enemies of the Peace of the Church and State.* London: E.G. for Iohn Rothwell, 1641.

Doyle, John P. "Francisco Suarez on the Law of Nations." In *Religion and International Law*, edited by Mark W. Janis and Carolyn Evans, 103–20. The Hague: Martinus Nijhoff Publishers, 1999.

Drysdall, Denis L. "Alciato and the Grammarians: The Law and the Humanities in the Parergon Iuris Libri Duodecim." *Renaissance Quarterly* 56, no. 3 (2003): 695–722.

Duncan-Jones, Katherine. *Sir Philip Sidney: Courtier Poet.* London: Hamish Hamilton, 1991.

Dust, Philip. "Alberico Gentili's Commentaries on Utopian War." *Moreana* 37 (1973): 31–40.

Dzelzainis, Martin. "The Politics of *Paradise Lost.*" In *The Oxford Handbook of Milton*, edited by Nicholas McDowell and Nigel Smith, 547–68. Oxford: Oxford University Press, 2009.

Edelstein, Dan. "War and Terror: The Law of Nations from Grotius to the French Revolution." *French Historical Studies* 31, no. 2 (Spring 2008): 229–62.

Eden, Kathy. *Poetic and Legal Fiction in the Aristotelian Tradition.* Princeton, NJ: Princeton University Press, 1986.

Elderfield, Christopher. *The Civil Right of Tythes.* London: Tho. Newcomb, for John Holden, 1650.

Ellison, James. *George Sandys: Travel, Colonialism, and Tolerance in the Seventeenth Century.* Cambridge: D.S. Brewer, 2002.

Empson, William. *Milton's God.* Rev. edn. London: Chatto & Windus, 1965.

Empson, William. *The Complete Poems of William Empson.* Edited by John Haffenden. Gainesville, FL: University Press of Florida, 2001.

English, Peter. *The Survey of Policy: Or, A Free Vindication of the Commonwealth of England, against Salmasius, and Other Royallists.* Leith, 1654.

Erasmus, Desiderius. "The Complaint of Peace." In *The Praise of Folly and Other Writings: A New Translation with Critical Commentary*, translated by Robert Martin Adams. New York: Norton, 1989.

Erlich, Ludwik. "The Development of International Law as a Science." *Recueil Des Cours* 105 (1962): 173–262.

Erskine, Toni, and Richard Ned Lebow, eds. *Tragedy and International Relations.* New York: Palgrave Macmillan, 2012.

Euben, J. Peter. *The Tragedy of Political Theory: The Road Not Taken.* Princeton, NJ: Princeton University Press, 1990.

Eyffinger, Arthur. "'La Plus Belle Des Histoires'. Grotius' Drama on Joseph in Egypt in the Tradition of the Theme." *Grotiana* 8, no. 1 (1987): 80–90.

Eyffinger, Arthur. "Introduction." In *Sophompaneas, 1635*, by Hugo Grotius, translated by Arthur Eyffinger. *The Poetry of Hugo Grotius*, 4 [A–B]. Assen: Van Gorcum, 1992.

Eyffinger, Arthur. "The Fourth Man: Stoic Tradition in Grotian Drama." In *Grotius and the Stoa*, edited by Hans W. Blom and Laurens C. Winkel, 117–56. Assen: Royal van Gorcum, 2004.

Fallon, Robert Thomas. *Milton in Government.* University Park, PA: Pennsylvania State University Press, 1993.

Fallon, Stephen M. *Milton's Peculiar Grace: Self-Representation and Authority.* Ithaca, NY: Cornell University Press, 2007.

Fassbender, Bardo. "Stories of War and Peace: On Writing the History of International Law in the 'Third Reich' and After." *European Journal of International Law* 13, no. 2 (2002): 479–512.

Fawcett, James, and Peter North. *Cheshire and North's Private International Law.* London: Butterworths, 2005.

Felperin, Howard. "'Tongue-Tied Our Queen?': The Deconstruction of Presence in The Winter's Tale." In *Shakespeare and the Question of Theory*, edited by Patricia Parker and Geoffrey Hartman, 3–18. London: Methuen, 1985.

Ferguson, Arthur B. *Clio Unbound: Perceptions of the Social and Cultural Past in Renaissance England.* Durham, NC: Duke University Press, 1979.

Filmer, Robert. *Patriarcha and Other Writings.* Edited by J. P. Sommerville. Cambridge: Cambridge University Press, 1991.

Fish, Stanley. "The Law Wishes to Have a Formal Existence." In *The Fate of Law*, edited by Austin Sarat and Thomas R Kearns, 159–208. Ann Arbor: University of Michigan Press, 1991.

Fish, Stanley. "Why Milton Matters; Or, Against Historicism." *Milton Studies* 44 (2005): 1–12.

Fish, Stanley. "How Hobbes Works." In *Visionary Milton: Essays on Prophecy and Violence*, edited by Peter E. Medine, John T. Shawcross, and David V. Urban, 65–88. Pittsburgh, PA: Duquesne University Press, 2010.

Fitzmaurice, Andrew. *Humanism and America: An Intellectual History of English Colonisation, 1500–1625.* Cambridge: Cambridge University Press, 2003.

Fitzmaurice, Andrew. "Moral Uncertainty in the Dispossession of Native Americans." In *The Atlantic World and Virginia, 1550–1624*, edited by Peter C. Mancall, 383–409. Chapel Hill, NC: The Omohundro Institute, 2007.

Flemion, Jess. "The Struggle for the Petition of Right in the House of Lords: The Study of an Opposition Party Victory." *Journal of Modern History* 45, no. 2 (1973): 183–210.

Flemion, Jess. "A Savings to Satisfy All: The House of Lords and the Meaning of the Petition of Right." *Parliamentary History* 10, no. 1 (1991): 27–44.

Florio, John. *Queen Anna's New World of Words, or Dictionarie of the Italian and English Tongues, Collected and Newly Much Augmented by Iohn Florio*. London, 1611.

Flynn, Dennis O., and Arturo Giraldez. "Globalization Began in 1571." In *Globalization and Global History*, edited by Barry K. Gills and William R. Thompson, 232–47. New York: Routledge, 2006.

Ford, John. "The Law of the Sea and the Two Unions." In *Anglo-Scottish Relations from 1603 to 1900*, edited by T. C. Smout, 127–41. Oxford: Oxford University Press, 2005.

Forman, Valerie. *Tragicomic Redemptions: Global Economics and the Early Modern English Stage*. Philadelphia, PA: University of Pennsylvania Press, 2008.

Foucault, Michel. *The Order of Things: An Archaeology of the Human Sciences*. New York: Vintage Books, 1970.

Foucault, Michel. *The History of Sexuality, Volume 1: The Will to Knowledge*. Translated by Robert Hurley. 3 vols. London: Penguin Books, 1990.

Franssen, Paul. "Canute or Neptune? The Dominion of the Seas and Two Versions of *The Tempest*." *Cahiers Élisabéthains* 57 (2000): 79–94.

Frye, Northrop. *Narrative Dynamics: Essays on Time, Plot, Closure, and Frames*. Edited by Brian Richardson. Columbus, OH: Ohio State University Press, 2002.

Fuchs, Barbara. "Conquering Islands: Contextualizing *The Tempest*." *Shakespeare Quarterly* 48, no. 1 (1997): 45–62.

Fulbeck[e], William. *A Parallele or Conference of the Ciuill Law, the Canon Law, and the Common Law of This Realme of England VVherein the Agreement and Disagreement of These Three Lawes, and the Causes and Reasons of the Said Agreement and Disagreement, Are Opened and Discussed*. London: [Adam Islip for] Thomas Wight, 1601.

Fulbeck[e], William. *The Pandectes of the Law of Nations: Contayning Severall Discourses of the Questions... of Law, Wherein the Nations of the World Doe Consent and Accord. Giving Great Light to the Understanding and Opening of the Principall Objects... of the Civill Law, and Common Law of His Realme of England*. London: Thomas Wight, 1602.

Fulton, Thomas Wemyss. *The Sovereignty of the Sea: An Historical Account of the Claims of England to the Dominion of the British Seas, and of the Evolution of the Territorial Waters*. London: W. Blackwood, 1911.

Gager, William. *William Gager: The Complete Works*. Translated by Dana Ferrin Sutton. 4 vols. New York: Garland, 1994.

Galloway, Bruce, and Brian P. Levack, eds. *The Jacobean Union: Six Tracts of 1604*. Edinburgh: Scottish History Society, 1985.

Galloway, Bruce. *The Union of England and Scotland, 1603–1608*. Edinburgh: J. Donald, 1986.

Garrison, James D. "War: Turnus and 'Pietas' in the Later Renaissance." In *Pietas from Vergil to Dryden*, 161–204. University Park, PA: Pennsylvania State University Press, 1992.

Gayton, Edmund. "The Lawyer's Duel, or Two Sonnets Composed on Grotius's Mare Liberum and Selden's Mare Clausum." 1655.

Gellinek, Christian. *Hugo Grotius*. Boston: Twayne Publishers, 1983.

Gentili, Alberico. *De Legationibus Libri Tres*. London: T[homas] Vautrollerius, 1585.

Gentili, Alberico. *De Iure Belli Commentatio Secunda*. London: Iohannes Wolfius, 1588.

Gentili, Alberico. *De Jure Belli Libri III*. Hanover: Guilielmus Antonius, 1598.

Gentili, Alberico. *Hispanicae Advocationis Libri Duo*. Translated by Frank Frost Abbott. 2 vols. New York: Oxford University Press, 1921.

Gentili, Alberico. *De Legationibvs Libri Tres*. Translated by Gordon Jennings Laing. 2 vols. Vol. II. Classics of International Law 12. New York: Oxford University Press, 1924.

Gentili, Alberico. *De Jure Belli Libri Tres*. Translated by John Carew Rolfe. 2 vols. Oxford: Clarendon Press, 1933.

Gentili, Alberico. *Commentary on the Third Law of the Title of the Code "On Teachers and Doctors."* Translated by J. W. Binns. In "Alberico Gentili in Defense of Poetry and Acting." *Studies in the Renaissance* 19 (1972): 224–72.

Gentili, Alberico, and John Rainolds. *Latin Correspondence by Alberico Gentili and John Rainolds on Academic Drama*. Edited and translated by Leon Markowicz. Salzburg: Institut für Englische Sprache und Literatur, Universität Salzburg, 1977.

Gentili, Alberico. *The Wars of the Romans: A Critical Edition and Translation of De Armis Romanis*. Edited by Benedict Kingsbury and Benjamin Straumann. Translated by David Lupher. New York: Oxford University Press, 2011.

Gentili, Scipione. *Scipii Gentilis Nereus Siue De Natali Elizabethæ Illustriss. Philippi Sydnæi Filiæ*. London: John Wolfe, 1585.

Gentili, Scipione. *Annotationi Di Scipio Gentili Sopra La Gierusalemme Liberata Di Torquato Tasso*. London: John Wolfe, 1586.

Gerard, John. *The True and Perfect Speeches of Colonel John Gerhard... Likewise, the Speech of the Portugal Ambassadors Brother upon the Scaffold*. London: C. Horton, 1654.

Gilbert, Sandra M., and Susan Gubar. *The Madwoman in the Attic: The Woman Writer and the Nineteenth-Century Literary Imagination*. New Haven, CT: Yale University Press, 1979.

Glanville, Luke. *Sovereignty and the Responsibility to Protect: A New History*. Chicago, IL: University of Chicago Press, 2014.

Glover, Henry. *Ekdikesis or A Discourse of Vengeance*. London: Henry Brome, 1664.

Godolphin, John. *Synēgoros Thalassios. A View of the Admiral Jurisdiction. Wherein the Most Material Points Concerning That Jurisdiction Are Fairly and Submissively Discussed. As Also Divers of the Laws, Customes, Rights, and Privileges of the High Admiralty of England by Ancient Records, and Other Arguments of Law Asserted. Whereunto Is Added by Way of Appendix an Extract of the Ancient Laws of Oleron*. London: Printed by W. Godbid for Edmund Paxton, 1661.

Goldie, Mark. "Edmund Bohun and Jus Gentium in the Revolution Debate, 1689–1693." *The Historical Journal* 20, no. 03 (1977): 569–86.

Goldie, Mark. "The Context of 'The Foundations.'" In *Rethinking the Foundations of Modern Political Thought*, edited by Annabel S. Brett, James Tully, and Hamilton-Bleakley, 3–19. Cambridge: Cambridge University Press, 2006.

Goodrich, Peter. "On the Relational Aesthetics of International Law." *Journal of the History of International Law* 10 (2008): 321.

Goodrich, Peter. "Law." In *Critical Terms for Media Studies*, edited by W. J. T. Mitchell and Mark B. N. Hansen. Chicago, IL: University of Chicago Press, 2010.

Gossett, Suzanne. "Introduction." In *Pericles*. London: Arden Shakespeare, 2004.

Grafton, Anthony. *What Was History?: The Art of History in Early Modern Europe*. Cambridge: Cambridge University Press, 2007.

Grafton, Anthony. *Worlds Made by Words: Scholarship and Community in the Modern West*. Cambridge, MA: Harvard University Press, 2009.

Graswinckel, Dirk. *Theod. J. F. Graswinckelii j.c. maris liberi vindiciae, adversus Petrum Baptistam Burgum Ligustici maritimi dominii assertorem.* Hagae-Comitum: ex typogr. Adriani Vlac, 1652.

Gray, Charles M. *The Writ of Prohibition: Jurisdiction in Early Modern English Law.* New York: Oceana Publications, 1994.

Green, Roland. "Fictions of Immanence, Fictions of Embassy." In *The Project of Prose in Early Modern Europe and the New World,* edited by Elizabeth Fowler and Roland Greene. Cambridge: Cambridge University Press, 1997.

Greenberg, Lynne A. "Dalila's 'Feminine Assaults': The Gendering and Engendering of Crime in Samson Agonistes." In *Altering Eyes: New Perspectives on "Samson Agonistes",* edited by M. R. Kelley and Joseph Wittreich, 192–219. Newark, DE: University of Delaware Press, 2002.

Greenblatt, Stephen. *Renaissance Self-Fashioning: From More to Shakespeare.* Chicago, IL: University of Chicago Press, 1980.

Greenblatt, Stephen. *Shakespearean Negotiations: The Circulation of Social Energy in Renaissance England.* Berkeley, CA: University of California Press, 1989.

Greenblatt, Stephen. "What Is the History of Literature?" *Critical Inquiry* 23, no. 3 (1997): 460–81.

Greenblatt, Stephen, Jean E. Howard, and Katharine Eisaman Maus, eds. *The Norton Shakespeare.* London: W. W. Norton & Company, 1997.

Greenfield, Matthew. "1 Henry IV: Metatheatrical Britain." In *British Identities and English Renaissance Literature,* edited by David J. Baker and Willy Maley, 71–80. Cambridge: Cambridge University Press, 2002.

Gregoire, Abbe. "Declaration of the Law of Nations." In *The Progressive Development of International Law; Proposed Declaration on Rights and Duties of States,* translated by Manley O. Hudson, 1–2. Boston, MA: American Bar Association, Committee for Peace and Law Through United Nations, 1947.

Gregory, Tobias. *From Many Gods to One: Divine Action in Renaissance Epic.* Chicago, IL: University of Chicago Press, 2006.

Grene, David, ed. *The Peloponnesian War: The Complete Thomas Hobbes Translation.* Translated by Thomas Hobbes. Chicago, IL: University of Chicago Press, 1989.

Grossman, Edith. *Why Translation Matters.* New Haven, CT: Yale University Press, 2010.

Grotius, Hugo. *Christs Passion: A Tragedy. With Annotations.* Translated by George Sandys. STC 12397.5. London: John Letat, 1640.

Grotius, Hugo. *A Treatise of the Antiquity of the Battaver, Which Is Now the Hollanders.* Translated by Thomas Woods. London, 1649.

Grotius, Hugo. *Hugo Grotius His Sophompaneas, or Ioseph. A Tragedy. With Annotations.* Edited and translated by Francis Goldsmith. London: W.H., 1652.

Grotius, Hugo. *The Illustrious Hugo Grotius of the Law of Warre and Peace With Annotations. III. Parts. And Memorials of the Author's Life and Death.* Translated by Clement Barksdale. London: T. Warren, for William Lee, 1654.

Grotius, Hugo. *Opera Omnia Theologica.* Edited by Pieter de Groot. 3 vols. Amsterdam, 1679.

Grotius, Hugo. "Eclogues." In *Select Translations from the Works of Sannazarius H. Grotius, Bapt. Amaltheus, D. Heinsius, G. Buchanan, and M. Hier. Vida. To Which Is Prefix'd, Some Account of the Authors.,* translated by John Rooke. London, 1726.

Grotius, Hugo. *The Freedom of the Seas; Or, The Right Which Belongs to the Dutch to Take Part in the East Indian Trade;* Edited by James Brown Scott. Translated by Ralph Van Deman Magoffin. New York: Oxford University Press, 1916.

Grotius, Hugo. "Adamus Exul." In *The Celestial Cycle; the Theme of Paradise Lost in World Literature with Translations of the Major Analogues.*, translated by Watson Kirkconnell. Toronto: University of Toronto Press, 1952.

Grotius, Hugo. *Original Poetry, 1604–1608.* Edited by Edwin Rabbie. Assen: Van Gorcum, 1992.

Grotius, Hugo. *Sophompaneas, 1635.* Edited by Arthur Eyffinger and B.L Meulenbroek. Translated by Arthur Eyffinger. The Poetry of Hugo Grotius, 4 [A-B]. Assen: Van Gorcum, 1992.

Grotius, Hugo. *Hugo Grotius "Commentarius in theses XI": an early treatise on sovereignty, the just war, and the legitimacy of the Dutch revolt.* Edited and translated by Peter Borschberg. New York: P. Lang, 1994.

Grotius, Hugo. *The Free Sea.* Edited by David Armitage. Translated by Richard Hakluyt. Natural Law and Enlightenment Classics. Indianapolis, IN: Liberty Fund, 2004.

Grotius, Hugo. *The Rights of War and Peace.* Edited by Richard Tuck and Jean Barbeyrac. Translated by [John Morris]. 3 vols. Indianapolis, IN: Liberty Fund, 2005.

Grotius, Hugo. *Commentary on the Law of Prize and Booty.* Edited by Martine Julia Van Ittersum. Indianapolis, IN: Liberty Fund, 2006.

Guarini, Giambattista. "The Compendium of Tragicomic Poetry." In *Literary Criticism: Plato to Dryden*, edited and translated by Allan H. Gilbert, 504–33. Detroit: Wayne State University Press, 1962.

Guilhot, Nicolas. "American Katechon: When Political Theology Became International Relations Theory." *Constellations* 17, no. 2 (2010): 224–53.

Habermas, Jürgen. "The Horrors of Autonomy: Carl Schmitt in English." In *The New Conservatism: Cultural Criticism and the Historians' Debate*, translated by Shierry Weber Nicholsen, 128–39. Studies in Contemporary German Social Thought. Cambridge, MA: MIT Press, 1989.

Habermas, Jürgen. *The Divided West.* Cambridge, UK: Polity, 2006.

Haggenmacher, Peter. "Grotius and Gentili: A Reassessment of Thomas E. Holland's Inaugural Lecture." In *Hugo Grotius and International Relations*, edited by Hedley Bull, Benedict Kinsbury, and Adam Roberts. Oxford: Clarendon Press, 1990.

Hall, Henry Marion. *Idylls of Fishermen: A History of the Literary Species.* New York: Columbia University Press, 1912.

Hall, John. *Mercurius Politicus.* London: Robert White, 1650–1660, 1650.

Halliday, Paul D. *Habeas Corpus: From England to Empire.* Cambridge, MA: Belknap Press of Harvard University Press, 2010.

Hamilton, Donna B. *Virgil and The Tempest: The Politics of Imitation.* Columbus, OH: Ohio State University Press, 1990.

Hamilton, Donna B. "The Winter's Tale and the Language of Union, 1604–1610." *Shakespeare Studies* 21 (1993): 228–52.

Hammersley, Rachel. *French Revolutionaries and English Republicans: The Cordeliers Club, 1790–1794.* Rochester, NY: Boydell Press, 2005.

Hammond, Henry. *A Second Defence of the Learned Hugo Grotius.* London: J. Flesher, for Richard Royston, 1655.

Hampton, Timothy. *Writing from History: The Rhetoric of Exemplarity in Renaissance Literature.* Ithaca, NY: Cornell University Press, 1990.

Hampton, Timothy. *Fictions of Embassy: Literature and Diplomacy in Early Modern Europe.* Ithaca, NY: Cornell University Press, 2009.

Hanford, James Holly. "The Chronology of Milton's Private Studies." *PMLA* 36, no. 2 (1921): 251–314.

Hardin, Garrett. "The Tragedy of the Commons." *Science*, December 13, 1968: 1243–8.

Harding, Christopher. "'Hostis Humani Generis' – the Pirate as Outlaw in the Early Modern Law of the Sea." In *Pirates?: The Politics of Plunder, 1550–1650*. Basingstoke: Palgrave Macmillan, 2006.

Harlan, Susan. "'Certain Condolements, Certain Vails': Staging Rusty Armour in Shakespeare's *Pericles*." *Early Theatre* 11, no. 2 (2008): 129–40.

Harrison, Peter. "'Fill the Earth and Subdue It': Biblical Warrants for Colonization in Seventeenth Century England." *Journal of Religious History* 29, no. 1 (2005): 3–24.

Harrison, S. J. "Some Views of the Aeneid in the Twentieth Century." In *Oxford Readings in Vergil's Aeneid*, edited by S. J. Harrison, 1–20. Oxford: Oxford University Press, 1990.

Haugen, Kristine Louise. "A French Jesuit's Lectures on Vergil, 1582–1583: Jacques Sirmond between Literature, History, and Myth." *The Sixteenth Century Journal* 30, no. 4 (1999): 20.

Hayward, John. *A Treatise of Union of the Two Realmes of England and Scotland*. London: F[elix] K[ingston] for C[uthbert] B[urby], 1604.

Hearsey, Marguerite. "Sidney's 'Defense of Poesy' and Amyot's 'Preface' in North's 'Plutarch': A Relationship." *Studies in Philology* 30, no. 4 (1933): 535–50.

Heinsius, Daniel. *On Plot in Tragedy*. Translated by P. R. Sellin and J. McManmon. Northridge, CA: San Fernando Valley State College, 1971.

Helgerson, Richard. *Forms of Nationhood: The Elizabethan Writing of England*. Chicago, IL: University of Chicago Press, 1992.

Heller, Kevin Jon. *The Nuremberg Military Tribunals and the Origins of International Criminal Law*. Oxford: Oxford University Press, 2011.

Henke, Robert. *Pastoral Transformations: Italian Tragicomedy and Shakespeare's Late Plays*. Newark, DE: University of Delaware Press, 1997.

Henke, Robert. "Border-Crossing in the Commedia dell'Arte." In *Transnational Exchange in Early Modern Theater*, edited by Eric Nicholson and Robert Henke, 19–34. Burlington, VT: Ashgate, 2008.

Henke, Robert, and Eric Nicholson. *Transnational Exchange in Early Modern Theater*. Burlington, VT: Ashgate, 2008.

Heywood, Thomas. *The Captives*. Edited by Arthur Brown. London: The Malone Society, 1953.

Hill, Christopher. "Covenant Theology and the Concept of a Public Person." In *The Collected Essays of Christopher Hill*, 3: 300–24. Amherst: University of Massachusetts Press, 1985.

Hill, Christopher. "The English Revolution and the Brotherhood of Man." In *Puritanism and Revolution: Studies in Interpretation of the English Revolution of the Seventeenth Century*, 112–38. New York: St. Martin's Press, 1997.

Hill, L. M. *Bench and Bureaucracy: The Public Career of Sir Julius Caesar, 1580–1636*. Stanford, CA: Stanford University Press, 1988.

Hillier, Russell. "Grotius's Christus Patiens and Milton's Samson Agonistes." *The Explicator* 65, no. 1 (2006): 9–13.

Hillier, Russell. *Milton's Messiah: The Son of God in the Works of John Milton*. Oxford: Oxford University Press, 2011.

Hobbes, Thomas, trans. *Eight Bookes of the Peloponnesian Warre*. London: Henry Seile, 1629.

Hobbes, Thomas. *Behemoth, the history of the causes of the civil wars of England, from 1640 to 1660* in *Tracts of Mr. Thomas Hobbs of Malmsbury*. London: W. Crooke, 1682.

Hobbes, Thomas. *Leviathan*. Edited by C. B. MacPherson. Harmondsworth: Penguin Classics, 1968.

Hobbes, Thomas. *Leviathan: With Selected Variants from the Latin Edition of 1668*. Edited by Edwin Curley. Indianapolis, IN: Hackett, 1994.

Hobbes, Thomas. "Verse Autobiography." In *Leviathan: With Selected Variants from the Latin Edition of 1668*, edited by Edwin M. Curley, 1994.

Hobbes, Thomas, Noel Reynolds, and Arlene Saxonhouse. *Three Discourses: A Critical Modern Edition of Newly Identified Work of the Young Hobbes*. Chicago, IL: University of Chicago Press, 1995.

Hobbes, Thomas. *On the Citizen*. Edited by Richard Tuck. Translated by Michael Silverthorne. Cambridge: Cambridge University Press, 1998.

Hobbes, Thomas. *The Elements of Law, Natural and Politic: Part I, Human Nature, Part II, De Corpore Politico; with Three Lives*. Edited by J. C. A Gaskin. Oxford: Oxford University Press, 2008.

Hobbes, Thomas. *Translations of Homer*. Edited by Eric Nelson. 2 vols. The Clarendon Edition of the Works of Thomas Hobbes. Oxford: Clarendon Press, 2008.

Hoeflich, M. H. "The Lawyer as Pragmatic Reader: The History of Legal Common-Placing." *Arkansas Law Review* 55, no. 87 (2002): 88–121.

Hoekstra, Kinch. "The 'De Facto' Turn in Hobbes's Political Philosophy." In *Leviathan after 350 Years*, edited by Tom Sorell and Luc Foisneau, 33–74. Oxford: Oxford University Press, 2004.

Hoekstra, Kinch. "Gentili, Thucydides, and the Justification of Pre-Emption." In *Alberico Gentili: La Salvaguardia Dei Beni Culturali Nel Diritto Internazionale*. Milan: Giuffrè editore, 2008.

Hoekstra, Kinch. "Thucydides and the Bellicose Beginnings of Modern Political Theory." In *Thucydides and the Modern World*. Cambridge: Cambridge University Press, 2012.

Holland, Peter. "Coasting in the Mediterranean: The Journeyings of Pericles." In *Charting Shakespearean Waters: Text and Theatre*, edited by Niels Bugge Hansen and Søs Haugaard. Copenhagen: Museum Tusculanum Press, University of Copenhagen, 2005.

Holland, Thomas Erskine. *Studies in International Law*. Oxford: Clarendon Press, 1898.

Holsinger, Bruce W. *Neomedievalism, Neoconservatism, and the War on Terror*. Chicago, IL: Prickly Paradigm Press, 2007.

Hood, Kirsty. "Roots and Context of the Conflict of Laws Within the UK." In *The Conflict of Laws Within the UK*, 1st edn., 1–33. Oxford University Press, 2007.

Hooker, Richard. *Of the Laws of Ecclesiastical Polity: Preface, Book I, Book VIII*. Edited by Arthur Stephen McGrade. Cambridge: Cambridge University Press, 1989.

Horace. *Satires, Epistles and Ars Poetica, with an English Translation*. Translated by H. Rushton Fairclough. Loeb Classical Library. Cambridge, MA: Harvard University Press, 1926.

Hotman, François. *Quæstionum Illustrium Liber*. Paris, 1573.

Hotman, Jean. *The Ambassador*. London: James Shawe, 1603.

Hotman, Jean. *L'ambassadeur, Par Le Sieur de Vill. H.*, 1603.

Howard, Jean E. *Theater of a City The Places of London Comedy, 1598–1642*. Philadelphia: University of Pennsylvania Press, 2007.

Howell, Thomas Jones, William Cobbett, and David Jardine. *Cobbett's State Trials*. Vol. V. R. Bagshaw, 1810.

Huber, Ulrik. "De Conflictu Legum Diversarum in Diversis Imperiis." Translated by Ernest G. Lorenzen. *Illinois Law Review* 13 (1918): 375.

Hunt, Arnold. "Book Trade Patents, 1603–1640." In *The Book Trade & Its Customers, 1450–1900: Historical Essays for Robin Myers*, edited by Arnold Hunt, Giles Mandelbrote, and Alison Shell. Winchester: Oak Knoll Press, 1997.

Hunt, Lynn. *Inventing Human Rights: A History*. New York: W.W. Norton & Co, 2007.

Hutson, Lorna. *The Invention of Suspicion: Law and Mimesis in Shakespeare and Renaissance Drama*. Oxford: Oxford University Press, 2007.

Huxley, Andrew. "The *Aphorismi* and a *Discourse of Laws*: Bacon, Cavendish, and Hobbes 1615–1620." *The Historical Journal* 47, no. 2 (2004): 399–412.

International Commission on Intervention and State Sovereignty, Gareth J Evans, Sahnoun, and International Development Research Centre (Canada). *The Responsibility to Protect Report of the International Commission on Intervention and State Sovereignty*. Ottawa: International Development Research Centre, 2001. <http://site.ebrary.com/id/10119691>.

Isidore of Seville. *The Etymologies of Isidore of Seville*. Translated by Stephen A. Barney. Cambridge: Cambridge University Press, 2007.

Jackson, MacDonald P. *Defining Shakespeare: Pericles as Test Case*. Oxford: Oxford University Press, 2003.

James VI and I. *King James VI and I: Political Writings*. Edited by Johann P. Sommerville. Cambridge: Cambridge University Press, 1995.

Jameson, Fredric. *Archaeologies of the Future: The Desire Called Utopia and Other Science Fictions*. London: Verso, 2007.

Janis, M. W. "Jeremy Bentham and the Fashioning of 'International Law.' " *The American Journal of International Law* 78, no. 2 (1984): 405–18.

Jardine, Lisa, and Anthony Grafton. "'Studied for Action': How Gabriel Harvey Read His Livy." *Past & Present* 129, no. 1 (1990): 30–78.

Johns, Fleur, Richard Joyce, and Sundhya Pahuja, eds. *Events: The Force of International Law*. London: Routledge-Cavendish, 2011.

Johnston, David. *Roman Law in Context*. Cambridge: Cambridge University Press, 1999.

Jonson, Ben. "Ode to Himself." In *Ben Jonson: The Complete Poems*, ed. George Parfitt, 282–4. New York: Penguin Classics, 1975.

Jordan, Constance. "Woman's Rule in Sixteenth-Century British Political Thought." *Renaissance Quarterly* 40, no. 3 (1987): 421–51.

Jordan, Constance. *Shakespeare's Monarchies: Ruler and Subject in the Romances*. Ithaca, NY: Cornell University Press, 1997.

Justinian. *The Digest of Justinian*. Translated by Alan Watson. 4 vols. Philadelphia, PA: University of Pennsylvania Press, 1985.

Justinian. *Justinian's Institutes*. Translated by Peter Birks and Grant McLeod. Ithaca, NY: Cornell University Press, 1987.

Kahn, Victoria. *Machiavellian Rhetoric: From the Counter-Reformation to Milton*. Princeton, NJ: Princeton University Press, 1994.

Kahn, Victoria. *Wayward Contracts: The Crisis of Political Obligation in England, 1640–1674*. Princeton, NJ: Princeton University Press, 2004.

Kahn, Victoria. "Disappointed Nationalism: Milton in the Context of Seventeenth-Century Debates about the Nation-State." In *Early Modern Nationalism and Milton's England*, edited by David Loewenstein and Paul Stevens, 249–72. Toronto: University of Toronto Press, 2008.

Kahn-Freund, Otto. *The Growth of Internationalism in English Private International Law*. Jerusalem: Magnes Press, Hebrew University, 1960.

Kallendorf, Craig. *In Praise of Aeneas: Virgil and Epideictic Rhetoric in the Early Italian Renaissance*. Hanover, NH: University Press of New England, 1989.

Kallendorf, Craig. *The Other Virgil: "Pessimistic" Readings of the Aeneid in Early Modern Culture*. Oxford: Oxford University Press, 2007.

Kant, Immanuel. *Political Writings*. Edited by Hans Siegbert Reiss. Translated by Hugh Nisbet. 2nd edn. Cambridge: Cambridge University Press, 1991.

Kastan, David Scott. *Shakespeare After Theory*. New York: Routledge, 1999.

Kasten, Madeleine. "Translation Studies—Vondel's Appropriation of Grotius's Sophompaneas (1635)." In *Joost van Den Vondel (1587–1679) Dutch Playwright in the Golden Age*, edited by Jan Bloemendal and Frans-Willem Korsten, 249–69. Leiden; Boston: Brill, 2012.

Kavenagh, W. Keith, ed. *Foundations of Colonial America: A Documentary History*. New York: Chelsea House, 1973.

Kay, Dennis, ed. *Sir Philip Sidney: An Anthology of Modern Criticism*. Oxford: Clarendon Press, 1987.

Keblusek, Marika. "Commerce and Cultural Transfer: Merchants as Agents in the Early Modern World of Books." In *Kultureller Austausch: Bilanz Und Perspektiven Der Frühneuzeitforschung*, edited by Michael North, 297–307. Cologne: Böhlau, 2009.

Keeler, Mary Frear, Maija Jansson Cole, and William B. Bidwell, eds. *Proceedings in Parliament, 1628*. 5 vols. Vol. V. New Haven, CT: Yale University Press, 1983.

Keen, Maurice Hugh. *The Laws of War in the Late Middle Ages*. London: Routledge & Kegan Paul, 1965.

Keene, Edward. *International Political Thought: A Historical Introduction*. Cambridge, UK; Malden, MA: Polity, 2005.

Kelley, Donald R. *Foundations of Modern Historical Scholarship: Language, Law, and History in the French Renaissance*. New York: Columbia University Press, 1970.

Kelley, Donald R. "The Rise of Legal History in the Renaissance." *History and Theory* 9, no. 2 (1970): 174–94.

Kelley, Donald R. *François Hotman; a Revolutionary's Ordeal*. Princeton, NJ: Princeton University Press, 1973.

Kelley, Donald R. "History, English Law and the Renaissance: A Rejoinder." *Past and Present*, no. 72 (1976): 143–6.

Kelley, Donald R. "Law." In *The Cambridge History of Political Thought, 1450–1700*, edited by J. H. Burns and Mark Goldie, 66–94. Cambridge: Cambridge University Press, 1991.

Kelley, Donald R., and David Harris Sacks. "Introduction." In *The Historical Imagination in Early Modern Britain: History, Rhetoric, and Fiction, 1500–1800*. Cambridge: Cambridge University Press, 1997.

Kennedy, David. "Images of Religion in International Law." In *Religion and International Law*, edited by Mark W. Janis and Carolyn Evans, 145–53. The Hague: Martinus Nijhoff Publishers, 1999.

Kerrigan, John. *Archipelagic English: Literature, History, and Politics, 1603–1707*. Oxford: Oxford University Press, 2008.

Kidd, Colin. *Union and Unionisms: Political Thought in Scotland, 1500–2000*. Cambridge: Cambridge University Press, 2008.

Kiessling, Nicolas K, ed. *The Library of Robert Burton*. Oxford: Oxford Bibliographical Society, 1988.

Kingsbury, Benedict. "Confronting Difference: The Puzzling Durability of Gentili's Combination of Pragmatic Pluralism and Normative Judgment." *The American Journal of International Law* 92, no. 4 (October 1, 1998): 713–23.

Kingsbury, Benedict, and Benjamin Straumann, eds. *The Roman Foundations of the Law of Nations: Alberico Gentili and the Justice of Empire*. New York: Oxford University Press, 2011.

Kinney, Arthur F. "Sir Philip Sidney and the Uses of History." In *The Historical Renaissance: New Essays on Tudor and Stuart Literature and Culture*, edited by Heather Dubrow and Richard Strier, 293–314. Chicago, IL: University of Chicago Press, 1988.

Klein, Bernhard. "Staying Afloat: Literary Shipboard Encounters from Columbus to Equiano." In *Sea Changes: Historicizing the Ocean*, edited by Bernhard Klein and Gesa Mackenthun, 91–110. New York: Routledge, 2004.

Klosko, George, and Daryl Rice. "Thucydides and Hobbes's State of Nature." *History of Political Thought* 6, no. 3 (1985): 405–9.

Knafla, Louis A. *Law and Politics in Jacobean England: The Tracts of Lord Chancellor Ellesmere.* Cambridge: Cambridge University Press, 1977.

Knapp, James A. "Visual and Ethical Truth in The Winter's Tale." *Shakespeare Quarterly* 55, no. 3 (2004): 253–78.

Knop, Karen. "Citizenship, Public and Private." *Law and Contemporary Problems* 71, no. 3 (2008): 309–42.

Knox, Robert. "Marxism, International Law, and Political Strategy." *Leiden Journal of International Law* 22, no. 03 (2009): 413–36.

Komorowski, Michael. "Milton's Natural Law: Divorce and Individual Property." *Milton Studies* 53, no. 1 (2012): 69–99.

Kooijmans, P. H. "Protestantism and the Development of International Law." In *Recueil Des Cours, Collected Courses of the Hague Academy of International Law*, edited by Francesco Durante, IV: 79–118. Sijthoff & Noordhoff, 1976.

Korman, Sharon. *The Right of Conquest: The Acquisition of Territory by Force in International Law and Practice.* Oxford: Oxford University Press, 1996.

Koselleck, Reinhart. "Historia Magistra Vitae: The Dissolution of the Topos into the Perspective of a Modernized Historical Process." In *Futures Past: On the Semantics of Historical Time*, translated by Keith Tribe, 26–42. New York: Columbia University Press, 2004.

Koskenniemi, Martti. "The Hobbesian Structure of International Legal Discourse." In *Hobbes: War among Nations*, edited by Timo Airaksinen, Martin A Bertman, and Suomen Filosofinen Yhdistys, 168–78. Aldershot: Avebury, 1989.

Koskenniemi, Martti. *The Gentle Civilizer of Nations: The Rise and Fall of Modern International Law, 1870–1960.* New York: Cambridge University Press, 2001.

Koskenniemi, Martti. *From Apology to Utopia: The Structure of International Legal Argument.* 2nd edn. Cambridge: Cambridge University Press, 2005.

Koskenniemi, Martti. "International Law and Raison D'etat: Rethinking the Prehistory of International Law." In *The Roman Foundations of the Law of Nations: Alberico Gentili and the Justice of Empire*, edited by Benedict Kingsbury and Benjamin Straumann, 297–339. Oxford: Oxford University Press, 2011.

Koskenniemi, Martti. "The Political Theology of Trade Law: The Scholastic Contribution." In *From Bilateralism to Community Interest*, edited by Ulrich Fastenrath, Rudolf Geiger, Daniel-Erasmus Khan, Andreas Paulus, Sabine von Schorlemer, and Christoph Vedder. Oxford: Oxford University Press, 2011.

Koskenniemi, Martti. *The Politics of International Law.* Oxford: Hart, 2011.

Kuin, Roger. "Sir Philip Sidney and World War Zero: Implications of the Dutch Revolt." *Sidney Journal* 30, no. 2 (July 2012): 33–55.

Lactantius. *Divine Institutes.* Translated by Anthony Bowen and Peter Garnsey. Liverpool: Liverpool University Press, 2003.

Lake, Edward. *Memoranda: Touching the Oath Ex Officio, Pretended Self-Accusation, and Canonical Purgation Together with Some Notes about the Making of Some New, and Alteration and Explanation of Some Old Laws.* London: R. Royston, 1662.

Lang, Bernhard. *Joseph in Egypt: A Cultural Icon from Grotius to Goethe.* New Haven, CT: Yale University Press, 2009.

Laqueur, Thomas. "Bodies, Details, and the Humanitarian Narrative." In *The New Cultural History: Essays*, edited by Aletta Biersack and Lynn Hunt. Berkeley: University of California Press, 1989.

Latham, Robert, ed. *Catalogue of the Pepys Library at Magdalene College, Cambridge*. 7 vols. Vol. I. Woodbridge: D. S. Brewer, 1978.

Latour, Bruno. *Reassembling the Social: An Introduction to Actor-Network-Theory*. Oxford: Oxford University Press, 2005.

Lattimore, Steven, ed. *The Peloponnesian War*. Indianapolis: Hackett Pub Co., 1998.

Law, Jonathan, and E. A. Martin, eds. *A Dictionary of Law*. 6th edn. Oxford: Oxford University Press, 2006.

Lee, Sidney, and Victor Slater. "Cavendish, William, Second Earl of Devonshire (1590–1628)." *Oxford Dictionary of National Biography*. Oxford: Oxford University Press, 2004.

Leeson, Peter T. "The Laws of Lawlessness." *The Journal of Legal Studies* 38, no. 2 (2009): 471–503.

Lefroy, J. H., ed. *Memorials of the Discovery and Early Settlement of the Bermudas or Somers Islands, 1515–1685*. 2 vols. London: Longmans, Green, and Co., 1877.

Leibniz, Gottfried Wilhelm. *Political Writings*. 2nd edn. Cambridge: Cambridge University Press, 1988.

Leigh, Matthew. *Comedy and the Rise of Rome*. Oxford: Oxford University Press, 2004.

Leigh, Matthew. "Forms of Exile in the Rudens of Plautus." *The Classical Quarterly* 60, no. 1 (2010): 110–17.

Lesser, Zachary. *Renaissance Drama and the Politics of Publication: Readings in the English Book Trade*. Cambridge: Cambridge University Press, 2004.

Lesser, Zachary. "Tragical-Comical-Pastoral-Colonial: Economic Sovereignty, Globalization, and the Form of Tragicomedy." *ELH* 74 (2007): 881–908.

Levack, Brian. *The Civil Lawyers in England, 1603–1641: A Political Study*. Oxford: Clarendon Press, 1973.

Levack, Brian. "The Proposed Union of English Law and Scots Law in the Seventeenth Century." *Juridical Review* 20 (1975): 97–115.

Levack, Brian. "English Law, Scots Law and the Union, 1603–1707." In *Law-Making and Law-Makers in British History*, edited by A. Harding, 107–19. London: Royal Historical Society, 1980.

Levine, Bruce L. "The Tragedy of the Commons and the Comedy of Community: The Commons in History." *Journal of Community Psychology* 14, no. 1 (1986): 81–99.

Levy, F. J. "Philip Sidney Reconsidered." *English Literary Renaissance* 2, no. 1 (1972): 5–18.

Lewalski, Barbara Kiefer. *Paradise Lost and the Rhetoric of Literary Forms*. Princeton, NJ: Princeton University Press, 1985.

Lindenbaum, Peter. "Dispatches from the Archives." *Times Literary Supplement*, no. 5383 (2006).

Locke, John. *Two Treatises of Government*. Edited by Peter Laslett. 2nd edn. Cambridge: Cambridge University Press, 1988.

Lockey, Brian. *Law and Empire in English Renaissance Literature*. Cambridge: Cambridge University Press, 2006.

Loewenstein, David. "Milton and the Poetics of Defense." In *Politics, Poetics, and Hermeneutics in Milton's Prose*, edited by David Loewenstein and James Grantham Turner, 171–92. Cambridge: Cambridge University Press, 1990.

Louden, Bruce. "The Tempest, Plautus, and the Rudens." *Comparative Drama* 33, no. 2 (1999): 199–233.

Louis XIII. *Admirable and Notable Things of Note*. London: Francis Coules and Thomas Banks, 1642.

Lucretius Carus, Titus. *The Translation of Lucretius*. Edited by Reid Barbour and David Norbrook. Translated by Lucy Hutchinson. Vol. 1.1. The Works of Lucy Hutchinson. Oxford: Oxford University Press, 2011.

Lund, William R. "The Use and Abuse of the Past: Hobbes on the Study of History." *Hobbes Studies* 5, no. 1 (1992): 3–22.

Lupton, Julia Reinhard. *Thinking with Shakespeare: Essays on Politics and Life*. Chicago, IL: University of Chicago Press, 2011.

Luxemburg, Rosa. *The National Question: Selected Writings*. Edited by Horace B. Davis. New York: Monthly Review Press, 1976.

Lyne, Raphael. "Shakespeare, Plautus, and the Discovery of New Comic Space." In *Shakespeare and the Classics*, edited by Charles Martindale and A. B. Taylor. Cambridge: Cambridge University Press, 2004.

Maccioni, P. Alessandra, and Marco Mostert. "Isaac Dorislaus (1595–1649); the Career of a Dutch Scholar in England." *Transactions of the Cambridge Bibliographical Society* 8, no. 4 (1984): 419–70.

MacKenzie, W. Mackay. "The Debateable Land." *The Scottish Historical Review* 30, no. 110 (1951): 109–25.

MacKinnon, Catharine A. *Are Women Human?: And Other International Dialogues*. Cambridge, MA: Belknap Press of Harvard University Press, 2006.

MacKinnon, Catharine A. "Women's September 11th: Rethinking the International Law of Conflict." In *Are Women Human?: And Other International Dialogues*, 259–80. Cambridge, MA: Belknap Press of Harvard University Press, 2006.

MacKinnon, Catharine A. "Law in the Everyday Life of Women." In *Women's Lives, Men's Laws*, 32–43. Cambridge, MA: Harvard University Press, 2007.

Maclean, Ian. "Alberico Gentili, His Publishers, and the Vagaries of the Book Trade between England and Germany, 1580–1614." In *Learning and the Market Place: Essays in the History of the Early Modern Book*, 291–337. Leiden: Brill, 2009.

Maguire, Laurie E. *Shakespearean Suspect Texts: The "Bad" Quartos and Their Contexts*. Cambridge: Cambridge University Press, 1996.

Malcolm, Noel. "Hobbes, Sandys, and the Virginia Company." *The Historical Journal* 24, no. 02 (1981): 297–321.

Malcolm, Noel. *Aspects of Hobbes*. Oxford: Clarendon Press, 2002.

Malcolm, Noel. "Alberico Gentili and the Ottomans." In *Alberico Gentili: La Salvaguardia Dei Beni Culturali Nel Diritto Internazionale*, 65–89. Milano: Giuffrè editore, 2008.

Maley, Willy. "Postcolonial Shakespeare: British Identity Formation and Cymbeline." In *Shakespeare's Late Plays: New Readings*, edited by Jennifer Richards and James Knowles, 145–57. Edinburgh: Edinburgh University Press, 1999.

Malynes, Gerard. *Consuetudo: Vel, Lex Mercatoria, Or, The Ancient Law-Merchant . . . Necessary for All States-Men, Judges, Magistrates, Temporall, and Civill Lawyers, Mint-Men, Merchants, Mariners, and All Others Negotiating in All Places of the World*. London: Printed by W. Hunt, for N. Bourne, 1656.

Marcus, Leah S. *Puzzling Shakespeare: Local Reading and Its Discontents*. Berkeley, CA: University of California Press, 1988.

Marks, Susan. "Human Rights in Disastrous Times." In *The Cambridge Companion to International Law*, edited by James Crawford and Martti Koskenniemi, 309–26. Cambridge: Cambridge University Press, 2012.

Marsden, Reginald G., ed. *Documents Relating to Law and Custom of the Sea*. London: Printed for the Navy Records Society, 1915.

Martin, James. "Epistle Dedicatory." In *Vindiciae Sacrae. A Treatise of the Honor and Maintenance due to Ecclesiasticall Persons*, by Adrien Saravia, translated by James Martin. London: T. Cotes and R. Cotes for James Boler, 1629.

Martindale, Charles, and Michelle Martindale. *Shakespeare and the Uses of Antiquity: An Introductory Essay*. London; New York: Routledge, 1990.

Martinich, A. P. "Hobbes's Translations of Homer and Anticlericalism." *The Seventeenth Century* 16, no. 1 (2001): 147–57.

Marvell, Andrew. *The Poems of Andrew Marvell*. Edited by Nigel Smith. Rev. edn. London: Pearson Longman, 2007.

Maslan, Susan. "The Anti-Human: Man and Citizen before the Declaration of the Rights of Man and of the Citizen." *South Atlantic Quarterly* 103, no. 2/3 (2004): 357–74.

Masson, David. *The Life of John Milton: Narrated in Connexion with the Political, Ecclesiastical, and Literary History of His Time*. 7 vols. London: Macmillan and Co., 1859.

Mattingly, Garrett. *Renaissance Diplomacy*. Boston, MA: Houghton Mifflin, 1955.

McCoy, Richard C. *Sir Philip Sidney: Rebellion in Arcadia*. New Brunswick, NJ: Rutgers University Press, 1979.

McEachern, Claire. *The Poetics of English Nationhood, 1590–1612*. Cambridge: Cambridge University Press, 1996.

McKenzie, D. F., and Maureen Bell, eds. *A Chronology and Calendar of Documents Relating to the London Book Trade, 1641–1700*. 3 vols. Oxford: Oxford University Press, 2005.

Mentz, Steven. "Toward a Blue Cultural Studies: The Sea, Maritime Culture, and Early Modern English Literature." *Literature Compass* 6, no. 5 (2009): 997–1013.

Mentz, Steven. "Tongues in the Storm: Shakespeare, Ecological Crisis, and the Resources of Genre." In *Ecocritical Shakespeare*, edited by Lynne Bruckner and Dan Brayton, 155–71. Farnham: Ashgate, 2011.

Mercurius Melancholicus. *Mistris Parliament Brought to Bed of a Monstrous Childe of Reformation*. [London], 1648.

Meron, Theodor. "Shakespeare's Henry the Fifth and the Law of War." *The American Journal of International Law* 86, no. 1 (1992): 1.

Meron, Theodor. *Henry's Wars and Shakespeare's Laws: Perspectives on the Law of War in the Later Middle Ages*. Oxford: Oxford University Press, 1993.

Meron, Theodor. *Bloody Constraint: War and Chivalry in Shakespeare*. New York: Oxford University Press, 1998.

Merryman, John Henry, and Rogelio Pérez-Perdomo. *The Civil Law Tradition: An Introduction to the Legal Systems of Europe and Latin America*. 3rd edn. Stanford, CA: Stanford University Press, 2007.

Mezey, Naomi. "Law as Culture." *Yale Journal of Law & the Humanities* 13 (2001): 35.

Micanzio, Fulgenzio. *Lettere a William Cavendish (1615–1628)*. Edited by Roberto Ferrini. Translated by Thomas Hobbes. Rome: Istituto storico O.S.M., 1987.

Miéville, China. *Between Equal Rights: A Marxist Theory Of International Law*. Chicago, IL: Haymarket Books, 2006.

Miller, Leo. *John Milton & the Oldenburg Safeguard: New Light on Milton and His Friends in the Commonwealth from the Diaries and Letters of Hermann Mylius, Agonist in the Early History of Modern Diplomacy*. New York: Loewenthal Press, 1985.

Miller, Leo. *John Milton's Writings in the Anglo-Dutch Negotiations, 1651–1654*. Pittsburgh, PA: Duquesne University Press, 1992.

Miller, Peter N. *Peiresc's Europe: Learning and Virtue in the Seventeenth Century*. New Haven, CT: Yale University Press, 2000.

Miller, Peter N. "Major Trends in European Antiquarianism, from Petrarch to Peiresc." In *The Oxford History of Historical Writing*, edited by osé Rabasa, Masayuki Sato, Edoardo Tortarolo, and Daniel Woolf, 3: 1400–1800: 244–60. Oxford: Oxford University Press, 2011.

Mills, Alex. "The Private History of International Law." *International and Comparative Law Quarterly* 55 (January 1, 2006): 1–50.

Milton, Anthony. "Marketing a Massacre: Amboyna, the East Indies Company, and the Public Sphere in Early Stuart England." In *The Politics of the Public Sphere in Early Modern England*, edited by Peter Lake and Steven C. A. Pincus, 168–90. Manchester: Manchester University Press, 2007.

Milton, John. *Pro Populo Anglicano Defensio*. London: William DuGard, 1651.

Milton, John. *Letters of State Written by Mr. John Milton, to Most of the Sovereign Princes and Republicks of Europe, from the Year 1649, till the Year 1659*. London, 1694.

Milton, John. *A Common-Place Book of John Milton, and a Latin Essay and Latin Verses Presumed to Be by Milton*. Edited by Alfred J. Horwood. Rev. ed. Westminster: Camden Society, 1877.

Milton, John. *The Works of John Milton*. Edited by Frank Allen Patterson. 18 vols. New York: Columbia University Press, 1931.

Milton, John. *Complete Prose Works*. Edited by Don. M. Wolfe. 8 vols. New Haven, CT: Yale University Press, 1953.

Milton, John. *Paradise Lost*. Edited by Alastair Fowler. 2nd edn. London: Longman, 1998.

Miola, Robert S. *Shakespeare and Classical Comedy: The Influence of Plautus and Terence*. Oxford: Oxford University Press, 1994.

Mohamed, Feisal. *Milton and the Post-Secular Present: Ethics, Politics, Terrorism*. Stanford, CA: Stanford University Press, 2011.

Moloney, Pat. "Hobbes, Savagery, and International Anarchy." *American Political Science Review* 105, no. 1 (2011): 1–16.

More, Thomas. *Utopia*. Edited by David Harris Sacks. Translated by Ralph Robynson. New York: Bedford/St. Martin's, 1999.

Moretti, Franco. "The Great Eclipse: Tragic Form as the Deconsecration of Sovereignty." In *Signs Taken for Wonders: Essays in the Sociology of Literary Forms*, Revised edition, 42–82. London: Verso, 1988.

Moretti, Franco. *Graphs, Maps, Trees: Abstract Models for Literary History*. Verso, 2007.

Morgan, Edward. *The Aesthetics of International Law*. Toronto: University of Toronto Press, 2007.

Morley, Henry. *The Cleansing of the Leper Discoursed*. London: H[umphrey] L[ownes] for Clement Knight, 1609.

Morrow, David. "Local/Global Pericles: International Storytelling, Domestic Social Relations, Capitalism." In *A Companion to the Global Renaissance: English Literature and Culture in the Era of Expansion*, edited by Jyotsna G. Singh, 355–77. Chichester: John Wiley and Sons, 2009.

Mosley, Charles. "The Literary and Dramatic Contexts of the Last Plays." In *The Cambridge Companion to Shakespeare's Last Plays*, edited by Catherine M. S. Alexander. Cambridge: Cambridge University Press, 2009.

Moyn, Samuel. *The Last Utopia: Human Rights in History*. Cambridge, MA. Harvard University Press, 2010.

Mueller, Janel. "The Figure and the Ground: Samson as a Hero of London Nonconformity, 1662–1667." In *Milton and the Terms of Liberty*, edited by Graham Parry and Joad Raymond. Cambridge: D. S. Brewer, 2002.

Muldoon, J. "Medieval Canon Law and the Formation of International Law." *Zeitschrift Der Savigny-Stiftung Für Rechtsgeschichte. Kanonistische Abteilung* 125 (1995): 64–82.

Mullaney, Steven. *The Place of the Stage: License, Play, and Power in Renaissance England.* Chicago, IL: University of Chicago Press, 1988.

Müller, Jan-Werner. *A Dangerous Mind: Carl Schmitt in Post-War European Thought.* New Haven, CT: Yale University Press, 2003.

Murdoch, Steve. *The Terror of the Seas?: Scottish Maritime Warfare, 1513–1713.* Leiden: Brill, 2010.

Myers, Albert Cook, ed. "Affidavit of Four Men from the Key of Calmar, 1638." In *Narratives of Early Pennsylvania, West New Jersey and Delaware, 1630–1707*. New York: C. Scribner's Sons, 1912.

Myriell, Thomas. "To the Right Worshipfull Mr. Maurice Abbott, Governor of the East-India Companie." In *The Stripping of Ioseph . . . With a Consolatorie Epistle, to the English-East-India Companie, for Their Vnsufferable Wrongs Sustayned in Amboyna, by the Dutch There*. London: W[illiam] S[tansby] for Hen. Holland and Geo. Gibbs, 1625.

Nairn, Tom. "Internationalism: A Critique." In *Faces of Nationalism: Janus Revisited*, 25–46. London: Verso, 1998.

Nelson, Eric, ed. *Translations of Homer.* Translated by Thomas Hobbes. 2 vols. The Clarendon Edition of the Works of Thomas Hobbes. Oxford: Clarendon Press, 2008.

Nelson, Herbert B. "Amidas v. Bracidas." *Modern Language Quarterly* 1 (1940).

Netzloff, Mark. *England's Internal Colonies: Class, Capital, and the Literature of Early Modern English Colonialism.* New York: Palgrave Macmillan, 2003.

Neville, Cynthia J. "Remembering the Legal Past: Anglo-Scottish Border Law and Practice in the Later Middle Ages." In *North-East England in the Later Middle Ages*, edited by Christian D. Liddy and Richard H. Britnell, 43–55. Woodbridge: Boydell Press, 2005.

Newman, Jane O. " 'Race', Religion, and the Law: Rhetorics of Sameness and Difference in the Work of Hugo Grotius." In *Rhetoric and Law in Early Modern Europe*, edited by Victoria Kahn and Lorna Hutson, 285–317. New Haven, CT: Yale University Press, 2001.

Newman, Jane O. "Tragedy and Trauerspiel for the (Post-)Westphalian Age." *Renaissance Drama* 40, no. 1 (2012): 197–208.

Ng, S. F. "Global Renaissance: Alexander the Great and Early Modern Classicism from the British Isles to the Malay Archipelago." *Comparative Literature* 58, no. 4 (2006): 293–312.

Nicolson, William, ed. *Leges Marchiarum, or Border-Laws: Containing Several Original Articles and Treaties, Made and Agreed upon by the Commissioners of the Respective Kings of England and Scotland, for the Better Preservation of Peace and Commerce upon the Marches of Both Kingdoms.* London: Tim Goodwin, 1705.

Norbrook, David. "Macbeth and the Politics of Historiography." In *Politics of Discourse: The Literature and History of Seventeenth-Century England*, edited by Kevin Sharpe and Steven N. Zwicker, 78–116. Berkeley, CA: University of California Press, 1987.

Norbrook, David. *Writing the English Republic: Poetry, Rhetoric and Politics, 1627–1660.* Cambridge: Cambridge University Press, 1999.

Norbrook, David. *Poetry and Politics in the English Renaissance.* Revised edition. Oxford: Oxford University Press, 2002.

Norbrook, David. "Republican Occasions in Paradise Regained and Samson Agonistes." *Milton Studies* 42 (2003): 122.

Nussbaum, Arthur. "The Significance of Roman Law in the History of International Law." *University of Pennsylvania Law Review* 100, no. 5 (1952): 678–87.

Nussbaum, Arthur. *A Concise History of the Law of Nations*. New York: Macmillan, 1954.

Nussbaum, Martha Craven. *The Fragility of Goodness: Luck and Ethics in Greek Tragedy and Philosophy*. Cambridge: Cambridge University Press, 1986.

Nyquist, Mary. "Contemporary Ancestors of de Bry, Hobbes, and Milton." *University of Toronto Quarterly* 77, no. 3 (2008): 837–75.

O'Connor, Marie Theresa. "A British People: Cymbeline and the Anglo-Scottish Union Issue." In *Shakespeare and the Law: A Conversation Among Disciplines and Professions*, edited by Bradin Cormack, Martha Nussbaum, and Richard Strier, 231–55. Chicago, IL: University of Chicago Press, 2013.

O'Driscoll, Cian. "Thucydides and the Just War Tradition: Unlikely Bedfellows?." In *A Handbook to the Reception of Thucydides*, edited by Christine Lee and Neville Morley, 373–90. John Wiley & Sons, 2014.

Ohlmeyer, Jane. " 'Civilizinge of Those Rude Partes': Colonization within Britain and Ireland, 1580s–1640s." In *The Oxford History of the British Empire*, 124–47. Oxford: Oxford University Press, 1998.

Oldman, Elizabeth. "Milton, Grotius, and the Law of War: A Reading of Paradise Regained and Samson Agonistes." *Studies in Philology* 104, no. 3 (2007): 340–75.

Oppenheim, Lassa. *International Law: A Treatise*. London: Longmans, Green, 1920.

Orford, Anne. "Jurisdiction without Territory: From the Holy Roman Empire to the Responsibility to Protect." *Michigan Journal of International Law* 30 (2008): 981.

Orford, Anne. *International Authority and the Responsibility to Protect*. Cambridge: Cambridge University Press, 2011.

Orford, Anne. "The Past as Law or History?: The Relevance of Imperialism for Modern International Law." *International Law and Justice Working Papers*, IILJ Working Papers, no. 2 (2012). <http://www.iilj.org>.

Orgel, Stephen. "Prospero's Wife." *Representations*, no. 8 (1984): 1–13.

Osborn, James Marshall. *Young Philip Sidney, 1572–1577*. The Elizabethan Club Series 5. New Haven, CT: Published for the Elizabethan Club [by] Yale University Press, 1972.

Osler, Douglas J. "Budaeus and Roman Law." *Ius Commune* 13 (1985): 195–212.

Owen, John. *Vindiciae Evangelicae or The Mystery of the Gospell Vindicated, and Socinianisme Examined*. Oxford: Leonard Lichfield, 1655.

Pade, Marianne. "Thucydides." In *Catalogus Translationum et Commentariorum: Mediaeval and Renaissance Latin Translations and Commentaries*, edited by Virginia Brown, James Hankins, and Robert A. Kaster, 8:104–81. Washington, DC: Catholic Univ. of America Press, 2003.

Pade, Marianne. "Thucydides' Renaissance Readers." In *Brill's Companion to Thucydides*, edited by Antonios Rengakos and Antonis Tsakmakis, 779–810. Leiden: Brill, 2006.

Pagden, Anthony. *The Fall of Natural Man: The American Indian and the Origins of Comparative Ethnology*. Cambridge: Cambridge University Press, 1982.

Pagden, Anthony. *Lords of All the World: Ideologies of Empire in Spain, Britain and France C. 1500–C. 1800*. New Haven, CT: Yale University Press, 1995.

Päivärinne, Meri. "Translating Grotius's De Jure Belli Ac Pacis: Courtin vs Barbeyrac." *Translation Studies* 5, no. 1 (2012): 33–47.

Palfrey, Simon. *Late Shakespeare: A New World of Words*. Oxford: Oxford University Press, 1997.

Pallant, Anne. "Scipione Gentili: A Sixteenth Century Jurist." *The Kingston Law Review* 14–15 (1984–1985).

Panizza, Diego. *Political Theory and Jurisprudence in Gentili's De Iure Belli: The Great Debate between "Theological" and "Humanist" Perspectives from Vitoria to Grotius.* New York: Institute for International Law and Justice, New York University School of Law, 2005 <http://ssrn.com/abstract=871754>.

Panizza, Diego. "The 'Freedom of the Sea' and the 'Modern Cosmopolis' in Alberico Gentili's De Iure Belli." *Grotiana* 30, no. 1 (2009): 88–106.

Parfitt, Rose Sydney. "The Unequal Equality of Sovereigns: A Brief History of 'Peripheral Personality.'" *Jean Monnet Working Papers Series* 20, no. 13 (2013). <http://www.jeanmonnetprogram.org/papers/13/documents/Parfitt.pdf>.

Parkin, Jon. "Hobbism in the Later 1660's: Daniel Scargill and Samuel Parker." *The Historical Journal* 42, no. 1 (1999).

Parmelee, Lisa Ferraro. *Good Newes from Fraunce: French Anti-League Propaganda in Late Elizabethan England.* Rochester, NY: University of Rochester Press, 1996.

Patterson, Annabel M. *Censorship and Interpretation: The Conditions of Writing and Reading in Early Modern England.* Madison, WI: University of Wisconsin Press, 1984.

Pavel, Thomas G. *Fictional Worlds.* Cambridge, MA: Harvard University Press, 1986.

Peck, Francis. *Memoirs of the Life and Actions of Oliver Cromwell: As Delivered in Three Panegyrics of Him, Written in Latin.* London, 1740.

Penaguião, João Rodrigues de Sá e Meneses. *Panegyrici Cromwello Scripti. Vnus À Legato Portugallici Regis. Alter À Quodam Iesuita.* [Leyden]: [Louis Elzevier], 1654.

Pérotin-Dumon, Anne. "The Pirate and the Emperor: Power and the Law on the Seas, 1450–1850." In *The Political Economy of Merchant Empires: State Power and World Trade 1350–1750*, edited by James D. Tracy, 196–227. Cambridge: Cambridge University Press, 1997.

Peters, Julie Stone. "A 'Bridge over Chaos': De Jure Belli, Paradise Lost, Terror, Sovereignty, Globalism, and the Modern Law of Nations." *Comparative Literature* 57, no. 4 (2005): 273–93.

Peters, Julie Stone. "Law, Literature, and the Vanishing Real: On the Future of an Interdisciplinary Illusion." *PMLA* 120, no. 2 (2005): 442–53.

Peters, Julie Stone. "'Literature,' the 'Rights of Man,' and Narratives of Atrocity: Historical Backgrounds to the Culture of Testimony." *Yale Journal of Law & the Humanities* 17, no. 2 (2005).

Pettit, Philip. *Republicanism: A Theory of Freedom and Government.* Oxford: Oxford University Press, 2000.

Pettit, Philip. "Legitimate International Institutions: A Neo-Republican Perspective." In *The Philosophy of International Law*, edited by Samantha Besson and John Tasioulas. Oxford: Oxford University Press, 2010.

Pettit, Philip. "A Republican Law of Peoples." *European Journal of Political Theory* 9, no. 1 (2010): 70–94.

Phillips, Edward. *Theatrum Poetarum, Or, A Compleat Collection of the Poets Especially the Most Eminent, of All Ages.* London: Charles Smith, 1675.

Picciotto, Joanna. "The Public Person and the Play of Fact." *Representations* 105, no. 1 (2009): 85–132.

Picciotto, Joanna. *Labors of Innocence in Early Modern England.* Cambridge, MA: Harvard University Press, 2010.

Pitts, Jennifer. "Empire and Legal Universalisms in the Eighteenth Century." *American Historical Review* 117, no. 1 (2012): 92–121.

Plato. *Laws*. Translated by Robert Gregg Bury. 2 vols. Cambridge, MA: Harvard University Press, 1984.

Plautus, Titus Maccius. *Plautus integer cum interpretatione Joannis Baptistae Pii*. Edited by Joannes Battista Pio. Mediolani: per Uldericum Scinzenzeler, 1500.

Plautus, Titus Maccius. *Plautus: with an English translation*. Translated by Paul Nixon. 5 vols. Vol. 4. Loeb Classical Library. New York; London: G.P. Putnam's Sons; W. Heinemann, 1916.

Plutarch. *The Lives of the Noble Grecians and Romanes*. Translated by Thomas North. London: Thomas Vautroullier, 1579.

Plutarch. *Plutarch's Lives*. 11 vols. Vol. IX. London; Cambridge, MA: Heinemann, 1914.

Pocock, J. G. A. *The Ancient Constitution and the Feudal Law: A Study of English Historical Thought in the Seventeenth Century*. Cambridge: Cambridge University Press, 1957.

Poole, Robert. *Time's Alteration: Calendar Reform in Early Modern England*. London: UCL Press, 1998.

Posner, Richard A. *Law and Literature*. 3rd edn. Cambridge, MA: Harvard University Press, 2009.

Posthumus Meyjes, G. H. M. *Jean Hotman's English Connection*. Amsterdam: Koninklijke Nederlandse Akademie van Wetenschappen, 1990.

Potter, Lois. "Pirates and 'Turning Turk' in Renaissance Drama." In *Travel and Drama in Shakespeare's Time*, edited by Jean-Pierre Maquerlot and Michèle Willems, 124–40. Cambridge: Cambridge University Press, 1996.

Powell, Jason. "Astrophil the Orator: Diplomacy and Diplomats in Sidney's *Astrophil and Stella*." In *Authority and Diplomacy from Dante to Shakespeare*. Edited by Jason Powell and William T. Rossiter. Burlington, VT: Ashgate, 2013.

Power, Samantha. *A Problem from Hell: America and the Age of Genocide*. New York: Basic Books, 2002.

Prestage, Edgar. "The Anglo-Portuguese Alliance." *Transactions of the Royal Historical Society*, Fourth Series, 17 (1934): 69–100.

Price, Polly J. "Natural Law and Birthright Citizenship in Calvin's Case (1608)." *Yale Journal of Law & the Humanities* 9 (1997): 73.

Pufendorf, Samuel. *De Jure Naturae et Gentium Libri Octo*. Edited by Walter Simons. Translated by C. H. Oldfather and William Abbott Oldfather. 2 vols. Oxford: Clarendon, 1934.

Puttenham, George. *The Art of English Poesy*. Edited by Frank Whigham and Wayne A Rebhorn. Ithaca, NY: Cornell University Press, 2007.

Quine, Willard V. "On What There Is." *The Review of Metaphysics* 2, no. 5 (1948): 21–38.

Quint, David. "'Alexander the Pig': Shakespeare on History and Poetry." *Boundary 2* 10, no. 3 (1982): 49–67.

Quint, David. *Epic and Empire: Politics and Generic Form from Virgil to Milton*. Princeton, NJ: Princeton University Press, 1993.

Quintilian. *The Orator's Education*. Translated by D. A. Russell. Cambridge, MA: Harvard University Press, 2001.

Rabkin, Jeremy A. *Law without Nations?: Why Constitutional Government Requires Sovereign States*. Princeton, NJ: Princeton University Press, 2007.

Rae, Thomas I. *The Administration of the Scottish Frontier, 1513–1603*. Edinburgh: Edinburgh University Press, 1966.

Raitiere, Martin N. *Faire Bitts: Sir Philip Sidney and Renaissance Political Theory*. Pittsburgh, PA: Duquesne University Press, 1984.

Rajan, Balachandra. "Milton and Camões." *Portuguese Cultural and Literary Studies* 9 (2002): 177–87.

Raleigh, Walter. *The History of the World*. London: [William Stansby] for Walter Burr, 1617.

Ramachandran, Ayesha. "A War of Worlds: Becoming 'Early Modern' and the Challenge of Comparison." In *Comparative Early Modernities, 1100–1800*, edited by David Porter, 15–46. New York: Palgrave Macmillan, 2012.

Rawls, John. *The Law of Peoples; With, The Idea of Public Reason Revisited*. Cambridge, MA: Harvard University Press, 1999.

Raymond, Joad. "The King Is a Thing." In *Milton and the Terms of Liberty*, edited by Graham Parry and Joad Raymond, 69–94. Cambridge: D. S. Brewer, 2002.

Reik, Miriam M. *The Golden Lands of Thomas Hobbes*. Detroit, MI: Wayne State University Press, 1977.

Relihan, Constance C. "Liminal Geography: Pericles and the Politics of Place." *Philological Quarterly* 71, no. 3 (1992): 281–301.

Riles, Annelise. "A New Agenda for the Cultural Study of Law: Taking on the Technicalities." *Buffalo Law Review* 53 (2005): 973–1033.

Robbins, Bruce. *Feeling Global: Internationalism in Distress*. New York: New York University Press, 1999.

Rorty, Richard. "The End of Leninism and History as Comic Frame." In *History and the Idea of Progress*, edited by Arthur M. Melzer, Jerry Weinberger, and M. Richard Zinman, 211–26. Ithaca, NY: Cornell University Press, 1995.

Rose, Carol. "The Comedy of the Commons: Custom, Commerce, and Inherently Public Property." *The University of Chicago Law Review* 53, no. 3 (Summer 1986): 711–81.

Rosenberg, Daniel, and Anthony Grafton. *Cartographies of Time: A History of the Timeline*. New York, NY: Princeton Architectural Press, 2010.

Rosenberg, Eleanor. *Leicester, Patron of Letters*. New York: Columbia University Press, 1955.

Rosenblatt, Jason. *Torah and Law in Paradise Lost*. Princeton, N.J: Princeton University Press, 1994.

Rosenblatt, Jason. *Renaissance England's Chief Rabbi: John Selden*. Oxford: Oxford University Press, 2006.

Rosenblatt, Jason. "Milton, Natural Law, and Toleration." In *Milton and Toleration*, edited by Sharon Achinstein and Elizabeth Sauer, 126–43. New York: Oxford University Press, 2007.

Rosenstock, Bruce. "Against Sovereign Impunity: The Political Theology of the ICC." In *After Secular Law*, edited by Winnifred Fallers Sullivan, Robert A. Yelle, and Mateo Taussig-Rubbo, 160–77. Stanford, CA: Stanford University Press, 2011.

Rowland, Richard. "The Captives: Thomas Heywood's 'Whole Monopoly off Mischeiff.'" *The Modern Language Review* 90, no. 3 (1995): 585–602.

Rubin, Gayle. "The Traffic in Women: Notes on the 'Political Economy' of Sex." In *Toward an Anthropology of Women*, edited by Rayna Reiter, 157–209. New York: Monthly Review Press, 1975.

Runciman, David. "What Kind of Person Is Hobbes's State? A Reply to Skinner." *Journal of Political Philosophy* 8, no. 2 (2000): 268.

Russell, Conrad. "1603: The End of English National Sovereignty." In *The Accession of James I: Historical and Cultural Consequences*, edited by Glenn Burgess, Rowland Wymer, and Jason Lawrence, 1–14. Basingstoke: Palgrave Macmillan, 2006.

Russell, John. "A Treatise of The Happie and Blissed Unioun." In *The Jacobean Union Six Tracts of 1604*, edited by Bruce Galloway and Brian P. Levack, 75–142. Edinburgh: Scottish History Society by C. Constable, 1985.

Rymer, Thomas. *Foedera: Conventiones, Literae, Et Cujuscunque Generis Acta Publica, Inter Reges Angliae, Et Alios Quosvis Imperatores, Reges.* 20 vols. Vol. 18. London: A. & J. Churchill, 1726.

Sá, Pantaleão. *A Narration of the Late Accident in the New-Exchange, on the 21. and 22. of November, 1653.* London, 1653.

Sacks, David Harris. "The Promise and the Contract in Early Modern England: Slade's Case in Perspective." In *Rhetoric and Law in Early Modern Europe*, edited by Victoria Kahn and Lorna Hutson, 28–53. New Haven, CT: Yale University Press, 2001.

Salmon, J. H. M. "Catholic Resistance Theory, Ultramontanism, and the Royalist Response, 1580–1620." In *The Cambridge History of Political Thought, 1450–1700*, edited by J. H. Burns and Mark Goldie. Cambridge: Cambridge University Press, 1991.

Salmon, J. H. M. "Precept, Example, and Truth: Degory Wheare and the Ars Historica." In *The Historical Imagination in Early Modern Britain: History, Rhetoric, and Fiction, 1500–1800*, edited by Donald R. Kelley and David Harris Sacks. Cambridge: Cambridge University Press, 1997.

Sauer, Elizabeth. "The Politics of Performance in the Inner Theater: 'Samson Agonistes' as Closet Drama." In *Milton and Heresy*, edited by Stephen B. Dobranski and John Peter Rumrich. Cambridge: Cambridge University Press, 1998.

Sauer, Elizabeth. "Closet Drama and the Case of Tyrannicall-Government Anatomized." In *The Book of the Play: Playwrights, Stationers, and Readers in Early Modern England*, edited by Marta Straznicky. Amherst, MA: University of Massachusetts Press, 2006.

Sauer, Elizabeth. "Pious Fraud: Extralegal Heroism in Samson Agonistes." *Studies in English Literature 1500–1900* 53, no. 1 (2013): 179–96.

Scafuro, Adele C. *The Forensic Stage: Settling Disputes in Graeco-Roman New Comedy.* Cambridge: Cambridge University Press, 1997.

Scaliger, Julius Caesar. *Select Translations from Scaliger's Poetics.* Translated by Frederick Morgan Padelford. New York: H. Holt, 1905.

Scarry, Elaine. "The Made-Up and the Made-Real." In *Field Work: Sites in Literary and Cultural Studies*, edited by Marjorie Garber, Paul Franklin, and Rebecca Walkowitz, 214–24. New York: Routledge, 1996.

Schlatter, Richard. "Thomas Hobbes and Thucydides." *Journal of the History of Ideas* 6, no. 3 (1945): 350–62.

Schmitt, Carl. "On the Barbaric Character of Shakespearean Drama: A Response to Walter Benjamin on the Origin of German Tragic Drama." Translated by David Pan. *Telos* 72, no. June (1987).

Schmitt, Carl. *The Concept of the Political.* Translated by George Schwab. Chicago, IL: University of Chicago Press, 1996.

Schmitt, Carl. *Land and Sea.* Washington, DC: Plutarch Press, 1997.

Schmitt, Carl. *The Nomos of the Earth in the International Law of the Jus Publicum Europeaum.* Translated by G. L. Ulmen. New York: Telos Press, 2003.

Scott, David. *Conscripts of Modernity: The Tragedy of Colonial Enlightenment.* Durham, NC: Duke University Press Books, 2004.

Scott, Jonathan. "The Peace of Silence: Thucydides and the English Civil War." In *The Certainty of Doubt: Tributes to Peter Munz*, edited by Miles Fairburn and W. H. Oliver, 90–116. Wellington: Victoria University Press, 1996.

Scott, Jonathan. *When the Waves Ruled Britannia: Geography and Political Identities, 1500–1800.* Cambridge: Cambridge University Press, 2011.

Scott, Jonathan. "Maritime Orientalism, or the Political Theory of Water." *History of Political Thought* 35, no. 1 (2014): 70–90.

Sebek, Barbara, and Stephen Deng, eds. *Global Traffic: Discourses and Practices of Trade in English Literature and Culture from 1550 to 1700*. New York: Palgrave Macmillan, 2008.

Seddon, P. R., ed. *Letters of John Holles, 1587–1637*. 3 vols. Vol. II. Nottingham: Derry and Sons for the Thoroton Society, 1975.

Seed, Patricia. "'This Island's Mine': Caliban and Native Sovereignty." In *"The Tempest" and Its Travels*, edited by Peter Hulme and William Howard Sherman. Philadelphia, PA: University of Pennsylvania Press, 2000.

Selden, John. *Of the Dominion, Or, Ownership of the Sea*. Translated by Marchamont Nedham. London: William DuGard, 1652.

Selleck, Nancy Gail. *The Interpersonal Idiom in Shakespeare, Donne, and Early Modern Culture*. Basingstoke: Palgrave Macmillan, 2008.

Serjeantson, R. W. "Testimony and Proof in Early-Modern England." *Studies in the History and Philosophy of Science* 30A, no. 2 (1999): 195–236.

Serjeantson, R. W. "Samson Agonistes and 'Single Rebellion.'" In *The Oxford Handbook of Milton*, edited by Nicholas McDowell and Nigel Smith, 613–31. Oxford: Oxford University Press, 2009.

Shakespeare, William. *The Norton Shakespeare*. Edited by Stephen Greenblatt, Jean E. Howard, and Katharine Eisaman Maus. London: W. W. Norton & Company, 1997.

Shakespeare, William. *Pericles*. Edited by Suzanne Gossett. London: Arden Shakespeare, 2004.

Shannon, Laurie. "Poor, Bare, Forked: Animal Sovereignty, Human Negative Exceptionalism, and the Natural History of King Lear." *Shakespeare Quarterly* 60, no. 2 (2009): 168–96.

Shapiro, Barbara J. "Classical Rhetoric and the English Law of Evidence." In *Rhetoric and Law in Early Modern Europe*, edited by Victoria Ann Kahn and Lorna Hutson, 54–72. New Haven, CT: Yale University Press, 2001.

Shaw, L. M. E. *The Anglo-Portuguese Alliance and the English Merchants in Portugal, 1654–1810*. Aldershot: Ashgate, 1998.

Shawcross, John T. "John Milton and His Spanish and Portuguese Presence." *Milton Quarterly* 32, no. 2 (1998): 41–52.

Sheets, George A. "Conceptualizing International Law in Thucydides." *American Journal of Philology* 115 (1994): 51–73.

Shelley, Percy Bysshe. "A Defense of Poetry." In *Shelley's Poetry and Prose*, edited by Neil Fraistat and Donald H. Reiman. New York: Norton, 2002.

Sheppard, Steve. "The Laws of War in the Pre-Dawn Light: Institutions and Obligations in Thucydides' Peloponnesian War." *Columbia Journal of Transnational Law* 43 (2004–2005): 905.

Sherbo, Arthur. *Shakespeare's Midwives: Some Neglected Shakespeareans*. Cranbury, NJ: Associated University Presses, 1992.

Sherman, William H. *John Dee: The Politics of Reading and Writing in the English Renaissance*. Amherst, MA: University of Massachusetts Press, 1995.

Sherman, William H. "Sir Julius Caesar's Search Engine." In *Used Books: Marking Readers in Renaissance England*, 127–48. Philadelphia, PA: University of Pennsylvania Press, 2008.

Shore, Daniel. "WWJD? The Genealogy of a Syntactic Form." *Critical Inquiry* 37, no. 1 (2010): 1–25.

Shore, Daniel. *Milton and the Art of Rhetoric*. Cambridge: Cambridge University Press, 2012.

Shuger, Debora Kuller. *The Renaissance Bible: Scholarship, Sacrifice, and Subjectivity*. 2nd edn. Baylor University Press, 2010.

Sidney, Philip. *The Countesse of Pembrokes Arcadia*. London: [by John Windet] for William Ponsonbie, 1590.

Sidney, Philip. *The Countess of Pembroke's Arcadia (the New Arcadia)*. Edited by Victor Skretkowicz. Oxford: Clarendon Press, 1987.

Sidney, Philip. *The Countess of Pembroke's Arcadia: (The Old Arcadia)*. Edited by Katherine Duncan-Jones. Oxford: Oxford University Press, 1999.

Sidney, Philip. *An Apology for Poetry, Or, The Defence of Poesy*. Edited by Geoffrey Shepherd and R. W. Maslen. 3rd edn. Manchester: Manchester University Press, 2002.

Sierhuis, Freya. "Therapeutic Tragedy: Compassion, Remorse, and Reconciliation in the Joseph Plays of Joost van Den Vondel (1635–1640)." *European Review of History: Revue Europeenne D'histoire* 17, no. 1 (2010): 27–51.

Silvestrini, Gabriella. "With Grotius against Grotius: Jephtha's 'Appeal to Heaven' in John Locke's Two Treatises of Government." In *The Roots of International Law: Liber Amicorum for Peter Haggenmacher*, edited by Pierre-Marie Dupuy and Vincent Chetail, 59–94. Leiden: Martinus Nijhoff, 2014.

Simmonds, K. R. *Alberico Gentili at the Admiralty Bar, 1605–1608*. Tubingen: J. C. B. Mohr, 1958.

Simpson, Percy. *Studies in Elizabethan Drama*. Oxford: Clarendon Press, 1955.

Sims, James H. "Camoens' 'Lusiads' and Milton's 'Paradise Lost': Satan's Voyage to Eden." In *Papers on Milton.*, edited by Philip Mahone Griffith and Lester F. Zimmerman, 36–46. Tulsa, OK: University of Tulsa, 1969.

Singh, Jyotsna G., ed. *A Companion to the Global Renaissance: English Literature and Culture in the Era of Expansion*. Chichester: John Wiley and Sons, 2009.

Skinner, Quentin. *Reason and Rhetoric in the Philosophy of Thomas Hobbes*. Cambridge: Cambridge University Press, 1996.

Skinner, Quentin. *Liberty before Liberalism*. Cambridge: Cambridge University Press, 1998.

Skinner, Quentin. "John Milton and the Politics of Slavery." In *Visions of Politics*, 2: 286–307. Cambridge: Cambridge University Press, 2002.

Skinner, Quentin. "Meaning and Understanding in the History of Ideas." In *Visions of Politics*, I: 57–89. Cambridge: Cambridge University Press, 2002.

Skinner, Quentin. "Moral Ambiguity and the Renaissance Art of Eloquence." In *Visions of Politics*, II: 264–85. Cambridge: Cambridge University Press, 2002.

Skinner, Quentin. *Visions of Politics*. 3 vols. Cambridge: Cambridge University Press, 2002.

Skinner, Quentin. "Hobbes on Representation." *European Journal of Philosophy* 13, no. 2 (2005): 155–84.

Skinner, Quentin. "Surveying 'The Foundations': A Retrospect and Reassessment." In *Rethinking the Foundations of Modern Political Thought*, edited by Annabel S. Brett, James Tully, and Hamilton-Bleakley, 236–61. Cambridge: Cambridge University Press, 2006.

Skinner, Quentin. *Hobbes and Republican Liberty*. Cambridge: Cambridge University Press, 2008.

Slaughter, Joseph R. "Enabling Fictions and Novel Subjects: The *Bildungsroman* and International Human Rights Law." *PMLA* 121, no. 5 (October 2006): 1405–23.

Slaughter, Joseph R. *Human Rights, Inc.: The World Novel, Narrative Form, and International Law*. New York: Fordham University Press, 2007.

Slomp, G. "Hobbes, Thucydides, and the Three Greatest Things." *History of Political Thought* 11 (1990).

Sommerville, J. P. *Politics and Ideology in England, 1603–1640.* London: Longman, 1986.

Sommerville, Johann P. *Thomas Hobbes: Political Ideas in Historical Context.* Basingstoke: Palgrave Macmillan, 1992.

Sowerby, Robin. "Thomas Hobbes's Translation of Thucydides." *Translation & Literature* 7, no. 2 (1998): 147–69.

Spenser, Edmund. *A View of the State of Ireland: From the First Printed Edition (1633).* Edited by Andrew Hadfield and Willy Maley. Oxford: Blackwell, 1997.

Spenser, Edmund. *The Faerie Queene.* Edited by A. C Hamilton, Hiroshi Yamashita, and Toshiyuki Suzuki. New York: Longman, 2001.

Springborg, Patricia. "Hobbes, Heresy, and the Historia Ecclesiastica." *Journal of the History of Ideas* 55, no. 4 (1994): 553–71.

Springborg, Patricia. "Leviathan, Mythic History, and National Historiography." In *The Historical Imagination in Early Modern Britain: History, Rhetoric, and Fiction, 1500–1800,* edited by Donald R. Kelley and David Harris Sacks. Cambridge: Cambridge University Press, 1997.

Springborg, Patricia. "Classical Translation and Political Surrogacy: English Renaissance Classical Translations and Imitations as Politically Coded Texts." *Finnish Yearbook of Political Thought* 5 (2001).

Springborg, Patricia. "Hobbes, Donne, and the Virginia Company: Terra Nullius and the 'Bulimia of Dominion.'" *History of Political Thought* 36, no. 1 (2015): 113–64.

Srigley, Michael. *Images of Regeneration: A Study of Shakespeare's The Tempest and Its Cultural Background.* Uppsala: Academiae Upsaliensis, 1985.

St. Leger, James. *The "Etiamsi Daremus" of Hugo Grotius: A Study in the Origins of International Law.* Rome: Typis Pontificiae Universitatis Gregorianae, 1962.

Stephens, Walter. "Reading Tasso Reading Vergil Reading Homer: An Archeology of Andromache." *Comparative Literature Studies* 32, no. 2 (1995): 24.

Stern, Philip J. *The Company-State: Corporate Sovereignty and the Early Modern Foundations of the British Empire in India.* Oxford: Oxford University Press, 2012.

Stevens, Paul. "Paradise Lost and the Colonial Imperative." *Milton Studies* 34 (1996): 3–22.

Stevens, Paul. "Heterogenizing Imagination: Globalization, The Merchant of Venice, and the Work of Literary Criticism." *New Literary History* 36, no. 3 (2005): 425–37.

Stevens, Paul. "How Milton's Nationalism Works: Globalization and the Possibilities of Positive Nationalism." In *Early Modern Nationalism and Milton's England,* edited by David Loewenstein and Paul Stevens, 273–301. Toronto: University of Toronto Press, 2008.

Stone, Lawrence. *An Elizabethan: Sir Horatio Palavicino.* Oxford: Clarendon Press, 1956.

Strain, Virginia. "*The Winter's Tale* and the Oracle of the Law." *ELH* 78, no. 3 (2011): 557–84.

Straumann, Benjamin. "'Ancient Caesarian Lawyers' in a State of Nature: Roman Tradition and Natural Rights in Hugo Grotius's De Iure Praedae." *Political Theory* 34, no. 3 (2006): 328–50.

Straumann, Benjamin. "The Corpus Juris as a Source of Law Between Sovereigns in Alberico Gentili's Thought." In *The Roman Foundations of the Law of Nations: Alberico Gentili and the Justice of Empire,* edited by Benedict Kingsbury and Benjamin Straumann, 101–25. Oxford: Oxford University Press, 2011.

Straznicky, Marta. *Privacy, Playreading, and Women's Closet Drama, 1550–1700.* Cambridge: Cambridge University Press, 2004.

Strier, Richard. *Resistant Structures: Particularity, Radicalism, and Renaissance Texts.* Berkeley, CA: University of California Press, 1995.

Subrahmanyam, Sanjay. "On World Historians in the Sixteenth Century." *Representations* 91, no. 1 (2005): 26–57.

Suganami, Hidemi. "A Note on the Origin of the Word 'International.'" *British Journal of International Studies* 4, no. 3 (1978): 226–32.

Tamm, Ditlev. *Roman Law and European Legal History*. Copenhagen: DJØF Pub., 1997.

Tang, Chenxi. "Re-Imagining World Order: From International Law to Romantic Poetics." *Deutsche Vierteljahrsschrift Fur Literaturwissenschaft Und Geistesgeschichte* 84, no. 4 (2010): 526–79.

Tang, Chenxi. "The Transformation of the Law of Nations and the Reinvention of the Novella: Legal History and Literary Innovation from Boccaccio's Decameron to Goethe's Unterhaltungen Deutscher Ausgewanderten." *Goethe Yearbook: Publications of the Goethe Society of North America* 19 (2012): 67–92.

Tasso, Torquato. *Jerusalem Delivered (Gerusalemme Liberata)*. Edited and translated by Anthony M. Esolen. Baltimore, MD: Johns Hopkins University Press, 2000.

Taylor, Charles. "The Politics of Recognition." In *Multiculturalism and "The Politics of Recognition": An Essay*, edited by Charles Taylor and Amy Gutmann, 25–73. Princeton, NJ: Princeton University Press, 1992.

Test, Edward M. "*The Tempest* and the Newfoundland Cod Fishery." In *Global Traffic: Discourses and Practices of Trade in English Literature and Culture from 1550 to 1700*, edited by Barbara Sebek and Stephen Deng, 201–19. New York: Palgrave Macmillan, 2008.

"The Answer to a Dutch Pamphlet." In *A True Relation of the Vniust, Cruell, and Barbarous Proceedings against the English at Amboyna in the East-Indies, by the Neatherlandish Governour and Councel There*. London, 1624.

The Petition and Articles Exhibited in Parliament against Doctor Heywood, Late Chaplen to the Bishop of Canterburie, by the Parishioners of S. Giles in the Fields. With Some Considerable Circumstances (worth Observing) in the Hearing of the Businesse before the Grand Committee for Religion, and of His Demeanour Since. London, 1641.

Thompson, E. P. *Whigs and Hunters: The Origin of the Black Act*. New York: Pantheon Books, 1975.

Thomson, Erik. "France's Grotian Moment? Hugo Grotius and Cardinal Richelieu's Commercial Statecraft." *French History* 21, no. 4 (2007): 377–94.

Thorowgood, Thomas. *Jewes in America, Or, Probabilities That the Americans Are of That Race*. London: W. H. for Tho. Slater, 1650.

Thurloe, John. *A Collection of the State Papers of John Thurloe*. Edited by Thomas Birch. 7 vols. London: Thomas Woodward, 1742.

Tierney, Brian. "Vitoria and Suarez on Ius Gentium, Natural Law, and Custom." In *The Nature of Customary Law*, edited by Amanda Perreau-Saussine and James Bernard Murphy, 101–24. Cambridge: Cambridge University Press, 2007.

Treherne, Matthew. "The Difficult Emergence of Pastoral Tragicomedy: Guarini's *Il Pastor Fido* and Its Critical Reception in Italy, 1586–1601." In *Early Modern Tragicomedy*, edited by Subha Mukherji and Raphael Lyne, 28–42. Woodbridge, Suffolk, UK: D. S. Brewer, 2007.

Trim, D. J. B. "'If a Prince Use Tyrannie towards His People': Interventions on Behalf of Foreign Populations in Early Modern Europe." In *Humanitarian Intervention: A History*, edited by Brendan Simms and D. J. B. Trim, 29–66. Cambridge: Cambridge University Press, 2011.

Trubowitz, Rachel. *Nation and Nurture in Seventeenth-Century English Literature*. Oxford: Oxford University Press, 2012.

Tuck, Richard. *Natural Rights Theories: Their Origin and Development*. Cambridge: Cambridge University Press, 1979.

Tuck, Richard. *The Rights of War and Peace: Political Thought and the International Order from Grotius to Kant*. Oxford: Oxford University Press, 1999.

Tuck, Richard. "The Making and Unmaking of Boundaries from the Natural Law Perspective." In *States, Nations, and Borders: The Ethics of Making Boundaries*, edited by Allen E. Buchanan and Margaret Moore. Cambridge: Cambridge University Press, 2003.

Tuck, Richard. "Alliances with Infidels in the European Imperial Expansion." In *Empire and Modern Political Thought*, edited by Sankar Muthu, 61–82. Cambridge: Cambridge University Press, 2012.

Tuori, Kaius. "The Reception of Ancient Legal Thought in Early Modern International Law." In *The Oxford Handbook of the History of International Law*, edited by Bardo Fassbender and Anne Peters, 1012–33. Oxford University Press, 2012.

Urueña, Rene. *No Citizens Here: Global Subjects and Participation in International Law*. Leiden; Boston, MA: M. Nijhoff Publishers, 2012.

Vallance, Edward. "Oaths, Casuistry, and Equivocation: Anglican Responses to the Engagement Controversy." *The Historical Journal* 44, no. 01 (2001).

Van der Molen, Gesina H. J. *Alberico Gentili and the Development of International Law: His Life, Work and Times*. 2nd rev. edn. Leyden: A.W. Sifthoff, 1968.

Van Dorsten, J. A. *Poets, Patrons, and Professors: Sir Philip Sidney, Daniel Rogers, and the Leiden Humanists*. Leiden: University of Leiden, 1962.

Van Ittersum, Martine Julia. "'Three Moneths Observations of the Low Countreys, Especially Holland': Owen Felltham and Anglo-Dutch Relations in the Seventeenth Century." *LIAS: Sources and Documents Relating to the Early Modern History of Ideas* 27 (2000).

Van Ittersum, Martine Julia. "Hugo Grotius in Context: Van Heemskerck's Capture of the Santa Catarina and Its Justification in De Jure Praedae (1604–1606)." *Asian Journal of Social Science* 31, no. 3 (2003): 511–48.

Van Ittersum, Martine Julia. "Mare Liberum Versus the Propriety of the Seas? The Debate between Hugo Grotius (1583–1645) and William Welwood (1552–1624) and Its Impact on Anglo-Scotto-Dutch Fishery Disputes in the Second Decade of the Seventeenth Century." *Edinburgh Law Review* 10, no. 2 (2006): 239–76.

Van Ittersum, Martine Julia. "The Long Goodbye: Hugo Grotius' Justification of Dutch Expansion Overseas, 1615–1645." *History of European Ideas* 36, no. 4 (2010): 386–411.

Vattel, Emer. *The Law of Nations: Or, Principles of the Law of Nature, Applied to the Conduct and Affairs of Nations and Sovereigns, with Three Early Essays on the Origin and Nature of Natural Law and on Luxury*. Indianapolis, IN: Liberty Fund, 2008.

Venning, Timothy. *Cromwellian Foreign Policy*. New York: St. Martin's Press, 1995.

Venuti, Lawrence. "Translation, Community, Utopia." In *Translation Changes Everything: Theory and Practice*, 11–31. London: Routledge, 2013.

Vickers, Brian. *Shakespeare, Co-Author: A Historical Study of Five Collaborative Plays*. Oxford: Oxford University Press, 2002.

Virgil. *Virgil*. Edited by G. P. Goold. Translated by H. Rushton Fairclough. Rev. Ed. with new introduction. 2 vols. Cambridge, MA: Harvard University Press, 1999.

Visconsi, Elliott. *Lines of Equity: Literature and the Origins of Law in Later Stuart England*. Ithaca, NY: Cornell University Press, 2008.

Visconsi, Elliott. "Vinculum Fidei: The Tempest and the Law of Allegiance." *Law and Literature* 20 (2008): 1.

Vitkus, Daniel J. *Turning Turk: English Theater and the Multicultural Mediterranean, 1570–1630*. New York: Palgrave Macmillan, 2003.

Vitoria, Francisco de. *Political Writings*. Edited by Anthony Pagden. Translated by Jeremy Lawrance. Cambridge: Cambridge University Press, 1991.

Voet, Paul. *The Selective Paulus Voet: Being a Translation of Those Sections Regarded as Relevant to Modern Conflict of Laws, of De Statutis Eorumque Concursu Singularis (Amstelodami, 1661)*. Translated by A. Basil Edwards. Pretoria: University of South Africa, 2007.

Waithe, Marcus. "Empson's Legal Fiction." *Essays in Criticism* 62, no. 3 (July 1, 2012): 279–301.

Waldron, Jeremy. "Foreign Law and the Modern Ius Gentium." *Harvard Law Review* 119, no. 1 (2005): 129–47.

Waldron, Jeremy. "Ius Gentium: A Defence of Gentili's Equation of the Law of Nations and the Law of Nature." In *The Roman Foundations of the Law of Nations: Alberico Gentili and the Justice of Empire*, edited by Benedict Kingsbury and Benjamin Straumann, 283–96. Oxford: Oxford University Press, 2011.

Walker, David M. *A Legal History of Scotland: The Sixteenth Century*. Vol. III. Edinburgh: W. Green, 1995.

Walker, David M. *A Legal History of Scotland Vol. IV, The Seventeenth Century*. Edinburgh: T&T Clark, 1996.

Walker, R. B. J. *Inside/outside: International Relations as Political Theory*. Cambridge: Cambridge University Press, 1993.

Wallace, John M. " 'Examples Are Best Precepts': Readers and Meanings in Seventeenth-Century Poetry." *Critical Inquiry* 1, no. 2 (December 1, 1974): 273–90.

Warren, Christopher N. "When Self-Preservation Bids: Approaching Milton, Hobbes, and Dissent." *English Literary Renaissance* 37, no. 1 (2007): 118–50.

Warren, Christopher N. "John Milton and the Epochs of International Law." *European Journal of International Law* 24, no. 2 (May 1, 2013): 557–81.

Warren, Roger. "Introduction." In *A Reconstructed Text of Pericles, Prince of Tyre*. Oxford: Oxford University Press, 2003.

Weinberg, Bernard. *A History of Literary Criticism in the Italian Renaissance*. Chicago, IL: University of Chicago Press, 1961.

Welwood, William. "Of the Community and Propriety of the Seas." In *The Free Sea*, edited by David Armitage. Indianapolis, IN: Liberty Fund, 2004.

Wheare, Degory. *The Method and Order of Reading Both Civil and Ecclesiastical Histories in Which the Most Excellent Historians Are Reduced into the Order in Which They Are Successively to Be Read, and the Judgments of Learned Men Concerning Each of Them, Subjoin'd*. Translated by Edmund Bohun. London: M. Flesher for Charles Brome, 1685.

White, Hayden. *Metahistory: The Historical Imagination in Nineteenth-Century Europe*. Baltimore, MD: Johns Hopkins University Press, 1973.

White, Hayden. *The Content of the Form: Narrative Discourse and Historical Representation*. Baltimore, MD: Johns Hopkins University Press, 1987.

Whitrow, G. J. *Time in History: The Evolution of Our General Awareness of Time and Temporal Perspective*. Oxford: Oxford University Press, 1988.

Whittington, Leah. "Milton's Poetics of Supplication." *Milton Studies* 55 (forthcoming).

Wickham, Glynne. "From Tragedy to Tragi-Comedy: 'King Lear' as Prologue." In *Shakespeare Survey*, edited by Kenneth Muir, 33–48. Cambridge: Cambridge University Press, 1973.

Wijffels, Alain. *Alberico Gentili and Thomas Crompton: An Encounter between an Academic Jurist and a Legal Practitioner*. Leiden: Ius Deco Publications, 1992.

Wijffels, Alain. "Ius Gentium in the Practice of the Court of Admiralty around 1600." In *The Roman Law Tradition*, edited by A. D. E. Lewis and D. J. Ibbetson, 119–34. Cambridge: Cambridge University Press, 1994.

Wijffels, Alain. "Sir Julius Caesar and the Merchants of Venice." In *Geschichte der Zentraljustiz in Mitteleuropa: Festschrift für Bernhard Diestelkamp zum 65. Geburtstag*, edited by Bernhard Diestelkamp, Friedrich Battenberg, and Filippo Ranieri. Weimar: Böhlau, 1994.

Wijffels, Alain. "A British Ius Commune? A Debate on the Union of the Laws of Scotland and England during the First Years of James VI/I's English Reign." *Edinburgh Law Review* 6 (2002): 315–55.

Wilkinson, Henry C. *The Adventurers of Bermuda: A History of the Island from Its Discovery until the Dissolution of the Somers Island Company in 1684*. 2nd edn. London: Oxford University Press, 1958.

Williams, Raymond. *The Sociology of Culture*. 2nd edn. Chicago, IL: University of Chicago Press, 1995.

Williamson, Arthur. "Radical Britain: David Hume of Godscroft and the Challenge to the Jacobean British Vision." In *The Accession of James I: Historical and Cultural Consequences*, edited by Glenn Burgess, Rowland Wymer, and Jason Lawrence, 48–68. Basingstoke: Palgrave Macmillan, 2006.

Wilson, Luke. "Drama and Marine Insurance in Shakespeare's London." In *The Law in Shakespeare*, edited by Constance Jordan and Karen Cunningham. New York: Palgrave Macmillan, 2007.

Winks, Robin W. *Cloak & Gown: Scholars in the Secret War, 1939–1961*. New Haven, CT: Yale University Press, 1996.

Wiseman, Robert, Sir. *The Law of Laws, Or, The Excellencie of the Civil Law above All Humane Laws Whatsoever*. London: R. Royston, 1664.

Wittreich, Joseph Anthony. *Shifting Contexts: Reinterpreting Samson Agonistes*. Pittsburgh, PA: Duquesne University Press, 2002.

Wolin, Sheldon S. *Hobbes and the Epic Tradition of Political Theory*. Los Angeles, CA: William Andrews Clark Memorial Library, University of California, 1970.

Woodfield, Denis B. *Surreptitious Printing in England, 1550–1640*. Charlottesville, VA: University of Virginia Press, 1984.

Woolf, D. R. *Reading History in Early Modern England*. Cambridge: Cambridge University Press, 2000.

Worden, Blair. "Milton's Republicanism and the Tyranny of Heaven." In *Machiavelli and Republicanism*, edited by Gisela Bock, Quentin Skinner, and Maurizio Viroli. Cambridge: Cambridge University Press, 1990.

Worden, Blair. *The Sound of Virtue: Philip Sidney's "Arcadia" and Elizabethan Politics*. New Haven, CT: Yale University Press, 1996.

Worden, Blair. *Literature and Politics in Cromwellian England: John Milton, Andrew Marvell, Marchamont Nedham*. Oxford: Oxford University Press, 2007.

Wormald, Jenny. "James VI and I: Two Kings or One?" *History* 68, no. 223 (1983): 187–209.

Wright, Abraham. *Delitiae Delitiarum Sive Epigrammatum*. Oxford: Leonard Lichfield, 1637.

Wright, Herbert F. "Some Less Known Works of Hugo Grotius: Consisting of a Translation of His Works on Fisheries in His Controversy with William Welwood; a Translation of Extracts from His Letters Concerning International, Natural Law and Fisheries; an Account of His Controversy with Johan De Laet on the Origin of the American Aborigines; And, a Translation of Peerlkamp's Appreciation of His Ability as a Poet." In *Bibliotheca Visseriana Dissertationum Ius Internationale Illustrantium*, Vol. VII. Leiden, 1928.

Wyatt, Michael. *The Italian Encounter with Tudor England: A Cultural Politics of Translation*. Cambridge: Cambridge University Press, 2005.

Yaeger, Patricia. "Sea Trash, Dark Pools, and the Tragedy of the Commons." *PMLA* 125, no. 3 (2010): 523–45.

Yoo, John. "Introduction." In *De Legationibus*, by Alberico Gentili. Delran, NJ: Legal Classics Library, 1997.

Yoo, John. "Memo 14. August 1, 2002, Memorandum for Alberto R. Gonzales Counsel to the President." In *The Torture Papers: The Road to Abu Ghraib*, edited by Karen J. Greenberg and Joshua L. Dratel, 172–222. New York: Cambridge University Press, 2005.

Yoo, John, and Robert J. Delahunty. "Memo 4. January 9, 2002, To: William J. Haynes II, General Counsel, Department of Defense, From: John Yoo, Deputy Assistant Attorney General, U.S. Department of Justice, Office of Legal Counsel and Robert J. Delahunty, Special Counsel, U.S. Department of Justice, Re: Application of Treaties and Laws to Al Qaeda and Taliban Detainees." In *The Torture Papers: The Road to Abu Ghraib*, edited by Karen J. Greenberg and Joshua L. Dratel, 38–79. New York: Cambridge University Press, 2005.

Ziskind, Jonathan. "International Law and Ancient Sources: Grotius and Selden." *The Review of Politics* 35, no. 4 (1973): 537–59.

Zurcher, Andrew. *Spenser's Legal Language: Law and Poetry in Early Modern England*. Woodbridge: D. S. Brewer, 2007.

Index